The Masjid in Contemporary Islamic Africa

The masjid, fundamentally defined as a "place of prostration," is a concept that has long underscored Islamic approaches to spiritual space. Now in the contemporary period, Muslim populations across Africa are redeploying the masjid to navigate the murky waters of globalization and modernity through the development of emergent, progressive spaces that take form across a spectrum of cultural landscapes. Drawing from multiple disciplines and diverse case studies, this book uses the masjid to reflect on the shifting realities of Islamic communities as they engage in processes of sociopolitical and cultural transformation. Specifically, it focuses on how contemporary interpretations of the masjid have catalyzed the growth of forward-thinking, flexible environments that highlight how Muslim communities are developing unique solutions to the problem of performing identity within diverse contexts. In doing so, these spaces provide evidence that contemporary globalization processes and Islamic practice are not necessarily disparate.

Michelle Apotsos is Associate Professor in African Art History at Williams College, specializing in Afro-Islamic architectural sites and landscapes. She is the author of *Architecture, Islam, and Identity in West Africa: Lessons from Larabanga* (2016) and has published in various journals including *African Arts*, *Material Culture Review*, and the *International Journal of Islamic Architecture*. She is also a member of the African Studies Association, the Arts Council of the African Studies Association, the Society of Architectural Historians, and the Global Architectural History Teaching Collaborative based at MIT.

The Masjid in Contemporary Islamic Africa

Michelle Apotsos
Williams College, Massachusetts

CAMBRIDGE
UNIVERSITY PRESS

University Printing House, Cambridge CB2 8BS, United Kingdom

One Liberty Plaza, 20th Floor, New York, NY 10006, USA

477 Williamstown Road, Port Melbourne, VIC 3207, Australia

314–321, 3rd Floor, Plot 3, Splendor Forum, Jasola District Centre, New Delhi – 110025, India

103 Penang Road, #05–06/07, Visioncrest Commercial, Singapore 238467

Cambridge University Press is part of the University of Cambridge.

It furthers the University's mission by disseminating knowledge in the pursuit of education, learning, and research at the highest international levels of excellence.

www.cambridge.org
Information on this title: www.cambridge.org/9781108473347
DOI: 10.1017/9781108573931

© Michelle Apotsos 2021

This publication is in copyright. Subject to statutory exception and to the provisions of relevant collective licensing agreements, no reproduction of any part may take place without the written permission of Cambridge University Press.

First published 2021

A catalogue record for this publication is available from the British Library.

Library of Congress Cataloging-in-Publication Data
Names: Apotsos, Michelle, author.
Title: The Masjid in contemporary Islamic Africa / Michelle Apotsos.
Description: New York : Cambridge University Press, 2021. | Includes index.
Identifiers: LCCN 2021008484 (print) | LCCN 2021008485 (ebook) | ISBN 9781108473347 (hardback) | ISBN 9781108573931 (ebook)
Subjects: LCSH: Mosques – Social aspects – Africa, North. | Mosques – Social aspects – Africa. | BISAC: HISTORY / Africa / General | HISTORY / Africa / General
Classification: LCC BP187.65.A355 A65 2021 (print) | LCC BP187.65.A355 (ebook) | DDC 297.3/56–dc23
LC record available at https://lccn.loc.gov/2021008484
LC ebook record available at https://lccn.loc.gov/2021008485

ISBN 978-1-108-47334-7 Hardback

Cambridge University Press has no responsibility for the persistence or accuracy of URLs for external or third-party internet websites referred to in this publication and does not guarantee that any content on such websites is, or will remain, accurate or appropriate.

I dedicate this book to my family, whose love, life, and laughter probably made it take longer than it should have.

Contents

List of Figures	*page* viii
Preface: Framing the Masjid in Contemporary Islamic Africa	xi
Acknowledgments	xvii
Introduction: "A Place of Prostration": The Concept of Masjid in Contemporary Africa	1
1 Spaces Both Radical and Revolutionary: The Intersectional Masjid	28
2 Monument, Memory, and Remembrance: Rethinking the Masjid Through Contemporary Heritage Regimes	79
3 "All the Earth Is a Mosque": The Masjid as Environmental Advocate	132
4 Masjids on the Move: Mobility and the Growth of "Portable" Islamic Space	184
Conclusion: Looking to the Future: The Masjid as a Space on the Edge	255
Bibliography	260
Index	278

Figures

i.1	Theoretical rendering of the House of the Prophet Muhammad (*pbuh) (c. 632).	page 7
i.2 a and b	Prayer rug with a compass embedded in the fabric; a merchant stand in Dar es Salaam selling Muslim religious paraphernalia, Tanzania, 2018.	9
1.1 a and b	Exterior and interior views of the Open Mosque, Wynberg, Cape Town, South Africa, 2018.	31
1.2	Detail of the *Shahada*, Open Mosque, Wynberg, Cape Town, South Africa, 2018.	33
1.3	The People's Mosque (Masjidul Umam), Wynberg, Cape Town, South Africa, 2018.	46
1.4	Work space adjacent to prayer space, the People's Mosque (Masjidul Umam), Wynberg, Cape Town, South Africa, 2018.	48
1.5	Sankoré Masjid, Timbuktu, Mali.	65
1.6	The sacred gate of the Sidi Yahya Mosque, Timbuktu, Mali, after Ansar Dine destroyed its wooden entrance, 2012.	69
1.7	Members of Ansar Dine, Timbuktu, Mali, 2012.	72
2.1	Aerial view of Harar Jugol, Ethiopia.	83
2.2 a and b	Harar *bari* (gate) and wall section, Harar Jugol, Ethiopia, 2018.	87
2.3 a and b	Grand Jami Mosque and detail of horseshoe arches adorning the primary entrance, Harar Jugol, Ethiopia, 2018.	93
2.4 a and b	Shrine of Emir Nur bin Mujahid, containing the emir's whip, Harar Jugol, Ethiopia, 2018.	97
2.5	Shrine of Sheikh Ay Abida, Harar Jugol, Ethiopia, 2018.	99
2.6 a and b	New Gourna Mosque and floorplan, Luxor, Egypt. Image by Marc Ryckaert (MJJR).	109

List of Figures

2.7 a and b	Dar al Islam (aerial view) and interior, Abiquiú, New Mexico, 2018.	113
2.8	Süleymaniye Mosque, Istanbul, Republic of Turkey c. 1550.	118
2.9 a and b	Akra Furqan, or the National Mosque of Ghana, Accra, Ghana, 2016.	121
3.1 a and b	Kramat of Sheikh Abdurahman Matebe Shah, Constantia, South Africa, 2018.	144
3.2 a and b	Kramat of Sayed Mahmud, Constantia, South Africa, 2018.	148
3.3 a and b	The Great Mosque of Djenne. Image by BluesyPete.	158
3.4 a and b	Visual comparison between Djenne's Great Mosque and a West African termitarium from Ghana. Image of Great Mosque of Djenne by Francesco Bandarin.	164
3.5 a and b	Eco-mosque, children's village, Kisemvule, Tanzania, 2018.	174
4.1 a and b	Views of *car rapides*, Dakar, Senegal, 2018.	193
4.2 a and b	Bole International Airport, Addis Ababa, Ethiopia, masjid and ablution station, 2018.	213
4.3 a and b	O. R. Tambo International Airport, Johannesburg, South Africa, women's masjid, 2018.	217
4.4 a and b	Blaise Diagne International Airport, Dakar, Senegal, masjid interior and exterior, 2018.	219
4.5 a and b	Cape Town International Airport, interior and exterior of the multifaith prayer space, Cape Town, South Africa, 2018.	222
4.6	The Great Mosque of Touba and the Lamp Fall minaret, Touba, Senegal, 2018.	235
4.7 a and b	Images of Chiekh Amadou Bamba on a shop building in Dakar and the home page of the Hizbut Tarqiyya, Senegal, 2018.	242

Preface
Framing the Masjid in Contemporary Islamic Africa

This volume constitutes one of the first dedicated surveys of contemporary Islamic spiritual spaces in Africa, a topic whose breadth, complexity, and diversity requires an interpretive lens that not only addresses established architectural forms and traditions, but can also accommodate the emergent, liminal spaces of contemporary and, some might say, future-facing practice. To this end, this study utilizes the trans-Islamic spatial medium of the *masjid*, whose definition as a "place of prostration" can yield multiple spatial interpretations and thus constitutes a useful interrogative approach for the growing number of diverse, flexible, Islamic environments on the continent, each of which reflects the shifting realities of Muslim life and spiritual identity in the contemporary period. In exploring how contemporary masjids are taking form on the continent, this study also highlights how Muslim communities are developing unique solutions to the problem of performing identity within Africa's diverse contexts and navigating the murky waters of the contemporary condition through a purposeful renovation of Afro-Islamic spiritual space.

In exploring this topic, however, it is important to provide justification for its existence. In other words, why is a study of masjid space in Africa important, even crucial, to understanding Islam in the contemporary period? For one, this study engages in a revisionist dialogue that refutes previous studies of Islam in Africa as a fossilized movement on the periphery of the contemporary Islamic world. Within the context of this volume, Islam in Africa is positioned according to its reality as an active participant in contemporary global conversations about the faith. In doing so, this study frames Islam's spatial environment in Africa as one that favors the flexibility and adaptability in form and meaning, and the individuals who participate in the faith as intersectional beings who are both the authors of their own spirituality and able to project images of themselves, their history, and their spiritual identity into the world that is of their own manufacture.

The masjid, thus, acts as an important apparatus in this enterprise as a multi-tiered construct shaped by time and context, and thus a spatial "working through" of this history in terms of the ongoing identity projects of various communities around the continent, whose diverse and sometimes contested political, social, and cultural identities generate the fabric of everyday contemporary life and existence. As both the product and producer of such identities in these contexts, the masjid reflects and refracts the events, influences, and interruptions that constitute what it means to be a Muslim located within a particular space, time, and context, and subsequently becomes an archive of the dialogues, encounters, and interactions both past and ongoing that have occurred between multiple social, political, cultural, and spiritual contingents.

In addition, while masjid spaces obviously aren't specific to Africa, the diversity of the continent and the size and longevity of its Muslim population means that masjid spaces are equally varied and attuned to their particular contexts. Along these lines, increased access to technology, communication, transportation, and methods of mobility has generated new spaces that are in many ways challenging established ideas of what architecture can be in the contemporary period. Such spaces "carry within them a world of ... relationships," whose identity "creates some variety of Muslim space whenever they are present," to borrow from Barbara Metcalf (Metcalf 1996, 3). Thus, as spaces that increasingly exist as symbol, statement, object, sense-scape, process, text, intervention, and even nonspace, one could rightly question whether this study constitutes a study of architecture at all. As a "place of prostration," the masjid occupies any number of spatial realities with architecture constituting only one of the numerous spatial manifestations that a masjid can take. As such, beyond being merely a three-dimensional constructed space, the masjid also acts as a mode of organizing bodies in space and thus supports a fluid, adaptive mode of existence that shifts one's focus from iconic structural monuments that represent "large-scale explicative narratives of history and culture" toward sites that privilege "the contingent, the temporary, and the dynamic," spaces that focus on "processes rather than structures, on hybridity rather than consistency, on the quotidian as well as the extra-ordinary, on the periphery as well as the center, on reception as well as production" (Stieber 2003, 176). In doing so, the masjid becomes a space that is fundamentally generative and pluralistic, which in turn promotes a more inclusive view of the faith as not only a worldview, but a "system of action" (Elias 2012, 18).

Such realizations are particularly important when one considers the fact that the experience of Islam as a faith and a worldview is fundamentally intersectional. In other words, individuals come to Islam and its spaces of practice/performance with different, overlapping perspectives and socioeconomic, political, and cultural positions. This is an important consideration with regard to the study of Islam in Africa given the diversity of Africa's Muslim community and the questions it raises about how space can be molded to fit their multidimensional contours. As sites defined by "everyday habits and behaviors, ... environmental belief[s], attitudes, and practice, ... social mobility, hybridity and identity," contemporary masjids function as a spatial extension of societies increasingly defined by "geopolitics and territorial imaginations" (Della Dora 2015). In addition, as geographic boundaries are more and more being recognized for the leaky, porous containers that they are, and contemporary ideas of identity are becoming progressively untethered to such artificially demarcated terrains, the reality of being Muslim itself is becoming acknowledged as a condition in which spirituality, class, race, ethnicity, gender, sexuality, socioeconomic status, cultural identity, and more not only shape the contours of spiritual experience but also dictate how spiritual space is constructed, utilized, and subsequently interpreted as a mode of Muslim self-fashioning that enables the faithful to be the protagonists of their own centralized narrative.

As a representative mechanism, thus, masjids actively support diverse iterations of Islamic identity in Africa over time and space, but also evolve in response to the influences, ideologies, and interventions that continuously reshape the contours of Afro-Islamic identity and practice over time and space. And it is through these purposeful renovations of space that the masjid continues to represent and reaffirm a community's ability to engage in meaningful spiritual practice, identity, and performance over time.

In light of this, the case studies addressed in this volume focus on new, emergent masjid spaces in conjunction with historical sites as collective, active participants in broader "global" conversations and discussions occurring within the wider Muslim world. In addition, each case study speaks to the diverse modes through which Islam has been able to thrive in different areas of the continent over its 1500-year history, some located within perceived centers of Afro-Islamic history, belief, and practice, while others occupy peripheral spaces in society. Each, however, is privileged for their contribution to a holistic understanding of the shape of Islam as it has existed as a continental spiritual movement.

Another important note concerning the case studies surveyed in this volume is that rarely are the architects responsible for these spaces addressed at length. Because masjid space is inherently generated through the prayer act rather than the construction of a dedicated space, the role of the architect is tangential to the function of the space. To this end, this volume redirects attention "from the design and construction of buildings to the question of how people use them, from production to consumption" (Vellinga 2011; in Verkaaik 2013, 11). While some might argue that the design and authorship of spatial elements fundamentally affect and control the performance of prayer, the fact remains that anyone who prays at a site becomes the architect of the space and it is because of this that these spaces, to quote Melanie van der Hoorn, "can embody the claims, hopes or frustrations of entire groups of people" (van der Hoorn 2009, 193).

By distributing the authorship role to multiple individuals and populations, this study privileges the layers of dialogue and negotiation that lay behind its associated meanings, pointing to the fact that "buildings may have different meanings or even 'lives' to different groups of people in different periods of time" (Verkaaik 2013, 11). Thus, the current focus on space tends less toward the meanings, messages, and definitions attached by the architect, commissioner, and critic, and more toward those systems of identity-making and meaning creation that occur in the interactive relationships that form between structure and user. Thus, the "identity" of space becomes less a fossilized tribute to artistic genius and more a result of encounters with inhabitants "who not only organize their spatial practices in response to them ... but who also come to understand [space] as symbols of wider social order" (Jones 2011, 27).

Moving beyond discussions of architects and authors, though, another aspect of this study that needs to be addressed is the collective grouping of the case studies in this volume under the title *The Masjid in Contemporary Islamic Africa*. With regard to the qualifier "Islamic" and its oft-positioned synonym "Muslim," the fundamental difference between these two adjectival descriptors has been the subject of great debate. Scholars such as architectural historian Spahic Omer note that "Islamic" designates that which is judged to be the "epitome of the Islamic message, or a major portion of it" and "the spirit of Islam," whereas the descriptor "Muslim" refers to a "segment of life's spiritual paradigm" and a certain Islamic mentality that, in contrast to "Islamic," is inevitably informed by the flaws and faults of human nature (Omer 2008, 504–505). As such, a category such as "Muslim architecture" can be defined according to geographic, stylistic, or temporal parameters, whereas "Islamic architecture manifests the ethos and ideals of Islam" (Omer 2008, 505) in a way that is collective in its multidimensionality in "facilitate[ing] Muslims' realization of the Islamic purpose and its divine principles" (Omer 2008, 510). Thus, with regard to this study, "Muslim" is used to describe a singular condition of being whereas "Islamic" describes a collective spiritual worldview that acknowledges all of its attendant sociopolitical, cultural, and economic components and diversities.[1]

With regard to these interpretive methods, however, it should be noted that the analyses and interrogative platforms in this volume are those of an individual who identifies as female, Caucasian, non-Muslim, CIS, heteronormative, and American, characteristics that inevitably generate perspectives at odds with both established and emerging schools of thought on this topic. As such, I have attempted as much as I am able to let the spaces and the individuals who use them speak for themselves and, to this end, it is my hope that this volume effectively pushes forward the idea of masjid as a forward-thinking flexible method of performing identity in the contemporary period that incorporates traditional and nontraditional genres of Islamic space as a catalyst in the fostering of thought-provoking ideas of what a place of prostration can entail under different social, political, and cultural conditions. Likewise, I hope this volume demonstrates how these spaces are in conversation with multiple contexts, practices, traditions, and histories across the world, supporting the idea that "no identity is ever complete" (Baydar 2004, 20) and privileging the fact that individuals are mobile in ways that push them to carry interior spatial templates that they reproduce as needed. To quote Barbara Metcalf, "people ... seem to transcend sites completely, caught up in global movements or proselytization and trade, so that they essentially exclude the outside world to carry with them a world of ritual, relationships, and symbols that create some variety of Muslim space wherever they are present" (Metcalf 1996, 3). These individuals subsequently generate "their own [spiritual spaces and] cartographies" by re-envisioning and reproducing masjid space in new places and geographies (Metcalf 1996, 4; 6–7).

---

[1] Along these lines, this study does not differentiate between Saharan/sub-Saharan regions given the fact that the divide is arbitrary from both an environmental and a geopolitical standpoint. There is little notable difference in environmental ecology between the Sahara and Sahelian regions, and the Sahara has never acted as an obstacle for the movement of people, goods, and ideas back and forth across it. In actuality, the "boundary" of the Sahara served as a strategic narrative for European colonial powers, who encouraged the supposed divide between North and sub-Saharan Africa, and by extension established an emergent Islamic space. This narrative effectively erased a long history of diverse Afro-Islamic existence and exchange as a mode of generating oppositional hierarchies between the two regions that enabled the European imperial regime to flourish.

Thus, as a spatial language that articulates Muslim identity and a fluid blueprint through which Muslim identity can be indefinitely reproduced, the concept of the masjid as it is deployed in this volume re-imagines major themes surrounding definitions of Islamic architectural space in the contemporary period in Africa and the nature of "Islamic identity" as it is currently unfolding across diverse contexts.

Acknowledgments

This volume would not have been possible without the help of a number of individuals and organizations who have acted in both informational and supportive capacities. First and foremost, I would like to thank Williams College for providing me with numerous Harry Powers Fund awards to complete the bulk of this research. I would also like to thank my editors, Maria Marsh and Daniel Brown, for their interest in this project and their encouragement. Within my department, I have benefitted from the feedback and support of Professors Holly Edwards, Catherine Howe, Murad Mumtaz, Kailani Polzak, Mari Rodriguez Binnie, and Guy Hedreen. Beyond Williams, Professors Barbara Frank, Michelle Craig, and Scott Siraj al-Haqq Kugle have been instrumental in fleshing out the various components and backgrounds upon which I have built.

Truly, however, this work is the result of the generous help and formative relationships I have had the privilege of building with the following people: Gegaw Haile (Dire Dawa, Ethiopia), Dr. Taj Hargey (Cape Town, South Africa), Mahmood Limbada (Cape Town, South Africa), Yusuf Mokada (Cape Town, South Africa), Anjam Hassan (Zanzibar), Mame Laye Mbengue (Dakar, Senegal), Serigne Abo Madyana Diakhate (Porokhane, Senegal), Serigne Thiaw (Ngor [Dakar], Senegal), Ahmed Thiaw (Ngor [Dakar], Senegal), Andul Ahmed (Harar Jugol, Ethiopia), "Nice" (Dakar, Senegal), Rughsaun Adams (Cape Town, South Africa), Kamran Fazil (Dar es Salaam, Tanzania), Saidi Ngolola (Dar es Salaam, Tanzania), Dr. Heinz Rüther (Cape Town, South Africa), Stephen Wessels (Cape Town, South Africa), Roshan Bhurtha (Cape Town, South Africa), Ralph Schröder, Muhsin Hendricks (Cape Town, South Africa), Voici (Soweto, South Africa), Janet Davis (Johannesburg, South Africa), and Lebo Sello (Soweto, South Africa).

I would also like to acknowledge and thank the numerous scholars who have provided many of the major historical and theoretical platforms on which my work is based. They include but are not limited to: Akel Ismail Kahera, Paul Jones, Roman Loimeier, Prita Meier, Rosa De Jorio, Talal Asad, Barbara Metcalf, James Clifford, Kimberlé Crenshaw, Veronica

Della Dora, Jamal Elias, Shamil Jeppie, Heinrich Matthee, Ali Mazrui, Gülru Necipoğlu, Bissera Pentcheva, Nasser Rabbat, Allen and Mary Nooter Roberts, Eric Ross, Mimi Sheller, John Urry, Nasseema Taleb, Abdulkader Tayob, and Goolam H. Vahed.

As always, my love and appreciation to my family, who may not always understand what I do but support it nonetheless. And to Alex, Will, and Rowan, my favorite people in the world.

Introduction
"A Place of Prostration": The Concept of Masjid in Contemporary Africa

This book is not about beautiful buildings, although some will be addressed. This book is also not necessarily about mosques, although they will be present as well. This book is about the masjid, an Islamic space that has over the course of its history existed at the threshold of numerous sociopolitical paradigms, geographical frontiers, and technological horizons. Defined conventionally as "a place of prostration" and often (problematically) embedded in the architectural category of the mosque, the masjid deserves reconsideration as a space not easily contained within such limiting structural frameworks due to its reality as a site in which emergent, often alternative, forms of Islamic practice have been and increasingly are being practiced. The masjid in fact constitutes a sophisticated bit of spatial technology that has been increasingly used in the contemporary period to generate unique solutions to the problems of performing Islamic identity within a variety of diverse societies, whose own complex, nuanced realities require forward-thinking, flexible environments that reflect the shifting realities of Islamic communities as they engage in processes of sociopolitical and cultural transformation. This is particularly the case in Africa, a space that contains one of the fastest growing, most diverse Muslim populations in the world. Within the intersectional spaces of the continent, the masjid has increasingly come to help Islamic communities spatially articulate what it means to be a Muslim in the contemporary period, often by adopting flexible, adaptive forms of spiritual practice and performance, and pushing back against traditional spatial forms like mosques and mausolea as incontrovertible statements of collective Muslim identity and presence. In many ways, the nature of the "masjid" as it is unfolding across the diverse contexts on the continent is reimagining basic ideas of what Islamic space entails through the creation of new cutting-edge spiritual sites that speak to the multiple modernities existing across the continent in the contemporary period. As such, this introduction aims to establish a theoretical and methodological platform for understanding how the masjid has come to function as a spatial articulation of what it means to be Muslim in modern Africa.

i.1 Defining the Masjid: Spiritual Spaces as Performative Places

Toward starting this conversation, the concept of the masjid must be unpacked in terms of both its conceptual history as well as the diverse realities it has occupied over time and space. In addition, it must also be separated from the architectural genre of the mosque, which has long stood as an inappropriate synonym for masjid space and a mode of collectivizing and subsuming masjid space under the generalized umbrella of a singular structural qualifier. Masjid space requires conceptualization in a way that privileges its reality as a concept that has been summoned time and time again by different stakeholders to define space for diverse identities.

So, what is a masjid in its most essential state?[1] From an etymological standpoint, the term "masjid" is a derivative of the Arabic word *sajada* (*sujūd*), which means "prostration" with masjid subsequently defined as "a place of prostration" or, more specifically, "a place in which ritual prayer (salat) is performed" (Sourdel, Sourdel-Thomine, and Higgitt 2007, 106).[2] Yet from a spatial standpoint, neither Islam's sacred text – the Qur'an – nor the hadiths dictate the nature of the masjid as it is made physically manifest in the world. As Ahmad notes, "If reduced to basics, [masjid] is no more than a wall at right angle to Qibla axis and behind or rather before that wall, there can be anything." Indeed, simplicity in the spatial design of the masjid is privileged by the words of the Prophet (pbuh),[3] who said "Wherever you pray, that place is a mosque" (Ahmad et al. 2016, 97).

Adding to its opacity is the fact that the masjid maintains a number of ambiguous identities and realities throughout its appearance in Islam's holy texts, with numerous verses in the Qur'an speaking of "masjid" generally without pinpointing specific mosque identities.[4] Although Islamic hermeneutics offers various interpretations in this regard, often identifying ambiguous masjids in various Qur'anic verses as one of three – the Masjid al-Aqsa

---

[1] It should be noted that the English plural of masjid – masjids – will be used throughout the volume rather than the Arabic plural, *masājid*.

[2] This is in contrast to the term "mosque," which is a derivation of the Spanish *mesquita* (Sourdel, Sourdel-Thomine, and Higgitt 2007, 115).

[3] When mentioning the Prophet Muhammad or other prophets in the Islamic faith, it is traditional and respectful to follow their name with the added phrase *'alayhi s-salām* (عليه السلام) or "peace be upon him." In English texts, sometimes one also sees the abbreviation PBUH (peace be unto him). While not appearing after each mention of the Prophet's name in this volume, it is my intent that such respect be accorded after each mention.

[4] In Qur'an Surah 2:114, the plural of masjid – *masājid* – is used to describe "Allah's Masjids," a cryptic description that potentially refers to either all masjids on earth, or a specific one on which no one can agree on which one.

i.1 Defining the Masjid 3

(the "Far Mosque"), the Masjid al-Haram (sanctuary at Mecca around the Ka'ba), or the Masjid al-Rasul (structure sited on the original location of the Prophet Muhammad's house) – this type of specificity is rarely supported by the verses themselves, which seem to frame "masjid" less as a specific structure in many cases and more of an idea, or ideal, to be followed and applied to one's life space. Similarly, there are numerous instances in which the masjid itself is known by other names. Qur'an Surah 24:36 reads "In house (*fi buyutin*) which Allah has ordered to be raised (to be cleaned and to be Honoured)." Here, the term for houses or dwellings – *fi buyutin* (sing. *buyut*) – in fact implies "all places of pure worship" or all prayer spaces on earth, hence all masjids (Sourdel, Sourdel-Thomine, and Higgitt 2007, 49–50).[5]

Such ambiguity is hardly surprising, given the fact that a number of other spatial concepts within Islamic tradition also exhibit similar interpretive ambiguities. Perhaps the most abstruse spatial entity within Islamic spatial practice outside the masjid itself, however, is the *mihrab*, often taking form as a concave niche in the *Qiblah* wall[6] of most mosque structures indicating the direction of Mecca. A majority of its descriptive uses in the Qur'an and other medieval Islamic texts are actually nonarchitectural in nature, gesturing loosely to an "honored location" and sometimes shifting identity from noun to adjective to describe the height or elevated nature of a space or structure (Nuha 1998, 8; 11). Its subsequent translation into a form of Islamic liturgical infrastructure is thought to have been influenced by non-Islamic spiritual architectures including Christian church apses, Judaic synagogue arks, and even the throne niches of early medieval palaces. Indeed, its pervasive presence within multiple religious and political infrastructures within the first millennium made it "both too common and too neutral a form to yield precise, incontrovertible sources of origin, let alone meaning" (Nuha 1998, 2). The word itself – *mihrab* – also has a complicated generative history, given its origin may in fact not be Arabic at all, but possibly Syriac, Hebrew, Ethiopic, or even Pahlavi, which also explains the fact that, like the

---

[5] Others feel that "*buyutin*" in this case actually refers to three "special" masjid spaces, namely Islam's three holy "mosques": the Ka'ba in Mecca, the House of the Prophet in Medina, and the Masjid Bayt al-Maqdis in Jerusalem (El-Khatib 2001, 49). It should also be noted that at least two out of the three "mosques" mentioned are not "mosques" in the most direct sense but occupy the position of "masjid" due to the venerative performances of prayer that occur there.
[6] The *Qiblah* has also not only occupied various conceptually ambiguous/fluid realities, but has also been absorbed and in many ways fossilized into architectural form. Yet within the Qur'an, it has also been identified as an indicator for directional orientation, a site of prayer, and even an actual place of worship, numerous realities that position it simultaneously as a physical construct as well as a metaphysical concept (Nuha 1998, 14).

masjid, the general meaning of the *mihrab* is open for debate.[7] Nuha notes that "the term mihrab contains no references to specific forms or functions. Rather, it operates primarily as a metaphorical and emphatic device that receives its function from its context" (Nuha 1998, 11). Thus, within its various definitions and utilizations, "the only constant is the word mihrab itself" and the subsequent intermingling and assimilation of the concept into the context of Muslim culture and religion went on to not only Islamize the term but also cement its physical reality in the form of an "indivisible architectural element that is singularly associated with mosques" (Nuha 1998, 13; 17). The application of the niche form to the *mihrab* concept would also inscribe the *mihrab* with a specific spatial identity that in many ways erased the term's past and essentially "transform[ed] all occurrences of the word *mihrab* in texts into niches." Thus, the *mihrab* has in many ways become cemented as a "verbal and visual signal of the presence of Islamic functions and values" (Nuha 1998, 18), just as the masjid has become architecturally calcified in the form of a mosque structure, hard-pressed to exist beyond this reality and entombed in a structural genre that does not do justice to its conceptual breadth.

This thus brings up an important question, indeed the key question: what is the difference between a mosque and masjid? The diverse spaces of prayer and prostration that exist in the world, informed as they are by numerous socioeconomic, political, and cultural conditions, generates natural push-back against their collapse within the space of a bound structural genre or essentialized formal envelope like the mosque. Thus, perhaps a better question is: what is the true relationship between the mosque and the masjid? The previous discussion would indicate that while all mosques are masjids, not all masjids are mosques, and this is supported in some ways by the various requirements different communities and bodies of belief place on a space for it to become "mosque." For some, permission must be given to pray in that space. For others, space must be *waqf* or the result of a donation provided for that purpose. Yet as a spiritual paradigm that is "spatially and temporally unbound," Islam is "not necessarily practiced only in officially designated spaces (or at allocated times)" (Della Dora 2015). As Kong notes, "there are many ways in which every-day spaces can be implicated in religious meaning-making, legitimating, maintaining and enhancing, but also challenging religious life, beliefs, practices and

---

[7] In various pre-Islamic fourth- and fifth-century inscriptions from Southern Arabia, one finds the term used to describe a fortress structure, while other sources use it to describe a royal court or palace (Nuha 1998, 6). In addition, some scholars have equated *mihrab*s to *majali*s, or spaces where one sits in the context of a meeting or council.

i.1 Defining the Masjid

identities" (Kong 2010, 758; in Della Dora 2015). Such "unofficial" spaces include professional venues, urban avenues, domestic spaces, and even mediascapes and this breadth of space lies at the heart of the masjid as a spatial concept that challenges the traditional binaries of sacred vs. secular in ways that speak to Islam's reality as a way of living and being in the world.

Thus, as a space articulated through practice and mobility, and one that can be "continuously made and dissolved" (Della Dora 2015), the masjid does not abide structural boundaries or infrastructures, which points to one of the most defining characteristics of a masjid space: its fundamental dependence on the presence of a performing, ritualized body for its existence. Indeed, as a place of prostration, it is the venerative act alone that can summon forth the masjid, transforming the individual into a channel through which masjid space is made manifest. Indeed, it is also this defining element that allows the whole of the earth to be interpreted as "masjid," a space that is accomplished rather than established through the ritualized movements of the body. In this way, to quote Oleg Grabar, "it is ritual and sanction practice that ... creates 'Muslim space'" (Metcalf 1996, 3).

This leads to a consideration of the performative process itself, a process that begins with the position of the sun, which provides cues for the body to begin its transition from "profane" to "purified." The pre-performing body undergoes a purification process with water (*wuḍū'*), which itself has a number of nuanced symbolic properties further explored in Chapter 3, toward cleansing the body of pollutants (Joseph 1981, 290). Thus, it is not only the performing body that establishes masjid space, but a performing body existing in a state or condition of purified being. The prayer act begins when the body engages in a series of motions, each designed to physically and symbolically transition the self from a profane to a spiritual plane of existence and, in doing so, differentiate one's spiritual self from that of the profane self. Roger Joseph, referencing Titus Burckhardt, notes thusly:

> the standing attitude distinguishes man from all other animals, investing him with a special status, while the reclining attitude recapitulates the notion of submission to God (cf. Burckhardt 1976, 87). The act of submission is made when one is closest to the ground, metaphorically recognizing man's biological status as earthbound just as the upright position is mimetic of his biological uniqueness. (Joseph 1981, 290)

These movements, according to Burckhardt, establish a type of spatio-spiritual cartography that maps the relationship between humanity and the divine through a bodily imprint. As movements unlikely to be replicated over the course of everyday existence, these actions create a space that stands apart from one's surroundings and together with a ritualized body in action, support and reaffirm each other as mutually constitutive elements of spiritual practice (Chidester and Linenthal 1995, 10).

Such practices constitute what David Chidester and Edward Linenthal define as a "particular type of embodied, spatial practice ... [that] ... can act out and embody perfectly the way things 'ought to be'" (Chidester and Linenthal 1995, 9). In these performances, the ritual manipulations of the human form as "formalized 'gestures of approach'" enable the body to become a portal through which masjid space emerges. Indeed, the specificity of the actions and movements undertaken by the body create a "habitus," to reference Pierre Bourdieu, in which ritual performance constitutes "a localized fusion of thought and action in and through which human beings negotiate the social relations and practical knowledge of their worlds." And through this ritual performance as "embodied practice," the masjid space that emerges not only acts as an apparatus of performance but represents "a dynamic spatial ordering of knowledge and power" (Chidester and Linenthal 1995, 10).

Similar repertoires of action, space, and performance are made manifest in other Islamic spiritual practices as well such as the Hajj, which according to scholar and architect Sami Angawi, symbolizes both "unity and continuity" through the Ka'ba as "constant," as well as "change and diversity" accomplished by the circumambulation of pilgrims around the Ka'ba and to various sacred sites in the Holy City (Hammond 2012, 216). Often interpreted as the "first true temple" (and one might exchange "temple" with "masjid" in this case), the Ka'ba's location is often viewed as "the center of the world ... where God's presence is felt the most on earth" and indeed "the heart of Islam" (Hammond 2012, 215).[8] Yet its power lies not only in its location and history, but in the performative elements of the Hajj itself, in which pilgrims circle the Ka'ba and visit a series of sacred sites in the area toward establishing a type of "cosmic order." Egyptian scholar Abdul Hakam al-Sa'idi notes that "the planets revolve around the sun, each in a separate orbit, with specific speed. In the same way, the Ka'ba which God made the first sanctuary for mankind is located at the center of the earth" (Hammond 2012, 216).[9] To return to the question of the relationship between the masjid and the

---

[8] The Ka'ba is thought to have been built by Abraham, the "genealogical father of the Arabs" (Hammond 2012, 216), and his son Ismail.
[9] However, the faithful are discouraged from privileging the Ka'ba as space or object, lest they end up venerating the structure and not the prayerful act in an exercise in idolatry. Indeed, Caliph Omar, senior companion to the Prophet Muhammad, once addressed the Ka'ba saying, "I know you are only a stone and can do neither good nor ill, and if I had not seen the Prophet kiss you, then I would not do so too" (Hammond 2012, 216).

i.1 Defining the Masjid

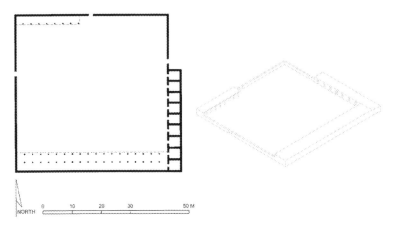

Figure i.1 Theoretical rendering of the House of the Prophet Muhammad (*pbuh) (c. 632).
Illustration by the author after Mortada 2011.

mosque, thus, it becomes apparent that mosque space in and of itself is not masjid full stop, but is at best a "masjid-in-waiting," an anticipatory yet fundamentally dormant space requiring a performative body to enable ascension/affirmation.

This thus begs the question of how mosques themselves came to occupy the role of "masjid made manifest." The mosque as a structural genre had rather inauspicious structural beginnings, with most scholars pointing to the house of the Prophet Muhammad as its original inspiration and the template upon which the essential blueprint of the mosque would develop as a genre (Figure i.1). The Prophet's house was a simple (theoretically), vernacular structure, composed of a rectangular courtyard whose north and south sides were bookended by hypostyle halls that offered shade during the heat of the day and a space to congregate, work, converse, and socialize.[10] The Prophet's house would also come to accommodate Friday communal worship and the *khutbah*, or sermon which would have been delivered by Muhammad from a raised platform that would serve as a proto-*minbar*. This space would also serve as a forum for discussing communal affairs and making decisions with regard to the congregation as a type of judiciary seat (Kahera 2008, 41).

Yet the Prophet's house was also a space of intimacy and family life. A series of rooms lining one of the two remaining sides housed the

---

[10] Because this was where the Prophet's companions would meet, they would eventually become known as the *ṣāhib al-ṣafa*, or "people of the portico" (Rizvi 2015, 10).

Prophet, his wives, and his children, who were protected from public view by curtains and screens, elements that would be made architecturally manifest in later mosque spaces in the form of female galleries and various partitions designed to separate space and control visibility. Given the fact that the Prophet's life is typically seen as providing the ideal model by which every Muslim should live, his home space, thus, came to be co-opted as a spatial ideal of the faith and thus an appropriate template on which to model subsequent spiritual spaces.

Such functions align with historian Gerard van der Leeuw's proposed correspondence between the "home, temple, settlement, pilgrimage site, and human body" in that "they can be discerned as transferable metaphors for the same kind of powerful space" (Chidester and Linenthal 1995, 7). Thus, the Prophet's home came to act not only as a space for prostration but also as "an agora, a courthouse, a learning center, and a refuge for the poor, homeless, and destitute" (Rabbat 2002, 2). This demonstrates the important fact that mosques from their very inception were designed to accommodate functions beyond that of just performative spiritual space as the "House[s] of the Nation (*Bayt al-Umma*)" and as such would subsequently become representative of a distinctive type of spatial program that symbolized derivative virtues associated with the Prophet himself. In addition, this space came to be the working template which later mosques would follow, structures that ranged from early formative "humble" spaces "determined for worship" such as the basic rock mosques of the Sahara region in North Africa (Kahera 2008, 44), to later mosque spaces that functioned as formidable political, socioeconomic, and aesthetic fortresses of faith and power, such as the contemporary Nizamiye Mosque in Johannesburg, South Africa.

Thus, in conceptualizing the relationship between the mosque and the masjid, the mosque represents one iteration of masjid space that, by its nature, also accommodates additional activities beyond that of performative prayer. Likewise, as a space that is "open-ended and constructed anew by each observer" (Erzen 2011, 130), masjid cannot by their nature be contained by structural boundaries and thresholds; in fact it is a space that expands and contracts within and beyond its surrounding environment according to the performative actions of the bodies within. This likewise gives masjids the ability to move, relocate, and re-emerge across multiple spaces, contexts, and conditions and assume multiple forms that are only loosely architectonic in nature.

One such example of this type of masjid space might be the prayer mat (Figure i.2a and i.2b). The prayer mat in many ways underscores the creation and mobilization of space in that its presence indicates intent. As first and foremost an anticipatory spatial tool kit – one might even say

i.1 Defining the Masjid

Figure i.2 a and b Prayer rug with a compass embedded in the fabric; a merchant stand in Dar es Salaam selling Muslim religious paraphernalia, Tanzania, 2018.
Images by the author.

a type of "pre-emptive" spiritual space – the value of the prayer mat object lies not in its quality per se, but in the fact that it is an object that can separate one space from another within the physical environment through its role as a mode of demarcation and a platform for performance. Able to move and exist in multiple locations, the prayer mat also acts as a *seede* or witness to both the creation of the space and the act of prayer carried out within. Such "witnesses" have also taken the form of rocks or pieces of wood laid on or stuck into the ground, so long as they were placed a single cubit from the space where the act of prayer was to occur (Dilley 2011, 191). The prayer mat improves on this demarcation scheme by not only establishing a perimeter but also ensuring that the space within the perimeter is free of debris and other filth that could invalidate the prayer act. As such, these mats establish a new space altogether by creating an island of purity temporarily displaced from its polluted surroundings.

Like the masjid itself, the use of prayer mats within the Islamic faith is not formalized by the Qur'an and the hadith in any specific sense. As a masjid space, prayer mats are comparable to sleeping mats, woven grass coverings, and even "the sands of the desert" when one is called to perform *salat* (Morris 1921, 253). Yet in the contemporary period, particularly in urban areas where continuous mobility often defines one's way of life, prayer mats have become a decidedly convenient mode of accommodating one's spiritual needs in a constantly shifting environment.

Prayer mats not only help establish masjid space, however; they can also expand it. This is particularly the case during Muslim religious festivals and holidays when prayer mats are deployed to extend masjid space beyond the physical containment of mosques into courtyards, sideyards, and even streets to accommodate the number of participants. In addition, prayer mat technology has advanced to the point where some incorporate mechanisms such as compasses sewn into the fabric of the rug itself and even alarms that erupt five times daily to remind the faithful of *salat* (*Economist* 2012).

Yet such qualities do not define most everyday prayer mats, which continue to be a vital piece of spiritual technology with regard to gaining "a sense of control over disruptive forces with the potential to undermine the experience of mystical union sought by the faithful" and streamlining the set of procedures needed to successfully perform prayer (Dilley 2011, 185). A city street, a side room, a sidewalk, a market stall, an alley: each of these spaces becomes suitable as a masjid space via the prayer mat which "spread out and qibla-directed ... defines the elemental place of prayer." The prayer mat is a masjid in one of its most simplistic forms, and through its utilization, becomes architectonic in nature, "ris[ing] out of its horizontal plane and wrap[ping] itself around the space" (Haider 1996, 42).

These mobile masjids can be seen everywhere in Islamic Africa, both in mosques themselves as well as on the carts of mobile sellers roaming the streets, lined up along numerous market stalls and boutique shops around various cities, and stashed within the buses, taxis, and other modes of transport that define contemporary life. One sees prayer mats stuffed under chairs, folded haphazardly on shelves, crammed in backpacks, sitting on the dashboards of buses, all functioning as "spaces in waiting," anticipatory masjids that are activated by time, place, and performance. In fact, they are almost a hegemonic presence that unfurls to claim space at numerous times during the day, suggesting that there is a place for the unexceptional, the mundane, and even the nonspace in masjid forms, whose very nature is again founded on the individual, and through said individual's purposeful action.

At its most fundamental level, a prayer mat as masjid enables a person to remove themselves from time and space through performative practice and mentally strip themselves bare of the politics of meaning and identity, yet remain embedded in these experiences as a human being and a Muslim. The masjid subsequently becomes a spatial indication of

i.1 Defining the Masjid

spiritual performance, a supplement to the work of worship which, in itself, supports the "human labor of [self] consecration" and reaffirms "what it means to be a [Muslim] human being in a meaningful world" (Chidester and Linenthal 1995, 6; 12). This pushes back against the assumed necessity of a pre-established site for "formalized repeatable symbolic performances" (Chidester and Linenthal 1995, 9), as is so often emphasized and used to justify the establishment of monumental mosque space. Indeed, what needs to be de-emphasized with regard to the masjid is the necessity of dedicated space to provide "an arena for the performance of controlled, 'extraordinary' patterns of action" (Chidester and Linenthal 1995, 9). Forms like the prayer mat act as masjids in that they are able to orient an individual within a particular spiritual reality through the simplest possible means, setting them apart yet keeping them in conversation with the social, political, and cultural geographies of life, an awareness that allows masjids to exist as multiple types of space and continuously rearticulate themselves in response to their particular environment and context. In each case, the masjid is oriented around the act of prayer, not the space, privileging lived reality over orthodox practice through its fundamental purpose to serve the needs of the individual in the state of *salat* rather than itself.

Thus, masjids are not only privileged in and of themselves as spatial constructions for prostration, but also act as participants in broader societal narratives in multiple spatial ways. As spaces of prostration, masjids not only include mosques, but also shrines, spiritual landscapes, and even natural formations as charged spaces primed for spiritual performance, a necessary interpretation lest the masjid be reduced to suffering containment within a fossilized mosque form and prevented from incorporating all of the sacred topography that Islam encompasses. This is a necessary interpretive maneuver in that it represents a clear path toward understanding how Islam as a lifestyle, a practice, a religion, and a way of life exists and is practiced within the contemporary realities of Africa, which are increasingly categorized by flux, impermanence, and mobility, and where Islam has over time and space developed and evolved in ways that speak to both its interpretive fluidity as well as its fundamentally adaptive/broadly applicable character.[11]

---

[11] Roman Loimeier's surprisingly concise essay entitled "Is There an 'African' Islam?" (in Loimeier 2013) does an admirable job in laying out not only the routes through which Islam found purchase in various areas all over the continent, but also the modes through which it not only gained a foothold but would also go on to become one of the dominant religious groups on the continent.

i.2 Islam in Africa: Culture, Context, and the Construction of a Continental Faith

At this point, it becomes important to address the numerous political, social, and economic contexts through which Islam has been filtered on the continent over 1400 years toward yielding the diverse spatial array of masjid types that currently define Islamic practice in Africa today. The Islamic realities that emerged from these diverse historical contexts and conditions were not embedded within the geographically inscribed identities of a particular territory or series of territories, but instead resided within the individuals moving into, out of, and within these territories, whose own intricate intersectional identities and realities would evolve into complex, sophisticated societies over time. These societies collectively maintained social, political, cultural, economic, and spiritual borders defined by porousness, adaptability, and resilience, which would allow a plurality of Islamic identity and practice to flourish through diverse channels of entry, flow, and evolution.

One of the earliest testing grounds for emergent Afro-Islamic practice and space was in northeast Africa, specifically seventh-century Egypt, which became one of the primary gateways for Islam to enter the continent from the Middle East via people, objects, images, and space less than fifty years after the Prophet's death (Loimeier 2013, 11). As a bridge between Africa and Asia, Egypt became a staging point for the armies of the Rashidun Caliphate under Arab general 'Amr ibn al-'Ās to advance into North Africa between 639 and 646 CE and defeat the occupying Byzantines, which would give birth to an emergent synthetic culture composed of Islamic elements and established indigenous and pre-Islamic Egyptian cultural components. Some such components included elements from Orthodox Christianity, which had gained a foothold in Egypt during the sixth century of the common era (Loimeier 2013, 11). Egypt's newly established Muslim capital, Fustat, would be home to one of the country's first mosques (dedicated to the aforementioned conquering commander al-'Ās), and would set the stage for a Nilotic Islamic architectural style to emerge, a combination of Middle Eastern masjid templates and Arabo-Egyptian domestic architectural elements and materials (see Apotsos 2016a).

Following the Rashiduns, the Umayyads would deploy yet another general – 'Uqba ibn Nafi – to pick up where al-'Ās left off and move Umayyad armies across the face of North Africa into the Maghreb. The presence of these armies would give rise to a nascent body of Muslim merchants who would subsequently travel with the military, not only supplying them with necessary resources and materials, but also information, which enabled these traders to act as "mobile units of knowledge and influence that deposited histories, cultural, identities, and value systems wherever they stopped" (Apotsos 2016a, 43). It was perhaps through such traders that the Umayyads were subsequently exposed to the influences of various indigenous groups within the Maghreb, including Amazigh and Judaic communities who maintained a strong presence in the region, and whose various material and spatial characteristics may have found their way into the Umayyad lived environment. Some of the Umayyads' earliest "frontier" mosque structures potentially represent a cross-pollination of such ideas and influences, constructed as they were at various military outposts across the northern Sahara. One such mosque is the Great Mosque of Kairouan, built in 670 CE by Nafi himself. Part *ribat* (fortress) and part religious landmark, the mosque was not only a symbol of Islamic presence in a "land of infidels," but also an important defensive structure against potential exterior attacks (see Apotsos 2016a). In addition, it also potentially pulled some of its structural influences from another great defensive structure present in the Maghreb at this time: the *ksour* (sing. *ksar*), which were large towered earthen fortresses built by groups like the Amazigh, which were often constructed along trade routes in the southern mountain ranges of the Maghreb.[12]

These developmental architectural templates would increasingly come to be associated with an Afro-Islamic way of life and, as Muslim merchants in the Maghreb began to follow pre-established trade routes south of the Sahara, these templates would travel with them. In fact, as early as the ninth century, one would see these templates being reproduced in modified form in the context of a series of powerful West African polities: the Ghanaian, the Malian, and the Songhai, for whom Islam would become an important political, spiritual, and socioeconomic system.

Within these contexts, Islam would inspire several vibrant centers of education, scholarship, and philosophy, with cities like Timbuktu coming to be known throughout the Islamicate in the fifteenth century for its extensive libraries, archives, and universities. Many of Timbuktu's institutions were housed in a variety of deftly engineered earthen architectural forms that would go on to define the spatial character of West African Islamic urbanized life more generally. The mosques, shrines, and tombs in this area would all utilize a composite design that signaled both the power of Islam as well as the presence of pre-Islamic value systems and

---

[12] Seeming to resemble the surrounding mountains themselves, these structures were shaped to contain large communities who received protection behind their high, thick earthen walls, which also protected trade goods arriving via routes leading south into the Sahel (see Apotsos 2016a).

belief structures, which remained active in society at this time through both formal and material architectural languages.

Over time, however, this Sahelian spiritual and sociopolitical model would continue to trickle south, this time into the forest regions of the Upper Volta and the Gold Coast via primarily mercantile activity, though occasionally military and raiding activities to the south would aid in this transfer as well. Here Islam would not gain the sociopolitical foothold that it held in the Sahel, but would maintain a small, dedicated community of followers, a state potentially symbolized by the rather diminutive Islamic mosque and shrine structures that would emerge in this area. As Labelle Prussin notes in her formative article "The Architecture of Islam in West Africa" (1968), the small, "squat" nature of mosques that came about as Islam moved south into the forest regions of West Africa was not just due to a more humid climate, which prevented the structures from achieving the iconic verticality of their Sahelian cousins, but also the fact that the proclamative aesthetic deployed in Sahelian mosques would have been inappropriate to the somewhat insubstantial status of Islam in this area.[13] Yet despite Islam's less-than-monumental structural manifestations within the Volta region, Islam would nonetheless constitute a distinctive area element that, due to its minority status, would become much more concentrated and potent in certain communities and centers (see Apotsos 2016a).[14]

Islamic activity was also afoot further west of the Volta as well, in areas like the Senegambia which was introduced to the Islamic tradition as early as the eleventh century. Strong Sufi traditions would develop later in the eighteenth and nineteenth centuries under the direction of local clerical personalities and in response to the trauma of both the trans-Atlantic trade in enslaved individuals and the presence of French colonial authorities. Because of this, many early mosques in the Senegambia area maintained church-like features, reflective of French institutional policies regarding building requirements in areas like the colonial capital of Dakar. The rise of Sufi brotherhoods such as the Tijaniyyah, Muridiyya, Qādiriyya, and Layenne orders, however, would eventually result in the establishment of various "capital cities" for each Sufi brotherhood within Senegal that not only actively asserted autonomy (to a degree) from various governmental structures in terms of establishing their own normative society, but would also create numerous iconic

---

[13] It was also further influenced by incoming Muslim Hausa traders from the east in what is today Muslim-majority northern Nigeria.
[14] See Apotsos 2016a.

i.2 Islam in Africa

religious environments such as Touba, which would become a spiritual beacon for the Muridiyya religious order. Thus the trajectory that Islam would follow into the Maghreb and various parts of West Africa would create a number of diverse origin narratives and catalyze the growth of numerous forms of Islamic identity, practice, belief, and importantly, space in these respective regions.

Similar to the narrative of Islam's introduction into West Africa is its introduction into East Africa, where Islamic practice was both spiritual and socioeconomic in nature. Historically, the shore between the uppermost tip of Kenya down through Tanzania and into Mozambique is known as the Swahili coast and has been a major point of commercial activity between traders from both southern Arabia and East Africa for millennia. Because these traders crossed the Indian Ocean on the winds of the seasonal monsoons, for at least half of the year they spent their time in either southern Arabia or on the East African coast. Thus, many Arabic merchants would eventually settle in the coastal areas of Kenya and Tanzania and begin communities, generating an Afro-Arabic population that became increasingly Islamized over time. By the eighth century, a distinctive culture had emerged along the coast that became known as the Swahili, after the Arabic word *sawahili* for "[language of] the coast" and this group not only came to define themselves according to a distinctive type of religio-cultural identity, but also through a unique architectural style that would subsequently be deployed on mosque structures, homes, and towns. This style was defined by a singular material – coral – and would form the basis of what would become known popularly as "stone architecture." Distinctive for its brilliant white walls, this architecture was not only notable for its exterior but also for its interiors, which were often richly decorated in ways intended to represent the wealth and sociopolitical capital of their owners. This decorative style would also find purchase in neighboring areas like Ethiopia, whose own Islamic population was far less dominant but nonetheless still intimately connected and active in similar economic enterprises.

Yet Ethiopia deserves to be singled out for a moment due to its interesting and largely unique history with regard to Islamic presence. Early narratives detail the arrival of a small group of persecuted Muslim refugees sent by the Prophet Muhammad to be given sanctuary by the Christian King Armah (Negash) of Ethiopia (then Abyssinia) in Aksum around the beginning of the seventh century. This kindness would earn Ethiopia the title of *Dar al Hiyad*, meaning "neutral area" or area exempted from Islamic expansion and jihad, and thus gestured to the uniquely amiable relationship between Muslims and the people of Abyssinia. Although Muslims would never become a sizable population in Ethiopia, the country would nonetheless go on to be home to the fourth holiest city in Islam – Harar Jugol – whose distinctive shrines, mosques, and houses enclosed within a defensive wall represent a uniquely Islamo-Ethiopic identity, which has allowed this area and Ethiopia more broadly to maintain an important place in Islamic history.

Looking further to the south, however, Islam would also enter African continental space through less equitable means. The Dutch colonization and agricultural domestication of southern Africa, particularly in the area of the Western Cape, required the import of a great deal of manual labor. Thus, enslaved individuals and political prisoners, many of whom were Muslim, were shipped from areas such as Malaysia and Indonesia to the southern tip of the African continent to work on newly established Dutch farms. Later arrivals from India and East Africa would create an increasingly diverse Muslim population whose intricate cultural, social, and later political identities would go on to be shaped by the segregationist policies of the South African Apartheid regime. Islamic space in this context became more than just an area in which to perform one's Muslim identity. Early on, it became a political space often prohibited from existence by oppressive governmental powers and thus necessarily transient, secretive, and fundamentally politicized. Later, many of these spaces would continue to act in a sociopolitical manner, appropriating architectural elements from historically colonial architectural systems and redeploying them on Islamic facades as a mode of reclamation.

To zoom out a bit from this continental narrative, however, the idea of an Islam "assimilated" into these various regions of the continent does not mean that Islam as a practice and a worldview did not generate certain interventions on its own behalf over the course of its history on the continent. Indeed, Islam as a politicized movement has a lengthy history in Africa, taking multiple forms and having multiple implications depending on context. The growth/revitalization of Sufi orders in both West and East Africa in the nineteenth and twentieth centuries not only represented new modes of seeking enlightenment with regard to the righteous path, but were also organized as social reform movements that aimed to challenge clan and culturally based ties in favor of religious ones (Grosz-Ngate, Hanson, and O'Meara 2014, 115). There are also histories of more militant interventionist activity in the form of various conflicts, wars, and jihads (defined broadly as "religious effort or struggle") that have been both violent and nonviolent in nature (Grosz-Ngate, Hanson, and O'Meara 2014, 115). In the nineteenth century, for example, Tijaniyya leader Umar Tal in present-day Senegal would take a leaf out of the book of an earlier Muslim leader, Uthman dan Fodio (founder of the Islamic Sokoto Caliphate in northern Nigeria), and launch a jihad in what is today Mali against non-Muslim elites toward establishing an

Islamic state, a campaign that achieved significant success (Grosz-Ngate, Hanson, and O'Meara 2014, 115).

Islamic interventions were also accomplished in other ways, however. The presence of European colonial regimes in many areas around the continent from the eighteenth century onwards resulted in the promotion of Christianity as the "true" religion and the foundation of "civilized" society; subsequent conversions to Christianity would generate tension between Muslim and Christian populations that continue to exist today in many areas, largely due to lingering disparities in education (converted Christians often had access to schools run by European missionaries where they were able to learn European languages) and Christian tolerance for secular ways of life that stand in opposition to those of Islam (Grosz-Ngate, Hanson, and O'Meara 2014, 118). These elements have generated contemporary reformist movements in a number of areas in the contemporary period, some of whom, like the Sufi Muridiyyas in Senegal, continue to expand their influence through economic growth and a highly mobile population of believers, and others like Ansar Dine, which attempted to stamp out the "heretical Sufist practices" of Timbuktu by destroying the city's religious architecture in 2012. Numerous other groups, both passive and activist, exist throughout the continent, but importantly, their identities, like so many others, reflect the continuous negotiations that are currently going on between local and global currents. And these conversations are read not in the fossilized monumental mosque structures that decorate guidebooks and architectural history volumes, but emerge in the ephemeral spaces that proliferate in the nooks and crannies of urban spaces during prayer times, in the vehicles that zoom down urban streets, their Islamic decorations waving in the wind as they go, and even the forgotten, ruined spaces of history whose decay somehow still carries charge as a site of memory and performative spirituality. Such spaces collectively represent the avenues through which Islam has managed to establish itself on the continent over time and space, reflective of the fact that Islam is not, nor has it ever been, a single narrative, but a matrix with multiple centers and shifting parameters whose relations are in a constant state of flux, as are the spaces that define them.

Such spaces also provide a platform from which to think about Islam's current success on the continent and the complexity inherent in understanding the spectrum of identities and realities it maintains. Because it has been built, crafted, and refined over time and space within individuals, communities, and nations on the continent, Islam's contextually defined reality in Africa has naturally given rise to a seemingly endless degree of variation, framing it less as a "normative system with clearly

18   Introduction

defined boundaries" and more a "flexible system of reference with blurred conceptions of exclusion" (Desplat 2005, 483). This makes conversations about an "essential" nature of Islam in Africa as a cohesive concept both problematic and ambiguous.

i.3   Islam or Islam(s)? A Question of Faith, Religion, and Identity

The question of "Islams" is one that has been taken up by scholars such as Talal Asad who, in his astute article on the anthropology of Islam, offers a series of common answers for the question "What is Islam?" Such answers include the idea that there is no such "theoretical object" as Islam; that Islam is an "anthropologist's label for a heterogeneous collection of items, each of which has been designated Islamic by informants"; and lastly, that Islam is less a concept/object and more of a collective history/totality that has been deployed as an organizational mode for social life (Asad 2009, 2). Asad also references anthropologist Abdul Hamid El-Zein (1977) who ultimately arrives at the conclusion that there are multiple Islams, each "equally real, each worth describing" yet all nonetheless constitutive of "an underlying unconscious logic" (Asad 2009, 2). Yet the fact that there is no universal consensus among Muslims concerning what and what is not Islamic often positions different "Islams" in binary relationships, which means that this theory is inherently problematic. In addition, various hierarchies have been established over time between these so-called "Islams" that is largely the result of "the virtual equation of Islam with the Middle East," which has disenfranchised other "Islams" such as those in Africa by placing them in the spaces of the metaphorical Islamic "frontier" (Asad 2009, 7). Other hierarchies have been established between so-called "orthodox" and "folk" Islams (Asad 2009, 8), a binary that gives itself to associated opposites including urban vs. rural, normal vs. unconventional, literate vs. illiterate, center vs. periphery, and importantly for studies of Islam in Africa, popular vs. official, whose only point of connection seems to be an adherence to Qur'anic doctrine. The implicit value judgments evoked with regard to those Muslims who occupy the "folk," i.e. rural, peripheral, popular, etc. means that they are rarely if ever positioned as the protagonists in their own centralized narratives, seen as unable to participate in their own modes of self-fashioning and recreate and represent themselves as intersectional beings and the authors of their own spirituality.

Yet in the contemporary period, the "popular" has been increasingly applied to multiple types of nonuniform, dynamic, everyday Islamic practice composed of multiple frameworks, institutions, and dimensions, which all intersect, interact, and define themselves both with and against one another. It is also becoming increasingly recognized that such developments are the rule rather than the exception precisely because "Islam by definition encompasses both the mundane and the spiritual" and thus "the language of Islam is ... deeply embedded in the fabric of both official functions and everyday activities" (Gaffney 1992, 41). Don Yoder also points out that such "unofficial" or "popular" religious practices do "not oppose a central religious body in an organized form ..., but represent unorganized practices and ideas that have a dynamic relationship to official religion" (Primiano 1995, 39). Perhaps most importantly, this concept of faith, organized as it is around individual experience and interpretation, focuses on the importance, authenticity, and legitimacy of individual spiritual experience as based on one's lived reality, an idea intimately associated with fundamental conceptualizations of the masjid.

Many of these elements, particularly as they have existed in Afro-Islamic belief and practice, subsequently create what Don Yoder terms "a unified organic system of belief" in which elements of contemporary life that at first seem discordant and even antithetical to one another are continuously negotiated and reinterpreted until they form a new flexible reality (Yoder 1974, 13; Yoder 1990, 80; in Primiano 1995, 44). And with regard to Islam in Africa in the contemporary period, individuals are actively expanding and redefining "the nature and limits of what is religious in the Muslim society" (Tayob 1999, 10), a movement that ranges from progressive interpretations of Qur'anic verses to the creation of alternative spaces to accommodate alternative Muslim realities, all of which position one's self in modern society as a complete, authentic individual of faith.

These elements are not only demonstrative of the way that religion "articulates relations between society, the individual and modernity" (Vered and Garsten 2015, 23), but also offer frameworks through which to potentially view religions such as Islam in Africa as a system rather than a thing, less a static, rigidly constructed entity and more a fluid, dynamic medium for performing one's spiritual identity. In fact, the term "Islam" itself, according to Matthee, "designates a constellation of dynamic discourses that constitute sacred orders and also serve as the flexible vehicles of a collective identity and a universalist message, often with political dimensions and effects" (Matthee 2008, 25). This enables Muslim communities not only in Africa but around the world to act as a global body of followers connected by a religious paradigm that provides not only spiritual but also political, social, and cultural guidance as well, not only allowing Islam to spread into diverse areas but also resulting in the religion itself "tak[ing] as many forms ... as there are individual believers" (Primiano 1995, 51). In this case, Oskar Verkaaik notes, "it is no longer self-evident what religious means within a particular historical moment" (Verkaaik 2013, 13). Thus, the various material and structural expressions of faith become a key component in its identification and interpretation and, importantly, reflect the fact that neither Islam nor the spiritual spaces associated with it are pristine, contained, or preserved. If Islam as a spiritual system can be thought of in this way, then the masjid must be recognized for what it is: a sometimes beautiful, sometimes mundane, occasionally gritty space of everyday life, which constitutes the essence of contemporary spirituality.

i.4 Re-Narrating the Masjid Through an Afro-Centric Lens

As space undefined by structure, "experienced through embodied performance" (Della Dora 2015), and thus both the product and producer of Muslim identity, the masjid becomes a stable and thus transportable spatial ideal, individualized and diversified yet nonetheless maintaining a certain invariable character based on a Muslim's sense of "being in the universe" (Bokhari 1980, 77). Thus, the masjid becomes "a physical manifestation of man's attempt to approach cosmological ideals and divine concepts" with the "inner" being much more important than the "outer" (Bokhari 1980, 76). Such interpretations have had deep impacts on current scholarship oriented toward the study of Afro-Islamic space and form, which makes the topic of this volume not only timely but also pivotal in the contemporary period in that both Islamic studies in Africa and studies of the built environment are currently experiencing a transformative disciplinary moment. Historical discussions of Islam in Africa have been crafted along the lines of centers and peripheries in both geographic and intellectual senses, binaries that have subjected African Islam and its attendant spaces of practice to a type of "third world-ism," existing peripherally and thus subject to multiple simultaneous oppressions. Subsequently, masjid spaces in Islamic Africa have come to occupy a "third space" in scholarship, considered legible or acceptable only when they mimic first or second spaces, i.e. those of the West or, in Islam's case, the East. These replications aim to make Islamic spaces in Africa familiar and thus knowable/legible, while simultaneously becoming tolerable and able to be absorbed into an established canon.

Yet Islamic space in Africa is receiving increasingly nuanced scholarly attention in the contemporary period toward engaging in a revisionist project, motivated by the faith's rapid and widely publicized growth across the continent in recent decades. The statistics are telling in that, currently, one in three Africans identify as Muslim and loose figures have the Muslim population on the continent hovering at around 40%, numbers that belie Islam's long historical presence on the continent and its significant contribution to African spatial culture and religious identity over the course of its tenure. Existing as an African phenomenon almost as long as it has been a Middle Eastern one, Islam is a deeply entrenched cultural and religious presence, whose followers have affected many of the most dramatic sociocultural, spiritual, and material developments on the continent, shaping landscapes and mentalities for over a millennium and establishing a powerful network of identities on the continent in the process.

Further, approaches to Islamic space in Africa are evolving beyond the paradigm of "stylistic description" toward a consideration of Afro-Islamic space and form as an "operative category" (Bhatt and Patel 1998, 47), using individuals to construct architecture, not the architecture to construct the individual. The nature of architectural history as it has been applied to "third spaces" thus far has been a methodology of assembling cultures through architectural objects, whereas current studies like the present one aim to position individuals as operators and consumers rather than passive inhabitants and recipients (Verkaaik 2013, 11). Participants in other words become the protagonists of their own sociospatial narrative.

To this end, this volume views Islamic space and form through the lens of the idea of Afro-centricity, or a retelling of history that places Africa in the center rather than the periphery, which in turn focuses on those elements "authentic" to African history, experience, and identity (Mazrui 2005, 77). Although this paradigm has been traditionally hostile to "alien forces" like Islam, contemporary thinkers are moving in directions that view these elements as contributions to the diversity and uniqueness of the continent as a whole. In addition, such a view has enormous potential in the contemporary period to privilege the continent's histories and identities by recognizing the multiple forms and directions that modernization is taking on the continent today, particularly with regard to Islamic space and the contemporary realities of being Muslim in Africa. As such, this volume addresses the concept of the masjid from the basis of its existence within conditions of sociopolitical, cultural, and economic flux, underscoring the ways in which space is not only able to accommodate the needs and desires of variegated Muslim communities firmly situated in the canons of their faith, but also enable these communities to engage in constructive dialogues with the contemporary global influences that are currently shaping Islamic cultural and spiritual identity on the continent.

Such a model of the masjid, to quote Hasan-Uddin Khan, is both "contemporary and timeless" (Khan 1990, 126), maintaining its reality as an independent, individual space while also embedding itself within the broader physical, sociocultural, political, and spiritual fabric of its environment. In this way, the masjid not only reaffirms Islam's presence and identity within an area but also reflects associated values back to the Muslim community as well as others who share it. Toward analyzing the contemporary reality of the masjid as it lies at the intersection of multiple Islams existing within African spaces, the case studies in this volume are oriented around four major contemporary analytical lenses that address the key spatial attributes of existence that constitute contemporary modern life both on the continent and around the world.

The first lens is that of intersectionality, which privileges the intertwined reality of identities that exist within the space of a single individual or a group. Theories of intersectionality hold that because of these multiple realities and identities, an individual or group can not only experience multiple simultaneous realities at once but also multiple oppressions and disenfranchisements as a result of bias or discrimination against the various components of their identity. Taking intersectionality as an interrogative platform, the first chapter in this volume explores three different case studies involving the intersectional condition, the first being the current position of Muslim women within mosque/masjid congregations throughout South Africa, whose history of exclusion, disenfranchisement, and marginalization has crafted the ideological contours of South African mosque space and thus hindered its function as masjid or a "space of prostration" for all. This situation has led to the development of new spaces such as the Open Mosque in Cape Town, South Africa, which actively promotes the originary function of the masjid by providing a space where men and women alike can engage in performative spirituality in an equitably oriented spatial environment. This discussion continues into the next case study with a consideration of the Al-Fitre Foundation, located only a block away from the Open Mosque, which is currently the continent's first openly LGBT+ congregation and moves beyond gender-equitable spaces to promote an environment for Muslims whose sexual identity does not conform to that traditionally interpreted by Islamic doctrine. This space not only acts as a place of prostration, but also an affirmational space for LGBT+ Muslims to perform spiritual identity from the basis of a largely marginalized existence. Yet just as masjid spaces can empower identity, they can also be deployed toward disrupting, intervening, and even destroying it as well, as was the case in 2012 when the extremist group Ansar Dine engaged in a broad-based destructive campaign that targeted the predominantly Sufi environment of Timbuktu and aimed to eliminate the spatial touchstones of this historical identity. Not only did this iconoclastic campaign touch on

i.4 Re-Narrating Masjid Through Afro-Centric Lens

issues of Islamic orthodoxy but it also used existing tensions with regard to Mali's national heritage campaign in the northern region to catalyze this iconoclastic response. Ansar Dine's campaign subsequently transformed Timbuktu's masjid landscape into a space of ruin, a "counter-masjid," that in many ways actively traumatized not only the physical landscape but the human landscape as well. Collectively, however, these case studies reveal the masjid for its function as a spatial text that articulates the specific sociopolitical character of the context that shapes it and it is in this way that these spaces are able to either "contest unequal power relationships ... [and] ... affirm the existence of inequality in the struggle of life" or "simply ... confirm the social status quo" or in some cases erase it toward crafting one anew (Primiano 1995, 47).

Following intersectionality, the next interpretive lens deployed within this volume toward understanding masjids in contemporary Islamic Africa is critical heritage studies, a natural continuum of the intersectional discussion in that heritage, as a physical or immaterial legacy, not only plays an important role in the establishment of identity but is also created through a continuous process of compromise, concession, mediation, and sometimes intervention. As a "production of the past in the present" (Harrison 2013, 32), heritage is subject to continuous renovation and reimagining as a result of the nature of the existent relationships between people and the value systems and priorities that are operating at any one time within society. The case studies addressed in Chapter 2, thus, explore situations where heritage has taken spatial form in the masjid and how the two exist in a somewhat uneasy relationship with regard to heritage's need to conserve and the masjid's need to adapt. The Islamic holy city of Harar Jugol in Ethiopia, as the first case study in this chapter, reflects the particular work that masjid forms do in organizing the "life" of Harar's Muslim community through the creation of a spiritual topography that makes the entire town not only a masjid area, but also a community space. However, Harar is also an important Islamic heritage site, making the city "a social space characterized by many different symbolic and material struggles" (Jones 2011, 12). These struggles are actively and simultaneously inscribed on the physical condition of the spatial environment, particularly the city's shrine and mosque structures, which serve as spiritual touchstones for many Muslims in East Africa. The case of Harar subsequently begs the questions of how preservation affects perception and performativity within the masjid space. The second case study of this chapter focuses on mid-twentieth-century Egyptian architect Hassan Fathy and his design of the planned Muslim community of New Gourna, a space intended to both function as a sustainable community for its inhabitants while also celebrating Egypt's architectural, cultural, and spiritual legacies through the use of ideas of "appropriate technology" (AT) deployed in a socially and culturally resilient manner. The structural keystone of this community was to be the mosque structure, whose formal and social centrality would anchor the community's identity. Yet New Gourna would ultimately achieve limited success, and Fathy would take his ideas and apply them to a later project located in Abiquiú, New Mexico, called Dar al Islam. Part masjid, part educational center, Dar al Islam maintains a strong embeddness in the local cultural and ecological environment through its commitment to producing a light footprint on the surrounding desert landscape and, importantly, structurally and materially referencing historical Native American traditions in the area as well, tapping into their structural legacy to inform its own. Yet this case study also highlights the fact that, just as heritage traditions and ideas can be exported out of an area, they can also be imported in. This is a particularly interesting situation in that conventional ideals of heritage tend to evoke ideas of "authenticity" through local embeddedness. Yet such conventions are being challenged in the contemporary period by expanding networks of influence that are connecting people, communities, and environments across the globe. The growth of "Afro-Ottoman" mosques in Africa represents one such example of this tension as a style embedded in Ottoman Turkish history and identity, yet experiencing a new reality within African space as it is being increasingly deployed to symbolize Afro-Islamic identity. Thus, the third and final case study in this chapter focuses on the National Mosque of Ghana, located in the capital city of Accra, which was completed in 2016 with funding from the Turkish government and is built in the style of Turkey's Sultan Ahmed Mosque, popularly known as the Blue Mosque. As a self-styled monument to Islamic identity in Ghana, this mosque oddly eschews Ghana's historical architectural tradition of mosque building, particularly in the northerly regions of the country, in favor of an imported style that raises questions with regard to the motivations behind its construction and its disregard for established national legacies.

This brings us to the next interpretive methodology used in this volume, a method also connected to ideas of conservation and preservation. Contemporary environmentalism and eco-criticism are experiencing global attention in the contemporary period not only as movements but as philosophies and, in Islam's case, as directives, given the role of man according to the Qur'an, as the steward of God's creation (the earth). Indeed, environmental concerns have long laid at the heart of Islamic spiritual and spatial practice in terms of how the masjid functions as an expression of the relationship between man and the natural environment. Thus, the case studies in Chapter 3 focus on the creation of sustainable

i.4 Re-Narrating Masjid Through Afro-Centric Lens

relationships between man and nature, and the construction of resilient spaces that not only complement the natural world but actively work to maintain it. This chapter begins with a discussion of the kramats or shrines of Cape Town, South Africa, which utilize what might be called a "natural aesthetic" given their locations throughout the diverse natural zones of Cape Town's environment (mountains, beaches, forests). In some cases, the kramats themselves are all but indistinguishable from the surrounding landscape, generating situations in which nature itself becomes the "architecture" of the kramat, not only privileging the idea that all of the earth is a masjid, but also reflecting a sensitivity to nature as something to be celebrated, venerated, and preserved. The next case study takes the relationships between man and nature in a more design-oriented direction, focusing on ways in which architecture can sometime utilize natural engineering solutions for the production of built form. The Djenne mosque in Mali, as the second case study, not only deploys historical building technology toward creating a fundamentally environmentally friendly structure made entirely out of mud, but also deploys natural engineering in the form of a biomimetic adaptation of the West African termite mound, whose superior heating, cooling, and organizational systems provide an excellent model on which to base a space meant to quite literally act as a byproduct of spiritual reality. Yet natural technology can also be supplemented by manmade technology as expressed in the final case study in this chapter: Tanzania's first "eco-mosque." Recently constructed on the outskirts of Dar es Salaam in the Mkurunga district, the mosque is located in the Children's Eco-Village, a sustainable community sponsored by the British NGO Islamic Help. Standing as a prototype for the application of ecologically and spiritually responsible living, the village's masjid and community is designed to promote green living and decreased environmental impact, privileging the idea of masjid as a fundamentally eco-friendly spatial concept that can manifest both with and without specific physical infrastructure. Yet the eco-masjid and its surrounding community use appropriate, locally sourced technology to accomplish its goal of living sustainably and self-sufficiently.

The final interpretive methodology utilized in this volume, however, points to the fundamental component that differentiates the masjid from so many other types of space, spiritual or otherwise: its ability to move. The inherent mobility of masjid space as it travels and evolves in response to changing conditions of being underscores what Mimi Sheller and John Urry term the "mobility paradigm," a system of "fluid interdependences" composed of the movement of people, ideas, objects, and visual culture that are connected along similar lines of transfer and exchange (Rizvi 2015, 8). Mobility paradigms are also increasingly utilized to mediate

26   Introduction

broad-based discussions of contemporary "globalization," whose breadth has made it difficult to define and unwieldy to use with any degree of accuracy or nuance.[15] The case studies in Chapter 4 address the ways in which mobility pushes discussions of space, especially masjid space, beyond considerations of three-dimensional shelter toward highlighting the fact that spaces embedded in contemporary conditions often leave conventional spatial models behind toward creating spaces that accommodate individuals and groups on the move. The first case study focuses on the brightly colored, icon-laden public transport buses or *car rapides* of the city of Dakar. These vessels in many ways act as mobile masjids through their exterior spiritual ornamentation, and as such become containers of blessing capable of transporting and possibly even depositing sanctification as they go. These "spaces" not only act as apparatuses for advertising and performing Muslim identity within the physical, social, and cultural fabric of Dakar, but also create spaces that simultaneously speak to the city's reality as one of the largest, most modernized cities in West Africa. Following this line of thought, the second case study in this chapter follows the growing popularity of air travel and the subsequent development of airport prayer spaces on the continent, whose spiritually ambiguous identities allow them to shift character in response to the bodies that inhabit them. The fleeting relationships established between transient bodies and space create a somewhat chimerical reality for the masjid as a spiritual space-in-waiting, a mirror of the ephemeral spiritual needs of individual inhabitants in motion and thus existing in a state of constant destabilization. This sense of destabilization is also present in the third case study, which addresses the holy city of Touba (Senegal) and its newest reality as a digital environment. "New Information and Communication Technologies" growth (Guèye 2003) has created a new spatial identity for the city that allows it to operate *beyond* its

---

[15] His study challenges broad-based contextualizations of globalization as a "universal" condition equitably distributed across numerous geographies by highlighting the global inequalities that govern one's access to the "tools of globalization" such as technology, communication, transportation, and of course space. It is because of this that Abdoulaye Saine holds that globalization is largely "incomplete," its "partial character" resulting from the fact that "only a few countries are fully integrated and receive most of the benefits from it" (Saine 2011, 405). At best, globalization has become "an ideology aimed at justifying American, as well as Western, hegemony in the global economy"; at worst, it acts as "a sanitized 'imperialism' used to conceal continued exploitation of weaker states by the powerful and the rich" (Saine 2011, 405). In many cases "globalization" is indicative of the presence of hierarchies of vulnerability and dominance; thus, when the term is used in the context of this volume, it is done so with an eye toward this reality. This conceptualization also challenges the West's domination over the definition of modernity as "a global condition affecting cultural life and institutional forms as much as capitalist cycles and hegemonic contentions" (Böwering, Crone, and Mirza 2013, 352).

i.4 Re-Narrating Masjid Through Afro-Centric Lens

geographic borders by expanding itself as a conceptual "territory" into a global digital environment. For followers of Mouridism, thus, Touba no longer exists only as a tangibly rooted masjid space, but now as a flexible, mobile, digital terrain that is able to realize itself virtually beyond the boundaries of the city's physical space. This in turn has the potential to "de-colonize" space or release it from established power hierarchies of presence vs. absence while also constituting a new frontier for religious practice as pure unadulterated space for a body freed from its sensual, i.e. mundane, fleshy dimensions.

Collectively, these chapters, their interpretive methods, and the case studies presented therein position the masjid as a space fundamentally rooted in the present, but also essentially anticipatory in nature as a space on the edge of multiple possible identities and realities, thriving at the thresholds of multiple sociopolitical paradigms, geographical frontiers, and technological horizons. The masjid in contemporary Islamic Africa thus not only actively reproduces diverse iterations of Muslim identity within the space of the continent, but also adapts within these contexts in response to an evolving spectrum of influences, ideologies, and interventions that each play important roles in shaping the contours of Islamic identity and practice within specific regional contexts. Thus, the masjid in contemporary Islamic Africa is a fundamentally flexible space, able to accommodate the needs and desires of a diverse Islamic community firmly situated in the canons of their faith, but which also allows communities to engage in constructive conversation with the modernizing influences that are increasingly shaping their contemporary condition. Through this exercise in reimagining, the masjid becomes a collective, multi-tiered cross section of how Islam exists in the contemporary period, and how Muslims are using space to navigate contemporary life in Africa as well as in a global contemporary world.

1 Spaces Both Radical and Revolutionary: The Intersectional Masjid

The masjid is composed of a set of representative frameworks that reflect its sociopolitical identity back to itself and to others.

1.1 Introduction

Masjids are intersectional precisely because the individuals who create them are intersectional, maintaining any number of complex identities that together generate the unique character of a person and position them as members of multiple communities or groups simultaneously. Yet with this simultaneous membership also comes the possibility of simultaneous oppressions stemming from bias and discrimination against one or more of an individual's identities. The fact that masjids are brought into being by the performative ritual action of an individual means that such spaces naturally respond to the lived reality of this individual by maintaining potentially infinite variations in form, space, and place, all fundamentally attuned to an individual's unique condition and their subsequent position within the space of society.

The term "intersectionality" was first coined by jurist and critical race theorist Kimberlé Williams Crenshaw in 1989 as an approach to human identity and experience that recognizes that individuals are composed of multiple identities that are not mutually exclusive. The combination of overlapping, combining, and intersecting identities that compose an individual in turn has the possibility of producing diverse, highly unique experiences of marginalization, disenfranchisement, and oppression. Thus, various modes of oppression, whether they be racism, sexism, xenophobia, etc., are not experienced as singular disenfranchising units, but as a broader interactive system of subjugation.[1] Intersectionality is

---

[1] In her landmark article "Demarginalizing the Intersection of Race and Sex: A Black Feminist Critique of Antidiscrimination Doctrine, Feminist Theory and Antiracist Politics," Crenshaw notes with regard to the experience of black women: "Black women are sometimes excluded from feminist theory and antiracist policy discourse because both

1.1 Introduction

also an evolutionary condition in that as social systems change and shift, new intersections of inclusion/exclusion/oppression are created. Along these lines, intersectionality as a mode of approach has also been broadened to focus on issues of gender and sexuality, which will be explored later in this chapter.

Theories such as intersectionality also maintain an interesting space within conversations of globalization, not only in terms of the modes through which individuals are constructing identities across various borders and boundaries but also how "social lives are constructed, not only in single countries, but in transnational spaces ... [or] ... tangible geographic spaces that exist across multiple nation-states *and* virtual spaces" (Purkayastha 2012, 56). Broad-based networks have led to the movement of goods, images, and ideas across space, enabling "many groups to create lives that extend far beyond the boundaries of single nation-states," settling in multiple sites around the globe as "transnational villagers ... engaging in politics in 'homelands'" (Purkayastha 2012, 56). Likewise, the growth of the digital realm has not only enabled the emergence of "cyber migrants" who utilize technology to "work" in the "global north" while being physically based in the "global south" but has also enabled a different type of existence through the physical elision of the "consequences of gendering, racialization, class, and other social hierarchies to which they are subjected in their tangible lives" (Purkayastha 2012, 56). Yet just as modes of living in the contemporary period have evolved in some ways to counteract established institutions of intersectional oppression, this has also led to the revamping of established institutions toward generating new sociopolitical forms of control and oppression as well as new modes of disenfranchisement that in some cases find form in the spatial environment.

With regard to situating masjids in contemporary Islamic Africa within this discussion, it is important to revisit the fact that being Muslim also exists as a component of one's intersectional identity, functioning within a larger Venn diagram of realities within an individual where religion in conjunction with ethnicity, culture, race, sexuality, gender, caste, and socioeconomic status all intermingle in unique, unpredictable, and somewhat uncontrollable ways. Within various Afro-Islamic societies, a broad spectrum of stakeholders have contributed to the meaning and messaging of masjid space over time as a site that has come to act as a mode of spatializing and thus legitimizing a group identity. Masjid space in the contemporary period is becoming both a key apparatus and a signifier of

---

are predicated on a discrete set of experiences that often does not accurately reflect the interaction of race and gender" (Crenshaw 1989, 140).

these various conversations, negotiations, and oppressions as a sociopolitical construct, informed largely by the histories and narratives that inform its particular context.

Toward exploring this topic, this chapter focuses on three case studies, two in South Africa and one in Mali, that illustrate the modes through which masjid space has been utilized to generate feelings of belonging and exile as a response to conditions of intersectional existence. In South Africa, masjid spaces have emerged as mechanisms with which to push back against institutional biases and discrimination that have enabled the spatial exclusion of women and LGBT+ members of the South African Muslim community from participation in mosque-based spiritual performances. In contrast, recently in Mali, masjid spaces (and specifically their destruction) have been deployed as tools of trauma toward disempowering Islamic identity, specifically Timbuktu's largely Sufi identity, through the transformation of the landscape into a spatial martyr. In each case, the masjid does not exist as a stand-alone space, but is an active representation of intersectional being, operationalized as a mechanism toward establishing and actively inserting identity and agenda onto the spatial environment.

1.2 Women in the Masjid: Gender Equity and Cape Town's Open Mosque

This story thus begins in South Africa with the Open Mosque, a masjid located in the suburb of Wynberg right outside of Cape Town, South Africa (Figure 1.1a and 1.1b). Housed in a repurposed autobody shop, the Open Mosque opened in 2014 and frames itself as a space "for all Progressive, Open-Minded, and Forward-Looking Muslims." The Open Mosque exists under the direction of Imam Taj Hargey, who has a PhD in religious studies from Oxford and became a highly controversial figure in Great Britain for his "Ban the Burqa" campaign in 2014.[2] Importantly, though, Hargey and by extension the Open Mosque has taken an aggressive stance on what it perceives to be the general condition of Islam in South Africa: a defunct religion based on "mindless rituals, superstitious legends, cultural mythology and a **blatant sexist contamination** of the **pristine faith** ... [based not on] ... Islam's supreme text but from suspect subsidiary sources" (bold face part of the original quote). It also targets growing Wahabist "distortions" of the Qur'an as being the

---

[2] Hargey has strong opinions concerning the practice of veiling, calling it a cultural rather than a religious practice. In a rather colorful comparison, Hargey notes: "If I want to put a bone through my nose – I have a right ... but then do I have a right to say a bone through my nose is an Islamic thing?" (Seemungal 2015).

1.2 Women in the Masjid

(a)

(b)

Figure 1.1 a and b Exterior and interior views of the Open Mosque, Wynberg, Cape Town, South Africa, 2018. Images by the author.

primary instigators for "growing Muslim alienation to and disaffection with contemporary religion." Along these lines, the Open Mosque also singles out various South African Islamic institutions like the Muslim Judiciary Council as instigators of this condition, specifically as a "**self-appointed, un-accountable** and **non-transparent body** of often poorly trained clergy" who offer "no **recognized haven** for progressive or **thinking Muslims** fed-up with a 'fairy-tale' faith or non-Qur'anic dogmas" (Open Mosque n.d.). In another move of ideological positioning, the mosque identifies "reason and logic" rather than "blind belief and robotic ritualism" as the path forward for Islam in South Africa.[3]

The Open Mosque offers an alternative space of Islamic practice through a forward path that, ironically, has its basis in historical Islamic practice, and much of this is represented through the spatial apparatus of the structure. The structure of the masjid, for example, "heeds the **original format** of the first house of prayer" by maintaining no gendered entrances and having no visual or physical barriers or partitions to separate the sexes. Along these lines, the mosque congregation holds that "sexual equality and gender parity is an unequivocal Qur'anic ordinance and that women's intrinsic rights are not subordinate to those of their male counterparts" (Open Mosque n.d.). Thus, there are no visual or structural divisions within the prayer hall itself, which is an open, square room that maintains a full 360-degree view of one's surroundings (and coinhabiters). The prayer hall and the study space are also not separate, but occupy side-by-side unpartitioned spaces, which gestures not only toward a general idea of transparency between worship and education but also the intimate connection between intellect and spiritual practice, an interpretation that stands as one of the foundations of the Open Mosque. The open plan of this structure also represents a spatialization of the mosque's theological position in that the Open Mosque is not affiliated with any specific school of Islamic thought and focuses on individual empowerment through a steady rotation of secular experts and religious specialists who act as sequential "Imams" and "ensure that the congregation benefit[s] from deliberate cross-pollination" (Open Mosque n.d.). As a side note, the fact that the Open Mosque is located in a repurposed autobody shop not only reflects the somewhat stark approach the congregation takes to Islamic practice and belief but also denies the necessity of

---

[3] I experienced the activistic ideology of Open Mosque members in my first inquiry. Upon asking if I could visit and whether I should dress a certain way, I was informed that I would be welcome to "witness liberal and progressive Islam in action" and that matters such as dress code were "merely the manufactured whims of a patriarchal clergy" and that the Open Mosque "has nothing to hide" (personal communication, Jamila Abrahams, 9/14/2017).

a purpose-built iconography-riddled structure which has traditionally been deployed to proclaim Islam in a landmark fashion. Indeed, the Open Mosque harkens to a "stripped bare" version of masjid space, characterized by a deemphasis of the space itself and a primacy placed on the structure as a functional container for the educated body engaged in a process of spiritual growth and enlightenment.

The sanctuary itself, with its lime-green walls and fluorescent lighting, underscores this progressive, content-oriented focus, as does the presence and calligraphic style of the *Shahada*, or the Islamic declaration that there is no God but God and that the Prophet Muhammad is his messenger, which is displayed along the mosque walls in a continuous banner (Figure 1.2). Unlike more traditional calligraphic styles that often represent the *Shahada* with flourish to the point of illegibility in aesthetic script styles ranging from *Kufic* to *Naskh*, *Thuluth*, etc., the *Shahada* displayed in the Open Mosque is done so using a highly modernistic, almost calligram-esque style that is organized in a continuous panel around the room in vacillating colors. Although the use of calligraphic panels is traditional within the decorative program of many historical and contemporary mosque spaces, they are rarely deployed as a singular unit. Rather, they are part and parcel of a larger aesthetic program in which textual elements are combined and

Figure 1.2 Detail of the *Shahada*, Open Mosque, Wynberg, Cape Town, South Africa, 2018. Image by the author.

manipulated into a variety of dizzying, often ambiguous combinations. The display of the *Shahada* in the Open Mosque is in stark style and, as the only decorative element in the room, pushes back against historically ornament-heavy interior programs in a way that emphasizes rather than obscures the message of the *Shahada* through its visual clarity, its singular presence, and its legibility, in turn underscoring the role of the space as functional and spiritual rather than an exercise in aesthetic experience. In many ways, the structure of the Open Mosque is the spatial equivalent of its mission statement: the masjid does not privilege useless ritualistic, fetishistic elements and instead aims to return to the fundamental elements of the faith as expressed in the Qur'an, in which both verses of the *Shahada* are found in Surahs 37:35 and 48:29, respectively. It is also in this way that the interior program emphasizes the supremacy of the Qur'an over complementary texts like the hadith as the sole source of Islamic guidance.

As one of the only gender-neutral masjid spaces in South Africa and the continent more broadly, the Open Mosque maintains an identity deeply embedded in both spiritual performance as well as sociopolitical messaging, a reality that is also reflective of the historical context of South Africa more broadly, whose historical narrative surrounding the politics of Islam, gender, and space is entrenched within a larger conversation concerning the relationship between space, history, and national identity in the pre-Apartheid, Apartheid, and now post-Apartheid period.

Islam arrived in South Africa only six years after the Dutch East India Company (Vereenigde Oostindische Campagnie) established a supply depot on the South African coast in 1652. The first Muslims to arrive in this colony did so from Southeast Asia and were composed of Amboyans ("Amboya" being an Indonesia island) and Mardyckers (free men, loosely translated) who were brought over to help defend the depot against indigenous San and Khoi groups along the coast. Eventually, additional Muslim populations were brought to the region as an enslaved workforce, the Dutch having pegged the indigenous San and Khoi peoples as being "unreliable" and subsequently decimating their numbers in short order. Additional non-Muslim enslaved individuals were also delivered from Angola and present-day Benin (Loimeier 2013, 249).

Among these early Muslims was 'Abdallāh Qādī 'Abd al-Salām, a.k.a. Tuan Guru ("Master Teacher"), a Moluccan religious scholar sent to the Cape in 1780 for conspiring with the British against the Dutch, who would subsequently become known as the father of South African Islam. He would be imam at the first mosque in the Cape Province, the Auwal Masjid, which would be the first of a steady stream of masjid spaces to branch off in its wake over the next few centuries.

1.2 Women in the Masjid

The Apartheid regime, however, would effectively curtail the rights, movements, associations, and access to spaces, spiritual and others, of nonwhite South Africans across the country, many Muslim communities included. Launched in 1948 under the direction of the newly elected National Party, Apartheid would also provide the impetus for Muslim communities to begin organizing and developing a more activist identity.[4] In 1961, Muslims in the Cape created the *Call of Islam*, an organization whose goal was to fight the oppression of Apartheid through the lens of Islamic ideology, declaring the political system *haram* or forbidden. The group was first led by Imam Abdullah Haroon, who died in police custody in 1969 and "became a renowned martyr for the anti-apartheid cause" (Sonn 1994, 15). Ten years later, the Muslim Youth Movement (MYM) emerged, followed by spinoff movements like the Women's Islamic Movement and the Islamic Da'wah Movement, and it was during this period that many young Muslims also began participating in political demonstrations and underground antigovernment groups like the African National Congress (ANC) and the Pan Africanist Congress (PAC) (Matthee 2008, 92); in fact, a handful of Muslim leaders such as Yusuf Dadoo, Ahmed Timol, Ismail Cachalia, and Fathima Meer became noted anti-Apartheid activist figures at this time (Khan 2017). Although the first Call to Islam eventually became defunct, it was revived in the mid-1980s by former members of some of the previous groups, the MYM and the United Democratic Front specifically, and has remained at the "forefront of Islamic social justice movements" (Sonn 1994, 15).

Yet this is not to say that the politicized identity that Muslim communities developed both before and during Apartheid was unified. Numerous cleavages occurred within this population, particularly with regard to politics, Islamic philosophy, race, ethnicity, and cultural identity. One particularly contentious issue was that of gender equality and inclusion, particularly with regard to the presence of women within the masjid space of the mosque. Numerous Muslim activist groups in the Apartheid and immediate post-Apartheid period have taken up this issue. Two aforementioned Muslim groups – the Muslim Youth Movement (established in 1970) and the Call of Islam, established thirteen years later

---

[4] It should be noted that this activist identity was also present before Apartheid. In the Cape Province during the period of the Dutch East India company (1602–1799), for example, the Muslim community at the time was actively engaged in creating a culture of resistance to both the company and the Dutch Reformed Church as a survival tactic to preserve their emergent identity. Muslim ritual practice and prayer in many ways became a mode of establishing "zones of freedom in a realm of legal, political and social oppression," largely because such activities were restricted. This also led to the creation of secret spaces of prayer or *langers* (prayer rooms), which came to act as the community's emergent masjids before the establishment of dedicated mosque spaces was approved (Loimeier 2013, 251).

in 1983 – positioned women as active members within these respective organizations and pushed for women's rights and equality within the parameters of Islamic practice (Hoel 2013a, 83). Indeed, by the 1990s, the feminist discourse within South African Islamic circles had become more confident. The Muslim Youth Movement established a "Gender Desk" in 1993 manned by noted activist Shamima Shaikh, who acted as the National Coordinator and promoted a broader Gender Equality Campaign (Jeenah 2001, 11). The MYM was also behind the notable "women in mosques" campaign, which advocated for women's right to use the space and for the mosques themselves to provide the necessary facilities for them to do so. Yet this movement in particular drew overwhelming criticism from the 'ulama or Islamic religious scholarly group, who felt such a move represented a stark deviation from Qur'an proscription (Jeenah 2001, 13–14) in addition to representing a general challenge to the body of scholars themselves as the foremost interpreters of Qur'anic law.

It should be noted as well that such conversations are not and have never been specific to South Africa or Africa more generally. The history of separating women and men in Islamic religious space is both common and has taken many different forms. One of the first spatial tools deployed to this end was the *hijab*, which was originally an architectural partition and only later came to refer to a head covering that women wear.[5] Indeed, *hijab* as it was first conceived was a broad concept intimately connected to principles of modesty (*haya* in Arabic) and was first mentioned in the Qur'an as a type of barrier or screen, which gave the wives of the Prophet protection against those looking to slander them as in Qur'an Surah 33:53, which states "and when ye ask (the Prophet's wives) for anything ye want, ask them from before a screen (*hijab*): that makes for greater purity for your hearts and for theirs." The verses dealing with these architectural forms were also crafted during a time when slander and gossip were serious concerns, gaining particular prominence during the time of Muhammed when the Prophet's wife Aisha was accused and found innocent of adultery (BBC 2009). *Hijab* thus came to refer to a curtain or screen placed between men and women within a space that allowed them to converse without having to dress appropriately, although this practice was more common historically.

---

[5] A woman's head covering more appropriately called a *khimaar*, which is a piece of cloth (sometimes two) which covers the hair, ears, and neck while outside the home. In the contemporary period, the *hijab* as an element of one's personal appearance has taken on numerous additional realities as a fashion accessory, a statement of identity, a tool of empowerment, and even as a vehicle of activism.

1.2 Women in the Masjid

Although practices in South Africa vary across congregations, many communities have tended to favor an outright ban on the presence of women within the space of the mosque. In the contemporary period, some mosques have adopted more progressive views that have allowed women space in the form of separate entrances and rooms for ritual ablution, and spaces for prayer that run the gamut from balconies and mezzanines to basements and even backyards (Hoel 2013b). Yet due to the secondary and largely undignified nature of many of these additive spaces, mosques in South Africa largely continue to perform in accordance with dominant ideologies in Islam and some might say even broader South African society, which not only favors traditionalist views of women in Islam but also actively implements and reinforces the dominant gender power hierarchies of society. Thus, mosque spaces in South Africa have both historically and in the contemporary period been shaped by and continue to shape "the progress of gender domination" (Taleb 2005, 13).

Such entrenched beliefs with regard to women, and the active control of female presence and movement within Islamic physical and social space, have been vigorously defended through the use of Qur'anic verses such as Qur'an Surah 2:228, which states "Women shall have rights similar to the rights against them, according to what is equitable; but men have a degree over them." Likewise, Qur'an Surah 4:34 states: "Men are in charge of women," and Qur'an Surah 33:33 commands: "And stay quietly in your houses, and make not a dazzling display, like that of the former times of ignorance" (Jeenah 2001, 9). Such verses have historically been interpreted to mean that women were not only of sub-par intellect and spirituality, but that they were inherently untrustworthy due to their tendency to gossip and their penchant for self-decoration (Jeenah 2001, 9). This is despite the fact that there are noted instances in the Qur'an when the Prophet not only advises men not to prevent women from attending prayers at the mosque, but also commands them to attend certain communal prayers such as that during the Eid. In addition, the prayer space of the Prophet himself included both men and women. Despite these elements, the presence of women within the spiritual space of the mosque is often positioned not only as a distraction, but also as inherently problematic in that their presence could potentially "desacralize or defile" space, regardless of the fact that mosque space as a space "set apart" is not endowed with a spirituality that would make such acts concerning (Hoel 2013b).

Specifically, it has been articulated that gender separation is a necessary contingent of a spiritually "pure" space. Unlike non-Islamic religious spaces that derive their spiritual capital from empowered relics/artifacts or geographic location/symbolism (as in the Christian tradition), the presence of sanitized bodies engaged in the committed performance of prayer generates the spiritual resonance of a masjid space; indeed, it is what gives the space its masjid identity and separates it from surrounded spaces. Yet the sanitized bodies that have historically been privileged with producing this spiritual space are historically gendered male and thus a hegemonic relationship has developed over time and space that equates the male body with the construction and configuration of spiritual space. The female body, in contrast, has innate sexual characteristics that must be either concealed or purged from the space in order for it to function appropriately and, in this case, the "body" is defined in multiple ways. The Muslim Judicial Council of South Africa indicated that a woman's voice is, in fact, part of her *'awrah* (literally translated as "nakedness") and thus constitutes a part of her "person" that should be publicly concealed. This element has been equated to a specific verse in the Qur'an in which Allah "appeals to the wives of the Prophet Muhammad to guard their speech in public so as not to stir desire in men" (Hoel 2013b). Thus, the voice of a woman should not only be *not* heard, but it should "be precluded from public consumption" and not address men within the sacred space of the masjid (Hoel 2013b). Interestingly, similar arguments arose with the establishment of *Radio Islam* in 1997, which allowed female speakers to participate on air. Even with the absence of a physical body, the "auditory" or vocal body of a woman was powerful enough to be considered an almost physical presence through the creation of a feminine sensescape (Hoel 2013b).

The notion of *'awrah* extends (obviously) to women's bodies and constitutes one of the main objections to the presence of women in the mosque. Women's bodies as constructs of desire have been regulated in numerous ways through the application of boundary-producing constructs ranging from the application of behavioral protocols as well as spatial divisions in the domestic space, public space, and masjid space. Based on this, "the need to conceal female corporeality," particularly in the masjid, "becomes essential, and in effect reinscribes the mosque spaces as normatively male" (Hoel 2013b). Along these lines, the presence of female congregants in a sacred (read male) space has thus been seen as detrimental and unsanctioned, largely due to the fact that this display of *'awrah* creates a sexualized space in which "a woman's modesty ... becomes compromised ... [through her contribution] ... to the sexualization of the mosque space" (Hoel 2013b). This also singles out women as "the primary repository of modesty" who, through their presence in the mosque, fall from this position of grace to become "hypersexualized objects of desire," which distract and dissuade men from being able to fulfill their roles as the

1.2 Women in the Masjid

producers and sanctifiers of sacred space (Hoel 2013b). Such responses seem to reduce male congregants to "pubescent voyeurs incapable of moral responsibility and spiritual dedication" (Hoel 2013b) and reduce female congregants to a physical body and a source of *fitnah* (corruption) that poses risk to men's spiritual condition. It also underscores the patriarchal implication that ritualized female bodies are incapable of producing masjid space.

Because these bodies do not function appropriately within the space of the masjid, the masjid supposedly ceases to function appropriately as well. The presence of women "introduce[s] impurity into the mosque" through their "female corporeality and imminence" (Hoel 2013b). More broadly, it also reflects on the masjid space as a microcosm of social relationships and society, produced by human activity and, once again, reflective and responsive to the desires of the dominant social unit. As such, views on women in mosques in the contemporary period tend to stem from social views of women in general in relation to their relationship with men, which range from views that women are naturally inferior to men, to the idea that men and women are "separate but equal" in a kind of "complementary" relationship, and lastly, that there is no disparity between men and women in terms of their inherent value or their general worth (Jeenah 2001, 8). The masjid has become a contested and discursive space in this arena as both a symbol of liberation/radicalism, and innovation/modernization, but at the same time an oppressive and disenfranchising space of exclusion, which continues to function as such in many contexts throughout South Africa, even in areas as progressive as Cape Town.

Yet a growth of female voices in the past few decades has begun to push back against these male hegemonic Islamic discourses in South Africa from a variety of perspectives, ranging from rereading the scripture from feminist perspectives to actively pushing for a presence in mosque space. Beginning largely in the early 1990s, feminist rereadings of Qur'anic verse have aimed to demonstrate that the equity exists between men and women in the Qur'an as faithful Muslims rather than women existing as unequal partners with men intended as the primary recipients of the word of God. One such rereading reads as follows:

Verily, for all men and women who have surrendered themselves unto God, and all believing men and believing women, and all truly devout men and truly devout women, and all men and women who are true to their word, and all men and women who are patient in adversity, and all men and women who humble themselves [before God], and all men and women who give in charity, and all self-denying men and self-denying women, and all men and women who are mindful of their chastity, and all men and women who remember God unceasingly: for them has God readied forgiveness of sins and a mighty reward. (Qur'an Surah 33:35; in Jeenah 2001, 1)

In addition, the Qur'an itself does not weigh in on female presence in mosque space with regard to a "specific spatial formula" for the masjid (Kahera 2008, 121). As Kahera points out, the term "masjid" is largely equated with the idea of "spatial sanctity" (Qur'an Surah 72:18) and orientation within the landscape (Qur'an Surah 2:149–150). In terms of the question of male/female interaction, the Qur'an encourages all of the *ummah* to perform *salat* (prayer), and because the Qur'an does not differentiate in this manner with regard to gender, anyone wishing to pray in a public masjid space must simply "be in a state of ceremonial purity and wear proper attire" (Kahera 2008, 134).[6] One can also glean interpretations regarding women in mosque spaces from the organization of the Prophet's home itself, which became a model after which most if not all mosque spaces are constructed and which had no dedicated space for prayer set aside for the women of his household or his female followers, which seems to indicate that partitioning was not considered until later periods.[7]

Yet one of the primary elements pushing these current rereadings has been the development of a nascent vision of South African Islamic feminism in which female scholars are increasingly taking up the task of defining its platform through explorations of how these two terms – "Islamic" and "feminism" – come together more broadly for all Muslim women in South Africa as an intersectional space.

Emergent additional reimaginings of contemporary feminism are increasingly making known the fact that so-called "feminist experience" has historically only ever been considered through the lens of white,

---

[6] There is also the fact that the hadiths, which are supposed recordings of the Prophet's words and deeds during his life, often contradict each other with regard to women's participation in the prayer space of the masjid. One hadith indicates that the primary place for women's prayer is in the "innermost part of her home" in an argument against female participation in a public masjid space and another recounts the Prophet saying: "Do not prevent God's female servants from [going to] God's mosque" (Ali and Leaman 2008, 84; in Hoel 2013b).

[7] Theologian Ibn Hazm (d. 456/1064) actually pins this shift in opinion on Abu Hanifa (d. 149/767) and Malik, who put forth the opinion that women would be better off praying in the privacy of the home, regardless of the fact that the mosque of the Prophet was a cogendered space (Kahera 2008, 122; 129) and that women were active participants in the public sphere of life. Importantly (albeit perhaps obviously) Akel Kahera also points out that most sources regarding rulings on female participation in masjid spaces are written by men and thus "are presented with a male-oriented vision" (Kahera 2008, 131), which is also a vision that fundamentally sexualizes the woman's body through its visibility and thus requires regulation so that the "spiritual balance" of men, those responsible for catalyzing and maintaining the purity of the sacred within the space, is not disrupted (Hoel 2013b).

1.2 Women in the Masjid

Western womanhood, which in some ways stands as an equivalent to masculinity in that the experience of it as "human" fundamentally identifies and excludes "others" (Hoel 2013a, 74–75). As scholars like bell hooks have pointed out, historical conceptualizations of feminism have ignored or disregarding diversity in the female experience related to race, class, religion, and a number of other qualities (hooks 1984). Likewise scholars like Chandra Mohanty note that Western feminist writings that *do* attempt to approach the experience of "Third World women" often "colonize the material and historical heterogeneities of the lives of women in the third world, thereby producing/re-presenting a composite, singular 'third world woman'" (Mohanty 1991).[8]

This creates an inappropriate homogenization of women that fails to recognize the unique, again intersectional, circumstances of their particular experience. This has especially been the case in parsing Muslim female experience, largely because of the grand, standing narratives that position Muslim women as the passive, disenfranchised victims of a universal, immovable patriarchal religion. Such a discussion is also inevitably inflected by, to quote Sa'diyya Shaikh, "a history of larger civilization polemics between the Islamic world and the West" (Shaikh 2003, 148). These discussions, in conjunction with international and largely conflicting concerns of female veiling (mark of oppression vs. mark of liberation vs. mark of religious identity), female excision, child/arranged marriages, honor killings, etc., have effectively "othered" Muslim women and cast them as impotent, agency-less characters within a larger oppressive socio-religious system (Hoel 2013a, 79). Not only does this point to the need for a more complex approach to the experience of Muslim women, but also the need for a repositioning of the narrative itself toward giving women the recognition they deserve as equally nuanced actors within their own diverse political, social, cultural, and religious realms of experience.

Such discussions have also come to rest on the problem of the mosque or masjid as the most tangible, physically present component of female disenfranchisement within South African Muslim space. Hoel cites Rita Gross who not only notes that women's religious lives are marked by "patterns of exclusion and participation," but that these patterns are often made most visible through the element of absence, whether it is absence from positions of leadership or absence from sacred spaces altogether (Gross 1977, 15; in Hoel 2013a, 76). Of the current existing mosques built both during and after Apartheid in South Africa, 75 percent are for

---

[8] The irony of the fact that I, as a white Western woman, am writing on a scholar who criticizes white Western feminist scholars for colonizing the "third world woman" experience is not lost on me.

males only (Matthee 2008, 122), with most of the mosques that allow women inside being located in the Western Cape. Because of the precedent set by this mosque tradition in South Africa, shock waves are felt even more broadly when the mosque as a spatial genre becomes a space of contestation.

The Open Mosque has experienced a great deal of pushback over the short period of its existence in terms of negative publicity but also actual physical acts of violence. In 2014, the Open Mosque was the target of three separate arson attacks, with members from area mosques weighing in heavily (and negatively) on its existence and message. Some members of the nearby Gatesville mosque, where women are separated by a barrier and pray from a balcony at the back of the mosque, have had rather choice things to say about the Open Mosque's imam. "Hargey's teaching and his philosophy is totally at variance with Islamic philosophy. Completely at variance," says Amien Gamza, a member of this congregation. Others have called him a "heretic" and an "imposter" (Seemungal 2015). Maulana Ebrahim Bham, a senior member of the Johannesburg-based Council of Muslim Theologians, when asked about his opinion regarding the Open Mosque, commented rather ambiguously "The Qur'an tells us to do whatever the Prophet tells you to and whatever the Prophet prohibits you from, then stay away from it" (Ismail 2015). Yet Bham also challenged the idea of an Open Mosque more generally in that, in his view, all mosques were in essence "open mosques." "I do not know of any mosque in South Africa where people stand at the gates of the mosque and say you have committed such and such sin, you are not allowed to enter. I have never seen it happen, it has never happened," Bham has said (Ismail 2015). Along these lines, Sa'diyya Shaikh comments wryly: "I like the fact that we've started conversations about this … I like the fact that people are falling over themselves to claim openness when in reality there are a number of mosques that simply don't have spaces for women" (Seemungal 2015). Hargey is not one to suffer silently and has fought back vehemently. "They have very little grounds theologically or otherwise to condemn this mosque," he has said, "what they are doing is scraping the bottom of the barrel" (Seemungal 2015).

The unique composition of those that attend the Open Mosque also reflects this approach. If one attends Qur'anic study on any given Tuesday evening, one will find a collection of men and women of different ethnicities, socioeconomic statuses, and even faiths (there is often an atheist or two in attendance) who have gathered to gain insight into a variety of issues ranging from learning more about the Qur'an and the faith, to engaging with an open faith-based community. The Open

Mosque has also become a haven for interfaith couples who have had difficulty finding acceptance in more traditional Islamic congregations; Dr. Hargey has officiated numerous interfaith marriages at the Open Mosque in the past few years.[9] There are also older couples, some of whom say that, for the first time in their spiritual lives, they feel a pull toward the faith because of the approach taken by the Open Mosque. Others strongly bond with the idea of equality between genders. One noted: "I come to this mosque every week because this is the only mosque that I know of where there's equality in the genders, where females sit and can actually view the sermon from the front and we're considered equals to men" (Seemungal 2015). There are also a sprinkling of Evangelical Christians who come to learn more about Islam and the Qur'an, one of whom Dr. Hargey even commissioned to decorate the interior of the mosque space.

Hargey is interested in expanding his masjid physically as well as socially. Plans for the future physical space of the Open Mosque include a central location that will act as a "hub for all inquiring Muslims." This future facility will be technologically sophisticated and will represent an architectural combination of "East and West," an admittedly vague conceptualization but aimed at creating a multivalent, multi-use complex that not only contains a masjid space, but also educational and community spaces that can accommodate social programs, including adult education, computer literacy, youth programs, a crèche, and possibly a Qur'anic school. Beyond this physical space, the Open Mosque also maintains an active online presence, utilizing multiple media landscapes in the form of Twitter, WhatsApp, Facebook, and "strategic adverts in the press and also the Internet" (Open Mosque n.d.) as a method of reaching out to like-minded members and establishing a virtual presence. In this way, the Open Mosque not only seeks to establish an intersectional community but also one deeply embedded in contemporary transnational dialogues made available via the extension of physical spaces like the Open Mosque into virtual space, a topic that will be addressed in more detail in Chapter 4.

Hargey's vision for the Open Mosque is one that has become increasingly popular around the world, with somewhat adjacent

---

[9] One recently married couple I spoke with came to the Open Mosque because the wife Sarah (pseudonym) who was a Christian had been pressured by her fiance's family to convert to Islam. She and her fiancé almost broke up because of it due to the fact that Sarah felt as if she was being forced into the faith and that little by little her own identity as being stripped away by the requirements of being part of a Muslim family. "Soon," she said, "I feared there would be nothing of me left." The Open Mosque, however, provided them with an alternate path. I would also note that her young husband chose not to speak once during this narrative.

congregations appearing on smaller scales in Canada, the United States, and France. There are even successful examples emerging on the African continent as well, with numerous "women's mosque" groups emerging in areas like the Sudan which have experienced growing success in having women's space prioritized in contemporary mosque-building projects (Nageeb 2007). Hussein Rashid, professor of religious studies at Hofstra University (Long Island) notes:

When we look at these new centers coming up, I think we have to see it – not as a trend . . . . But really it's a pattern of Muslims are now reimagining what these spaces could be like more largely. And so it's important because it's not the transformation of the tradition but it is the adaptation of the tradition. (Seemungal 2015)

Yet even though the Open Mosque has an open-door policy to all, its mission and value statement tend to focus heavily on gender equality and the position of women. In fact, the Open Mosque makes a point of crafting this distinction in the following statement: "We are a gender-equity institution where men and women are on par and equal in conformity with the Holy Qur'an's clear directives. Note: Gender-equal in this context does not refer to sexual orientation, it merely reinforces the fact that there is no sexist discrimination or traditional male chauvinism in our place of worship" (Open Mosque n.d.). The statement continues: "If anyone seeks to falsely portray the Open Mosque other than what we actually are by defaming, libeling and smearing us or to label us wrongly as gay or homosexual, we will institute legal proceedings against them and seek maximum punitive damages for such baseless accusations" (Open Mosque n.d.). Hargey himself does not endorse homosexuality as a practice, as he does not believe this is what the Qur'an teaches, although he notes that he does not have the right to cast judgment. "It is not our business to decide who enters this mosque or not and the Koran is very specific that judgement belongs to God alone, so if the homosexual or the lesbian comes in known to me or unknown to me, we don't have the right to exclude them from this gathering" (Seemungal 2015).

Yet this also raises the question of whether or not contemporary masjids should not only act as spaces of contestation and equity, but also spaces of safety, particularly for other groups "othered" by Islamic ideology. This is particularly relevant when considering the LGBT+ community in South Africa and the next case study of this chapter, the LGBT+-oriented Al-Fitre Foundation. Issues of sexuality in South Africa and on the continent more broadly have a history as equally fraught as those of racism and gender inequality.

1.3 Muslims on the Margins: Spatializing LGBT+ Rights at the Al-Fitre Foundation

As Ashley Currier notes, the "homosexuality-is-un-African discourse [has long] functioned as a specter in national and continental sociopolitical imaginaries" (Currier 2012, 122). Components of this discourse include the assertion that same-sex sexuality does not exist in Africa and that "there were no African lesbians or gay men" (Epprecht 2004; in Currier 2012, 121), or that it was a factor of Western "gay imperialism" (Barnard 2004, 7; in Currier 2012, 122). This discourse has become so historically embedded that even in the contemporary period in South Africa, LGBT+ rights get little support, with a 1995 survey revealing that only 38 percent of South Africans supported LGBT+ rights and that a full 41 percent believed that homosexuality was "un-African" (Reid and Dirsuweit 2002; in Currier 2012, 185). In fact, "homosexuals" as an undifferentiated metonymic group in South Africa was ranked as the "third most hated group in the country" after a far-right movement called the Afrikaner Resistance Movement (Afrikaner Weerstandsbeweging or AWB), and the anti-ANC Inkatha Freedom Party, an opposition party that had created a great deal of unrest during the 1994 democratic transition (Gibson and Gouws 2003, 18–19; 49–50; in Currier 2012, 186).

As such, LGBT+ Muslim affirmational groups like the Al-Fitre Foundation, founded by Imam Muhsin Hendricks, have become increasingly important in not only affirming the legitimacy of a Muslim LGBT+ identity but also providing a safe space for spiritual performance in which one can comfortably inhabit this identity as an LGBT+ Muslim. Founded in 1998, the Al-Fitre Foundation is located in Wynberg, a suburb of Cape Town, down the road from the Open Mosque in a repurposed industrial area. Hendricks categorized Al-Fitra as a foundation rather than a congregation, possibly for reasons relating to the fundamental meanings of both "Al-Fitra" and "foundation." Scott Siraj al-Haqq Kugle notes that the Arabic term "*fitra*" refers to an individual's "essential nature" and is deployed in the context of the Qur'an to "describe how God created all things, distinct in their individuality yet making up a harmonious whole" (Kugle 2014, 25). Qur'an Surah 30:30 says "So set your face towards the moral obligation in a true way, according to the essential nature granted by God, upon which God fashioned people, for there is no changing the creation of God!" (Kugle 2014, 25). From the perspective of nonheteronormative Muslims, this verse provides proof that Allah has given each individual a singular nature that is not only inherent but fundamentally harmonious with the path to righteousness. This perhaps makes the term "foundation" as opposed to

46   1 The Intersectional Masjid

"congregation" appropriate in that in addition to denoting an organization, the term "foundation" also references the load-bearing component of a structure or the underlying basis/principle of an idea.

Originally housed in Hendrick's garage as a "safe space for queer Muslims" to perform their spiritual identity (Pellot 2016), the Al-Fitre Foundation is now located in a walled complex with a handful of other businesses, a low profile that has enabled the foundation to perhaps avoid some of the more violent responses that have afflicted the Open Mosque thus far. Yet like the Open Mosque, the innocuous exterior appearance of Al-Fitre – that of a repurposed autobody shop akin to that of the Open Mosque – belies the environment that lies within: a humble space, yet one that is both affirmational and activistic in its design. On the first floor, immediately to the right of the entrance, is Al-Fitre's masjid space, also known as the People's Mosque (Masjidul Umam), whose humble aesthetic nonetheless utilizes a mosque spatial "toolkit" that generates a feeling of familiarity and comfort for those in attendance as well as enabling a type of psychological access to a spiritual space that has been denied to many whose sexuality is out in the open (Figure 1.3). Light green walls and industrial/track lighting are softened not only by

Figure 1.3 The People's Mosque (Masjidul Umam), Wynberg, Cape Town, South Africa, 2018.
Image by the author.

multicolored prayer mats but also pink pillows lined up along each side of the wall as an invitation to not only sit within the space but also move around within it as an active participant. A simple but beautiful *mihrab* niche occupies one corner of the room, next to which is positioned a small *minbar*. Stylized framed verses from the Qur'an also decorate the walls sparingly but with decorative flourish.

Simple in design, aesthetic, and execution, the masjid nonetheless deploys these "trappings of Islamic identity" very strategically toward becoming more than just an emblem of Islamic identity; through them, the masjid becomes an affective environment that allows individuals to inhabit a specific sense of self, which in turn has the potential to transform one's sense of "established" mosque space from that of an oppressive, potentially intimidating site to a welcoming, nurturing space. Indeed, such is the point of the Masjidul Umam. Imam Hendricks notes that the inspiration for this masjid in fact came from a conversation he had with one of his congregants, who had been sitting in on a Friday sermon focused on homosexuality at a different mosque. This particular congregant noted that the sermon made him feel as if the ground in front of him was going to open up and he was going to fall in and disappear. This clued Hendricks into the fact that space is a key element to the success of Al-Fitre as a:

> forum where people can just feel that they can be their own people, because they can't be themselves outside. You need a place where you can be gay and you can be a Muslim at the same time ... to build your self-esteem and to know that you belong somewhere, that you have a place in Islam and a place in this world. (Kugle 2014, 30)[10]

Along these lines, many of the practices that endow a space with spiritual identity are practiced at Al-Fitre but in accordance with the identity of its congregation. For example, Professor Scott Siraj al-Haqq Kugle relates how he attended a *dhikre*, which is a devotional practice that involves repeated rhythmic repetitions of the name of God or specific verses from the Qur'an, with Al-Fitre congregants. The Qur'an Surah recited was that of 8:62, which reads "If they intend to deceive you, surely God is sufficient for you – the One who strengthened you with divine aid along with the believers, and united their hearts." Following this Surah, congregants chanted the following: "O Prophet, God is sufficient for you and those believers who follow you" repetitively as a way for the meaning of the idea – "God is sufficient for

---

[10] This is particularly important for some of the congregants, who have been the victims of unspeakable violence. For example, one congregant – a local art teacher who remains unidentified – sought out the Inner Circle not only for spiritual nourishment but also for counseling after being the victim of a traumatic "corrective ritual" conducted by a traditional medical practitioner in Cape Town (AFP 2016).

us" – to become more firmly spiritually engrained. Such Surahs, however, have added meaning in the context of Al-Fitre in that they not only affirm the Muslim faith and in many ways create a spiritual space through their manifestation, but they also provide spiritual fortitude for members of the congregation who have suffered oppression, violence, and disenfranchisement due to their sexual or gender identity. Thus these ceremonial elements not only transform the site into a masjid space, but also an affirmative and intersectional sanctuary that promotes feelings of belonging not only to one's faith but also to one's community (Kugle 2014, 53).

Such affirmational space is also accomplished in the Al-Fitre masjid by putting its purpose as a platform of spirituality, identity, and community on display. One of the most powerful elements of this somewhat modest masjid space is the fact that, first and foremost, the masjid is a working space, "working" moving beyond elements of spiritual performativity to include the social work of LGBT+ Muslim rights and safety. Indeed, one side of the room is devoted to spiritual acts while the other side contains an easel with paper, a small sideboard for coffee and water, and a whiteboard overlaying the entire far side of the wall, covered with notes (Figure 1.4). A projector hangs from the ceiling facing this wall,

Figure 1.4 Work space adjacent to prayer space, the People's Mosque (Masjidul Umam), Wynberg, Cape Town, South Africa, 2018. Image by the author.

1.3 Muslims on the Margins

which also indicates it can be used for presentation-oriented purposes, and a set of speakers standing to the side undoubtedly supplement this function. In addition to prayer, the space is also used for *madrasa* classes on Tuesday (usually taught by members of the congregation or LGBT+ imams who are able to teach the Qur'an in a sensitive way), as well as various seminars and retreats during which members engage in multiple types of group work. The space is also used for Al-Fitre's annual retreat, a seven-day event in Cape Town that brings together queer Muslim activists from different organizations across the globe, many of whom come from largely intolerant societies. Al-Fitre and Hendricks create a temporary spiritual "safe space" for these figures to discuss spiritual and social matters, as well as modes of collaborative activism.[11] For many attendees, the retreat itself is a form of emotional therapy as well, not only due to its location in Hendricks' organization but also (ironically) due to its location in Cape Town and in South Africa more generally. South Africa is considered to be one of the more tolerant countries, not only on the continent but also across the globe, a characteristic which has drawn international Muslims to the country not only from other areas in Africa but even from spaces like the United Kingdom and Europe, where many Muslims are the victims of government suspicion and repressive surveillance on the one hand and growing conservative Islamic doctrines on the other (Tayob 2011, 23). Aissa Amazigh, who attended the annual retreat in 2016, notes "Once the plane landed in Cape Town, I just relaxed.... The spiritual context here is just so liberating" (Pellot 2016). This is precisely the type of spatial atmosphere that Hendricks hopes to craft, seeing the annual meeting as a "refuge for those who feel ostracized by LGBT+ communities because of their Muslim faith and shunned by Muslim communities because of their sexual orientation or gender identities" (Pellot 2016). In fact, Hendricks describes the "beautiful space" of the retreat as a space created through a combination of physical environment, social relationships, and politically liberal society (Pellot 2016). Having a physical space for both the retreat and for members of the organization more broadly is key because, in many cases, the spiritual space of the masjid as an open equitable space is something that has been either physically, spiritually, or psychological denied to them for most of their lives, either as a result of rejection or being forced to exist within an unsafe congregational space. In fact, the intensity of the connection that people develop for the space of the retreat is such that many attendees

---

[11] One individual who attended this annual retreat runs a support program in Tanzania for queer youth and asked not to be named for fear of reprisals in a country where homosexual acts can yield a life imprisonment sentence (Pellot 2016).

often experience "withdrawal symptoms and [even] separation anxiety" when they prepare to return to their home contexts at the conclusion of the retreat (Pellot 2016). The psychological power of these spaces is such that it affects people in a powerful sociospiritual way.[12]

Thus, all major events at the foundation occur in the masjid space, which is located on the ground floor, with the offices upstairs. This buttresses the identity of this space as a space of purpose, while also giving architectural form to the idea of the Muslim *ummah* or community of God which "transcends boundaries, frontiers, nationalities, citizenships, linguistic differences and all other form of cultural, political, economic or social differences" (Taleb 2005, 5). Through these avenues of organization and performance, Al-Fitre's masjid becomes the spatialization of a desired identity and a desired reality, made "real" through the creation of a collective space that acts as a platform on which individuals can construct a contemporary Islamic vision of themselves.

This space and how it is utilized in this context reveal the importance of space in the construction and affirmation of marginalized identities, particularly those of the LGBT+ community in South Africa. Such spaces have been key components in crafting strategic visibilities/invisibilities with regard to creating communal identities and generating empowerment and security for the LGBT+ population in the face of contemporary hardships. Such spaces in South Africa have taken many forms, ranging from proclamative spaces of resistance and empowerment to hidden, innocuous spaces designed to shelter, protect, and in many cases hide. The Forum for the Empowerment of Women (FEW), a black lesbian organization located in Johannesburg, set up their office in the Women's Gaol section of the Old Fort in 2005, which was recently renamed Constitution Hill and was at one point a prison for both men and women during the Apartheid era. The Constitutional Court of South

---

[12] Despite the intersectional strength of spaces like the Inner Circle, there are still groups within the Muslim queer community who feel disenfranchised for other reasons, and gender continues to play a large role in this aspect. Because women in Islam have traditionally been spatially marginalized in spiritual spaces like the mosque, in addition to public spaces outside the home and private spaces within the home, the fact that many queer "safe" spaces in South Africa are still largely dominated by gay men, some of whom still adopt fairly patriarchal attitudes to women, is doubly disenfranchising. This has led activists like Midi Achmat to craft additional safe spaces for this particular subgroup of the Muslim queer population through the creation of virtual space in the form of a Facebook page entitled Unveiling the Hijab. Achmat is no longer a practicing Muslim and has been estranged from her family for many years; yet she completed her honors thesis on the queer Muslim community and the particular challenges they face with regard to the multiple traumas and aggressions they must contend with on numerous fronts, ranging from being a Muslim and a woman to being part of the queer community, among others (Collison 2017).

Africa, the equivalent of the United States' Supreme Court, and an Apartheid museum are also housed within this complex. "The Old Fort," notes Ashley Currier, "has been reimagined as a place in which all South Africans can seek legal redress for injustice" (Currier 2012, 2) and the symbolic presence of a black women's lesbian organization in this space is not only purposeful, but highly strategic in terms of its location and visibility. In an interview with Currier, Nomsa, a black lesbian and FEW member, noted, "Women used to be locked up here; now women are coming out and saying, 'We're free, and we're speaking our minds,' in the same place that people were locked up" (Currier 2012, 2).

Sites such as the FEW office represent the spatialization of an agenda of empowerment, deriving power from the symbolic capital of its historical location. It also stands as a space of resistance, providing a counter to the site's history of oppressive power relationships and underscoring this history as a way to highlight its own resistance/empowerment agenda. As such, the location and implications of space provide, according to Taleb:

a sense of where one is in the world – a sense gained from the experiences of history, geography, culture, self and imagination – mapped through the simultaneously spatial and temporal interconnections between people, but also the political definition of the grounds on which struggles are the be fought. (Taleb 2005, 82)

Yet not all spaces are so proclamative. Spaces of invisibility also remain relevant and necessary, particularly with regard to establishing a site where one can comfortably exist in the "skin" of one's sexual and intersectional identity. Some organizations like FEW and the Triangle Project, based in Cape Town, have opened up satellite offices in various area townships to facilitate the provision of services to the surrounding community on a more accessible and also potentially less visible scale. Unfortunately, this does not appear to be working; many of the satellite offices are visited infrequently, if at all, due to the fact that many individuals fear their sexual status will become public knowledge within their community if they are seen. In fact, many members have reported being harassed on the streets outside of these offices because of their association with them (Currier 2012, 193).

Organizations have also attempted to mediate these elements through physical and psychological infrastructures of security. "Visibility routines" have been developed in which activists surveil problematic spaces and subsequently "defin[e] who could access organizations" (Currier 2012, 19). This creates a sense of security for individuals using these spaces, which subsequently become "sanctuaries" for comfortable and unsurveilled socialization and a space that caters to the "psychological needs of insecure and harassed gays and lesbians" (Palmberg 1999, 267; in Currier 2012, 19). Along these lines, these spaces also empower members "to learn a new self-respect, a deeper and more assertive group identity, public skills, and values of cooperation and civic virtue" (Evans and Boyte 1992, 17; in Currier 2012, 19–20). Part of the inherent security of these spaces, of course, is their controlled access, which allows them to function as sites of invisibility when viewed from the exterior and sanctioned visibility within the interior (Currier 2012, 20). Such boundaries and "territorializations" are also formed and reformed over time to accommodate shifting needs, populations, and politics.

But perhaps underscoring this conversation more fully is the fundamental relationship that space maintains with and between bodies, an interaction fundamental to the establishment of meaningful place. Likewise, it is also space which acts as a lens through which bodies are read in an approved manner. As Judith Butler notes: "Although we struggle for rights over our own bodies, the very bodies for which we struggle are not quite ever only our own. The body has its invariably public dimension; constituted as a social phenomenon in the public sphere, my body is and is not mine" (Butler 2004, 21; in Currier 2012, 182). One such example of this are Moffies, a nonheteronormative "subculture" or "local variant of gayness" within Cape Town. Composed of "Coloured" men who are defined by their effeminate mannerisms, Moffies are appreciated primarily for their "entertainment value," which is on display during events like Carnival where "social codes are reversed and participants act out personas considered unacceptable in 'conventional' society" (Iziko Museums 2017). This has made Moffies an acknowledged and somewhat tolerated segment of the LGBT+ population, and people have lined up to watch and be entertained by them during Carnival since the 1940s. Taking inspiration from cultural figures such as Carmen Miranda, Moffies cross-dress and "perform their personas as cross-dressers with humor and self-parody … an example of the subversive nature of Carnival" (Iziko Museums 2017). Interestingly, however, this seems to imply that Moffies are only accepted in society when they fashion their identities as a comedic enterprise to be performed and subsequently interpreted as a form of entertainment for others. Much of the stigma against nonheterosexuality stems from historically embedded social views of the dominance of masculinity, a dominance that has not only cast women but also effeminate men like Moffies and others who do not meet prescribed societal gender and sexual roles as nonnormative (Hendricks 2010, 34). In this way, the body becomes a construct within public spaces, built up and interpreted through the gaze of an audience that interrogates it through the lens of the social space that it occupies, which is all very much in line with theories in social and feminist fields that equate the viewed with the powerless and the viewer with dominance. The nonnormative status of many LGBT+ communities in South Africa like Moffies often gives them a "hypervisibility" or "a condition in which visible traits become interpreted as excessive in ways that attract the derision and gaze of a privileged group" (Currier 2012, 6). In some cases, this requires such bodies to use hidden spaces to escape those who would apply such unsanctioned readings and surveillance to their form and identity. Within hidden spaces, sanctioned social constructions and readings of the body can occur through the implementation of a controlled visibility that moves against the visual deconstruction of one's body into a single sexualized being; instead, this visibility promotes a more intersectional interpretation of the body not just as a body but a comprehensive individual.[13]

Along these lines, space and constructions of visibility/invisibility with regard to the body are also strategically deployed in the public arena, as with the offices of FEW, who combine bodies and space to create a powerful, highly symbolic, public statement. Thus, as Gordon notes: "Visibility is a 'complex system of permissions and prohibitions, of presence and absence'" (Gordon 2008, 15; emphasis removed, in Currier 2012, 6), a narrative that has a deep history in South Africa not only in terms of the contemporary conditions that are currently confronting the country's LGBT+ community, but the history that informs them.

Historically, heteronormativity in South Africa has been largely institutionalized and privileged as normative, with alternate forms of sexuality largely viewed as deviant and even politically dissident (Currier 2012, 176). This is despite the fact that South Africa is currently the only country on the continent to allow same-sex marriage, with Cape Town acting as the "continent's playground for queer expression" despite various acts of violence that have been directed toward the South African LGBT+ community both within the city and around the country (Pellot 2016). These intolerant attitudes and the deeply entrenched sense of political homophobia that they have created were potentially introduced during the colonial period by Christian missionaries and then later European scientists who, as part of their program to ensure racial purity, "prescribed that people should have sex with individuals of the opposite gender but of the same race and class" (McClintock 1995; in Currier 2012, 27). Anne McClintock notes that "boundaries were felt to be dangerously permeable and demanding

---

[13] Ashley Currier relates how, during her observation of an antiviolence workshop, she was asked to refrain from observing groups sharing personal narratives of violence and physical abuse because her physical presence might in effect generate a closed, self-protective atmosphere (Currier 2012, 193).

continual purification, so that sexuality, in particular women's sexuality, was cordoned off as the central transmitter of racial and hence cultural contagion" (McClintock 1995, 47; in Currier 2012, 28). Since then, political homophobia has been adopted by political leaders on the continent to "overcome colonial emasculation and to mark a new pathway to national, cultural, and racial authenticity" (Currier 2012, 176).

Such heteronormative ideologies would be present in the Apartheid era as well, during which sexuality was strictly regulated and actively policed. Anti-sodomy laws were set in place targeting gay men, whom policy makers thought of as an "alien threat to the Afrikaner domain of masculinity" (Jones 2008, 403; in Currier 2012, 29), and "'low key surveillance' of gay areas" began in the 1940s (Botha and Cameron 1997, 21; in Currier 2012, 29). Yet ironically no action was taken to prevent sexual activity between white women; Bacchetta notes that sex between women was not prohibited because "it [was] not imagined to exist" (Bacchetta 2002, 951; in Currier 2012, 29). To quote Currier, "their homosexuality was not acknowledged and remained invisible" (Currier 2012, 29). Nonwhite homosexuality, however, was dealt with in largely arbitrary inconsistent ways, largely because most of the anti-homosexuality policies were aimed at the white population and this was revealed via the presence of "some quietly sanctioned black men's same-sex sexual practices" which were practiced in the context of marginal spaces like single-sex housing hostels in townships and near mining operations, and condoned largely because Apartheid officials believed they "limit[ed] the possibility of sexual activity with white women" (Tucker 2009, 110; in Currier 2012, 29–30). That being said, however, black men "were three to four times more likely to be convicted than whites" of homosexual crimes, with black men being almost "ten times more likely to be prosecuted for sodomy" than white men between the 1970s and 1980s (Botha and Cameron 1997, 16; 18; in Currier 2012, 29). This in many ways highlights the importance of space and strategies of visibility/invisibility with regard to identity and acknowledging one's sexuality in a highly oppressive violent environment and how space can function in such climates as platforms of oppression and exclusion.

Yet such spaces also worked in opposite ways as well. With the passing of the Sexual Offenses Act in 1957, "private gatherings of two or more gay men" were prohibited, which effectively criminalized gay restaurants and clubs and created an underground spatial networks of "bars, social spaces, [and] 'health clubs'" (Reddy 1998, 69; Gevisser 1995; in Currier 2012, 30). As Currier notes, "These cultural spaces also acted as 'indigenous' free spaces that nurtured the formation of sexual subjectivities that would serve as the basis for mobilizable lesbian and gay collective identities" (Polletta 1999, 10–11; in Currier 2012, 30). These spaces thus existed as spatial niches of controlled and carefully guarded visibility within an oppressive administrative and social landscape whose survival depended on a strict control over who was allowed access and who wasn't. In this way, according to Currier, "gender and sexual minorities found ways to control their public visibility by retreating into safe spaces" (Currier 2012, 16).

Although the white gay and lesbian community would burst into public consciousness at various intervals during the last few decades of Apartheid, most notably in 1968 when they proposed the Homosexual Law Reform Fund in opposition to a newly strengthened Sexual Offenses Act (Currier 2012, 31), the LGBT+ community kept out of the limelight, with the nonwhite gay and lesbian community being all but invisible. Even in the 1980s, when momentum behind anti-Apartheid movements began to pick up steam, organizations associated with the gay and lesbian community remained apolitical, even with Western organizations pushing these groups to become interracial and oppose Apartheid (Currier 2012, 34). Eventually, in 1986, the Rand Gay Organization (RGO) was formed as a black-led gay and lesbian organization, followed by the Lesbians and Gays Against Oppression (LAGO) organization, also formed in 1986, which began taking an active role in Apartheid resistance through the view that "gay rights [were] human rights" (Nicol 2005, 72; in Currier 2012, 35).

Once it became clear that the days of Apartheid were numbered, this organization and others like it began to push the ANC to take a positive stance on gay and lesbian rights through their inclusion in the constitution. The ANC, seeing this as a positive strategy to continue their anti-oppression agenda, agreed, although this move did little to eliminate the pervasive homophobia that in many ways has continued to define South African culture, even within the ANC itself (Currier 2012, 35–36). This was also the era when HIV/AIDS had become a major concern within the LGBT+ community and was variously politicized/racialized in South Africa, first as a "white" disease framed as such in order to ingratiate the country into the global sphere as a "fellow sufferer" within this "world" crisis, then as a "migrant" disease brought by those coming in from other African countries, and then as a "black" disease emerging from the townships and moving to affect (white) heterosexuals elsewhere (Currier 2012, 37).

Eventually various organizations in South Africa merged to create the National Coalition for Gay and Lesbian Equality in 1994, a largely male-dominated organization tasked with ensuring that the protections established by the new constitution concerning gay and lesbian rights were safeguarded. It is also important to point out that other equally legitimate categories of sexual self-identification, including queerness, bisexuality, transgender, intersex, and the like, were either not recognized or acknowledged at this point, although they were in many ways unceremoniously folded into the conversation as peripheral nondescript elements. Even now, although there has been some discussion/advocacy with regard to transgender individuals in the post-Apartheid period, it has largely been irregular and inconsistent. Likewise, public policy with regard to social and political protections for members of these communities has been spotty. In 1992, legislation was passed that no longer allowed the state "to change the legal documents [transgender persons] need to function in society" (Swarr 2003, 65; in Currier 2012, 41). Eventually, a decade later, another piece of legislation was passed called the Alteration of Sex Description and Sex Status Act 49, which allowed individuals identifying as both transgender and intersex to "apply for legal adjustment of [their] sex description without genital surgery" (Klein 2008, 5; in Currier 2012, 41–42).

In the contemporary period, the LGBT+ community at large still faces a number of obstacles in society ranging from anti-lesbian violence[14] to rampant poverty to widespread crime to continued racial and ethnic divisions within society. Regarding the safeguarding of LGBT+ rights and the criminalization of hate speech against these groups,[15] little has been done to enforce these policies at the community level. Brutal attacks against individuals due to "homophobic and transphobic" attitudes have not only created a community that lives in constant fear of violence but have also increased the odds of many in the community of contracting HIV/AIDS (Currier 2012, 16–17).[16] In addition, there is also a strong sense of pessimism among some members of this community about the progression of LGBT+ rights moving forward. During the 1994 Johannesburg Lesbian and Gay Pride March, South African author and journalist Mark Gevisser interviewed a black South African drag queen regarding her opinions about "her new empowerment" associated with the election of Nelson Mandela and the ANC's passage of the country's new constitution in which specific protections were outlined for individuals of all races, genders, religions, and sexual orientations. "My darling," she replied, "it means sweet

---

[14] Ashley Currier notes that utilizing the phrase "antilesbian violence" as opposed to "corrective rape" is important in that it encompasses all forms of violence against women because of their sexual identity and differentiates its specific motives from those that define the broader fields of gender-based violence (Anguita 2011; in Currier 2012, 189).

[15] Antigay hate speech was made illegal in South Africa in 2000 when the Promotion of Equality and Prevention of Unfair Discrimination Act was passed (Currier 2012, 190).

[16] In her work *Thinking Through Lesbian Rape*, Zanele Muholi interviewed forty-seven self-identified lesbians in terms of their experience with violence. She found that twenty of the forty-seven had been raped because of their sexual identity, with seventeen experiencing physical assault, eight experiencing physical abuse, four experiencing attempted rape, and two experiencing kidnapping. Over half of them knew their attackers, yet only a fourth of these attacks were reported because they feared being victimized further (Currier 2012, 190–191).

1.3 Muslims on the Margins

motherfucking nothing at all. You can rape me, rob me, what am I going to do when you attack me? Wave the constitution in your face? I'm just a nobody black queen" (Gevisser 2000, 136; in Currier 2012, 17).

LGBT+ Muslims in South Africa also have the added burden of existing in a largely ambiguous spiritual and ideological space. In many Muslim communities, not only in South Africa but around the globe, homosexuality is interpreted as a sin and, under Shari'a law in more conservative areas, it is a sin punishable by death (Hendricks 2010, 31). This judgment is often defended by citing interpretations of various verses in both the Qur'an and the hadith that seem to condemn same-sex relationships. There is general agreement among Sunni and Shi'a scholars that "homosexuality is an adulterous act for which *Hadd* punishment applies," *Hadd* referring to a disciplinary genre that applies to specific crimes – theft, consumption of alcohol, fornication, and apostasy – and are said to be the "claims of God" (Hendricks 2010, 33; 49). Many scholars also address the issue on historical grounds, claiming without foundation or substantiation that homosexuality was nonexistent during the time of the Prophet and that it is a corrupting contemporary influence that has been imported from the West (Hendricks 2010, 33).

Such judgments have led many nonheteronormative Muslims to experience abuse and rejection at the hands of family, friends, and the religious community and subsequently turn to various self-destructive behaviors including drug abuse, unsafe sexual practices, and self-harm /suicide in response (Hendricks 2010, 32). As previously mentioned, after the end of Apartheid, protections were put in place for the gay and lesbian community; however, it seemed that only the "white and prosperous" were positioned to take advantage of these, while the nonwhite majority and religious minorities such as Muslims were left in the shadows to "emerge" for themselves, saddled with additional prejudices and socioeconomic disenfranchisement. It was this situation that would lead to gay and lesbian nonwhite Muslims turning to alternate and/or "secular" institutions (churches, social clubs, etc.) for support, and it was during this period that Imam Hendricks would become active in his ministry. Imam Hendricks,[17] who identifies as a nonheterosexual Muslim man,[18] has achieved compatibility between his faith and his sexual identity,

---

[17] While there is a slowly growing movement toward the creation of other inclusive congregations such as that of Ludovic Mohammed Zahed, who founded the first inclusive mosque congregation in Europe (Paris) and married his partner in South Africa, it is a very slow-moving process.

[18] Mushin himself notes that he "doesn't really identify as gay." "I'm a multiplicity of complexities and a vast ocean of possibilities," he says. "God created me, but he ain't finished with me yet" (Pellot 2016).

a state of being that he wishes to share with others, which was one of his primary motivations for both starting the Al-Fitre Foundation and becoming an activist (Kugle 2014, 23). Yet before becoming the imam of the People's Mosque (a career choice perhaps unsurprising considering that the funding for his *madrasa* training in Pakistan came from the aforementioned Call of Islam, which again was a branch of the Muslim Youth Movement (Kugle 2014, 24), Hendricks began an informal support group to keep nonheteronormative Muslims within the fold of the faith (Kugle 2014, 29). Hendricks and a small group of colleagues first created Gay Muslim Outreach, which eventually evolved into the Al-Fitra Foundation. At its formation this group was predominately social in nature, an identity that would in fact lead to its ultimate demise. The more dedicated members of the group would eventually join others in Cape Town to craft a group known as the Inner Circle, which would later become the Al-Fitre Foundation, whose focus would be on "developing an Islamic spirituality for gay and lesbian Muslims through structured discussion of the Qur'an but balanced with more informal social gatherings" (Kugle 2014, 30).[19]

Hendricks crafted the foundation as a "spiritual tool[s] towards personal development" (Kugle 2014, 32), a motivation arising from his own experience of rejection and expulsion from the Claremont Mosque, which "judged his being an openly gay Muslim to be too risky" (Kugle 2014, 34). After the release of the 2007 documentary *A Jihad for Love*, which focused on the difficulties of being a queer Muslim and in which Hendricks appeared, the Muslim Judicial Council (MJC) issued a *fatwa* for Hendricks, casting him "out of the fold of Islam" and characterizing his work as "propaganda." Yet it has been Hendricks in the context of Al-Fitre, among others, who has paved the way for alternative viewpoints and interpretations of the Qur'an that challenge the idea that nonheteronormative sexuality is forbidden. Along these lines, Hendricks has noted that the poetic nature of Qur'anic verse and the inconsistencies and contradictions that exist within collections of hadith create multiple possible interpretations with regard to Islamic views on same-sex or alternative sexual relationships (Hendricks 2010, 32–33). Indeed, this is one of the reasons that Qur'anic and hadith ideologies have remained relevant in the contemporary period in the sense that they allow for "human development, … diversity within humanity … [and] … social and spiritual growth (Hendricks 2010, 32). Likewise, there

---

[19] Language and terminology for Hendricks is also something of a problem with regard to the group that the Inner Circle is meant to support. Labels like "gay" and "homosexual" are not only sociopolitically powerful but also potentially divisive, according to Hendricks, who has settled on the term "queer" as an umbrella term for the identity of the Inner Circle congregation (Pellot 2016).

are in fact a number of arguments to be made against the idea that non-heterosexuality is condemned by the most holy book of Islam. Kecia Ali notes that marriage between those of the same sex has no basis in the Qur'an, but instead stems from legal and cultural views of marriage as a social institution (Hendricks 2010, 32). There are also issues with using the hadiths as an authoritative source for moral guidance in this manner, largely due to the fact that these documents, supposed recordings of the sayings and doings of the Prophet Muhammed, were not compiled until many years after his death. Indeed, the creation of these recordings was not sanctioned by the Prophet, who himself forbad their creation. Yet by the second century following his death, many of his lived experiences were being strategically manipulated and distorted, and Caliph Umar Ibn Abdul-Aziz permitted their inscription as a mode of standardization (Hendricks 2010, 32–33). Within this collection exist many of the same contradictions and distortions that had plagued this body of work in its oral form. It is also primarily from the hadith that people derive most of their arguments against nonheterosexuality.

It would also seem that, while such viewpoints are by no means the norm among South African Muslim communities, there are a handful of individuals who have come to terms with their existence. Ebrahim Desai, the *mufti* or Islamic legal expert who is the head of a Muslim seminary outside of Pietermaritzburg, notes that while he does not condone sexuality from a religious basis, its protection in the South African constitution must be respected (Tayob 2011, 20). The Open Mosque's Taj Hargey, while also not condoning nonhetero-based sexual identity, nonetheless notes "who am I to judge?" But Hendricks' readings of the Qur'an are key to his ministry and the success of Al-Fitre more broadly in that they help the foundation's members understand that it is possible to be both gay and Muslim and that one should not have to live a dual life as a public Muslim on the one hand and a private nonheteronormative individual on the other. Hendricks defends this position through specific interpretations of the Qur'an, which, he says, are often where interpretive mistakes are made (Kugle 2014, 31). He points to the fact that different interpretations of the Qur'an inevitably arise due to its interpretation through the lenses of multiple cultures, peoples, and experiences, a factor which also ironically allows the Qur'an to maintain relevance in the contemporary period through its ability to be crafted to fit into multiple social, cultural, and political contexts (Hendricks 2010, 33). Hendricks also stresses the fact that the Qur'an first and foremost stresses equality among peoples. Surah 2:179 of the Qur'an, for example, states: "In the Law of Equality there is the saving of life to you, o you men of understanding; that you may restrain yourselves." Likewise, Qur'an Surah 5:8 states: "O ye who believe! Stand out firmly for Allah, as witnesses to fair dealing, and let not hatred of others to you make you swerve to wrong and depart from justice. Be just: that is next to piety: and fear God. For God is well-acquainted with all that ye do."

Supporting his readings and interpretations of the faith is the mosque space of Al-Fitre itself, which again actively underscores the fact that the masjid as a space and the mosque as an institution do not just function as spaces of prayer and specifically religious activity, but can be and often are deployed for numerous political, social, and cultural activities and purposes toward making it a collectively representative ideological construct. As previously noted, the importance of this element is not only that space itself represents a distinct religious identity, but an identity that is intersectional in nature and therefore the potential target of multiple simultaneous oppressions. Thus, space becomes a mode of establishing and affirming the structural and ideological parameters of the group not only by acting as a space of gathering, but also as a space with its own established hierarchies of value and belonging that in turn connect and protect individuals along the lines of a shared lifeway.

Hendricks' vision of the future of the foundation is largely philosophical in nature: he hopes to reveal that Islam is not an intolerant religion. In fact, his goal is to push back against Islam as a traditionally patriarchal institution through a "care-frontational" approach, one oriented around generating dialogue and advocacy.[20] Likewise, Hendricks has little interest in building "satellite" spaces or expanding into other areas, although he hopes to grow his congregation not only in terms of gaining LGBT+ members but also gaining straight allies who come in support and unity. Hendricks notes that currently half of his congregation falls into that category. Hendricks aims to make the Al-Fitre mosque a safe spiritual masjid space, particularly for those who have had previous traumatic experiences within the religious institution by transforming the space into not only a space of religion but also a space of activism that occupies multiple different affirmational spaces. To this end, Al-Fitre is also involved in creating additional satellite "safe" sites where individuals can visit and receive counseling with "unprecedented anonymity" (Kugle 2014, 22). Such spaces are fundamentally transformative in the sense that they provide an active environment in which to attain "spiritual

---

[20] This differs in some ways from the approach taken by Dr. Hargey at the Open Mosque, which ironically is located only a couple hundred feet away. At one point, there was talk of a potential alliance between the two congregations and Hargey even came to the organization as a guest speaker and ally. Yet his views on homosexuality created tension between the two organizations, as did the fact that Hargey himself is a somewhat confrontational figure, which goes against the approach favored by Hendricks.

growth ... [by] ... stripping away the accumulated layers of 'false self' ... in order to free the 'true self' that had long been buried but through which they can sincerely turn to God" (Kugle 2014, 26).

Along these lines, spaces like Al-Fitre, and the Open Mosque as well, have the potential to encourage a rethinking about how various spaces and histories in the country relate to the citizens they signify, and how such forms are due for an intersectional reimagining that takes into consideration South Africa's diverse cultural and religious landscape and the various ideologies that have been structurally rendered over time to make such identities manifest. At the core of this discussion is the belief that not only do spaces and histories speak to the mechanics of lived reality, but that individuals living in this reality have multiple identities and narratives that coexist within shared spaces and contexts. Thus space as "a form and a set of practices through which social meanings are communicated and visions of the social world are sustained" needs to be reconsidered as a lens through which to also consider the evolving ambiguous social parameters of a nation currently in a state of flux (Jones 2011, 29).

Masjid spaces like the Open Mosque and the Inner Circle carry "a powerful potential to touch, draw upon and assimilate shared need, and in [their] cultural gestures, to give structure and form to aspirations" (Ahrends 1996, 72). How values are attached to space becomes, like the identities of their inhabitants, fluid and everchanging, with the spaces themselves becoming intersectional in their ability to produce and be the product of multiple identities and realities, challenging orthodoxies in form, function, and meaning with regard to the masjid. In doing so, these structures become structures of action, affirming bonds through visibility/invisibility and acceptance/inclusion in a way that has shaped South African society from the seventeenth century on into the present day. Taleb rightly notes that identity and geographic location are intimately entwined elements in one's identity: "knowing oneself is an exercise in mapping where one stands," she says (Taleb 2005, 54). In doing so, the individual in many ways also becomes a spatialized construct that is only "momentarily complete." Like the aforementioned spaces, the individual "is always partially constituted by the forces that oppose it ... [and] ... always contingent on surviving the contradictions that it subsumes" (Taleb 2005, 54).

As Adam Nathanial Furman notes, built form should represent the process by which "a fragmenting society and a diffuse urban realm is given new symbolic anchors that neither ignore the deep veins of difference, nor impose an arbitrary uniformity, but celebrate the constant tensions, debates and engagement that keep any one aspect of society from eclipsing the others" (Furman 2017). Indeed, some would argue that ambiguity in identity that South African Islam has been navigating for the past two decades represents the ideal opportunity to reconstruct one's identity both conceptually and architecturally. "In crisis," Furman notes, "lies the greatest opportunity for reinvention" (Furman 2017). Thus, it might be that masjid spaces like the Open Mosque and the Inner Circle are necessary to loosen the suffocating hold of traditional sociospiritual and architectural/spatial regimes by reflecting back – in stark fashion – the problematic politics of existence that define both South African Muslim lived reality in the contemporary period and those of the global *ummah*. In doing so, such spaces forcibly and often times uncomfortably provoke necessary discussions and confrontations not only with the traumatic elements of South Africa's past but also the continuity of these elements in the present.

1.4 Masjid as Martyr: Iconoclasm and Timbuktu's Traumatized Spiritual Landscape

Yet, zooming out, these spaces of the Open Mosque and the Inner Circle are fundamentally defined by their reality as emergent spaces of responsiveness and empowerment that represent the changing face of Islamic identity in southern Africa. Masjid space, however, also has the potential to be both politicized and even potentially weaponized when catalyzed by situations that threaten active hegemonies (Matthee 2008, 42). In such situations, space is just as able to be used as an oppressive device as an affirmational one, installing systems of oppression and disenfranchisement that actively disempower one group in favor of another. In such situations, space can even function as a tool of trauma and ideological aggression, targeting multiple communities and identities at once as part of a broader exercise of sometimes asymmetric warfare. Through the violence committed against these structures, a similar type of violence is symbolically inflicted on the community, and thus through this connection spiritual spaces become apparatuses of trauma.

Such was the case in northern Mali in 2012[21] when a military coup deposed then-president Amadou Toumani Touré and opened the door for a revolutionary group known as the National Movement for the Liberation of Azawad (MNLA) to seize control of the northern parts of

[21] The following writing on Timbuktu first appeared in "Timbuktu in Terror: Architecture and Iconoclasm in Contemporary Africa," *International Journal of Islamic Architecture*, 6 (1) (March 2017): 97–120, https://doi.org/10.1386/ijia.6.1.97_1. The author wishes to thank the editors and reviewers at IJIA for their invaluable feedback and contributions to this work.

1.4 Masjid as Martyr

the country.[22] Composed of various members of an ethno-cultural group known as the Tuareg or Kel Tamasheq, MNLA was joined two months later by fellow Tuareg members of Ansar Dine, a militant Islamist group endorsed and funded by North Africa's Al-Qaeda cell, who together with the MNLA formed a coalition that declared the northern part of Mali an Islamic state.[23] The group then proceeded to impose a highly conservative form of Islamic governance known as Shari'a law on the region and perpetrated numerous devastating and highly publicized acts of violence upon the architectural landscape in and around Timbuktu in the name of that doctrine (Tharoor 2012). Numerous mosques, tombs, shrines, and other structures of historical, cultural, and religious significance were damaged, vandalized, and/or despoiled during their occupation, and the intensity of the destruction was such that, less than a month after it was formed, the MNLA dissolved its merger with Ansar Dine, stating "[We] accepted the idea of an Islamic State but it should have been written that we will practice a moderate and tolerant Islam, with no mention of Shari'a" (McGregor 2012). Ansar Dine continued their program of violence in northern Mali for the next nine months, until French and Malian troops were able to force the militants out of most of the major areas in and around Timbuktu in early 2013.

The ferocity and targeted nature of these attacks, however, seemed to signal something specific about the architectural environment of Timbuktu, particularly the spiritual structures, whose purposeful destruction and desecration seemed to signify that they were occupying roles beyond that of mere casualties of war in the fight for Islamic orthodoxy, or convenient structural canvases on which Ansar Dine could paint its militant message. In fact, the careful selection and choreographed destruction of Timbuktu's built environment allowed Ansar Dine to accomplish multiple tasks simultaneously. It allowed Ansar Dine to engage in a campaign of radical self-fashioning, constructing a purposefully public image of militancy on par with similar globally recognized iconoclastic brands like Al-Qaeda and the Taliban. But it also allowed the group to perpetrate numerous ideologically based traumatic acts upon the landscape of Timbuktu at once, desecrating the area's historical Sufist identity of which most of Timbuktu's spiritual spaces were a part, while also making a strong disavowal of these sites as national and international heritage

---

[22] The MNLA, founded in 2011, is composed of ethnic Tuaregs, some of whom served in the Libyan army under Muammar Qaddafi. Its aim is the secession of the Azawad region, long framed as a Tuareg homeland, from the control of the Malian government and the establishment of an independent Tuareg state in the northern regions of the country.

[23] Ansar Dine is also connected to the group MUJWA, or the Movement for Unity and Jihad in West Africa.

spaces, an identity that some across the global Islamicate have come to view as pseudo-idolatrous. Along these lines, the performative sophistication of the destruction of these sites by Ansar Dine also seems to catalyze a different kind of space, what one might call a "counter-masjid" or even an "anti-masjid," in the sense that these acts of ritualized violence created sites of ruin rather than spirituality, erasing space rather than generating it through a performative spiritualism aimed at destruction rather than creation. Put another way, these acts had the effect of transforming masjid space in Timbuktu from a venerated vehicle of identity into an apparatus of trauma, using languages of extremist violence and a highly performative iconoclastic technique to do so.

Yet the success of Ansar Dine's campaign was fundamentally dependent on Timbuktu's intersectional identity as both a Sufist spiritual territory and a celebrated national and international heritage site. For over half a millennium, Timbuktu was a hub of multiple international networks of political, economic, and spiritual influence, achieving particular fame in the medieval period as a center for scholarship on Sufism, despite its inauspicious beginning as a small seasonal settlement in 1100 CE for nomadic peoples to graze their cattle. Timbuktu would eventually become a centralized location of the powerful Malian polity (thirteenth–fifteenth centuries) followed by the later Songhai polity (fifteenth–sixteenth centuries),[24] whose collective wealth and emphasis on Islamic cultural and economic modes would allow the area's reputation as the center of a vast intellectual, spiritual, and mercantile network to spread from Africa into the Middle East. This process was helped by notables such as Malian *Mansa* (king) Kanku Musa (c. 1280–c. 1337), who undertook a pilgrimage to Mecca in the early fourteenth century and spent so much gold along the way that he single-handedly influenced the global economy. Eventually Timbuktu would also become a major center of Sufi learning and spirituality that drew scholars and clerics from around the Islamic world to collaborate at the city's increasingly well-known educational institutions. Timbuktu's Islamic schools, or *madrasa*s, were numerous, supported by the development of libraries, both public and private, as well as an active book-making culture. Timbuktu's established university system was also among one of the most renowned in the Islamicate, composed of three primary institutions: the Sankoré (c. 1400), the Djinguere Ber (c. 1327), and the Sidi Yahya (c. 1440) schools, which attracted learned men such as famed

[24] I use "polity" in this case rather than "kingdom" or "empire" because the latter two terms are somewhat problematic in that they imply a centralized system of rule, a top-down form of governance that may not have been the case with regard to the sociopolitical structure at the time.

1.4 Masjid as Martyr

Figure 1.5 Sankoré Masjid, Timbuktu, Mali. Image by Lazare Eloundou Assomo. UNESCO World Heritage Site, listed as Timbuktu, CC BY-SA 3.0-igo.

Timbuktu scholar Ahmed Baba, known for his treatises on slavery and spiritual practice, to gather and exchange ideas (Dyke 2005) (Figure 1.5).[25]

Timbuktu's reputation as a site of Islamic power and learning was also buttressed by its architectural landscape and the spiritual cartography it generated through the organization of mosques, mausolea and, in particular, shrines into a type of charged topography. The construct of the tomb/shrine constituted one of the more direct expressions of the architectural humanism, or the connection between space and body, that lay at the heart of Timbuktu's urban ecology. Most tombs in Timbuktu are constructed in symbolically similar ways. Smaller tombs tend to be marked by a stone, which indicates the presence of the saint's body, as well as a terracotta pot indicating the location of the head. In addition, the head is positioned toward the Ka'ba in Mecca, as is traditional Islamic

[25] For additional history, see Labelle Prussin, *Hatumere: Islamic Design in West Africa* (Berkeley: University of California Press, 1986), and Timothy Insoll, *The Archaeology of Islam in Sub-Saharan Africa* (Cambridge: Cambridge University Press, 2003).

practice (de Jorio 2016, 118). Larger tombs or mausoleums often maintain a similar symbolic architectural language that often pulls from languages of domestic architecture to create a multi-tiered spiritual space. In fact, the tomb of Muslim scholar Cheick Sidi Mahmoud (1498–1548) was actually the original entrance vestibule into his domestic space and was transformed into his tomb at his death (de Jorio 2016, 118). Many of the shrines of the more venerated saints are visited daily, and this is because the saints play such an active role in the spiritual life of the community (de Jorio 2016, 118–120), their proximity conveying added protection and blessing, and further protecting the city from exterior threats. Because of this, numerous cemeteries have arisen next to the tombs of these saints largely because "proximity to a saint is believed to protect the deceased 'from the dangers of the afterlife'" (Becker 2009, 429; in de Jorio 2016, 119). Saints are also buried under Timbuktu's three primary Friday mosques – the Djinger Ber, Sankoré, and Sidi Yahya – and it is said that individuals visit these mosques when they have specific predicament and need intervention (de Jorio 2016, 120).[26] Thus, the architectural landscape of Timbuktu functions as an interconnected, mutually dependent ecological system in which spirituality has saturated every structure to generate a type of religious habitat and subsequently making the entire city a type of masjid environment (see Apotsos 2016a).

Regarding this masjid environment, at Timbuktu's height as an international spiritual society, its architectural landscape translated incoming influences and identities into a *métissage* of structural and spiritual forms whose weighty, monumental, earth-based construction merged Islamic structural genres like the mosque with Maghrebian styles seen in the aforementioned *ksar*, whose surface decoration and monumental, fortress-like appearance not only enabled its original inhabitants in the Sahara oases to defend against desert raiders, but also created a psychological sense of permanence, stability, and immovability.[27] Likewise, the earth-based styles of the Niger Bend, whose unique emphasis on structural pillars and pinnacles made manifest meaningful and powerful statements about the area's diverse spiritual and cultural

---

[26] Rosa de Jorio's field research notes that those with issues "related to the conquest of power" are pointed to the Djingarey Ber Mosque, while others having relationship issues should go to the Sankoré Mosque. Others who are concerned with finances should pray at the Sidi Yahya Mosque (de Jorio 2016, 120).

[27] A *ksar* is a pre-Islamic domestic compound typically located around oasis areas along trade routes in northern Africa. Multiple families live together within these large complexes, which have high, thick walls and corner towers to protect against nomadic raiders. These forms are thought to have influenced architectural developments south of the Sahara.

1.4 Masjid as Martyr

legacy, maintained a natural synergy with these incoming styles (to be addressed further in Chapter 3).

It is also this spiritual charge and the symbolic capital that accompanied it that ensured the continued survival of this environment into the contemporary period as well, not only as a spiritual space but also a space of historical and religious heritage. Timbuktu's history as a center for not only the production of Sufi spiritual space but also the subsequent dispersal of Islamic thought and identity throughout the Sahara and Sahelian regions has allowed international heritage organizations like UNESCO to claim it as an emblem of the Islamic "golden age under Songhai occupation (ca. 1468–1591)" (de Jorio 2016, 117). This project has been helped by the presence of numerous architectural artifacts that have been renovated and in some cases reimagined for a contemporary heritage tourism project. Timbuktu's heritage project was given new energy by President Amadou Toumani Touré who, following in the footsteps of his predecessor Alpha Oumar Konaré,[28] made Timbuktu's revitalization "a government priority" due to his "personal attachment to the religious patrimony of the city" and as part of his larger project of generating a sense of national identity and unity (de Jorio 2016, 121).

Yet Timbuktu's new reality as a World Heritage Site also meant that many of Timbuktu's great architectural institutions and events were no longer just spiritually oriented, but were also to assume the additional role of articulating local history to a broader public. Thus, the identities of its masjid spaces as vessels of ancestral presence and repositories of memory came to share conceptual space in the contemporary period with their new function as global heritage sites.[29] Importantly, this dual identity would become a keystone in Ansar Dine's destructive campaign, which framed Timbuktu not only as a site whose historical practices and belief systems could be interpreted as heretical by more orthodox Islamic sects, but also as a space that smacked of "Western" ambition and idolatrous behavior. As such, Timbuktu had much to offer Ansar Dine as an intersectional space that could be ideologically assaulted from multiple perspectives.

Another important, indeed principle, component in Ansar Dine's campaign, however, was the participation of one of the region's largest marginalized groups, the ethnic Tuareg. As a group, the Tuareg had historically been disenfranchised by the Malian government, whose

---

[28] For more information on Konare's heritage projects, see Mary Jo Arnoldi, "Bamako, Mali: Monuments and Modernity in the Urban Imagination," *Africa Today*, 54 (2), Visual Experience in Urban Africa (Winter, 2007): 3–24.

[29] This has generated a number of problems relating to heritage tourism and its treatment as a type of developmental model for the region. See Apotsos 2016a.

systematic neglect of Tuareg political, social, and economic matters has buttressed Tuareg views of the state as a corrupt, highly nepotistic entity.[30] This belies the fact, however, that Mali has long been a nation divided geopolitically between a perceived north and south, a division first created during the colonial period when the French imposed arbitrary geographic boundaries that alienated the Tuareg as a historically nomadic group and denied the legitimacy of traditional Tuareg clan-based political and cultural practices (Khan 2014). Ansar Dine's arrival in northern Mali offered the Tuareg an opportunity, to quote Dario Gamboni, for "radical measures of self-reestablishment," the chance to make a strong statement against this systemic cycle of neglect and marginalization (Gamboni 2011, 129). Indeed, in doing so, Ansar Dine followed a common script of "jihad-minded groups" such as Boko Haram and Al-Shabab in playing on the political, economic, social, and ethnic disenfranchisement of various groups by promising "a better allocation of resources and an end to discrimination and marginalization" (Loimeier 2016, 298). In addition, many regions vulnerable to such groups are generally geographically isolated with little governmental control and security, giving such movements "the chance to act as alternative sources of authority and security" (Loimeier 2016, 294), which has allowed extremist groups around the world to accomplish similar iconoclastic projects to a highly transformative end.

With regard to Ansar Dine's presence in Timbuktu, over the nine months of their occupation, the extremists leveled monuments and structures around the city in an unrelenting wave of destruction as a mode of both establishing ownership over this space as well as legitimizing themselves as an ideological authority using the interpretive lens of the Shari'a.[31] Through this lens, the selection of sites for destruction was not only deliberate but communicative, largely because violence, according to Riches, is "highly appropriate *both* for practical (instrumental) *and* for symbolic (expressive) purposes: as a means of transforming the social environment (instrumental purpose), and dramatizing the importance of key social ideas (expressive purpose)" (Riches 1986, 11; in van der Hoorn 2009, 24). It was the relationship between the spiritual and its human

---

[30] The feeling appears to be mutual. Tuaregs have an extraordinarily negative reputation among those living in the southern areas of the country due to their historic enslavement and mistreatment of "black" Malians (Tuareg are typically thought to be light-skinned and Arab in appearance, a largely incorrect but nonetheless pervasive belief).

[31] Increasingly, this approach to lived reality has fallen under the rubric of "fundamentalism," which not only applies the teachings of the Qur'an quite literally to any and all aspects of life, but also reflects the tendency to perceive an imagined Islamic past as being "purer" or more "spiritually authentic" than that of the contemporary period, which is often associated with Western influence and global imperialism (Leichtman 2015, 146).

1.4 Masjid as Martyr

community that underscored the particular choices being made as well toward generating an anti-masjid space (van der Hoorn 2009, 26).

Ansar Dine demolished more than sixteen mausoleums designated as both World Heritage Sites and key spiritual markers, while also inflicting significant damage to numerous other funerary areas, religious sites, and cemeteries (Figure 1.6). Tombs embedded in the exterior surface of the Sidi Yahya mosque, thought to have been built contemporaneously with the Sankoré during the Songhai Empire, were vandalized in conjunction with many neighboring tombs that were either booby-trapped with mine devices or despoiled with feces (ANCBS 2014, 5). Yet the fact that these tombs were not destroyed is also an important strategic element in that

Figure 1.6 The sacred gate of the Sidi Yahya Mosque, Timbuktu, Mali, after Ansar Dine destroyed its wooden entrance, 2012.
Image courtesy of MINUSMA/Sophie Ravier.

their defacement as opposed to demolition "make[s] [them] a token of the violence [they were] subjected to and of the infamy of anything with which [they were] associated" (Gamboni 1997, 19).

In fact, none of Timbuktu's mosques were razed. However, their annual plastering maintenance was prohibited due to the fact that it was accompanied by various ceremonies[32] that occupiers deemed "un-Islamic" (de Jorio 2016, 125). This was another strategic decision on the part of Ansar Dine in that Qur'anic tenets prohibit the destruction of a mosque, yet there are precedents for eliding this proscription, particularly within this region of Mali. One example is that of the Great Mosque in Djenne (addressed in Chapter 3), which in the eighteenth century was targeted by jihadist Sekou Amadou, ruler of the Massina Empire, who classified the building as a profane structure and a symbol of heresy due to its assumed expression of religious pluralism. As a way of circumventing the aforementioned Qur'anic tenets against mosque destruction, Amadou plugged the gutters of the earthen structure before the rainy season began and subsequently allowed it to "melt," not only finding a loophole in Islamic doctrine but also potentially framing it as an act of God itself. Ansar Dine's approach to these mosques, while not complete acts of destruction, were nonetheless intended to deconstruct the sanctity of the landscape by erasing structures through environmental attrition and preventing the transformative rituals that kept them solvent both physically and spiritually from taking place. In other words, these were not physically obliterative gestures, but spiritually obliterative ones that reached their crescendo with the dismantling of an ancient door located at the site of the Sidi Yahya mosque, which was said to open only at the end of days. The destruction of this door, but not the mosque on which it was located, again reflects Ansar Dine's strategy of psychological manipulation through the active and controlled transformation of Timbuktu's spiritual environment.

In addition to these spiritual sites, however, any "innovative" sites or sites that departed from "the conditions under which Islam was practiced in the seventh century" (O'Dell 2013, 510; in de Jorio 2016, 127) were also targeted, which included non-Sufi spaces like the Catholic church of Timbuktu, which was completely destroyed and its large wooden icon of the Virgin Mary defaced quite literally as she lay on the church altar. Other nonreligious sites were also damaged, including the El Farouk Monument at the entrance of the city and the Flame of Peace or Flamme de la Paix monument, which had been erected at the end of

---

[32] Such ceremonies occur in many other parts of Mali with regard to maintaining earth-based religious structures.

1.4 Masjid as Martyr

the second Tuareg rebellion in the 1990s (ANCBS 2014, 5). In doing so, Ansar Dine effectively reimagined Timbuktu's past by not only renovating ideas of the city's spiritual being through the erasure of important spiritual sites, but also attempted to renarrate Timbuktu's sociopolitical history through the censure of sites that not only spoke to Timbuktu as a space of political revolution but also cultural and spiritual tolerance.

Perhaps one of the most notable destructions, however, was that of thousands of historical manuscripts, some more than four hundred years old, that were destroyed at the Institute Ahmed Baba, Timbuktu's premiere library and research center on Sufi scholarship. Many manuscripts were despoiled where they were found, others were burned, and more would have undoubtedly succumbed to this fate had not a number of them been locked in the institute's vault. Many more manuscripts were saved through the ingenious smuggling activities of a handful of the conservators and their families (Rihouay 2014)

Beyond the instrumentalist objective of this destruction, however, the expressive processes or rituals through which these obliterative acts were undertaken are also key to understanding the creation of anti-masjid space. As van der Hoorn notes, "Architectural deaths have a great potential to fascinate people and have often been accompanied by a range of rituals." Quoting Neil Harris, she notes that "The death of particular buildings has, within the past hundred years or so, been invested with a new and elaborate set of rituals, reflecting the values of societies that are simultaneously energetic reshapers of their physical environments and elegiac about the settings and structures they are efficiently reducing to rubble" (Harris 1999, 134; in van der Hoorn 2009, 20). Regarding Timbuktu, eyewitness accounts report the presence of a well-oiled choreography of violence (Figure 1.7) that characterized these acts, typically beginning with the dramatic entrance of a militant-laden truck caravan flying the black flags of the organization with the *Shahada* or Islamic creed inscribed in white upon them. Chanting "*Allahu Akbar*" or "God is Great," these militants would then disembark and surround the targeted site with their trucks, blocking onlookers from interfering with the destruction itself but maintaining clear avenues of visibility so that onlookers would become involuntary participants in the action as well. Then, using shovels and pickaxes, the militants would proceed to systematically dismantle the targeted structure, continuing to cry "*Allahu Akbar*"over and over again until the job was done, at which point they would revel in a type of militant ecstasy. After this reaffirmation of faith, the militants would leave the site in much the same way that they had come, in a cloud of dust and sand, with their message indelibly etched in the rubble left behind.

72　1 The Intersectional Masjid

Figure 1.7 Members of Ansar Dine, Timbuktu, Mali, 2012.
Image by Magharebia. flickr, CC BY 2.0.

In these acts perpetrated by Ansar Dine, destruction was a key function not only as an act of piety but also as, to quote van der Hoorn, an "expression and acquisition of power" gained through "the conspicuous waste of goods" (Conor 1992, 75; in van der Hoorn 2009, 39), in this case, the built environment. This is of course in direct opposition to the notion of ruin where "the works of man ... were gradually reappropriated by nature"; destroyed buildings in contrast exist as "mere waste" (van der Hoorn 2009, 28). But importantly, the theatrical arrivals, the systematic or formulaic dismantlings, and the subsequent celebratory festivities that characterized these events point to the presence of a script, even a ritual, of destruction whose dramatic enactment reemphasizes the strategic nature of the spiritual built landscape in this drama (van der Hoorn 2009, 50). Indeed, the "symbolic potency" of these acts was directly related to the "symbolic properties" of the building (van der Hoorn 2009, 28) in which the purposeful destruction of buildings often acts as an equivalent to a type of sacrifice in that the aim is to "get rid of an impure status or to reach a superior one ... [through the eradication of] ... three-dimensional representatives of a dark period in history, to remove the stain on their collective identity, get rid of the burden of corruption, and attain a new, 'clean,' status" (van der Hoorn 2009, 50). Along these lines, due to the absolute union between "signifier" and "signified" in such cases, "people hardly perceive the difference between the object and what it embodies" (van der Hoorn 2009, 29).

It was in this way that these sites came to function as anti-masjids or counter-masjids, active disavowals and reversals of the spiritually performative actions that bring masjid space into being. In addition, such rituals targeted the particular nature of Timbuktu's masjid environment as an image of society, whose living human component had an important role to play in this drama, not only as makers of masjid space but as potential tools in its destruction. It is interesting to think that these targeted dismantlings would have failed in their purpose had there not been an audience there to witness it, the audience being a necessary element not only for their witnessing but also for the psychic pain they contributed to the event as coerced witnesses to these attacks. During the destruction of one of the mausoleums, one anonymous person reported: "There are many of us watching them destroy the mausoleum. It hurts but we can't do anything. These madmen are armed, we can't do anything but they will be cursed for this for sure" (Thomassen 2012).

Other testaments of vulnerability and disenfranchisement support the general feeling of helplessness that many of these acts of destruction evoked within the populace. Local journalist Yeya Tandina, speaking to Reuters via telephone, reported: "They are armed and have surrounded the sites with pick-up trucks. The population is just looking on helplessly" (Ewing 2012). As van der Hoorn notes, "Martyred edifices, typically, fell prey to their executioners while bystanders did not, or could not, do anything but witness" (van der Hoorn 2009, 175). Additional physical and psychological torture was also inflicted on the human population itself during this period, most of which was committed under the aegis of Shari'a law. As detailed in a report by the United Nations High Commissioner for Human Rights in 2012, crimes against humanity occurring under Ansar Dine included "summary executions, rape, torture, the recruitment of child soldiers, violations of freedom of expression and of right to information and violations of the right to education and health" (AFP 2012). These attacks began within the first few weeks of Ansar Dine's presence in northern Mali, and like those committed against the architectural environment, they were notable for their very public, very performative dimensions. The UN reported the stoning of a young couple who were accused of having children out of wedlock. The couple were tied together, buried up to their necks in a pit, and then stoned to death in front of a crowd of over 300 people who had been gathered specifically for this purpose. Likewise, ten cases of amputations occurred in the region during Ansar Dine's incursion, three of which were in Timbuktu, and most were public events. One individual, Al Hader Ag

Al Mahmoud, detailed the account of his amputation as happening in the public square where militants had rounded up people for the event. Sexual violence, typically inflicted as a result of violations of dress code or inappropriate public behavior, was rampant and highly visible during this period. The assaults, which targeted women and female adolescents alike, often occurred in homes and in the presence of relatives as a method of demoralization and psychic torture (AFP 2012, 10–11).

Within this context, the line between human and architectural iconoclasm begins to blur as the symbolic dimensions and the public trauma associated with these "punishments" generated a powerful type of collective horror. Both masjid and the human body became synonymous as canvases for Ansar Dine's art of war, their destruction made all the more potent by the social and spiritual connection between humanity and architecture that had long existed within the landscape of Timbuktu. Through Ansar Dine's supplementation of architectural iconoclasm with similar fragmentary acts against the human body, the group attacked multiple landscapes and identities in Timbuktu at once, simultaneously altering and transforming these environs into "appropriate" social entities through intersectional violence. One of the strategies for accomplishing this was through a systematic program of rebranding. When Ansar Dine entered Timbuktu in 2012, one of their first iconoclastic acts was to vandalize, *but not destroy*, a shelter that marked the entrance to the town, on which was originally written "Timbuktu: City of 333 Saints." The militants promptly scratched out the "333" and replaced it with a 0, erasing most of the word "saint" in the process. They then proceeded to construct and plant signboards proclaiming various Salafist slogans like conquering flags along the major roads that connected Timbuktu to the rest of the world. One of the larger signs posted on a major road leading to Timbuktu's small airport read "Timbuktu: The Gateway to the Application of Shari'a law, welcome" (Rihouay 2014). These written markers represent attempts by Ansar Dine to quite literally paper over established identities and entrench more acceptable ones in their place, thereby reassigning the sociospiritual landscape of Timbuktu a new, more suitable Salafist identity.[33] The human counterpart to this act involved the institution of strict dress codes on the population at large. Females

---

[33] Salafism takes a very literal approach to Islam that is highly orthodox and supports jihad against perceived "enemies of Islam." Also known as Wahhabism, it is thought that this particular school of Islamic thought began in the eighteenth century on the Arabian Peninsula with Sheikh Mohammed Ibn Abdelwahhab. Some explanations for its growth in North Africa in the contemporary period point to the wave of uprisings leading up to and following the Arab Spring, which created a vacuum that many "hard-liners" from Saudi Arabia and other Arabic states have attempted to fill.

1.4 Masjid as Martyr

over the age of five were forced to cover their bodies from head to toe, and the institution of dress codes for men of all ages required them to roll their trousers up to their ankles (AFP 2012, 13). This rebranding of human and architectural form marked a process of "overwriting" Timbuktu by stamping bodies and the surrounding landscape with new, more ideologically conservative identities.

Yet this merging of human and architectural bodies into a collective anti-masjid landscape in Timbuktu would result in a type of dual martyrdom that would eventually generate a posthumous power, underscoring the point that "destruction is less an end-point ... than the beginning of a process of meaning-making" (Mancini, Bresnahan, and Schwenkel 2014, 3). These "casualties," marked as they are by violence and trauma, "refuse[d] to let historical narratives of completion stand. Memories of the war are deeply encoded in them, marked literally and figuratively in their flesh.... The wound gives evidence of the act of injuring" (Sturken 1991, 132–133; in van der Hoorn 2009, 160). Such ideas also underscore Bruno Latour's conceptualization of "iconoclash" in that every image broken is also in fact an image made, and even acts aimed at "removal, negation or obliteration" are ultimately productive and generative in creating new spaces, images, and ideas imprinted within the memory and message of the act (McClanan and Johnson 2005, 3). Indeed, the "afterlife" of such bodies can take two forms: the first where "attempts can be made to clear the edifice of its impure status," and the second in which "efforts can be made to grant the edifice superior status" in the form of rehabilitation, replacement, reconstitution, or even reframing in a more optimistic manner (van der Hoorn 2009, 166).

Yet an important element in the "afterlife" of a body is the word "life." Ansar Dine's actions fundamentally transformed Timbuktu's masjid spaces, architectural and human alike, into spaces and bodies "set apart" or separated from one another; yet in singling them out for this unique type of attention, destructive as it may have been, these spaces became sites defined by a type of reverent anti-attention, conveying ambiguousness to the nature and power of the destroyed object that make it unclear "whether the object consists of 'mere stones' or has a power of its own." Latour also points out that "[N]o one knows whether those idols can be smashed without any consequences ... or whether they have to be destroyed because they are so *powerful,* so ominous" (Latour 2002, 21; in van der Hoorn 2009, 30). In such cases, the materiality of the structure and the body becomes supercharged, almost alive, and thus the lack of regard for the "remains" of them make them a source of deep unease (van der Hoorn 2009, 34). In this way, the "killing" of the masjid structures in Timbuktu specifically, paradoxically reconferred liveliness on them as well by giving them an "excess of meaning" (Buchli 2015, 168).

This excess subsequently bled into the spatial voids left behind by Ansar Dine, and over time became new localities of identity and reverence, their meaning deriving from their reality as indexes of absence and loss to become recharged with a newfound sense of religiocultural relevance. The last of the demolitions took place only three months before a combined force of French and Malian troops retook Timbuktu and routed Ansar Dine's remaining forces from the area in April 2013. Following this, rebuilding began, with Ansar Dine's destructions conceptually refashioned in the Timbuktu mental landscape as the latest contributions to the cultural and structural narrative of city. Through such physical and metaphorical evolutions, the destroyed sites of Timbuktu have come to embody yet additional identities to those already established, identities that now reflect a timely globalized "radical" element that puts Timbuktu in dialogue with many other areas of the world that have experienced similar atrocities. The choice to reconstruct rather than memorialize or commemorate also speaks to the new roles that these forms now occupy. In addition to acting as functional spiritual and historical spaces, they also now stand as a new material landscape representing a new post-Ansar Dine sociopolitical reality and thus are "more related to the present than to the past" (van der Hoorn 2009, 172; 180). Along these lines, Robert Bevan has noted: "Rebuilding can be as symbolic as the destruction that necessitates it . . . . What were once unintentional monuments – the places of worship, libraries and foundation of everyday life – by their rebuilding can become new, intentional monuments to the events that caused their destruction" (Bevan 2006, 176; in van der Hoorn 2009, 172). In fact, rebuilding can sometimes promote unintentional symbolic realities. On the one hand, it potentially cements a structure's martyred status by preserving the structure in stasis in a perfect preconflict authentic utopian state. Contributing to this in Timbuktu's case is the reconstruction process itself, which has used traditional methods and, importantly, earthen materials to reconstitute these edifices. In reaffirming this material link with Timbuktu's architectural heritage (rather than rebuilding in cement or another material that is more physically permanent) and even using materials left at the foundation site, these reconstructions are also in the process of becoming/creating new reliquaries not only out of the bodies entombed within but out of the structures themselves. In addition, as van der Hoorn notes, "When relics originate from a martyr this is seen to increase their power – and thus also the power of those who possess, touch or worship them" (van der Hoorn 2009, 183).

Yet reconstruction also has the potential to make "previous transformations [destructive and otherwise] undone" and actually denies the existence of various scars and destructive elements that would give the building its martyred status in the first place (van der Hoorn 2009, 177; 179). Through this process, reconstruction as a process of remembering in some ways also promotes active forgetting in that it seems to "heal wounds by creating an impression of completeness" and that it remains somehow "untouched" (van der Hoorn 2009, 180; 189). These areas are in the process of becoming new sites of spiritual identity and renovated repositories of memory. From this perspective, it becomes apparent that identity can never be created or destroyed; it can only be transformed into new iterations through generative and degenerative histories that both layer a site and allow it to accrue additional physical, conceptual, and symbolic patinas.

Lastly, there have also been various conversations and conflicts with regard to the reconstruction of the mausolea and the vision of the heritage stakeholders versus the vision of the community in terms of the role that these structures should play moving into the future (de Jorio 2016, 117). This is in specific reference to these structures acting as contemporary spiritual sites of saint veneration versus commemorative secular sites of historical memory (de Jorio 2016, 132). Interestingly, this seems to reflect changing views with regard to how one should appropriately interpret these spaces. Rosa de Jorio even notes that some of Timbuktu's religious leaders who were adamant defenders of Sufi devotional traditions regarding these structures have, post-conflict, been far more restrained in their support (de Jorio 2016, 133). Thus it begs the question as to whether this architectural incursion not only changed the fundamental nature of these sites as masjid but also now how they function and signify for the broader community. Yet the spiritual malleability of these sites also reveals the inherent flexibility and adaptive nature of Islamic spiritual and spatial codes as, to quote Naomi Davidson, "an ensemble of precedents and general principles, interpreted by different and mutable narratives in diverse contexts" (Davidson 2012, 39).

1.5   Conclusion

Increasingly, shifting contexts and conditions are crafting secondary and even tertiary identities for spiritual sites as masjids, monuments, memorials, commodities, and increasingly battlefields. This is largely a result of the fact that culture (and I would argue the modern condition), according to Humphrey, is not just a condition that helps underscore and clarify how one connects to a spiritual object or structure; it is also a social element that remains unfixed and recreated continuously through interaction with one's material environment. Thus, to quote van der Hoorn, "Rather than *symbolizing* something unambiguously, buildings *embody* a number of things successively and simultaneously" (van der Hoorn 2009, 18). As such, buildings, or perhaps spaces, are by their very nature both intersectional and, I would argue, radical in their ability to generate or advocate for a type of essential change. The masjid environments within this chapter have functioned as structures, symbols, environments, and methods of being in the world. In addition, the masjid in each case is not only being utilized as a site of spiritual capital and efficacy but also as a means to a particular end, which in some ways reduces its power as an independent agent and rechannels it toward a new function as a support mechanism for particular agendas. However, the masjid also acts as a type of sociospatial battlefield for intersectional conditions of being, a space of action and agency not only through the conditions of its production but through its destruction as well, each speaking to the value systems, social dynamics, and political disruptions present in society in which masjid space can either participate or attempt to counteract. The masjid thus becomes an ally/advocate/accomplice through the generation of change or the reinscription of normativity based on intersectional modes of existence, deployed as a mode through which Islam renovates, rehabilitates, or reconstitutes worldviews using spiritual space in its constructed or destructed form as a vehicle. As such, the masjid becomes the ultimate affirmation of intersectional identity, according power and authenticity to those who inhabit the space.

2 Monument, Memory, and Remembrance: Rethinking the Masjid Through Contemporary Heritage Regimes

The masjid constructs the past through the present and thus is fundamentally situated in the time of its making, even as it references historical narratives.

2.1 Introduction

Nasser Rabbat notes that the role of architecture is not only to contain human activity and value systems embedded within a particular segment of space and time, but to function as a "branch of human creativity that is relied upon to frame, embody, and preserve memories" (Rabbat 2002, 56). Indeed, architecture as a medium of memory maintains a multitude of modes of transmitting historical narratives, recollections, and remembrances through spatial means that range from the material and the symbolic to the intellectual and the ideological (Rabbat 2002, 57). Yet history itself has never been a medium of the "past"; it exists completely in the present and thus actively aids in constructing the lenses through which individuals not only look back and interpret past events but also present realities as they relate to these events. This also means that memory, and by association, history is rarely fixed but can be adjusted, clarified, and/or manipulated over time and often through interpretations of mediums like architectural form as a mode of artifactual evidence (Rabbat 2002, 57).

Such conversations inform the field of critical heritage studies, which not only focuses on how heritage space is used to represent the value systems, ideologies, and agendas of the present, but also how these elements reflect ongoing relationships between history and memory, both of which have a foot in the past while being manufactured in the present and deployed toward "construct[ing], reconstruct[ing], and negotiat[ing] a range of identities and social and cultural values and meanings in the present" (Smith 2010, 3). To this end, heritage has increasingly come to reflect various power hierarchies active in society, hierarchies that in many ways dictate who currently controls the historical narrative of an area. Heritage, in other words, becomes "a struggle over power ... because heritage is itself a political resource" (Smith 2010, 281).

Yet, importantly, these elements make heritage an inherently fluid construct, a dynamic legacy that experiences shifts in meaning and relevance as a result of ongoing negotiations, discussions, and contestations in societal discourse that in turn affect continuous reimaginings of history and the various stories that heritage should be telling. Thus, heritage, like the masjid as it has been thus far addressed, is a verb as much as it is a noun, and these two spatial concepts have experienced numerous intersecting moments on the continent in the form of sites and traditions that actively bring history, identity, and spirituality into conversation.

Yet before engaging in the conversation fully, it is important to establish the current state of heritage as it is being defined in the contemporary period and the landscape of critical heritage studies in practice with regard to its deployment in the contemporary period. The United Nations World Heritage Convention Concerning Protection of the World Cultural and Natural Heritage divides spatial/structural heritage into groups that encompass both "monuments," which include architecture, monumental sculpture/painting, and archeological sites which include rock art and associated productions, and then composite built landscapes, representing a collaboration between man and nature. Yet all of these sites "represent combinations of features that are of outstanding universal value from the point of view of history, art or science" (Nuryanti 1996, 251–252). Interestingly as well, many of these elements seem to muddy the definition of "architecture" in the traditional sense in that, as a work of heritage, it is further nuanced to incorporate "human-made, fixed elements, possessing historical values and meaning derived from the settings in which they occur and societal values that ascribe worth to them" (Nuryanti 1996, 252). International heritage bodies like the World Monuments Fund and especially UNESCO (United Nations Educational, Scientific and Cultural Organization) have also been at the forefront of these conversations, not only creating guidelines for the establishment of heritage programs around the world but also playing a role in definitions of heritage writ large as they currently stand.

This has particularly been the case in Africa, which currently contains over one hundred UNESCO World Heritage Sites, about 10 percent of which are either Muslim sites or sites affiliated with Islamic culture. This is significant due to the fact that Islamic sites have a unique relationship with the idea of a material heritage, largely because materiality in both art and architecture is something that has been in many cases actively deemphasized or problematized within discussions of potential *haram*

2.1 Introduction

behaviors including idolatry and excessive materialism. Yet as one of the oldest religions in the world and one that experienced a very dramatic early spread across the globe, the spatial heritage of Islam incorporates a vast number of sites that are diverse in form, function, and history and not only offer alternatives to what one might consider the "physical" environment but also what the preservation of that environment might look like. Likewise, regarding preservation, many verses in the Qur'an evoke the verb "*amara*" which in translation means "to build, to maintain, to restore, to preserve, to refurbish." Concerning spiritual forms, Kahera interprets the presence of this verb to mean that the *ummah* is responsible for not only the construction and maintenance of structures like mosques and shrines, but also their quality, so that they can continue to serve as appropriate spaces of spiritual devotion or *masjid* (Kahera 2008, 36). Thus, Islamic heritage, particularly in diverse contexts like Africa, is complex and multi-tiered, and contemporary foci on heritage and material preservation are having an increased effect on the identity and reality of these sites as they continue to exist in the contemporary period beyond their role as spaces of spirituality.

To this end, this chapter looks at three case studies from the continent in which masjid spaces have found active counterparts within contemporary conceptualizations of heritage. Within these case studies, forms and landscapes not only function as sites of spiritual performance but also as symbols of local histories and identities, narratives that are not always universal in their construction, application, or reception. The first case study is located in Ethiopia, an area with one of the earliest histories of contact with Islam on the continent, and specifically within the walled city of Harar Jugol, the fourth holiest city of Islam. The history and unique structural character of Harar Jugol enables the city to function in a dual capacity as both a highly charged masjid and a heritage site, a collective identity that is actively affirmed and celebrated by those who live there. That being said, the growth of "new" Harar on the outskirts of the older city and questions regarding Harar's "living museum" status have put some pressure on the city's established heritage narrative even as residents remain committed to maintaining its unique spiritual and historical character. The second case study addresses Hassan Fathy's New Gourna project, which was begun in 1945. Specifically, this chapter focuses on the two lives of this project, the first beginning in Luxor, Egypt, where Fathy constructed a community that attempted to tap into architectural and spiritual traditions embedded within Egyptian history toward creating a self-sustaining, culturally sensitive society. New Gourna's second life began in 1981 when Fathy utilized knowledge gained from New Gourna to construct Dar al Islam, a masjid and educational center currently located in the community of Abiquiú, New Mexico. Fathy's Egypt-based design has found an excellent complement here, largely due to the synergies between Egyptian architectural heritage and that of the area's Native American adobe architectural legacies. In contrast to this export of architectural and spiritual heritage, the final case study of this chapter focuses on the import of contemporary Ottoman masjid spaces in Africa, specifically Ghana, which has generated pushback with regard to the possibility of a foreign cultural form being imposed on one's sociocultural and spiritual identity.

Collectively, these case studies illustrate the dynamic but selective nature of heritage as a process of remembering/forgetting and selective assimilation, which in turn positions the masjid space under study as not only a place of prostration but "simultaneously a memorial to the past and an aspiration towards what is to come" (Rizvi 2015, 4).

2.2   Lived Heritage and the Sacred Topography of Harar Jugol, Ethiopia

One of the central complexities that many Islamic sites have assumed under the weight of their world heritage status in both Africa and elsewhere is that they are often located in the midst of active contemporary communities. As Nuryanti notes, "Local people interact with these structures directly as they go about their everyday lives" (Nuryanti 1996, 256). As such, relationships that exist between contemporary populations and these heritage sites are also important with regard to the "interdependencies" that subsequently exist between them, particularly given the fact that such sites must now perform multiple roles for their dedicated audience (Nuryanti 1996, 256).

The walled medieval Islamic city of Harar Jugol constitutes one such example; yet the town is also unusual in terms of Islamic settlements in East Africa for a number of reasons. Located in the Harari district of Ethiopia, Harar Jugol is one of the only settlements that is not located on the coast, which has been a popular route for influences coming into East African cultural and religious space. In addition, Harar is also Ethiopia's only walled city, having an area of around 48 hectares and the world's highest concentration of mosques, earning it the title "Africa's Mecca" (Figure 2.1). This title is supported by the fact that Harar's spirituality is embedded in both its structures and layout, each of which contributes to the creation of a fractalized spiritual topography at micro- and macroscopic levels. Specifically, its repetition of similar structural and spiritual elements ranges from the establishment of boundaries at both the city and the compound level to the creation of spiritual shrine spaces ranging from the Jami Mosque to backyard familial shrines and tomb spaces.

2.2 Lived Heritage

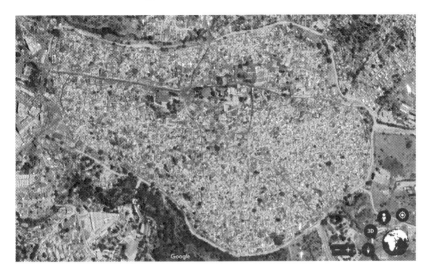

Figure 2.1 Aerial view of Harar Jugol, Ethiopia.
Image courtesy of Ó Maxar Technologies CNES/Airbus Landsat/Copernicus, Google, 2019.

Harar Jugol's history and ethnic composition is equally complex, the city itself actively contributing to Ethiopia's title as "the despair of the compulsive classifier," home to an ancient Christian civilization yet having a Muslim population that represents over a third of the national population (Demoz 1969, 49). Although Ethiopia was never officially colonized by European powers, its cultural history nonetheless places it at the center of various intersecting flows of imperial activity, from ancient Byzantine, Middle Eastern, and Egyptian Coptic influences to eighteenth- and nineteenth-century French, Italian, Greek, Yemeni, and Turkish presences.[1] Ethnically speaking, the country is also quite diverse, sometimes called a "museum of peoples" and is home to over eighty different ethnic groups and over two hundred different linguistic dialects (Demoz 1969, 49).

Such categorizations are important particularly when considering Ethiopia's current heritage project. Ethiopia's official tourism moniker is "The Land of Origins," which not only speaks to its general sociocultural diversity but also the fact that, at the national level, the country maintains thousands of registered heritage sites, including nine UNESCO World Heritage Sites, which is the most of any country on the continent (Selamta

---

[1] Currently, Asia, particularly China, is making large-scale inroads into the country through economic and infrastructural projects.

2018, 39). In addition to natural areas and archaeological sites, Ethiopia's UNESCO heritage sites also include a number of architectural sites, such as the rock-hewn churches of Lalibela (inscribed 1978), which were completed in the thirteenth century under the direction of King Lalibela, who aimed to create a "New Jerusalem" in Ethiopia. There is also the fortified city of Fasil Ghebbi, which was built in the sixteenth century and is sometimes known as the "Camelot of Africa" (Selamta 2018, 43).

Harar Jugol, however, stands out amongst this list as one of the only Islamic heritage sites in the country, and its importance both locally and in the context of the broader global Islamicate is significant. Not only is Harar Jugol considered the fourth holiest city in Islam, after Mecca, Medina, and Jerusalem, but its spiritual importance took form during a key moment in early Ethiopian history in 615 CE when the emperor of the reigning Ethiopian Axsum Empire al-Najāshī Ashāma (also known variously as al-Najāshī al-Asham, Ella Gabaz, or Ellä Säham) welcomed refugee Muslims at the request of the Prophet Muhammed who were fleeing persecution from the Quraysh of Mecca (Cuoq 1981, 32; in Loimeier 2016, 263). These refugees remained in Aksum for over twenty years and the event itself would become known as the first *hijra* (*al-hijra al-ūl*), not to be confused with the *hijra* undertaken by the Prophet in 622. This kindness was rewarded by the Prophet declaring Abyssinia (present-day Ethiopia) *dār al-aiyād (hiyād)*, or a land exempt from Islamic incursion, and the following saying has been attributed to the Prophet, granting Ethiopia immunity from jihad: "leave the Abyssinians as long as they leave you [in peace]" (Ahmed 2007, 263). There are even rumors that the Christian emperor himself converted to Islam and transformed his kingdom into an Islamic state, a move that was quickly squashed by his subjects, who deposed him and reestablished Christian rule. It is thought that because of this, Abyssinia forsook its *dār al-aiyād* status, catalyzing later Muslims in the sixteenth century under the rule of Ibrāhīm al-Ghāzī (also known as Ahmad Grañ, 1506–1543) to "liberate" the empire through jihad (Erlich 2010, 3; in Loimeier 2016, 263). Yet, most point to Emperor Ashāma's initial charitable act as laying the foundation for the generally positive attitude of tolerance and acceptance that has for the most part existed between Christians and Muslims within Ethiopia over time.

With regard to Harar, the history of its establishment is less certain. It is thought that the original inhabitants of Harar were composed of seven Argobbas villages – known respectively as Eskhanti Gey, Hassan Gey, Tukhun Gey, Ferqa Gey, Harawe Gey, Ruqiya Gey, and Samti Gey[2] – which joined together to become one mutually dependent

---

[2] "Gey" is Harari for "town."

2.2 Lived Heritage

polity as a result of their individual susceptibility to natural elements and disasters. Yet there is some inconsistency with regard to both the timing and the impetus behind this joining given that this would place the founding of Harar long before the arrival of Sheikh Abadir Umar ar Rida, who is widely considered to be both the "political and spiritual father of the Harari" (Harari Regional State Cultural Heritage and Tourism Bureau 2015). Others cite a local myth regarding 405 sheikhs arriving from the Arabian Peninsula in 1256 and choosing the site for this soon-to-be trading post due to its defensibility; the subsequent organization of the city into its five sections was undertaken by Abadir.[3]

Despite the inconclusive nature of Harar's origin story, however, most historians are confident that the history of Harar and Islam in Ethiopia was one characterized by regular transfers of power. At the end of the ninth century, the Muslim Sultanate of Ifat was established, ruled by the Makhzum Dynasty, whose seat of power would stretch across the plains to what would eventually be Harar (Revault et al. 2006, 57). It is thought that the first mosques in Harar – Aw Mansur and Garad Muhammad Abogh in Jugol, and Aw Machad Mosque outside the city walls – date from this period (Revault et al. 2006, 22). The Ethiopian Solomonic Dynasty, which existed simultaneously with the Ifat Islamic dynasty, would generate a period of continuous unrest between the thirteenth and sixteenth centuries (Harari Regional State Cultural Heritage and Tourism Bureau 2015), although this was also a period when Harar became a major center of Islamic learning and trade in the Horn of Africa.[4] It was also during this time (1551/2) that Harar's walls were built by Amir Nur bin Mujahid who, after realizing that the city's defenses had been exhausted by Grañ's fourteen-year campaign, commissioned city architect Yacine Aït al-Barak to not only build watchtowers with each city gate, but also organize the streets in a "zigzag" fashion to thwart enemy invaders (Revault et al. 2006, 56). Nur's significance to the defensive character of the city has given his tomb, which lies at the center of one of the oldest neighborhoods in the fortified city, particular spiritual significance. In fact, it is said that its presence effectively "consecrated the place [Harar] as holy, closed to non-Muslims up until the conquest of the

---

[3] In either case, these villages were composed of individuals of the Harla ethnic group, a now extinct group from which the Harari cultural group are considered to be the sole descendants (Revault et al. 2006, 56).

[4] In the late thirteenth century, Christian emperor Yekouna-Amlak of the Solomonic Dynasty would defeat a coalition of oppositional Muslim states and then three hundred years later the aforementioned Ibrāhīm al-Ghāzī would launch a jihad against Ethiopia's Christian dynasty and establish Harar as the capital of the Adal Sultanate in the sixteenth century.

region by Menelik in 1887" (Revault et al. 2006, 59). During the seventeenth century, Harar would eventually become an independent emirate under Ali Ibn Daud until the city was conquered and incorporated into the empire of Ethiopia in 1887.

The nineteenth and twentieth centuries would also bring Harar into contact with various European powers which were moving into East African space at the time. Harar and many of the settlements around it would be occupied by a shifting cast of international characters that ranged from French and Italian, to Egyptian, Greek, Turkish, and Indian, each of which inscribed not only their economic influence on the area, but their cultural and architectural influences as well, despite not establishing an "official" colonial governance system in the region.

Yet Harar's current character is very much in dialogue with the political events of Ethiopia in the 1970s and 1980s. The 1972 coup, carried out by the DERG Revolutionary Committee, would sink the country into a twenty-year period of violence that had far-reaching ramifications for populations all over Ethiopia, including Harar, which not only lost a number of citizens to the violence of the DERG regime but also had many of its cultural and material heritage objects cast aside as part of the DERG's general disinclination toward history and the nation's past. Another coup in 1991 ended the DERG's reign and set Ethiopia on the path that it currently follows, which has seen both Christianity and Islam accorded equal constitutional positions under Ethiopian law, as well as the lifting of prohibitions on religious activities and press freedoms established by the DERG. This has resulted in a significant rise in mosque and religious school (*madrasa*) buildings not only in Harar but also in other areas in the country, as well as an increase in Muslims making the pilgrimage to Mecca (Loimeier 2016, 260).

Currently one of the more prominent Islamic movements in Ethiopia is Sufism (*tasawwuf*), whose adherents concentrate on attaining a more intimate relationship with Allah through a series of collective ritual practices (Abbink 2008, 117). The Qadiriyya is currently one of the most popular Sufi brotherhoods in Ethiopia, specifically in Harar, having arrived there from Yemen in the sixteenth century before spreading throughout the rest of the country (Zeleke 2014, 198). Sufism as it developed in Harar mirrored similar trajectories of Islam more broadly on the continent in that it was adopted, adapted, and assimilated into the city's social and cultural systems in a way that made Harari Islam unique to its context. As such, the Islamic identity that would develop in Harar was a cultural identity as much as it was a religious one, as can be seen in its various architectural types that effectively combine Harari cultural and

2.2 Lived Heritage

Figure 2.2 a and b Harar *bari* (gate) and wall section, Harar Jugol, Ethiopia, 2018.
Images by the author.

Islamic Sufi identity into one harmonious cultural/spiritual/heritage-oriented whole.

Harar's Islamic identity begins with the city walls (Figure 2.2a and 2.2b); the term "Jugol" in actuality refers both to the walls themselves that wrap around the city and to the enclosed space itself. The walls also maintain a number of symbolic elements that enable them to bestow spiritual charge to Harar's interior space. The architect of the wall, Fakhraddin Yonis, constructed them according to the Abjad system of mathematics, which allowed the length of the wall – 6666 cubits – to correspond to the letter "M" of the Arabic alphabet in reference to the Prophet Muhammed as a mode of eliciting bərəkä or blessing (Revault et al. 2006, 18). In addition, the walls themselves were originally pierced by five gates – the Suqutat bari, the Argob *bari*, the Assumiy *bari*, the Asma-addin *bari*, and the Badri *bari*[5] – that corresponded to the five primary avenues extending from the central point out of the city and again have spiritual significance in referencing the five pillars of Islam and the fingers of the hand of Fatima (Revault et al. 2006, 18). A saint's tomb was placed in the vicinity of each gate to enable further spiritual protection of the town (Revault et al. 2006, 19) and provide the first layer of sanctity through which one passes when entering the space. In addition, in the past, incoming visitors were forced to leave their weapons at the gates, which were traditionally closed at night, although not presently.

These walls are important also because they bring the concept of "boundary" into play. These ramparts actively establish not only a sense of spiritual place but a differentiation between city and country and, one could argue, spiritual and secular space (Santelli and Revault 2004, 164) as a mediator between exterior to interior. This aspect was also emphasized by the fact that, historically, "polluting" materials including the dead, water (which was considered "noxious"), trash/rubbish, and bodily excrement were to be left outside the city walls; along these lines, there were no water sources within the city and rubbish dumps were often located right outside of the gates. As Serge Santelli notes, "The ramparts thus defined the limits of a city for values of purity, cleanliness and health that opposed it to the dirty values of the near outskirts" (Santelli and Revault 2004, 166). In addition, the wall and gate system of Harar created a "contained" spiritual element that not only preserved the interior physically and psychologically from exterior forces but also encouraged the differentiation of adjacent "secular" areas like "new" Harar, which has grown up along the outskirts of the old city. This system also separated the city socially from sister cities like Dire Dawa, which accommodated *haram* or forbidden activities not acceptable within the holy space of Harar.[6]

---

[5] *Bari* means "gate" in Harari.

[6] Along these lines, the walls of Harar Jugol have undergone various evolutions at the hands of foreign intruders, with the Egyptians fortifying the walls and building additional twenty-four guard towers along the walls in the mid-nineteenth century, and the Italians restoring and rebuilding some parts of the wall and gates, in addition to renovating the basic style of

2.2 Lived Heritage

Thus, the walls of Harar Jugol do not simply define the town as a "Muslim town," but more broadly as a spiritual space where in more recent years worshippers of other faiths, particularly Christianity, are able to not only traverse its boundaries via the various gates that pierce its borders, but also access Harar's most sacred spaces as universal spiritual sites. Indeed, once within Harar's spiritual space, borders between faiths are erased as one is absorbed into the universal spiritual sanctity of the city. Christian women can be found praying at various Islamic shrines within the city walls for help with pregnancy, and members of multiple faiths visit the area to participate in the week-long festivals that occur at an annual basis around various shrines in the city, with Christians "leaving only to attend Sunday service in their own church" (Desplat 2005, 487). The custodian of one of the city's most important shrines, the founder of the city Sheikh Abadir Umar ar Rida, had this to say about the multitude of different types of worshippers that visit his shrine:

Abadir is the father of all of us. He does not distinguish between nationalities and religions. Boundaries between followers don't make sense, because there are Christians who are Muslims at heart and there are Muslims who are Christians, the only importance is that you are pure. Allah knows you and on the final day of judgement you will be separated. As human beings, we are not capable of marking difference by ourselves. (Desplat 2005, 487)

This again positions Harar as not only as a collective space of veneration, but also a multivalent masjid space, whose spirituality is read through the lens of one's own belief system and whose spiritual applications are "flexible, absorbent, and heterogenous" (Gibb 1999, 90; in Desplat 2005, 488).

Yet interestingly, it is the presence of walls like that of Harar Jugol that have led many such sites to be inscribed as heritage sites, these walls acting as authenticating architectural elements to the cultural and religious "purity" of the city within and "contain" heritage elements within easily definable (physical) parameters. In Harar's case especially, the wall is interpreted as simultaneously gesturing toward "diverse cultural influences" while nonetheless embodying a singular social, ethnic, and spiritual identity (Creighton 2007, 343). This type of interpretation has allowed Harar Jugol's walls to become "monuments" to the city's assumed identity, a "cherished" symbol "of civic prestige and vitality in the context of the heritage industry" (Creighton 2007, 348). Yet with regard to how the walls are actually functioning in the contemporary period, they also actively separate the city into two distinctive areas – the "old" area and the "new"

the Badri *bari* (the south gate) by constructing an arched entrance portal bookended by crenellated semicircular towers in the 1930s (Revault et al. 2006, 19).

area – which is a demarcation that has in certain ways led to perceived class-based bias, with "old" section inhabitants viewing themselves as more "authentically" Harari than other members of the community. In addition, there are questions as to whether these physical boundaries are preventing potentially constructive dialogue with various global movements and are instead transforming the city's inhabitants into living actors playing on an economically motivated "stage set" of Harar's heritage narrative (Creighton 2007, 349). This possibility seems likely given Harar's current moniker as a "living museum where the past embraces the present" (Harari Regional State Cultural Heritage and Tourism Bureau 2015). Similar processes have been noted at other UNESCO-inscribed sites, such as Djenne (Mali) and Zanzibar. Yet the walls and gates of Harar must be contextualized as only one of a number of architectural heritage infrastructures that exist within this city that all contribute to the city's spiritual and heritage-saturated identity.

Another architectural infrastructure notable within the city is the mosque forms. Although the number varies depending on the source, the official number of mosques within the walls of Harar Jugol is eighty-two, each sited to accommodate forty households (Harari Regional State Cultural Heritage and Tourism Bureau 2015, 46), although many of these mosques are owned by families and typically only visited by their members. It is commonly believed within the city that building a mosque ensures one is admitted into heaven. According to Harar's oral histories the first mosque was established between the eleventh and twelfth centuries and coincided with the arrival of founder Abadir. After this developed the larger communal mosque, of which Din Agobarar Mosque, which translates as "great religion," is thought to be the first of five *jami* or congregational mosques in Harar before the thirteenth century (Revault et al. 2006, 57). Each mosque was built in one of the five neighborhoods established by Abadir and his patrons (forty-four in number), which in addition to Din Agobara include the Imam Ardin Mosque (neighborhood/kebele 4), the Aw Mansur Mosque (neighborhood/kebele 5), the Aw Machad Mosque near the Asmaadin *bari*, and the Kazir Abogn Mosque (neighborhood/kebele 7) (Revault et al. 2006, 57).

In the contemporary period, although the established number of mosques within Harar's walls is eighty-two, word-of-mouth rumors generally swell the number to around ninety-nine, a number that has multiple potential origins. One source suggests that Jugol originally had ninety-nine mosques but that some were demolished during the periods of urban modernization projects in the twentieth century (Revault et al. 2006, 29). Others note that there are in fact seventeen additional mosques outside the walls, which gives Harar a total of ninety-nine mosques. Closer

2.2 Lived Heritage

inspection reveals that the total number of contemporary mosques in Harar actually exceeds this number, but the religious symbolism of the number ninety-nine after the ninety-nine names of Allah points again to the Harari penchant for religious numerology. Either way, it is an enormously high number, and it is believed that the multitude of mosques within Harar is one reason why the city is the fourth holiest in Islam, the mosques in this case acting as consecrating edifices that deploy spirituality in equivalent measures to their quantity toward transforming the entire city into a collective masjid.

In addition, the mosques in Harar contribute to the structural harmony that generally characterizes the city's urban fabric via their democratic sprawl across the landscape, in accordance with Abadir's initial organizational impetus; in many ways, this generates the unique religious cartography that overlays the town and gives it its particular spiritual character. The mosques themselves are also diverse in form, some constituting urban landmarks within the city space and others only recognizable by the loudspeakers perched precariously on the rooftop or the bright green plaques adorning their doors. These plaques typically have the name of the owner of the mosque on them, as well as the number assigned to them by the regional tourism office. One might also occasionally see a small minaret or cluster of minarets and a niche form on the exterior wall indicating the *Qiblah* on these structures.

Regarding the general construction of mosques in Harar, most were constructed using local building materials, particularly local stone (typically granite) and lime. With the advent of cement, mosques have followed the trend of most other urban areas in incorporating a cement coating to the exterior and in some cases tilework if the expense can be accommodated. The mosques in Harar also range in size and population, from small familial mosques to the large iconic *jami* (congregational) mosques whose minarets rise above the city skyline like pins on a map. Perhaps the two most centralized mosque structures in this regard are the Din Agobarar Mosque and the Medhane Alem Church, an Ethiopian orthodox church that was established by Menelik II on the site of Harar's early Central Mosque in 1887. Designed by Italian engineer Luigi Robecchi-Briccheti (Revault et al. 2006, 13), the church stands as an island in the center of the city, built in a typical centralized orthodox design with concentric circular ambulatory halls and a bell tower that was previously the central minaret. Located on Faras Magala ("horse market") square at the central round point of the city, the church occupies a strange dual religious space in Harar and has been an object of continuing tension, particularly within the Harari population, who continue to view the site as spiritually resonant and hope that the structure will be converted back to a mosque.

A little way down Amir Ug street, forming an uneasy conversation with the church, is the Din Agobara Mosque, also known as the Grand Jami Mosque, a large sixteenth-century structure that has seen multiple renovations and alterations over its long life (Figure 2.3a and 2.3b). The mosque itself is a two-story structure, the lower story defined by a series of embellished horseshoe arches traditionally associated with Southeast Asian architectural practice and the upper story maintaining the true horseshoe arch of Arabo-Islamic tradition; this is also the site of a recently added women's prayer space. The structure itself is foregrounded by a large rectangular courtyard and ablution station to the right that acts as a spatial extension of the prayer hall during communal prayers on Friday. The first-floor prayer hall is accessed first through the aforementioned series of arches that lead to a covered area that also acts as an extension of the prayer hall. From this area, one goes through the doors leading into the main prayer hall, doors that are also adorned with painted arch forms. The women's entrance is in the back.

Another recent addition to the structure is the exterior surfacing, which was funded by the DERG regime in the 1980s, a group not particularly interested in seeing past historical sites preserved. This surfacing and additional renovations that have occurred in more recent years have in many ways actively disguised the age of the mosque, coating it with the façade of a fairly new modern building, much to the irritation of many Hararis. Yet many of its historical aspects still remain and continue to actively charge the structure. The minarets of the mosque, for example, although they are now tiled, are said to have appeared miraculously, an oral history that not only reaffirms the structure's historical spirituality but also connects it to a deeply established Islamic tradition in which miraculous events acts as modes of sanctifying a structure or space. During Friday prayers, the mosque prayer space extends beyond the interior into the street out front, a regular occurrence that gestures to the fact that spirituality in Harar is the primary orienting force within this city; religious practice thus even trumps vehicular traffic patterns in terms of spatial priorities.

Many of these elements and spiritual priorities are also repeated on smaller scales throughout Harar, where a series of smaller, less obvious mosques operate, sometimes anonymously, within a neighborhood space. Such mosques are often stumbled upon while wandering through the labyrinthine areas of the city off the primary thoroughfares and are woven seamlessly into the general structural fabric of the area. Some of these mosques are connected to saint tombs and therefore not

Figure 2.3 a and b Grand Jami Mosque and detail of horseshoe arches adorning the primary entrance, Harar Jugol, Ethiopia, 2018. Images by the author.

only act as spaces for daily prayer, but also spaces of veneration, pilgrimage, and various ceremonial cycles throughout the year. Others are more inward-looking and oriented toward the family that owns them; sometimes, these mosques are even located within the family compound itself, the compound courtyard acting in a dual capacity as a space of ablution and preparation for prayer within the masjid space itself.

Most of these spaces are also extremely small; in fact, many require visitors to duck when entering, an activity that also reinforces ideals of humility and the necessity of coming to God in a humble manner. Typically such spaces are composed of one prayer room with a small courtyard (either the familial courtyard or a separate one) for ablutions and a staircase leading to the rooftop for the *adhan* or the call to prayer (Revault et al. 2006, 14). In the interior, many of these spaces have nooks and niches where Qur'ans, candles, and other paraphernalia are kept, as well as spaces for shoes and extra prayer mats. In many cases, these mosques also contain *nabada*, or raised seating platforms or benches where students or elders can sit and discuss various religious matters and philosophies (Revault et al. 2006, 30).

While the interiors of these spaces have tended to remain the same over the years, many of the exteriors reflect general trends within the city regarding appearance and material. Most mosque exteriors are painted green in recognition of the color's relevance in Islamic religion, but many of the shades of green that now grace the surfaces are almost neon in color. In addition, color schemes often shift as Ramadan draws closer and beautification very much becomes the order of the day. As such, colors beyond green, especially those that are new and unusual within the environment, are often introduced. One such structure recently utilized a particularly flamboyant purple, which apparently raised some eyebrows within the community. In some cases, paint is also used to draw architectural details on the walls, including Islamo-Arabic iconographies such as arch forms, which not only connects these spaces to other spiritual sites like the Jami Mosque, but also gesture toward the function of these spaces as spiritually oriented sites, a two-dimensional compliment to other three-dimensional markers like the minaret.

Another important function that these structures often assume is memorial in nature. Many of these mosques are named after their creators, famous Harari personages, religious figures, emirs, etc. in ways that actively remind contemporary Harari inhabitants not only of the history of these figures and their importance in the community, but also the important role that Harar as a whole plays as a cultural, historical, and spiritual landmark, not only in Ethiopia but within the wider global

2.2 Lived Heritage

Islamicate. It is a way to keep memory and identity animate within the environment, using spatial means and apparatuses to establish heritage.

These memorial elements are perhaps even more dominant within Harar's shrine practice, whose structures speak to the power of Sufi practice in this area. Shrine "culture," as one might call it, has reached great spiritual and architectural heights in Ethiopia and Harar in particular, and is oriented around the veneration of saints (*wälī*), who are seen to act as both mediators and intercessors for the faithful through their possession and distribution of blessing (*bərəkä* or *baraka*) (Zeleke 2014, 199). Ethiopia has come to be known for its vast topography of shrine sites, which appear across central and northern areas of the country and take a number of forms, ranging from unmarked spaces in the landscape or stones marking a grave that only those with intimate knowledge of the site can discern, to large spaces of retreat, reflection, and religious study that almost resemble Christian monasteries in both form, function, and purpose (Abbink 2008). These shrines function as "mechanisms of remembrance" and constitute a spatial practice and process that involves "the continuous contextualization and re-contextualization of elements that must be classified as innovations in relation to the local context" (Desplat 2005, 491).

Harar is seen as a "'hub' of Muslim saints" (Gibb 1997, 92; in Zeleke 2014, 199); in fact, the city itself is typically considered a shrine, with one arriving on "holy ground" when one enters one of the gates into the city (Mohamed 2018). The shrines within thus constitute a "sub-shrine" system oriented around numerous saints that together with the mosques, houses, and other sites in the town generate a spiritual (masjid) overlay within the walled area. The process of shrine (*awaach*; pl. *awaaches*) creation begins with the death of a *shaykh*, which is followed by the construction of a grave by their followers, "usually under a tree where he used to teach, and henceforth venerated him as a saint." In addition, this grave, in conjunction with others around it both in Harar and beyond, served as "a kind of communication network" (Desplat 2005, 492), a type of mnemonic device for followers and, over time, the space and the saint associated with it would experience continuous recontextualization as political, social, and spiritual conditions within the town would catalyze the saint's fundamental message to evolve in order to resonate.

Individuals whose shrine is awarded the title of *awaach* are those who were impeccable in their piety and because of this were able to perform either miraculous acts or good deeds within society. As such, their shrines are considered "protectors of the city" (Harari Regional State Cultural Heritage and Tourism Bureau 2015, 50). Although the number of *awaach*s present in Harar seems to vary depending on the source, Harar's cultural heritage bureau states that there are currently 438 identified shrines in the city, both inside and outside the wall. Yet other local sources indicate that there either are 405, the number of sheikhs that supposedly arrived from Arabia in 1256, or 403, which some Islamic scholars say is the numerical translation of the name "Harar." Despite disputes regarding the number of shrines within the city, however, the network of shrines that exists both inside the walls of Harar Jugol and just outside of them creates a spiritual landscape or a type of spiritual topography that is powerful enough to transcend the borders of the town itself and provide a template that has been recreated within other spiritual areas around the country. The town of Wällo, for example, is home to the tombs of a number of Harari religious scholars (*awliya*ý) whose presence creates a "powerful 'mental infrastructure' for Muslim life in rural Ethiopia" (Abbink 2008, 123).

The shrines themselves come in a variety of forms, ranging from natural elements such as trees and rocks to domed structures that typically range between three and six meters in height. Some scholars like Braukämper (1984) have speculated that the use of natural objects to mark these spiritual sites is pre-Islamic in origin, potentially referencing the assimilation and repurposing of early Cushite cult practices by incoming Islamic adherents (Revault et al. 2006, 35; 113). Similar types of adaptations have been noted in Islamic practice across the continent, particularly with regard to the *Qubbah* dome form, a type of tomb architecture that may have been brought to Harar from the southern Arabian peninsula as early as the twelfth century (Revault et al. 2006, 114). Such forms have extensive history in East Africa, particularly the Sudan, where numerous *Qubbah* tombs not only act as burial sites for important sheikhs but are also spaces of pilgrimage and historically were sites of sanctuary for travelers. Thus, the use of various forms from multiple traditions to generate syncretic spiritual edifices have a complex history throughout the region.

These domed spaces as they exist in the context of Harar's shrines are usually painted green (or sometimes white with green piping) as a symbol of their Islamic spiritual function and typically contain a small door about one meter high that forces an adherent to bend when entering, yet another reminder that humility is a virtue (Revault et al. 2006, 101). These structures typically blend in with the general landscape of the city both in terms of the materials used – local stone (*hashi*), lime (*nora*), and a specific type of local wood (*darbi inchi*) which is also used to build houses and other structures in the city – and their formal elements (Revault et al. 2006, 35). Some shrines, such as that of Aw Hamid, are actually part of the general landscape of the city; the *awaach* is literally embedded within the exterior wall of a house on a main thoroughfare in Harar.

2.2 Lived Heritage

One can potentially read the architectural nature of the *awaach* as an indication of the particular type of spirituality that infuses the site. The tomb of forty-forth emir, Nur bin Mujahid, the commissioner of Harar's wall (Figure 2.4a and 2.4b), for example, is covered with ninety-nine

Figure 2.4 a and b Shrine of Emir Nur bin Mujahid, containing the emir's whip, Harar Jugol, Ethiopia, 2018.
Images by the author.

stones that not only act as a scaffolding for the annual painting of the shrine dome (which occurs at most shrines and houses every year just before Ramadan), but also reference the ninety-nine names of Allah. Interestingly, there is also a burial place for his horse, allowing this site to not only gesture toward his spiritual capacity but also his military role as a sixteenth-century warrior in the jihad against the Solomonic Dynasty. Within the shrine itself, one finds further evidence of his spiritual and political life. In it lays his tomb, which is covered with a wooden scaffolding that resembles a bed and is covered with a green cloth inscribed with Qur'anic inscriptions and identification information. Likewise, two ostrich eggs hang from the ceiling as a mode of preventing erosion by channeling water from the ceiling as it drips. The interior also holds a glass vitrine containing ropes that the Emir owned, as well as whips that in Harar tradition had the dual role of animal control (the emir would have undoubtedly used them for his horse) and spiritual cleansing (it is thought that if one is possessed, being whipped will expel the evil within through the tears that one sheds throughout the process; this practice is no longer followed, although the whips are often kept as spiritual and cultural artifacts). The emir's sword also previously resided in this shrine but has since been removed to Harar's national museum. Within this shrine it is apparent that various secular and cultural objects have now assumed the status of sacred relics, memorial remnants that have attained bərəkä within the context of this holy space. In this way, the emir is presented as a religious, political, and historical figure, with the shrine acting not only as a religious text, but also one deeply embedded in Harar history and identity.

Some shrines also gesture toward some of the social structures present in Harari culture with regard to their particular personages and architectural manifestation. The Shrine of Sheikh Ay Abida is one of the only shrines dedicated to a female (Figure 2.5). Abida's shrine is a space for women who come to this shrine to ask for her blessing/intercession in matters relating to marriage, children, and other traditionally feminine topics in Harar culture. As a space of empowerment, it is also the women who, with few exceptions, govern the maintenance of the shrine and its role moving into the future. Unlike her male counterparts, Abida does not enjoy a domed structure or a wooden mausoleum, but instead was interred directly into the ground within a walled compound with a tree planted above her grave. This tree, now incredibly large and lush, is an indication of her continuous life and blessing within Harar. Importantly, her shrine is tended by her female descendants, not her male descendants, with men more generally only being allowed on the grounds of the shrine during Qur'anic readings on her pilgrimage day or to ritually slaughter

2.2 Lived Heritage

Figure 2.5 Shrine of Sheikh Ay Abida, Harar Jugol, Ethiopia, 2018. Image by the author.

animals. Yet this shrine makes an interesting statement with regard to traditional gender structures in Harar on a social and symbolic level. In each case, saints are seen as living beings who actively affect the lives of their followers. Yet this liveliness is expressed in remarkably different gender-infused ways. All shrines incorporate green as a color symbol of the Islamic faith, yet green appears on both the painted dome of the male shrines and on the rich textiles that cover their mausoleum. Yet the green of Abida's tomb comes from the natural growth of the tree itself, which also incidentally gestures to traditional, seemingly universal associations between femininity and fecundity that have created connection points in cultures all over the world between nature and women's bodies. This also gestures toward how animacy and life is represented with regard to these saints. The lush vitality of Abida's tree gestures toward her continuing liveliness within the contemporary realm, whereas within male shrines such as Nur's, the tomb is filled with active artifacts of his spiritual and political power.

Some shrines are also the site of multiple burials, such as the shrine of Sheikh Hashim. Within his complex, his teacher Sheikh Muhammad Kazim is also buried, as well as another student of Kazim's, Sheikh Nur Hussein. Sheikh Hashim, however, maintains his own domed shrine space as does the final sheikh buried in this space, Sheikh Idris. Interestingly, however, the styles of burial differ between these shrines, reflecting the evolution of "interment trends." The shrine of Sheikh Idris is by far the oldest shrine, located both away from and behind the other shrine buildings. Rather than having a wooden scaffold draped with a carpet or green shroud as most do, his grave is self-consciously terrestrial, i.e. below ground, and covered with a horizontal stone inscription rather than a vertical headstone. This was, in fact, the "traditional" way of burying a saint within a tomb. Yet over time and with changing practices, saints were eventually interred in above-ground tombs and covered with a green shroud. In addition, other accoutrements were added, including niches in the walls that mimic those in traditional Harar houses, as well as incense burners, items from the saint's life, and other significant artifacts. Such interment practices were seen as being more "dignified" than traditional ground burials and also more attuned to the fact that these saints are not truly "dead," but have merely passed into a different state of existence. Some have even interpreted the wooden structure over the saint's tomb as resembling a type of "bed," lending additional support for this liminal status of existence (Revault et al. 2006, 101). After all, a deceased individual cannot act as an intermediary and bestow bərəkä on his or her followers, let alone sleep. Thus, the infrastructures included in the tomb that make it more "house-like" in conjunction with objects associated with the everyday life and accomplishments of the saint are important reminders of their everlasting life.[7]

Yet the shrine itself is sometimes only the centerpiece of the broader architectural infrastructure of a shrine site, all of which contribute to its collective spiritual function. The shrine itself is often located within the domestic compound of the individual's descendants. Within this compound as well is often a cemetery that includes family members as well as students, teachers, and other important adherents of the saint, all of whom have been buried in the traditional Muslim way, facing east toward Mecca. Most graves are composed of a simple rectangular outline of stones, although some have elaborately carved stone tombstones indicating the name and dates of the deceased. Many of the older graves, however, do not have these markings and their identities have been lost

---

[7] One might even say that these infrastructures gesture toward the power of domestic space in Harar culture. The Harari house (*ge gar*) stands as a unique combination of culture, beauty, and spiritual identity, each element corresponding harmoniously in the organization, structure, and embellishment of the home. These homes also speak to contemporary Islamic identity as it exists within Harar. Although they will not be addressed in this volume, these domestic spaces privilege the fact that Muslim identity is one identity within the layers of identity that overlay the Harari house, each layer intersecting each other at various points toward creating a harmonious and symbolic whole.

2.2 Lived Heritage

over time, save for a rock placed in the center of a grave that would indicate the inhabitant is female. Some have interpreted this rock to be an abstraction of the female breast while others have given it more phallic symbolisms, although neither can be verified (Revault et al. 2006, 113).

There is also a dedicated space or hall (*galma*), usually next to the shrine and the cemetery, which collectively is known as a *Qabri*. The *Qabri* is thought to be of pre-Islamic origin, largely because the term does not have an Arabic root, and serves a number of functions. Ranging from an open, sometimes circular, space with a simple awning to a built rectangular space with multi-height platforms (*nadaba*) to accommodate hierarchical seating, the space might house religious students or it might act as a receiving space for gifts and offerings left by individuals who petition the saint to intercede on their behalf. These gifts also often contribute to the upkeep of the structure by the saint's descendants, and are usually forthcoming during one's annual pilgrimage to the shrine, which usually falls on the saint's date of birth. This is also why these places are known as places for *ziyara* – "visitations by the devout, or 'pilgrimage'" (Abbink 2008, 122). Typically, the office of the current sheikh is also located in this area, and it is here that people are able to access him for advice or intercession. Because of this, these spaces also act as Sufi centers and sites for religious discussions among learned individuals and religious scholars, who typically consume large quantities of *qat*[8] and engage in *zikre* (collective praising) during such discussions. It must be noted, however, that another important function of these spaces is the facilitation and advancement of Harari cultural identity (Revault et al. 2006, 42). Not only do learned discussions take place in these spaces, but also the transmission of Harar histories and historical narratives (Harar has an extensive oral tradition), as well as discussions concerning the city's saints, personal religious experiences and reflections, the state of spirituality in Harar and Ethiopia more broadly and, more recently, the fear of encroaching Wahhabism.

But for all the shrines in Harar that are known and celebrated, there are also a number of shrines in the city that have been forgotten, save the few who might recall their presence. Such shrines are often not marked or, if there are markers, they are somewhat obscure and unworthy of note. The shrine of Sharif Al-Hassan, for example, exists as a concrete lump in the middle of a small thoroughfare on the south side of town.[9] Having no complex or prayer hall, the shrine is unremarkable in every respect, save

---

[8] *Qat* is one of the area's main agricultural exports. It tends to affect one's mental state and has been compared to Adderall.
[9] I was required to ask a number of people living in this area of town exactly who the saint was buried underneath and few of them knew.

its rather strange presence in the middle of the road. It contains a small hole at the bottom for the insertion of incense, but in no other way, shape, or form is it differentiated from its surrounding landscape save its physical presence, a lack of separation that has given it a somewhat mundane, anonymous quality. Yet such structures, anonymous as they may be, continue to contribute to the composite spirituality and thus the collective masjid cartography that defines the spatial nature of Harar, each one representing an encoded narrative that intertwines Islamic belief with both a historical memorialization of an individual and a commemoration of their particular spiritual, political, and cultural role in the formation of Harar's unique identity. Indeed, Nasser Rabbat notes "A more mature architecture does not depend for its meanings on elaborate designs, large spaces, precious materials, or extensively circumscribed signs and relics" (Rabbat 2002, 57). The structures themselves are catalysts of memory and, importantly, do not fix these connotations in a rigid memorial structure; instead, they "consciously manifest ample possibilities of nonspecific functions and meanings in its forms and spaces so that the individual can make it his or her own architecture, the milieu of his or her own memories, while it retains its initial role as the repository of collective meanings and memories" (Rabbat 2002, 57). Thus, the shrines both as "individuals" and a collective spiritual landscape catalyze masjid space.

These structures actively represent processes of remembering and forgetting as part of Harar's spiritual culture. Indeed, the sheer variety of shrine forms, ranging from natural forms such as trees and rocks to mixtures of man-made and natural elements to the construction of formal domes, allow these sites further agency as spaces of "collective memory [that] not only reflect the past but also shape present reality by providing people with understandings and symbolic frameworks that enable them to make sense of the world" (Misztal 2003, 13; in Jones 2011, 99). These shrines thus act as fundamental structural anchors to the spiritual identity and culture of Harar, both through their physical presence and the rituals, performances, behaviors, and practices they catalyze, which in many ways promote a type of "museum aesthetic" in their display of artifacts and spiritual identity.

This museum aesthetic is important to Harar's sense of spiritual and cultural identity. As Camilla Gibb notes: "By making interpretations of history a part of daily life, incorporating them into aspects of dress and architecture and ultimately 'tradition' and culture, Ge usu [Harari] are reminded every day of their shared history in these particular terms" (1997, 383; in Tarsitani 2009, 69). The infrastructures of Harar, not only the wall, the mosques, and the shrines but also homes and areas of commerce, have played a leading role in Harar's heritage industry, as

2.2 Lived Heritage

previously mentioned. Harar is seen as a particularly successful and "complete" example of an Islamic urban landscape that has maintained both its history and its dynamic urban character over time and space, maintaining the traditional layout of an Islamic urban space and its separation of commercial and residential areas within a dense but strategic constellation of spiritual spaces scattered throughout the city. In fact, most Hararis would argue that it is part of their cultural and spiritual mandate to preserve their environment, given Qur'anic injunctions to not only restore but also preserve and maintain spaces of spirituality and worship. In addition to these elements, age, particularly as it relates to various architectural edifices throughout the city, also plays a role in some of these conversations, with older spaces held in higher esteem than newer spiritual spaces because they existed "closer" to the time of the Prophet (Golombek 1983, 95). As Lisa Golombek notes, "Theoretically speaking, the closer something was to the time of the Prophet, the better or holier it was considered to be." Such spirituality, continues Golombek, should "behoove the restorers to retain as much of the old mosque as possible and to treat the parts they could preserve as relics, as one would do for any object associated with the early years of Islam" (Golombek 1983, 101). The same could be applied to any of the architectural infrastructures of Harar as cogs in the spiritual machinery of the site.

With regard to the city's active heritage program, Harar was first officially recognized as a national heritage site in Ethiopia in 1974, with identified sites of interest being "principal monuments, important historic buildings, contextual urban fabric and 'out-of-context' buildings" according to the city management plan. It was successfully inscribed on the UNESCO world heritage list in 2006, meeting the following criterion: it "exhibits an important interchange of values of original Islamic culture, expressed in the social and cultural development of the city," it "bears exceptional testimony to cultural traditions related to Islamic and African roots," it represents "an outstanding example of a type of architectural and urban ensemble which illustrates the impact of African and Islamic traditions on the development of specific building types," and it represents "an outstanding example of a traditional human settlement, representative of cultural interaction with the environment" (UNESCO n.d.a).

Thus far Harar's preservation plan has been primarily implemented through the Centre for Research and Conservation of Cultural Heritage (ARCCH), which was established in 1976. In addition, the Jugol Heritage Conservation Office (JHCO, established in 2003) as well as various representatives from the city and local authorities from the community's *kebele*s (neighborhoods) and support services have also played important roles (UNESCO n.d.a). The main sources of funding for Harar's continued upkeep comes from governmental sources, although many members of the community also take it upon themselves to contribute. Should a shrine custodian or a house owner be unable to finance the necessary repair work, a maintenance fund has been theoretically established by UNESCO and the Harar cultural office, although there are reports that many of those funds have been pilfered (Ahmed 2018).

A majority of Harar's upkeep has involved preserving the physical infrastructure of the city, making changes when necessary to increase quality of life while not disturbing the fundamental framework of the buildings themselves, restoring elements of the physical setting when they degrade, repurposing existing physical elements for new functions to keep them relevant, and maintaining structures as close to their original condition as possible. The development of museum spaces has supplemented this preservation project, with the 1977 founding of the Harari National Museum, followed by the Harari Cultural Museum (1979), which is currently stocked with objects contributed by the Harari community (Harari Regional State Cultural Heritage and Tourism Bureau 2015, 35), and the Sheriff Harar City Museum, which was established by private citizen Mr. Abdulahi Ali Sheriff in his home in 1983.

Harar's walls, gates, spiritual infrastructures, and now heritage infrastructures create a landscape designed to channel human movement and perception into specialized repertoires of encounter and interpretation. Yet this also creates interesting and sometimes contested conversations around the area's history and concerning specific opinions on how heritage should be treated and represented. For example, some family compounds have erected new cement walls lining the exterior walkways that create a rather abrupt contrast with the irregular textural patterns of the original walls. There is also developing tension with regard to the materials used in Harar's architectural infrastructures, with many of the traditional wooden doors now being replaced by metal doors and many of the colors used to paint the interior walls of Harar generating consternation among the older generation. Lastly, there is also a question of the appropriate means through which to present Harari culture and religious identity. Many objects that currently stock Harar's museums have not only come from domestic and public spaces, but also from shrine spaces themselves. As previously mentioned, the sword of Emir Nur was removed from his shrine for inclusion in one of these area museums. While no one has expressed direct resentment at this removal, it does represent a certain fragmentation of the spiritual narrative behind some of these sites and begs the question of what happens to Harar as a "living museum" if its spiritual sites not only become fragmented but these fragments are subsequently reconstructed within what some might consider a decontextualized, lifeless museum space.

At the end of the day, these examples and others such as overcrowding, congestion, pollution, and geographic isolation represent the broader collision currently occurring between Harar, modernity, and globalization, and this has resulted in conversations about the balance of preservation and the quality of spiritual life in Harar. Harar Jugol has grown increasingly crowded over the years and the Harari, while constituting what some might consider the social and political elite of Harar, are no longer the majority cultural group. In addition, the youth of Harar are increasingly attracted to a more modern way of life, which results in a rather ambivalent attitude toward the older city, catalyzed by the fact that many Hararis are increasingly going abroad to countries like Canada for economic reasons and are returning with money to invest in infrastructure.[10] This has resulted in the development of a "modern" Harar outside Jugol's walls that has increasingly obscured the older city behind a rising skyline of buildings. It is also important to note here, however, that Harar has continued to delicately negotiate the path between integration into a broader global context and maintaining a localized sense of self within the physical and symbolic ramparts of Harar Jugol, drawing from both to construct a modern self that is both authentic and evolutionary in nature.

2.3 Searching for an Egyptian Heritage: Hasan Fathy's New Gourna and Beyond

It is important to note at this point, however, that heritage as a material object does not have to be preestablished; often times one can look to past trends and influences as a type of immaterial heritage. This is especially the case when designers take an active interest in past architectures whose simplistic design and material provide important insights for the contemporary period in terms of building a local, regional, or national legacy. This is particularly true in Islamic contexts where many feel that spaces of postmodernism represent largely unsuccessful attempts at establishing a type of imagined identity due to its separation from faith-based ideas of existence and engagement (Kahera 2008, 117–118). Egyptian Hassan Fathy (March 23, 1900–November 30, 1989) was one architect working to subvert this trend in the context of his own attempts to recognize and

---

[10] An estimated 85 percent of Hararis are involved in some sort of commerce-related occupation (Ahmed 2018).

generate pride in a national architectural/spiritual legacy. He is quoted as saying:

> In this ever-changing world of things, man is *in* need of relating himself to some fixed point of reference to get out of chaos into cosmos. He has ever been seeking to situate himself in space, time and the world of the spirit and the mind .... The architect has to remember that wisdom does not belong to a unique epoch, it belongs to all times. It is present today as it was yesterday, and can be realized by anyone who desires it and who deserves it .... Nowadays the procedure and methods of design and building have changed from Sufi master craftsman to the architect-contractor system in which design and execution of the work are split, and the canons of sacred art are lost. (Kahera 2008, 116)

Here Fathy is singling out the fact that Muslim architecture, and spiritual architecture in particular, is "a nexus of temporality," to quote Kahera, in which "man is not the center of the universe ... neither is he the measure of all things" (Kahera 2008, 116). Humanity must be treated as part of a broader realm and subsequently embedded in their environment from multiple cultural, historical, and moral standpoints.

To this end, Hassan Fathy dedicated himself to the idea of "appropriate cultural form" in architecture over the course of his professional career. In fact, Fathy has often been called a "humanitarian" architect and a "pioneer of Islamic architecture" in the sense that much of his work focused on rural building traditions in Egypt that were intended to be rehabilitative in both cultural and spiritual senses (Karnouk and Vatikiotis 1988, 57). Much of Fathy's focus during the mid-twentieth century was on creating housing for those living in rural and poverty-stricken areas in Egypt; within this context, he attempted to create forms that utilized Egypt's rich architectural history – forms that spoke to iconic monuments from Egypt's past such as the pharaonic pyramids and temples – in the context of complementary vernacular traditions that have long informed the built environment of North African communities across the continent. Earthen materials played a large role in this vision, as well as a sustainable and culturally embedded material for construction that also provided a material mode of pushing back against the onslaught of highly modernized though largely inappropriate imported materials being used in contemporary Egyptian construction. In terms of their inappropriateness, many of the contemporary building materials coming into Egypt were not only invasive from a sociocultural point of view, but were also climatically insufficient. The early twentieth century saw the arrival of metal sheeting and concrete, which quickly replaced earthen material in most modern buildings and subsequently came to be associated with inferior, lower-class building. In contrast, these new contemporary materials not only became emblematic of a type of worldly modernism that Egypt was hoping to achieve at that time, but they were also intended to be reflective of a type of architectural style that represented an engagement with global conversations and architectural discourses. Thus, localized Egyptian views of what Islamic architecture in contemporary Egypt should look like were largely ignored (Karnouk and Vatikiotis 1988, 61–62).

Likewise, the structures that were subsequently built using these materials were not even remotely historically, culturally, or environmentally suited to this landscape. Indeed, formal styles associated with stock "Islamic" structures like mosques were deployed indiscriminately toward a spectacle-based exotist effect. One significant example of this is the suburb of Heliopolis, constructed in the early twentieth century by French-Belgian industrialist and amateur Egyptologist, Édouard Louis Joseph, the first Baron Empain, who "dreamed of reviving the ancient city of Heliopolis in the form of a modern, and highly profitable development" (Karnouk and Vatikiotis 1988, 59). Toward making this dream a reality, he enlisted the help of Belgian architect Marcel Jasper, to whom he said: "You love mosques. You are an architect. Why don't you submit to me a proposal?" (Karnouk and Vatikiotis 1988, 59). Jasper later partnered with Alexandre Marcel, who had recently returned from India where he had built a "Renaissance Palace" for the Maharaja of Kapourtala, among numerous other orientalist projects he undertook for European nobility, including both a Chinese pavilion and a Japanese pagoda for King Leopold II of Belgium (Karnouk and Vatikiotis 1988, 60). Working together, the two produced an architectural concept for Heliopolis that some visitors would compare with the European mosque-based fantasies produced within the pavilions of various World's Fairs, which had become a popular enterprise in the late nineteenth and early twentieth centuries. The idea of mining historical Egyptian architectural styles for this project was quickly discarded in favor of a "Neo-Moorish" style composed of an assemblage of architectural parts from the Arab world, many of them from mosques, which subsequently created an essentialized "Arabicized" view of Egyptian history and culture that reflected little appreciation or understanding of the architectural, cultural, and spiritual identity of the country. On top of that, the materials used – predominantly concrete and steel – made climate control within the complex difficult, if not impossible. Despite this, Heliopolis would go on to inspire a number of emergent architects at the time, although some like Hassan Fathy would aim to shift the architectural trajectory of the country in favor of historically established Egyptian architectural traditions, which incorporated a sense of Egyptian Islamic spiritualism into structural programs and recognized that the imported materials and styles which had thus far been favored were largely inappropriate religiously, culturally, and historically. Only through this approach, Fathy felt, would a "modern national art" emerge (Karnouk and Vatikiotis 1988, 61).

In 1945, Hasan Fathy was asked by the Egyptian Department of Antiquities to design and construct a new village with a congregational mosque that would rehouse the 7000-strong inhabitants of the town of Old Gourna, located in "Egypt's most crowded archaeological site" – the Valley of the Kings – and home to "a community of amateur archaeologists" who according to UNESCO were largely responsible for much of the damage and theft that had occurred at proximate pharaonic sites (Karnouk and Vatikiotis 1988, 62).[11] Fathy viewed this project as a platform from which to launch a new solution to the plight of Egypt's rural poor through housing and community development. Fifty acres of land was devoted to the project and Fathy not only consulted Old Gourna's villagers (Gournawis) with regard to their lifestyles, habits, and requirements, but also tapped the expertise of various Nubian master masons, whose skill in the creation of efficiently simple yet deeply meaningful earth-based designs suited to their physical environment and allowed them to effectively combined domestic, social, and spiritual lifestyles into one composite structure (Haney et al. 2011, 6). This may also have been instrumental in Fathy's decision to use earth as a primary building material; its simplicity, its efficiency, its ready availability in the desert environment, and its history as a regional building material would be instrumental to the development of affordable, environmentally conscious, spiritually appropriate, "grassroots" housing in the poor, rural areas of Egypt. Thus, Fathy's vision for New Gourna was one of an "ideal" village that would speak to an Egyptian national identity based on embedded historical spatial traditions, practices, and materials (Karnouk and Vatikiotis 1988, 63).

From a formal perspective, New Gourna would be a space of domes and arches (Figure 2.6a and 2.6b), representing an "essential geometry" that was modernist yet still nonetheless rooted in an accessible Egyptian architectural vocabulary that not only used forms but also materials that connected it both physically and symbolically to the land (Karnouk and Vatikiotis 1988, 63). Also important was the uniquely Egyptian "sacred" aspect that Fathy managed to incorporate into the structural character of the town, a gesture toward New Gourna's proximity to the temple of Dayr al-Bahari, the funerary complex of Hatshepsut, who was the only know

---

[11] There is some debate as to whether these "thefts" were in fact crimes, given the defense of New Gourna's residents, who held that these relics belonged to their ancestors and thus to them.

Figure 2.6 a and b New Gourna Mosque and floorplan, Luxor, Egypt. Image by Marc Ryckaert (MJJR). Own work, CC BY 3.0. Floorplan by the author.

female leader in Egypt's Pharaonic history. Stylistically, New Gourna mimics many of the formal characteristics of Dayr al-Bahari, not only in terms of its material but also its ability to visually emerge from the landscape like a natural growth. Likewise, its repetitive arcades seen in New Gourna's major mosque in many ways mimic the repetitive post and lintel arcade formation of Hatshepsut's primary temple entrance. Here, Fathy created "an affinity between the temple and the village," utilizing the timeless yet aspirational quality to "magical" effect (Karnouk and Vatikiotis 1988, 63) and also contributing to the continuing legacy of Egyptian engineering and architectural advancement through the creation of this symbolic foothold.

The mosque at New Gourna in particular deploys many of these aesthetic principles and represents an exceptional balance between "Islamic" and "modern." Simple in design and relatively unadorned in appearance save the latticework adorning the windows (*mashrabiyya*) and the muqarnas-like squinches that accent the primary dome form, the mosque form deploys a series of geometric configurations in ways that seem intimately connected with historical Islamic aesthetic conventions. A series of semi-vaults are utilized to generate load-bearing walls that do not require additional infrastructure for stability and the domes themselves are not only symbolically significant but also provide a mode for passively cooling the structure and providing good insulation and ventilation, an innovative system found on numerous buildings scattered throughout the community.

The mosque itself has a series of key spaces strategically placed both within and around the structure. The mosque's only minaret is accessed by a single set of stairs that lead up to a domed space where the *muezzin* calls the faithful to prayer. The walls surrounding the mosque complex are pierced by small windows and open arches that are enclosed by brick latticework. One enters the mosque space either through a single entrance on the south side of the structure in the form of a sunken arch next to a store, or the ablutions entrance located on the eastern side of the complex. From the ablutions entrance, one follows a corridor that passes both a store and a small meditation space/chapel before entering into a larger courtyard which contains greenery in the form of trees and shrubs that provide much-needed shade from the heat of the day. This space can also be accessed from the south entrance via a small forecourt that is bordered by a long vaulted corridor which runs along the street and contains benches for sitting and informal socializing. Just off this courtyard is the sheik's office and one enters the prayer hall through a series of *iwan*s. The covered spaces of this structure are created by both repeated arches and arches extended into vault forms, with light primarily generated by a series of small but strategically spaced windows that punctuate

2.3 Searching for an Egyptian Heritage

the walls at regular intervals. Each window, however, is located high on the wall so as to not violate the private, meditative aspects of the space.

The prayer hall itself is carpeted, and electric lights and fans hang from the ceiling in orderly rows. Sparsely decorated and brown walled, visual and spatial interest is created predominantly by the emerging and receding architectural elements of the space itself in the form of free-standing pillars, pilasters, niches, and faux arches. As a hypostyle hall, thick earthen pillars create a forested space that effectively generates a sense of solitude and privacy through the pillars' powerful physical presence and effective separation of bodies in space. These pillars also support a series of domes that line the ceiling and generate a passive cooling effect in the interior space. The *Qiblah* wall is composed of a simple niche bordered by an equally simple *minbar* under the main dome, which is composed of a decorative pendentive/squinch system whose corners are composed of niche forms and dotted with small regularly spaced windows whose organization and number decreases as one approaches the dome apex. In addition, many of these structural elements are reproduced in the souk (market) structure across the street as well as the open-air theater.

The mosque's placement within the broader commercial community demonstrates that such forms were not intended to stand as islands in the midst of the community, but were visually and structurally integrated into the communal fabric as part of a larger whole composed of schools, markets, public baths, and even an outdoor performance area in a way that mimicked and supported traditional modes of interactive life in a village community. This comprehensive, collaborative design was intended to generate a type of ownership among the inhabitants, who were predicted to be able to maintain the structures of New Gourna subsequent to their completion using the availability of its primary resource material, earth, and communal labor. The mosque was intended to be a unifying element within this landscape as the sole space for "collective spiritual thought" and a monument to the "moral fiber of community identity" (Haney et al. 2011, 47).

Unfortunately, New Gourna would not become the success story that Fathy had hoped it would be. He received little support from the various government officials and offices he attempted to work through, largely because his project was based less on budgeting and the specialized expertise of architects, engineers, and government contractors and more on the traditional systems of apprenticeships necessary to teach the citizens of New Gourna how to self-sustain the community. Such a "backwards-looking" project was low on the priority list. And then there was the community itself. New Gourna, despite Fathy's sensitivity to the needs of its individual inhabitants, was ultimately an ill fit for these same inhabitants. The residents of New Gourna had long existed off the capital that archaeological artifacts in the area provided. Because of this, few of these individuals were invested in the idea of New Gourna, which aimed to generate self-sufficiency and the preservation of traditional architectural knowledge systems at the expense of their relocation to a less than "modern" built environment as part of a social housing experiment. Another potential problem with New Gourna was that there was little room to evolve from the preservation-oriented impulse that governed the creation of the project. Although materially conscious and culturally embedded, New Gourna did not maintain the necessary social connections to its population that would have made the project holistically sustainable. Specifically, the "museumification" of the city into a type of timeless Egyptian construct was seen as counter to Egypt becoming an active member in a modern global world. As such, New Gourna now currently exists as a heritage space and a conserved artifact that in many ways documents one of the earliest efforts in Egypt to create locally embedded, environmentally consciousness, culturally and spiritually sensitive housing. Unfortunately, many of New Gourna's original structures are failing and, in 2010, New Gourna was put on the World Monuments Fund Watch List. UNESCO justified its inclusion by saying:

> The main characteristics of New Gourna Village consist of its reinterpretation of a traditional urban and architectural setting, its appropriate use of local materials and techniques, as well as its extraordinary sensitivity to climatic problems. It demonstrated, within the era of "modern movement" that sustainability and social cohesion could also be met with vernacular architectures, local materials and techniques. For this reason, it is an outstanding example of sustainable human settlement and appropriate use of technology in architecture and planning. (UNESCO n.d.)

Fathy's original design for New Gourna failed to answer the question of "how to create a culturally and environmentally valid architecture that is sensitive to ethnic and regional traditions without allowing subjective values and images to intervene in the design process" (Ahmed and Elgizawi 2009, 696). To this end, the only structures currently remaining in Fathy's New Gourna are the mosque, the market, and a handful of homes, with many of the proposed infrastructures and community buildings falling to take form. That being said, New Gourna's mosque remains as evidence of Fathy's vision and legacy, an iconic singular space for the performance of communal and spiritual identity and a space that brings together the community in a way that Fathy originally envisioned. In addition, New Gourna would provide important lessons in emergent conversations concerning appropriate technology and cultural sustainability, lessons that ironically Fathy

2.3 Searching for an Egyptian Heritage

would go on to replicate in a masjid project he undertook *outside* of Egypt in New Mexico, USA, of all places, nearly forty years after he first began constructing New Gourna. In 1980, Fathy was commissioned to design both a masjid and a "traditional" Muslim village in Abiquiú, New Mexico. Called Dar Al-Islam, the community was the first "planned" Islamic community in the USA and was intended to be "the largest and most comprehensive of its kind" (Kahera 2002, 338) (Figure 2.7a and 2.7b). Co-

Figure 2.7 a and b Dar al Islam (aerial view) and interior, Abiquiú, New Mexico, 2018.
Aerial view by Abdullah Nooruddeen Durkee. CC BY-SA 3.0. Interior images by the author.

founded by Abdullah Naseef (former Secretary General of the World Muslim League), Sahl Kabbani (a Saudi businessman), and Nooruddean Durkee (an American convert), the organization commissioned Fathy to design the primary complex, which would subsequently be based on many of the principles of appropriate technology that Fathy himself had espoused.

Yet the project faced one major conceptual problem that needed to be considered in terms of creating a holistically sustainable space, and this had to do with the fact that Fathy was not only crafting an Islamic space within a Muslim minority context, but also that this was taking place in a context whose native history and heritage had been decimated by Western colonization. Before the arrival of the Spanish, the area of the Chama Valley where Abiquiú is located was populated by several different groups of native peoples including the Pueblo, the Tewa, and the Anasazi who would come into contact with Spanish settlers in 1598. These settlers would go on to form a core component of the Penitente Brotherhood or "Los Hermanos de la Luz" in the area, a movement that branched off of Roman Catholicism potentially as early as the thirteenth century and that was known for its intensive practices of self-mortification and flagellation (Kahera 2002, 338).

Interestingly, this area does share certain characteristics with New Gourna, particularly in terms of its proximity to important archaeological sites related to the area's ancient native history. The Chama Valley is home to the Puye cliff dwellings, which were built by the Pueblo over eight hundred years ago. Meaning "pueblo ruin where the rabbits assemble or meet," this construct is a National Landmark and is maintained by the Pueblo of Santa Clara as a cultural monument (Strom n.d.). Additional pueblo sites include those of Poshuouinge, Leaf Water, and Tsama, most of which are relatively preserved. The architectural traditions of this area also use earth as a primary building material, lending itself naturally to a largely harmonious aesthetic and functional relationship with the surrounding landscape. Thus, Fathy was able to apply many of the foundational principles on which he constructed New Gourna to craft a community whose complementary architectural legacy made for a harmonious collaboration and successful end result.

The structure of the mosque complex, which is composed of a mosque and a *madrasa*, is composed of arch and dome combinations similar to those of New Gourna. Made of adobe covered with white stucco and rounded arches and vault forms that generate a humped, undulating appearance, this complex has the added bonus of mimicking both the regional architectural traditions of the area as well as the surrounding topography, composed of rolling hills and sculpted white rock formations. These forms also create a structure whose parts flow seamlessly and

2.3 Searching for an Egyptian Heritage

organically together, punctuated occasionally by geometric window latticework, with geometric crenellations along the top wall that speak to regional Native American aesthetic influence. Occasional decorative wooden accents have been added in the form of windows and doors, which are beautifully carved into geometric patterns that not only complement the window latticework but provide brief explosions of decorative enthusiasm, bursting into consciousness against the stark white backdrop of the stucco. The interior of the mosque is also white, but the lack of windows creates a pleasantly dim space. Composed of rounded arches and rounded vault forms made from these arches extending into space, the interior does not maintain any decoration beyond smooth rounded walls and embedded niches and arches carved into the walls, very similar to the mosque at New Gourna. The *mihrab* itself is only denoted by the fact that it is a doubly embedded arch that is lit from above by an electric light and accented by a small wooden *minbar*, which sits nearby. Over this area is the main dome, which is pierced by four small elongated arch windows. The prayer hall extending from this area is composed of a series of domes and spaces similar to that of New Gourna, with the functional element of passive cooling in effect. This structure is built on a small, intimate scale, a human scale that stands in stark contrast to the mountainous sublime landscape that surrounds the complex. This in many ways speaks to the language of the mosque complex as being not only sensitive to but also intrinsically interwoven into the natural world around it as masjid space. Through its materials, its light footprint on the environment, its reflection of natural forms and figures from the natural landscape, and its location on a wilderness plateau overlooking river valleys and farm land (which incidentally mimics the environment of many parts of the Arab world), this masjid space stands as a physical and material representation of mankind's stewardship of nature, supported by the fact that the mosque currently owns most of the acreage surrounding the complex and is engaged in numerous projects intended to protect and rehabilitate the surrounding area which has been damaged by overgrazing, inappropriate agricultural cultivation, and the presence of invasive plant species. This mosque stands as a success story for the marriage of spiritual and heritage concerns not only through the creation of space that acts as an expression of architectural, spiritual, and cultural stewardship, but also through the fact that the community currently occupying the mosque has made the mission of the complex into one focused on cultural generosity, environmental sensitivity, and a respect for the history and traditions of the area. The mosque complex encourages a specific, mutually conducive relationship between humanity, history, environmentalism, and heritage which rests on the idea that individuals in harmony with nature and history are fundamentally individuals in harmony with themselves. This is perhaps why Dar al-Islam has succeeded where New Gourna failed, with the tenets of sustainability in design and continuing heritage legacies reflecting the core value systems of the users of the complex, who maintain active agency, dictating the path that the structure and the community will take into the future.

In both cases, "Fathy's balanced spiritual awareness of a sense of unity between building, landscape, and user imposes an intangible order on the building and the site." Dar Al-Islam, in contrast to New Gourna, "transcends *spatio-temporal* categories or labels" (original emphasis) in that it is not only a "place-making" enterprise, but it actively mines the human history of the area and utilizes this sense of identity in the separation and creation of a new yet complementary spiritual space within this context (Kahera 2002, 339). To quote Kahera at necessary length, Fathy's architecture:

> reminds us of the divine and pure and unadulterated sense of being, because his architecture is in harmony with the environment . . . . His architecture allows us to experience the being of things as they are naturally; it is not an artificial or abstract . . . . By making us aware of God as a Necessary Being, the Prime Mover and the Supreme creator his architecture speaks to the profound meaning of existence as reflected in the way we dwell. Hence, in the mosques he has built we see that the task of the architect, like the task of all humankind in general, is to return to our origin or at least to acknowledge our origin. For when we understand our origin, we are able to return to the One, who has created us from natural clay not reinforced concrete. (Kahera 2002, 339)

2.4 Accra's New National Mosque and the Problems of an Imported Spiritual Heritage

Yet just as architectural traditions and legacies can travel outside their point of origin to find complementary spaces, histories, and legacies, similarly architectural traditions can also travel inward, as has been the case in recent decades with the arrival of numerous mosque styles and types into African Islamic space from areas such as Southeast Asia and the Middle East. As a structural phenomenon, mosque spaces have increasingly come to act as spatial manifestations of the telescopic collisions that are occurring between local and global, a condition that is allowing the mosque as a genre to signify not only as a "sacred artifact," to quote Roger Joseph, but also as a "technological and social artifact" (Joseph 1981, 288). As many established mosque styles are becoming physically untethered from points of geographic origin, they are subsequently traveling to diverse Islamic spaces and embedding not-so-complementary cultural and historical legacies into foreign soil. One particular mosque

2.4 The Problems of an Imported Spiritual Heritage

style that has come to act in this capacity in the Afro-Islamic landscape is the Neo-Ottoman mosque style.

The growth of Neo-Ottoman or, more appropriately, Afro-Ottoman mosques in Africa in the contemporary period and the particular sociopolitical flows that have accompanied their presence is a complex, context-specific development. Yet as Eric Roose notes, the use of iconic mosque styles like the Ottoman rarely reflects a mere impulse to mindlessly reproduce nostalgic form. The design process itself is a "symbolic-political practice" in that signs, forms, and architectural components are actively and often strategically deployed toward making a specific statement. In the contemporary period, structural programs like the Neo-Ottoman mosque have in many ways become spatial actors in ongoing contemporary sociopolitical dialogues occurring throughout the continent between various governmental and financial institutions, dialogues that again subtly locate architectural space at the interstices of power, influence, and ideology (Verkaaik 2013, 11).

Yet Ottoman mosques in Africa, Neo- or not, are not a new occurrence. The first recognized Ottoman-Turkish mosque to be constructed on the continent was that of the Youssef Dey, located in the Medina area of Tunis (Tunisia). The mosque itself was built in 1615 and designed by Andalusian architect Ibn Ghalib, who incorporated an assortment of stylistic elements in the structure that speak to the range of iconographic programs available for reproduction at this time. The exterior structure features variegated brickwork arches that mimic those at Cordoba, which was built over eight hundred years earlier, and a single octagonal tiled minaret, which mirrors other Tunis-based "Turkish" minaret forms like that of the Hammouda Pacha Mosque, which was built in 1655 by Hammouda Pacha, the second *bey* of the Tunisian Muradid Dynasty. Both mosques were also located within a predominantly Turkish commercial area in Tunis, whose inhabitants were their primary patrons. Yet in the contemporary period, Turkish mosques built in the "Neo-Ottoman" style have become increasingly prevalent, their stylistic roots arising from what Gulru Necipolglu terms the "mature age" of Ottoman architecture, which came about at the hands of architect Mimar Sinan, the chief architect of the Ottoman court (1538–1588) (Necipoğlu 1993, 172–173).

The Ottoman Empire, which emerged in the fifteenth century, faced problems similar to those of earlier emergent Islamic empires from the seventh century onwards in that they were the direct inheritors of (and thus in competition with) a series of monumental cultural and architectural legacies and heritages. In the Ottomans' case, they were posed as heirs to one of the most powerful empires in history at the time – Byzantium. Yet such legacies, as they have occurred throughout the history of the Islamicate, have inevitably provided the catalyst needed for the innovation and reimagining of established modes of crafting state-sponsored architectural forms (Necipoğlu 1993, 171). Thus, the emergent Ottoman architectural style that would be crafted by Mimar Sinan would continue the iconic proclamative architectural languages of notable Byzantine structures like the Hagia Sophia, whose structural engineering and phenomenological power was somewhat unprecedented at the time, but would favor specific architectural characteristics such as verticality, scale, and phenomenological effects as direct correlates to the political power and prestige of the Ottomans (Necipoğlu 1993, 170). Thus, Ottoman architectural projects, particularly their state-sponsored imperial mosques, would not only take inspiration from Byzantine traditions, but would renovate this structural language system – "collapse it" if you will – into a standard "Ottoman-ized" architectural genre.

To this end, one of Sinan's most illustrious architectural accomplishments would be the Süleymaniye Mosque, a "direct answer to the challenge of Justianian's masterpiece [the Hagia Sophia]," to quote Necipoğlu, which had until then stood in the eyes of Sinan as the penultimate example of architectural statecraft (Necipoğlu 1993, 173) (Figure 2.8). In terms of its general structure, the Süleymaniye maintains four

Figure 2.8 Süleymaniye Mosque, Istanbul, Republic of Turkey c. 1550. Image by © José Luiz Bernardes Ribeiro. CC BY-SA 3.0.

2.4 The Problems of an Imported Spiritual Heritage

spindle minarets placed at each corner of the complex, which is itself composed of a series of semicircular, multidimensional domes supported by massive buttressing that seem to tumble down from the central dome, which covers a vast interior uninterrupted space. In addition, the mosque is punctured by a series of large windows that circle the dome and penetrate the side walls, which, in concert with multiple stained-glass compositions, create an abstract lightshow along the *Qiblah* wall among others within the prayer hall itself (Renard 1996, 65). As with many other mosque complexes being built at the time, the Suleymaniye complex is half covered and half uncovered, maintaining a large open courtyard adjacent to the prayer hall (Renard 1996, 66).

In addition to its interior and exterior aesthetic, the positioning of the mosque within the urban fabric of Istanbul was also tactical. Imperial mosques were often seen as "'urban sculptures' that guide[d] visitors through cities" (Erzen 2011, 126). Along these lines, mosques were typically located in a way that allowed them to be viewed either from all four sides and/or from specific distances and locations (Erzen 2011, 129). Located as it was just above the harbor, the Süleymaniye complex functioned as an awe-inspiring and intimidating introduction to the city, some even saying that the mosque was lit at night as a type of beacon for those at sea, acting from a distance as "a perfect symbol, a perfect object, which creates the visual focus for the city" (Erzen 2011, 129). Likewise, shifting conditions and positions also had the potential to create different and constantly varying viewing experiences for an audience. Such factors were exploited in some later Ottoman creations, such as the Sultan Ahmed Mosque or "Blue" mosque (1609–1616), which was constructed by architect Sedefhar Mehmet Aga, a pupil of Mimar Sinan, during the reign of Sultan Ahmed I, who ruled fifty years after Suleyman the Magnificent. It is said that the multidimensional shapes of the Blue mosque provide an unlimited number of changing views depending on one's vantage point (Erzen 2011, 130).

All of this to say that the repetition of recognizable, indeed, iconic structural elements in these early monumental mosque structures was politically strategic. Not only did they directly quote the iconic Hagia Sophia in many of their structural elements, but in doing so, they "enriched [the mosque's] imperial associations and its status as the most ambitious Ottoman mosque complex ever built" (Necipoğlu 1993, 173). Although stylistically derivative mosque structures may gesture toward an Ottoman fascination (even fetishization) of Byzantine forms like the Hagia Sophia, the reinterpretation of this form within the context of successive imperial mosques not only connected the Ottoman Empire with the legacies of a great imperial past, but also presented the Ottomans themselves as a forward-facing empire who were not intent on "reinventing the wheel" but interested in continuing the Islamic success story by drawing on established iconic genres and giving them new and exciting upgrades (Necipoğlu 1993, 170–171). This allowed the Ottomans to maintain a firm association with past legacies while projecting an image of progressive movement into the future, a perfect political encapsulation.

With this in mind, it is perhaps unsurprising that the contemporary period has seen a revival of this style by the current government of the Republic of Turkey, whose revitalization of Sinan's sixteenth-century "Ottoman style" has been a major spatial component of the Republic's contemporary political strategy. The standardization of this signature mosque type through the work of contemporary Turkish architects such as Hilmi Şenalp has generated a "museum aesthetic" for this style, designed to keep contemporary Neo-Ottoman mosque design as homogenous as possible (Rizvi 2015, 63; 67). Even the decorative material additions and encrustations that define the formal surfaces of a majority of these forms are typically manufactured in Turkey rather than being produced locally. This returned focus to the monuments of the past, and thus the glory of the Ottoman Empire, has not only been framed as an expression of pride in national identity and heritage by the Republic, but also points to certain agendas at work currently within the Turkish government. The fact that many of these "Neo-Ottoman" mosques are being built under the patronage of a national government rather than an individual ruler or monarch signifies a contemporary symbolic interpretation of the structure as a modern, collectively sanctioned structure rather than a project for personal vanity and political gain. This makes these mosques in many ways analogous to a government building.

Many of these "Neo-Ottoman" mosques are also appearing in sub-Saharan Africa, with one recent Turkish "donation" being that of the new National Mosque in Ghana (Figure 2.9a and 2.9b). Often called the Akra Furqan the structure is located in the capital city of Accra in the neighborhood of Kanda on a major thoroughfare through the capital city. Completed in 2016, the complex was designed by Turkish architect Erdiogan Getinkaya and has been framed as a gift from the Turkish population to the people of Ghana. Composed of 4,000 cubic meters of concrete and 700 tons of steel, the design is inspired by both Aga's Sultan Ahmed Mosque as well as Sinan's Selimiye Mosque, and is a stock example of the Neo-Ottoman style, with four fifty-eight-meter minarets placed at each corner of the mosque structure and over fifty domes cascading down from the central massive dome, which rests thirty-three meters from the ground. The mosque structure also combines a mix of open courtyards, arcades, and porticos, the main

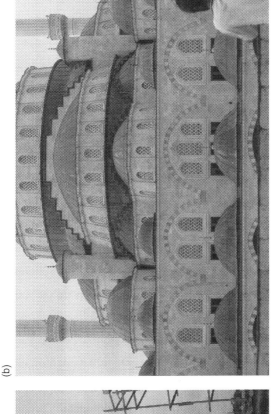

Figure 2.9 a and b Akra Furqan, or the National Mosque of Ghana, Accra, Ghana, 2016. Images by the author.

structure punctuated by window spaces that allow light to play across the interior mosaic tiles and epigraphic programs. This provides a counter to the exterior surface, which is clad in marble imported from Turkey in conjunction with a series of lead-covered domes. The mosque itself also contains three entrances and can accommodate over 5,200 congregants inside, with a total of 10,000 congregants both inside and outside at one time. But the mosque is only one part of a larger complex. The complex also contains a medical clinic, an auditorium, a conference center, a school complex, a library, a car park, and the residence of the National Chief Imam (Ghana Friendship and Solidarity Association 2017).[12] This new mosque also stands on the former site of Accra's Central Mosque, which was demolished for the construction of Accra's Rawlings Park. Although construction began with a donation of around $10 million from the Turkish government, the addition of ancillary facilities required more funds and thus partnerships were established with organizations like the Turkish Hudai Foundation, along with other nongovernmental organizations such as the Ghana Friendship and Solidarity Association (GANADER) and Human Development International (HUDAI) (GhanaWeb 2014).

Despite the beauty and success of this emergent space, a number of problems arose even before the mosque was completed. The first, perhaps most obvious question, is why Turkey would fund the construction of a Neo-Ottoman mosque in a non-Muslim majority country. Interestingly, this project is part of a larger trend on the part of the Turkish government, which has been building Neo-Ottoman mosques all over the world over the past few decades. Since 1975, the Republic has constructed over fifty mosques in twenty-five foreign countries and such projects appear to be growing in number. Some would argue that these Ottoman mosques are serving nationalistic functions abroad, as a way to continually express the existence, or at least appearance, of a unified state symbolized and reaffirmed via the architectural platform of an illustrious past. The presence of Ottoman mosques across the globe for example, gives the Turkish religious, political, and architectural brand unique global exposure, not only gesturing back to a uniquely Turkish history but also to a renewed Islamic national identity in the contemporary period, which, Rizvi notes,

---

[12] Previous Vice President Kwesi Bekoe Amissah-Arthur (August 6, 2012–January 7, 2017) noted that a little less than half the money budgeted for the complex went toward constructing a teacher training college, a senior high school, and two administrative buildings as a complement to the current government's program to produce more educators and fill the country's current gap in the education system. In addition, many of the Turkish engineers engaged in the project actively worked with their Ghanaian counterparts to pass on their expertise with regard to the technical knowledge associated with some of the structure's engineering components (GhanaWeb 2014).

2.4 The Problems of an Imported Spiritual Heritage

is a key component of the "condition of modernity in the contemporary Middle East" (Rizvi 2015, 22). Along these lines, Ulrich Beck notes "architecture is politics with bricks and mortar" (Beck 1998, 115; in Jones 2006, 550). The Ottoman mosque, over the time and space of its existence, has been made to exist parallel to discourses of Turkish national identity, acting as a mode through which to "'flag the nation' (Billig 1995), 'invent tradition' (Hobsbawm and Ranger, 1983), and 'discursively construct' identities (Wodak et al., 1999)" (Jones 2006, 550). Indeed, Ottoman structures as state-sponsored monumental or "landmark" architectures function in many ways as a nationalistic cipher, a response to the late modern development of increasing "fluid" cultural identities (Bauman 2004; in Jones 2006, 550) that have destabilized political control over the nationalistic image. As Paul Jones notes:

> Attempts by governments to reinvent state-driven collective identities in an era of diverse cultures within the nation means that the maintenance of identities linked to the nation-state is dependent on its ability to represent and symbolize diverse cultures in an appropriate and significant way. (Jones 2006, 550)

Thus, one of the many ways that the Turkish Republic has sought to control this image is not only through a meteoric rise in mosque-building projects in Turkey as an expression of pride in a national Islamic identity, but also in areas abroad as a form of international diplomacy (Rizvi 2015, 34). Run by the Directorate of Religious Affairs (Diyanet), the Turkish governmental body that oversees mosque projects both within the country as well as abroad, Sinan's iconic "Neo-Ottoman" mosques are exported as "architecture[s] of diplomacy" (Rizvi 2015, 60), allowing Turkey to join the ranks of Iran, Saudi Arabia, Qatar, the United Arab Emirates, and others, whose contemporary, large-scale transnational mosque projects signify,[13] on the one hand, the power of "global Islam" and its ideological composition, and on the other, the power of "donor countries" whose "exported" mosques act as extensions of their religiopolitical reach and thus potential sites "for propagating ideology, and ... [potentially] covert political machinations" (Rizvi 2015, 23).[14]

Yet additional questions remain as to the Akra Furqan that specifically revolve around the introduction of foreign architectural styles into a context that already has a strong history of localized mosque-building

---

[13] "Transnational" is defined by Rizvi as "buildings built through government sponsorship ... whose architectural design traverses geographic and temporal distances ... monumentalizing the political ambitions of their patrons" (Rizvi 2015, 5).

[14] Some donor countries have appointed imams to their gifted mosques and have provided educational literature/propaganda to these institutions as well.

practices. Ghana's historical tradition of earth-and-timber mosques is part of an architectural legacy that moved from the Sahel region of Mali during the medieval period into the forest regions of the Upper Volta and northern Ghana over subsequent centuries. Historic mosques like those of the towns of Larabnaga and Nakore, both potentially built as early as the seventeenth century, have been celebrated as unique examples of Ghanaian cultural and material heritage, replicated on postage stamps, government buildings, and even in a mural on the entrance terminal wall at the Kotoko International Airport. Yet these forms appear to have been ignored as contenders for the creative manifestation of Akra Furqan, potentially highlighting the inherent problems involved in the construction of an international-style mosque paid for by a foreign government with no points of connection in the architectural or cultural history of a space, a postcolonial space at that.

It also highlights the potential presence of a more symbolic type of communicative statement being made with this structure. Numerous mosques in Africa, both North and sub-Sahelian, were built after the end of the respective European colonial periods of their context and thus stand equally as nationalistic monuments as well as religious structures, despite the fact that, from an ideological standpoint, many of these monuments and the grand aesthetics they represent are somewhat inappropriate to the Islamicist functional framework (Verkaaik 2013, 8–9). Yet such structures nonetheless represent a past history that has become an element of national identity in the contemporary period, and gestures to a shared past of struggle and triumph that have subsequently been woven into the narrative fabric of a nation's narrative. Contemporary structures like the Akra Furqan, in contrast, are being constructed largely without regard for national histories/identities or established traditions and legacies, which makes the label of Accra's new mosque as the "National" mosque somewhat unsettling. Indeed, regarding Akra Furqan, one individual commented "Imagine if all regions can be inspired by their own traditional architecture and culture …. How unique it will be …. It will even encourage competition" (ACCRA 2014). The incorporation and replication of foreign forms within local landscapes can in some ways be interpreted as a type of international cultural incursion, particularly in the postcolonial landscapes of Africa, that gestures toward a wider global web of influence that countries like the Turkish republic maintain with other Islamic communities around the world.

Thus, political power operates heavily in this sphere with regard to the roles that structures like the mosque play in representing identity. Bourdieu notes that:

2.4 The Problems of an Imported Spiritual Heritage

[e]very power to exert symbolic violence, i.e. every power which manages to impose meanings and to impose them as legitimate by concealing the power relations which are the basis of its force, adds its own specifically symbolic force to these power relations. (Bourdieu and Passeron, 1977, 4; in Jones 2006, 551)

Thus, the construction of mosques like Akra Furqan, framed as it has been as a symbol of international collaboration, cannot be seen as neutral events, but as potentially gestures toward power and global influence, a spatialization of the politics of influence which sometimes also suggest the establishment of footholds across the global Islamicate. This power is made even more apparent by the fact that the southern region of Ghana where the capital city of Accra is located is a historically Christian area. Although Islam has made strides in the south as part of its larger regional foothold in West Africa over the past century, Muslims still nonetheless operate somewhat peripherally in both a cultural and spatial sense in this area, typically congregating within particular neighborhoods and locating mosques on roadsides primarily for visibility rather than as a representation of sociospiritual dominance. Indeed, some mosques in Accra function in a pseudo-missionary sense, perched in a religious "frontier" area and engaging in similar types of "outpost" outreach and tentative communal engagement. Thus, the size and proclamative nature of the Akra Furqan is fundamentally at odds not only with the location in which it appears but also with the dominant identity of the local community, which has generated some tensions within the city.

There is also the matter of historical correlations in the region that associate mosque size with localized Islamic power. As detailed in the introduction of the volume, when the large Sahelian-style mosque forms migrated from the predominantly Muslim north to the decidedly less Muslim south from the seventeenth century onwards, mosque forms became noticeably smaller not only because of climatic shifts between the Sahel and the forest that subsequently affected earthen building technologies, but also due to the fact that Islam ceased to be the sociopolitical power in the Volta that it had been in the Sahel. Thus, while the use of the Neo-Ottoman style for the Akra Furqan might underscore the Ghanaian government's stated commitment to maintain peaceable relations between the Muslim and Christian population in Ghana, the mosque's location in Accra rather than, say, Ghana's northerly Muslim capital of Tamale, and the fact that Muslim primacy in Accra does not fit the aggressively monumental presence of this massive structure, makes it a strange choice and begs the question of the presence of less visible motives behind its establishment.

In thinking through this situation, a quote from Ozlem Unsal, researcher at Istanbul's Kadir Has University seems particularly appropriate: "Every political power wants to leave a legacy on the urban landscape" (Daragahi 2015). In fact, many of the protests raised about the building of such mosques not only in Ghana but around the world gesture to the fact that these spaces are fundamentally *not* about religion or heritage, but about legitimating political power and authority (Daragahi 2015). Many feel that Turkey's current mosque-building program is directly related to the ambition of Turkey's current president, Recep Tayyip Erdogan. His critics suggest, in fact, that he is "constructing palaces to his power using his people's money in bizarre and irrelevant locations," particularly those whose Muslim population does not constitute a majority, as is the case in Ghana. Michael Bird and Zeynep Sentek also note that Erdogan's project mimics the same massive explosion of religious structures that occurred during the reign of the Ottoman emperor Sultan Sulieman the Magnificent in the sixteenth century, a figure to whom Erdogan has made direct references, as he did in 2014, saying "we [the Turks] are the grandchildren of Sulieman the Magnificent" (Bird and Sentek 2015). There is also the fact that in the last three decades, Turkey has come to dominate this "mosque-building diplomacy," in some cases outpacing Saudi Arabia and other Gulf nation-states in the process, which some speculate is due to the fact that Turkey has found a niche market for its type of moderate Islam in historically tolerant spaces like those of western and southern Africa. It also doesn't hurt that many of these mosque complexes often incorporate distinctly modern lifestyle amenities such as shopping centers, schools, cultural centers, and the like (Bird and Sentek 2015), creating a somewhat perilous framing for religious architecture as "an expression of contemporary global capitalism ... reflective of 'the structural interplay between equality, (dis) possession, consumption, and desire in our brave new world'" (Verkaaik 2013, 18).

But another potential motivation connected to this Neo-Ottoman focus is the desire to leave behind a legacy that consciously connects to Erdogan himself, particularly during a period of what some would consider Turkish "decline" as a result of Erdogan's shift toward a more authoritarian style of governance. As Dorian Jones notes: "Returning Turkey to the glories of its Ottoman past has been common theme of Erdogan's rhetoric throughout his long rule of Turkey, first as prime minister and now as president" (Jones 2015). Such imperialistic drives underscore the foreign policy behind these mosque-building programs as an "instrument of soft power[15] to widen Turkey's influence," according

---

[15] The idea of "soft power," taken from disciplines associated with international relations, holds that a country's power derives not only from its military, political, and financial strength, but also from its sociocultural and humanitarian image, particularly as it relates to international relations and action.

2.4 The Problems of an Imported Spiritual Heritage

to political scientist Beril Dedeoglu at Istanbul's Galatasaray University, thus framing Turkey as a universal and accessible brand for a global Islam (Seibert 2015).

The idea that these mosques stand as monuments to Erdogan himself[16] and to a Turkish brand of Islam is supported by the fact that, as previously noted, the style of these forms has been impervious to the influences of the local identities and architectural traditions in which they are built, remaining in their pristine Ottoman form. This has led some to interpret these mosques as tools of cultural imperialism, a stylistic "Turkish Trojan Horse" to quote Professor Nii-Adziri Wellington (Wellington 2017), and thus, at least in the case of the Akra Furqan, merely the latest instance of a general loss of Ghanaian identity to foreign influence, despite the rather awkward governmental claim that the mosque represents a "symbol of a country's history and its ideology" as well as "links to its Islamic past" (Rizvi 2015, 13; 16). In addition, within such diverse contexts, it is harder for the states to control the multiple meanings, identities, and significations that are attached to these structures, allowing them in some cases to become "sites of symbolic conflict and competition over identities" (Jones 2006, 551).

Interestingly, these elements and the conversations and contestations they have generated have also pushed one of the primary functions of such spaces to the backburner, namely their role as sites of prayer and spiritual practice. In the short time it has been in operation, the Akra Furqan has come to act more as a regional landmark attraction than a place of worship, whose ambassadorial role as a symbol of a Turkish "global" Islamic identity is, many would argue, negligible. Indeed, the Akra Furqan has in some ways become a soundstage for visiting Muslim dignitaries, Erdogan included, to stop and engage in international diplomatic posturing. Structures like the Akra Furqan and the almost mythic proportions they assume within the physical landscape seem to indicate that the Ottoman mosque style has become something of an aesthetic fetish object, its forms and spaces creating an "awe-chitecture" that overwhelms the senses in a way that has the potential to both completely negate the inner focus required for a successful prayer space and erase local architectural and spiritual histories in favor of what some might describe as an exercise in megalomania.

Along these lines, the Akra Furqan and other Neo-Ottoman styles emerging on the continent walk the dangerous line of being labeled as postmodern or even "kitsch," expressive of only the most blatant

---

[16] Erdogan has been accused of building "palaces to his own power," even going so far as to name a mosque in Somalia after his mother (Bird and Sentek 2015).

structural elements of a past style that do nothing beyond referencing the past (Rizvi 2015, 24). Kitsch has assumed a somewhat negative view in the contemporary period, at best associated with derivation, replication, and imitation of "the authentic"; at worst, seen as "simulacra or downright fakes, deliberately manufactured to exploit their associations of tradition and authenticity for political and economic reasons" (Vellinga 2006, 118). And, when viewed through the lens of spiritual forms like the masjid, architectural kitsch becomes a space that "distort[s] the imagination of the one who prays" (Haider 1996, 38). Regarding kitsch, Clement Greenburg (1939) once stated that kitsch:

is mechanical and operates by formulas. Kitsch is vicarious experience and faked sensations. It is the epitome of all that is spurious in the life of our times. (Greenburg 1965, 10; in Solomon 1985, 4)

Even more flamboyantly dire are Travis Price's thoughts on regional architecture whose "critical poetics ... [are] ... quietly being lost under the mud of homogenization ... where homogenized buildings augmented by nostalgically watered-down exterior decorating will shape our very human character into one mono-chromatic, bland whisper" (Price 2015, 249). Robert Solomon also calls out kitsch not only for the "glibness of its technique," but also for the motives behind it. Specifically, he says that kitsch is designed to be too pristine, too "ethically one-sided" (Solomon 1985, 4). Thus, structures like Akra Furqan as an institution framed for the benefit of humanity not only belie the structure's self-indulgent element and rather blatant consumerist function, but also the inherent political nature of the Ottoman style from a global perspective. To quote Solomon yet again, "Underlying all of these charges ... is the suspicion that kitsch ... [is a] ... mode[s] of distraction and self-deception, shifting our attention away from the world as it is" (Solomon 1985, 5).

All of this to say that architectural projects like the Akra Furqan and other "National" projects are "resultantly bound up with questions of nation, state, and culture, making them politicized statements articulating something of the wider state project of which they are a part" (Jones 2011, 552). Yet as Bauman (2004) notes, the contemporary period has seen the "contained" social and cultural identities reflected in such structures become increasingly porous, resulting in increased dynamism between the identities that these forms can contain and a collapse of state power to control them (Jones 2006, 551). Importantly, this also means that architecture does not have an innate identity or meaning, be it "democratic" or "Ottoman" or "global," but has the power to articulate the conversations, tensions, and transformations going on in society

2.4 The Problems of an Imported Spiritual Heritage

through its own shifting identities and connotations. In fact, as Paul Jones notes, "It is this capacity to articulate the many tensions within global and local identity projects that means that architecture continues to have a vital role in shaping the collective social imagination" (Jones 2006, 558). Regarding the Akra Furqan, one commentator noted: "What's local now, was new to Ghana from the beginning. So you should appreciate new things and stop this local stuff mentality. I'll bet you 5 yrs time, it will become local" (ACCRA 2014). Another notes:

Traditions have no end. It keeps changing all the time. So ... [do] ... Ghanaian traditions. We have not reached the climax. It will keep on changing. So that anything that doesn't look like what we know as such, shouldn't mean it is not Ghanaian tradition. Ghanaians are not people with limit and small imaginative prowess. Besides the traditions of the world are there for everyone to use. Be it food, clothes, architecture or dancing. I'm tired of these Ghanaian traditional tag thing. Why? Do we have to put a Ghana flag on every project we construct to look Ghanaian? Abaa! Me ni saani epo Nne. (ACCRA 2014)

Such views perhaps offer an emergent lens through which to view the growth of masjid spaces such as the Neo-Ottoman mosque in places like Ghana, which seem ill-connected to this new context and repetitive on a global scale. Homi Bhabha, in his influential deconstruction of the intersections of mimicry and colonial power (1994), notes that imperial powers exist perpetually at something of an impasse, wanting colonial subjects to be *like them*, i.e. "civilized," yet at the same time working to maintain a fundamental separation so that the boundaries between subjugator and the subjugated were clear (Ferguson 2002, 553). Yet progressing from this point, agency becomes an important and largely underrecognized element in these cases, particularly with regard to how "the subjugated" might subvert the trappings of an imperial power toward their own self-empowerment. I would defer to James Ferguson, who notes that acquisitions of forms such as Neo-Ottoman mosques could be interpreted as a manner of displaying full and equal participation in a global modern Islamic community as active contributors, "a membership hinged on a real, and not pretended, mastery of modern social and cultural forms" (Ferguson 2002, 557), and "pressing, by their conduct, claims to the political and social rights of full membership in a wider society" (Ferguson 2002, 555). Along the lines of what Rizvi calls the "mutability of religion and politics in the modern day" (Rizvi 2015, 26), the presence of a Neo-Ottoman mosque within Ghana's capital city as an iconic form associated with an illustrious global Islamic legacy not only firmly situates Ghana within the orbit of contemporary cosmopolitanism, but also makes a strong statement with regard to the presence of international relationships and dialogues circulating within Ghanaian space. A Neo-Ottoman mosque readily reads as symbolic of the presence of worldly relationships and heritage, elements that maintain great sociopolitical capital in the contemporary global period. And these heritages are made manifest through a merger between an architectural aesthetic of past and various aspirational goals of the future.

It is also important to emphasize that contemporary Islamic societies on the continent participate in a plethora of postmodernities that spring from diverse, social, political, and cultural situations/tensions. This complex condition also leads to the creation of spatio-political manifestations like the "Afro-Ottoman mosque," as I will now call it, as signifiers of this state of being whose presence denies, to quote Ferguson, "the sort of localization that ... [scholars] ... habitually force on their subjects and to speak, not for this or that local person in this or that circumstance, but for 'Africa' as a whole" (Ferguson 2002, 560).

As such, perhaps another way to interpret contemporary Afro-Ottoman mosque spaces like that of Akra Furqan beyond being kitsch or an exercise in soft power/political megalomania is to see it as a dynamic response to a contemporary global condition translated through the built landscape. Although this style, with its attendant connotations and symbolisms, has over time and space been reproduced through what some might call a system of "collective plagiarism" (Bonta 1979; in Jones 2011, 30), these forms are neither slavish reproductions of a historic heritage type, nor dynamic reinterpretations of this same type, but "distinctive cultural [and in this case spiritual] artifacts that are uniquely related to the particular social context in which they are found" (Vellinga 2006, 125). In other words, Neo-Ottoman mosques like Akra Furqan read outside of the Turkish context demand to be read as Afro-Ottoman mosques, an identity that privileges new realities, roles, and legacies within diverse new contexts toward becoming even more multivalent than they were before. As Jamal Elias notes, "the image [or structure] does not *copy* the prototype so much as it enters a discursive relationship with it" (Elias 2012, 28), following a lengthy history of architectural assimilation and reimagining within the Afro-Islamic tradition at local, regional, national, and international levels. Along these lines, these structures and the legacies, spiritual practices, and heritages they symbolize will continue to evolve and take on new forms and meanings that are embedded in the ebbs and flows of their unique sociopolitical contexts, leaving the mosque to maintain highly fluid meanings and emit subsequently evolving messages within its particular context.

2.5 Conclusion

Collectively, these case studies demonstrate ways through which masjids offer a mode of thinking through heritage beyond contemporary fetishizations of history and memory as a spatial site that indicates that "spirituality" is not only flexible and context-specific, but also, spatially speaking, requires an area to be "set apart" from its surroundings as a signal of nonnormative status. In thinking through heritage beyond the materiality of monuments, memorials, and other commemorative sites, perhaps a more abstract approach that favors the recognition of specific memories and events rather than their material reflection would create a more equitable relationship between these two components. The reality of the masjid, like many other heritage sites around the world, is that it is context-specific and sometimes indistinct. Potentially composed of natural elements like landscapes, parks, wilderness areas, etc., as well as human elements like built landscapes, monuments, works of art and sculpture, etc., heritage sites, like a masjid, are delineated both by the value ascribed to them as representations of identified legacies and spaces of venerative performance (Nuryanti 1996, 251).

3 "All the Earth Is a Mosque": The Masjid as Environmental Advocate

The masjid is environmental in the sense that it is oriented around man's position as a steward of God's creation according to the teachings of the Qur'an.

3.1 Introduction

Qur'an Surah 30:41 states: "Corruption has appeared on the land and in the sea because of what the hands of humans have wrought" (Abdul-Matin 2010, 19). Beyond contextualized socio-ideological developments and heritage programs currently operating on the continent, masjid spaces in Africa have also begun responding to broader global ecological issues as well, particularly those concerned with the growing impact of human behavior on natural systems around the world. Deforestation, desertification, increased acidification of the world's oceans, pollution, and climate change as a result of the emission of greenhouse gases have all been singled out by scientists as major components contributing to the contemporary global environmental/ecological crisis (Quadir 2013, 2). In fact, some have begun referring to these environmental phenomena as a "fifth nature," expanding the central definition of the "natural" beyond just that of cosmogenesis to incorporate the impacts of human waste and environmental pollution as "natural" byproducts of systematic human behavior (Jencks 2004, 105). Importantly, environmental degradation has also been shown to have various social effects, with the reduction of potable water and productive soil undermining the economic self-sustainability of those who depend on subsistence farming or who live in drought-prone areas.

Modern-day environmentalism has perhaps become mostly closely connected with the term "sustainability." Yet it was only in the 1980s that the term "sustainability" began to emerge as a solid concept associated with environmental and ecological issues, specifically in the context of a publication produced by the International Union for the Conservation of Nature (UCN) entitled *World Conservation Strategy*. This publication positioned sustainability, development, and economics as inextricably entwined, with environmentalism constituting one element of a larger whole (Steele 1997, 2). Further developments with regard to the concept of sustainability from an actual policy perspective began with the work of the World Commission on Environment and Development, which in 1983 defined the concept of sustainability in their now famous Brundtland Report[1] as "the principle that economic growth can and should be managed so that natural resources be used in such a way that the 'quality of life' of future generations is ensured" (Steele 1997, 5). Sustainable development, thus, should follow "those paths of social, economic and political progress that meet the needs of the present without compromising the ability of future generations to meet their own needs" (Steele 1997, 5). The next iteration of this conceptualization would emerge from the Rio Earth Summit in 1992, whose proceedings were published in a volume titled *Agenda 21*, after the century in which many of these recommendations would ideally be enacted. *Agenda 21* put forth a method for merging economics and environmental concerns via a series of sustainable development directives with the caveat that such developmental strategies should be subsidized by the developed world as a "redress [of] past inequities … and resource depletion" (Steele 1997, 8). One major area of concern was the management of human settlements and their impact on environmental and ecological wellbeing; within this context, correctives were offered by the American Institute of Architects and the International Union of Architects. Some areas of focus included the use of local materials and construction technologies, efficient design systems with regard to energy usage, appropriate siting, empowering local communities to have agency in the building process through subsidies, the use of "clean technologies," repurposing and recycling elements, and various methods of creating equity among stakeholders (Steele 1997, 17).

Yet one major criticism of the way "sustainable development" and its associated concepts were being deployed at the time was that it continued certain "growth-driven economic development model[s]" that effectively standardized and made hegemonic certain socioeconomic biases and inequities existing within both the model and the process (Wright and Ellis 2016). In addition, as James Steele notes in his work *Sustainable Architecture*, there were also a number of sociopolitical and cultural undercurrents running through these systems that went largely unrecognized, specifically the presence of various political, social, and cultural

---

[1] This report was named after Norwegian Prime Minister Gro Harlem Brundtland, who was the president of the panel at that time.

inequities hegemonic within such projects that established inherent power hierarchies along with flows of resources between the global north and south in a somewhat neo-imperialistic relationships. In addition, terms like "growth" and "development" remained largely undefined, and it remained unclear as to who precisely was the primary beneficiary from these developments. In other words, would the recipients of these initiatives be self-empowered by them or merely cast as subjects in the newest form of cultural and developmental colonialism?

Similar degrees of vague self-interest, or perhaps a lack of self-awareness, have emerged in contemporary discussions of the broader philosophy of sustainability as well, which have led to wide divergences of opinion surrounding the fundamental nature and value of the concept of sustainability. This has made the presence of sweeping policy decisions regularly crafted on sustainability's behalf somewhat troubling, with the perplexing condition of sustainability continuing to exist in a liminal state of both timeliness and prematurity. This encapsulates the problematic nature of "environmentalism" as it has thus far unfolded in developmental discourse.

Along these lines, other specific elements not nuanced in this brief yet accepted history of sustainability related to environmental consciousness includes the intersection of environment with gender, race, class, and religion. To address these elements individually, socioeconomic status or class often affects dualisms or binary types of approaches in which one stakeholder within environmental discussions is viewed as being of greater value than another. Within this "oppressive conceptual framework," according to Karen Warren, "wealthy people have the power and privilege to mobilize resources to self-determined ends" (Warren 2015), thus privileging higher socioeconomic solutions to environmental problems that disregard or ignore the fact that those with less access to resources and opportunities have a much harder time generating similarly successful resolutions. There also tends to be an implicit judgmental component to this situation in that "poor people may be viewed as inferior, and thereby undeserving of the same opportunities or rights of the wealthy, often on the grounds that their poverty is 'their own fault'" (Warren 2015).

Gender issues are also closely connected to socioeconomic issues in that women living in poor conditions are often the most direct victims of environmental catastrophe. This plight often goes unrecognized due to the fact that most environmental programs engage in "gender mainstreaming" through the universal application of environmental solutions across communities and individuals designed to focus on the symptoms rather than the causes of endemic situations that lead to such imbalances

3.1 Introduction

(Women's Environment and Development Organization 2013). The Women's Environment and Development Organization provides the following example: "a forest management program where gender balance is encouraged in decision-making structures – a positive but insufficient effort if little attention is paid to gender equality in land tenure laws, customary practices, or division of labor in forest activities and products" (Women's Environment and Development Organization 2013). Through a lack of understanding of the gendered issues that often form the basis of various sociopolitical relationships with the environment, sustainability-focused initiates often prove insufficient. In addition, in many areas of the so-called developing world, women play primary roles in generating the resources necessary for the survival of their families and communities in addition to providing a majority of the "reproductive labor." These divisions of labor often follow conventionalized or traditional modes of communal or cultural existence, which typically also result in different relationships and dependencies on the natural world that are rarely recognized in environmental discourse (Women's Environment and Development Organization 2013).

Similar issues affecting socioeconomic status and gender also arise with regard to race. Specifically, one must distinguish between the idea of environmental protection and awareness and equitable access to clean water and air. Not only are poor populations in Western countries like the United States often communities of color, but populations such as these are much more likely to be "exposed to various life-threatening environmental stressors" including multiple types of pollution (air, ground, water, etc.) as well as contaminants like lead and agricultural chemicals like pesticides (Belkhir and Butler 1998, 5–6). Similarly, when racially marginalized communities are exposed to such hazards, they rarely have the financial resources to alleviate their situation and may even depend on economic resources in the area to the extent that they are unable to leave. This cycle is often responsible for maintaining and even perpetuating existing oppressive systems.

Yet the last point of contention to be raised with regard to various gaps within the current environmental conversation is that few if any have examined the extensive connections that have long existed between religious systems and nature. Indeed, the philosophical nature of many religious systems has much to offer studies of "deep ecology," a phrase coined by philosopher Arne Naess to refer to the "deep conceptual roots of the environmental crisis" (Warren 2015). Deep ecology does not necessarily refer to the "applied" environmental crisis like air and water pollution but instead promotes:

an understanding of these issues in terms of false or problematic underlying assumptions, concepts, beliefs and values of canonical philosophy. Importantly as well, deep ecology stresses the impacts of Western culture's anthropocentric (human-centered) approach to nature and the environment. (Warren 2015)

Thinking through environmentalism as a spiritual issue, religions like Islam have defined environmentalism as an attention to nature as a creation of God and thus worthy of protection and veneration, a principle that has long guided Islam in its religious practice and material production. The specific principles through which Muslim life is ideally governed with regard to the environment can be found in both the Qur'an as well as the hadith, with hadith 10:10 recording the Prophet Muhammed declaring "The world is beautiful and verdant, and verily Allah, be He exalted, has made you His stewards in it, as He sees how you acquit yourselves" (Abdul-Matin 2010, 8). Likewise, the Qur'an notes that all creations of God "exist in a state of remembrance of the All-Mighty," the implication being that all of God's creations are in a constant state of prayer, i.e. the entire earth is essentially masjid space. Supporting this, Qur'an Surah 55:6 notes: "And the herbs and trees – both (alike) bow in adoration" (Abdul-Matin 2010, 12).

There are also fundamental principles within the faith that are intimately and naturally implicated in one's harmonious relationship with the environment. These principles form the basis of the philosophical views of Iranian philosopher Seyyed Hossein Nasr (b. 1933), who is typically considered one of the most important Islamic intellectuals of the contemporary era and has published widely on subjects that position Muslim philosophical doctrine within environmentalist discourse in terms of its "philosophical and religious dimension" (Quadir 2013, 4). Specifically, Nasr views nature and the environment as a type of "sacred" space in that it is "always in danger of desecration" (Chidester and Linenthal 1995, 21). In the mid-1960s, Nasr began producing a series of lectures at the University of Chicago designed to address the intimate relationship between man and the natural environment from a faith-based perspective, which would eventually become the basis for his book *Man and Nature: The Spiritual Crisis of Modern Man*, which was published in 1976. This volume essentially established Nasr as the "father of the modern Muslim environmental movement" (Abdul-Matin 2010, 42) and the founder of a contemporary brand of Islamic eco-theology, embedded in the contents of the Qur'an, which provided directives for the faithful with regard to their treatment of and interaction with the natural environment. The elements of this eco-theology evolved around

3.1 Introduction

several central tenets of the Islamic faith. The first, *tawhid*, holds that the oneness of God with his creations implies that his creations should receive commensurate respect. *Fitra*, understood as "the original state of creation" or "the original nature of things" implies that, when humans live in the state of *fitra*, they exist in natural harmony with the environment and thus have a responsibility to uphold that existence. The role of the faithful as *khalifah*, or stewards of God's creation, holds that humans have a responsibility to care for God's creation based on the trust God has given human beings. This plays into the idea of *amana*, which represents "the fulfilment of responsibility in all dimensions of life" and thus the role of *khalifah* which God bestowed upon humanity. Yet in addition to being the stewards of God's creation, the faithful also occupy the role of servants to God ('abd Allah) which in many ways places limits on the power of humankind as God's stewards. Muslim eco-theologists have also interpreted this to mean that "Muslims, in their role as servants of God, have to obey laws, including the care of Nature and the ecosystem and dealing properly with its resources." Last is the concept of *mizan*, or balance which, interpreted through the eco-theological lens, implies "ecological balance" and thus the careful management and, if needed, restoration of nature to balance out anthropogenic effects (Zbidi 2013). Importantly, the driving motivation behind these eco-theological premises is to honor God, with honoring nature being a type of devotional act. This is why Nasr and other Islamic environmentalists have emphasized a return to spiritual life as a mode of countering an environmental situation that has been largely brought about by consumerism and the "immoderate behavior[s]" of a modernist secular society (Zbidi 2013). This also plays into the performative act that is most connected with the honoring of God – prayer – with regard to the role the natural environment plays in formative conceptualizations of the space most directly connected to this act, the masjid. Hadith 1057:4 records the Prophet Muhammad saying: "Wherever you may be at the time of prayer, you may pray, for it [the Earth] is all a masjid." The implications of this are simple, as Abdul-Matin indicates. "The Earth is a mosque," he says, "the mosque is sacred; therefore, the Earth is sacred" (Abdul-Matin 2010, 2). Likewise, this hadith supports the broader belief that the earth is in fact a "divine manifestation," with the implications for the mosques being that "In the absence of a man-made enclosure set aside for worship, the immense structural dome of the sky can be perceived as a symbolic architectural form, which encompasses a worshipper in an open field" (Kahera 2008, 36).

Although the premises of an Islamic eco-theology are solidly grounded in accepted religious texts and interpretations, "eco-Islam" as a movement is still largely emergent and has suffered a number of false starts in various geographies for a variety of reasons. Yet one reason that has been identified in a number of contexts has been the utilization of environmental movements in many Islamic majority countries that have emerged from Western conservative approaches, resulting in largely unsuccessful and sometimes even negative outcomes. Quadir quotes Nigerian Islamic legal scholar Ali Ahmad, who noted that the "strategies and plans of action of [Nigerian Islamic environmentalists] completely adopt the Western framework, with little consideration for an Islamic input that will readily address local sensibilities"(Ahmad 2005, 81; in Quadir 2013, 26). Along these lines, many environmental projects in Africa are, ironically, sometimes handicapped by other projects focused on "sustainable development," which often ignore or even flagrantly violate environmental regulations (Quadir 2013, 26).

Fortunately, this problem is increasingly being recognized and a number of Islam-based environmental movements have been recognized and/or have begun to take form. The case studies in this chapter explore the different ways that Islam's spiritual relationship with nature and the current global environmentalist discourse have come together in the form of contemporary masjid structures on the continent which each approach the natural world through the diverse lenses of faith, nature, and built form. Specifically, the following case studies explore the intersection of space, spirituality, and the environment through the lenses of "natural" aesthetic, biomimetic design, and contemporary sustainable technology.

3.2 Nature's Aesthetic: The Kramats of South Africa's Cape Region

The kramats of Cape Town represent one "masjid" space where nature has found deeply conceptualized and aestheticized representation.[2] Like traditional mosque spaces, the kramats fulfill the role of a masjid as spaces of prayer and spiritual reflection while also having the social aspect of reaffirming one's membership within a broader community of believers

---

[2] Perhaps the most complete body of information on the kramats of South Africa has been compiled by the Cape Mazaar (Kramat) Society, which began in 1982 as the Robben Island Mazaar (Kramat) Society before growing to include the numerous additional kramat shrines located throughout the Cape in their maintenance, heritage. and education mission. The society tries to the best of its ability to fund and maintain the kramats and publishes educational materials for area Muslims and, increasingly, tourists who come to visit the kramats each year (Jaffer, Essack, and Davids 2010, 60). Much of the information on kramats in this chapter was taken from their informative guides and interviews with Cape Mazaar members Mahmood Limbada and Yusuf Mokada, who were kind enough to help me with this research.

through spiritual acts of devotion. Through the deployment of numerous structural and spatial strategies, these spaces become shrines to nature, deploying environment-based aesthetics to create a spiritual space/masjid that uses the natural world as the primary part of its spiritual/conceptual repertoire. According to area histories, a prophecy was made over 250 years ago by none other than Tuan Guru himself (see Chapter 1) who said that "a circle of Islam" would eventually form around the Cape composed of sites that would protect the city from any number of natural disasters (Binte-Farid 2013, 98). This circle was eventually made manifest through the emergence of a series of shrines called *kramat*, which can mean "a miracle of a saint" and additionally "a name commonly used in the Cape for the tomb of a saint" (Jaffer, Essack, and Davids 2010, 62). Shrines are often the result of specific types of patronage as well and are known for their almost universal spiritual accessibility (Rizvi 2015, 11). Shrines within the broader Islamicate also maintain a number of identities with regard to function and attribution. As was seen in Harar Jugol, some act as commemorative memorials to a historical/spiritual personage and in many cases contain the mausoleum of said personage. Likewise, they can also represent the site of a religiously significant event, or can even stand as a symbolic representation of a larger sociospiritual group or religious branch (Rizvi 2015, 12). In addition, some come into being as a result of dreams, visions, and other potentially divinely inspired events. It is perhaps ironic that Guru's tomb itself would become one of Cape Town's first kramats after which a number would follow to create a "sacred geography of Islam" in the region, the kramats themselves becoming "centers of local religiosity and shrine visits" (Loimeier 2013, 252).

Kramats in the Cape currently number around twenty-four (although there is some dispute about this tally) and take form in spaces ranging from "miniature mosques" (Davary 2016, 143) to open air spaces where the graves themselves and the landscaped areas around them act as the only site markers present. These spaces also occupy multiple roles. On the one hand, many of these sites act as symbols of political empowerment in the face of a history of Muslim oppression in the Cape. Many if not most of the shrines honor the remains of Muslim leaders, also known as *auliyah*s or "friends of Allah," who were originally brought to the Cape as enslaved individuals and political prisoners in the seventeenth and eighteenth centuries and were prohibited from practicing or propagating their religion (Binte-Farid 2013, 12). In addition to this function, however, these shrines are also national heritage sites, markers of history and spatial recognition of the contributions made by these "saints of Islam" through their contribution to the regional language of Afrikaans and their additions to contemporary Cape life, art, and culture. However, above all, these *kramat*s are fundamentally spiritual sites, maintaining an important role in the Cape Muslim community as spaces of spiritual charge, deriving their power not only from the individual interred in the spot but also often from the natural surroundings, real and manufactured, that categorize these sites and the spiritual performance of visitors within these spaces.

Regarding the *auliyah*s around whom the kramats are oriented, these were individuals who succeeded in reaching a stage of *wilaayet*, during which they effectively became a "beloved" of Allah or *Wali-Allah*. Following this achievement, all actions undertaken by the individual were interpreted as fueled by the power of the divine. Upon their physical passing, the bodies of these individuals did not decay; rather, they remained intact in a type of physical stasis derived from their spiritual status, which provides evidence of their blessed condition. The Prophet Muhammad is recorded as saying: "The bodies of the *Ambiyah* and *Auliyah* remain intact in their graves. Furthermore, the mercy and blessing of Allah continuously descends on them" (Jaffer, Essack, and Davids 2010, 12). This continuous blessing is not only made manifest in the spatial and environmental splendor that often surrounds these sites, but also in the variety of legends associated with each kramat that typically involve miraculous happenings occurring both during the life of the saint and after. Many of these occurrences happen within the area of the kramat, again providing evidence of the charge that the body of the *auliyah*, preserved in its pristine state, continues to emit. One visitor related an anecdote concerning his son, who was struggling in school. This visitor brought his son to the site of the kramat of Sayed Mahmoud, which is located in the Nova Constantia suburb of Cape Town, to pray. After this session, the son returned to school and not only ceased having problems in his studies, but rose to the top of his class.

In addition to the body of the *auliyah*, surrounding the grave are often additional graves of *asgaabs* or followers, most of whom are anonymous and buried in marked and sometimes unmarked sites around the *auliyah*. These bodies of the faithful contribute to the collective power of these sites and, as such, it is considered advantageous to one's own spiritual being to visit these kramats in order to "partake in their remembrance" which in turn generates blessings to those in attendance (Jaffer, Essack, and Davids 2010, 12). Reinforcing the designation of these sites as masjid spaces, many of the physical proscriptions for visiting a kramat are similar to those of a mosque: one must remove one's shoes and engage in *wudhu*, or the cleansing of one's person (there are typically ablution facilities provided for this). Likewise, visitors are instructed (often through notices at the site) that the mind must be solely focused on the spiritual intent at hand, avoiding unnecessary distractions or interactions. In addition, during one's meditation, one should ideally engage in reciting Qur'anic verses as a mode of devotional attention (Jaffer, Essack, and Davids 2010, 12–13).

The spiritual power of these sites is such that they have even generated small pilgrimage events throughout the year, often undertaken before individuals embark on the larger Hajj to Mecca as a type of "pre-Hajj" activity that prepares one's state of mind for the spiritual intensity one encounters in the Holy City. The sensuous aspects of the site are said to calm one's soul, and these components are derived not only from the presence of the *auliyah* themselves, but from the surrounding natural environment, which is often composed as a collaboration between natural and man-made complementary elements.

Each kramat is highly individual, and each lies in a unique natural location within a particular type of landscape (forest, coast, mountain, etc.). In addition, some kramats are individually patronized, which has largely governed the way they have been maintained and whether or not they have an architectural superstructure. Some remain largely out in the open and exposed to the elements, and in largely unpredictable locations, due to the proscription that saints should be buried close to the space of their death. Yet this too contributes to the natural, unmediated, and indeed sublime nature of these sites as spaces of spirituality embedded within the environment in a way that is spontaneous, seamless, and typically mutually beneficial. In addition, the spirituality and performativity that characterizes these sites is catalyzed by the nature of the site itself and the particular visual/sensual languages and vocabularies at work, of which the natural environment provides by far the most dominant aesthetic narrative.

These "natural" aesthetics are made manifest at these sites in a variety of ways. Sometimes they are evoked through the use of specific architectural vocabularies and conventions in the superstructure surrounding the tomb; at other sites, nature is deployed within the structural language of kramat itself as a type of aesthetic paradigm. Yet when thinking of nature as a type of architectural/aesthetic system, it is important to focus on the natural environment with regard to its history of distinctive symbolic language, particularly in Islamic traditions, and thus as a type of convention through which one not only experiences the sacred as an affirmational element of the Islamic faith but also as an intimate, individual experience that enables one to partake in numerous communions with this intermediary to God.

The history between nature and space in Islamic practice is one that has its roots in various pre-Islamic faiths and structural practices, particularly in pre-Islamic Arabia. Avni theorizes that in pre-Islamic Arabia, various nomadic travelers and groups, when they stopped to rest, would often create a type of spiritual shrine, first selecting four stones from a site, with the "finest" acting as their deity and the remaining three used to balance their cooking container. Thus, a site was created through the deployment of specific markers located in space and time, denoting both permanence and presence not through material means but through the very durability of the protocols governing their formation in the first place within a potentially undistinguished landscape. The pre-Islamic Nabataeans, for example, who were part of the nomadic Bedouin cultural group who inhabited Northern Arabia and the Southern Levant between the fourth century BCE and the second century CE, represented their deities primarily through the use of stele or an upright stone slab or column and importantly did not include any human figurative representation. The stones would be left behind when they moved on and the "ritual" would be reenacted at the next site (Avni 2007, 124–125), leaving behind a "'second order' space ... encompass[ing] the involuntary traces, remnants, and material leavings of actions and performances ... that provide symbolic evidence of past site-based events" (Apotsos 2016a, 11). While seeming to only represent "structural statements of presence," these remnants nonetheless serve an important role not only as "unspoken testimonials of previously inhabited space" but also evidence of specialized knowledge required to designate a site as "a place of action and habitation, whether it is ceremonial, ritual, or recreational." It also gestures to the fact that not only does every space contain elements of its symbolic/use value but also that such a "space" was at one point designated a "place" in that it was carved out of the surrounding natural environment and deployed for a specific purpose (Apotsos 2016a, 11). Along these lines, the Aramaic word gesturing toward these standing pillars – *msgd* – is a close affiliate of the now well-known Arabic term "masjid" (Avni 2007, 128).

Such practices of spatial creation and utilization in nature along the lines of what one might consider "appropriate technology" (AT) from an environmental perspective concerns the establishment of space that does not impact or disadvantage the surrounding ecology. Along these lines, AT may have acted as an inspiration for early mosque forms as well, which saw the emergence of the first open-air proto-Islamic spiritual sites in the Negev region of what is today southern Israel in the sixth century. Shortly after, such spaces spread throughout the Islamicate, including areas of North and West Africa, which experienced their own emergent spatial system based on nature itself as a type of construct for human space, activity, and spiritual performance. Ibrahim Abdul Ganiyu

3.2 Nature's Aesthetic

Jawondo indicates that early Muslims in Nigeria worshipped in open-space mosques called *masalasi jiji*, which were located under trees and thus "there by nature and not by design" (Jawondo 2012, 304). Eventually these spaces became cordoned off from the surrounding landscape using rocks, soil, and downed branches, some even being elevated through the construction of a sand-based platform, and subsequently demarcated by the planting of trees around the perimeter as a mode of more permanent demarcation (Jawondo 2012, 304). Soon half-walls built of earth began taking the place of trees, rocks, and soil, although the spaces were still located beneath trees for climate control, and eventually thatch roofing was applied to the structure, eliminating the need for tree shade. Importantly, the walls of these structures were painted with a green material known as *boto*, a combination of cow feces and vegetal matter that was soaked and fermented to act as both a waterproofing agent and a form of pest control (Jawondo 2012, 306). Skins and grass mats eventually covered the interior sandy floor, and water for ablutions was provided by nearby springs and rivers as well as rainfall (Jawondo 2012, 307). Thus, these forms become something of an evolution of the natural environment, a spatial appendage whose materials were derived from nature and reassembled to create a space mutually constitutive of natural and manmade systems.

Even today, open air mosques as they have existed both past and present are variously composed of open air and enclosed space. Some spiritual areas are composed of an outline of rocks with a larger standing stone at the head representing the *Qiblah* or direction of Mecca. Variations of this form appear across the Islamicate with some composed of an outline of a semi-circular *mihrab* section and a rock-lined division of space to demarcate male and female areas. Others are characterized by a simple line of stones behind which one prays with a standing stone positioned toward Mecca. The evolution of mosques over time has managed to maintain this flexible spatial paradigm as both interior/exterior by developing a collaborative relationship between open air and enclosed via the utilization of natural and environment-based themes (Avni 2007, 133–134).

This balance can be seen in a number of the kramats in the Cape region, one of which is that of Sheikh Abdurahman Matabe Shah (Figure 3.1a and 3.1b). Shah was a prominent Muslim leader and Malaccan Sultan from Indonesia who resisted Dutch domination (the Dutch gave him the name "Orange Cayen," which means individual of "influence and power," a particularly dangerous combination) and played an important role in establishing Islam in the Cape (Binte-Farid 2013, 12). Arriving in southern Africa in the mid-seventeenth century, the shah quickly became

Figure 3.1 a and b Kramat of Sheikh Abdurahman Matebe Shah, Constantia, South Africa, 2018. Images by the author.

an ally to the Cape's population of enslaved individuals, particularly those in the suburb of Constantia, and he began to propagate Islam among them. When he died in the 1680s, he was buried near a spot on the river where he regularly engaged in ablutions, prayers, and meditation. Originally his grave was sheltered by a small wooden building, but the structure eventually collapsed and was redesigned by one of Cape Town's formative architects, Gawie Fagan, with funds from the Cape Mazaar (Kramat) Society. Notable for his somewhat unusual focus on the interaction between architecture and the natural environment, Fagan designed the new superstructure with an eye toward incorporating it with the landscape which the shah had deemed so conducive to performing one's spiritual identity. The kramat itself is situated back from a side road on an estate in Klein Constantia, an ideal site whose tranquil atmosphere is supported by its surroundings of trees next to a running stream (the same stream where the shah would perform ablutions). As a "sacred spot filled with spiritualism" (Jaffer, Essack, and Davids 2010), the superstructure of the kramat was built to be in harmony with both the aesthetic and topographic reality of this space.

The kramat indeed is meant to flow with the natural topography of the area, sitting on an outcrop overlooking the stream and shaded by a variety of willow trees. As such, the kramat references two primary symbols often found in nature themes in masjid spaces: water and forests (Erzen 2011, 127). Water appears in almost every description of God's heavenly garden. "Allah has promised to the believing men and the believing women gardens, beneath which rivers flow, to abide in them, and goodly dwellings in gardens of perpetual abode; and best of all is Allah's goodly pleasure; that is the grand achievement" (Qur'an Surah 9:72). In addition, water has sacred value both as a life-giving substance and as a key resource in cleansing a human being in preparation for their communion with the divine. Trees also have an important symbolic significance as both a reference to the Tree of Life (Touba) and a gift from God, as well as being a powerful metaphor for correct faith. Qur'an Surah 14:24–25 notes: "Do you not see how God compares a good word to a good tree? Its root is firm and its branches are in the sky; it yields its fruit in every season by God's leave. God speaks in parables to mankind so that they may take heed. But an evil word is like an evil tree torn out of the earth and shorn of all its roots." In addition, trees were often treated as a type of segue between nature and architectural form, their shading providing a type of shelter that created a natural extension from exterior to interior.

Yet the undulated organization of the kramat space is also functional. The site itself is built on a series of platforms, again following the general topography of the area. The lower exterior platform holds the grave of the shah's wife, which lies directly adjacent to the stream, and the upper platform supports the superstructure containing the saint himself. Ablution facilities are also located on this level, outside of the main superstructure in the open air, overlooking the stream, and perhaps intended to mimic an experience similar to that which the shah would have experienced during his *wudhu*. In addition to containing the saint, the upper level also contains the graves of two followers, which are attached to the exterior of the superstructure. A tree has grown out of one of the graves "naturally," fusing the two in a way that has been interpreted as representative of the eternal liveliness and prosperity of the dedicated saint.

Interestingly, this type of symbolic melding can be seen in many other Islamic shrines, not only in South Africa but across the continent. The Shrine of Sheikh Ansar Ahmed outside the Argob *bari* gate in Harar Jugol, Ethiopia, for example, has a tree that has literally grown into the superstructure of the building itself so that the two are now inseparable; many also interpret this as a sign of his never-ending life, his body intimately entwined with that of the tree as an *ayat* or sign of God. Likewise, the Shrine of Sheikh Ay Abida, mentioned in Chapter 2 and one of the only shrines to female sheikhs in Harar Jugol, has a large tree that has grown directly out of her grave (which does not have a superstructure), and is also seen as evidence of the sheikh's ever-living reality and, importantly, her ability to bestow fertility and prosperity on women who come to give her prayers. This is one of the reasons that Abida is the favored saint of pregnant women and newly married couples in Harar's Islamic tradition.

To return to the kramat of Sheikh Abdurahman Matabe Shah, adding to the natural aesthetic is the color of the exterior of the structure, painted a deep green, as is the entire base of the building and the lower platform. Green is the primary color of God's creation and is "reflected all over the world," in addition to being the favorite color of the Prophet Muhammed, who said in Shamaa-il Timidhi, hadith 8: "Among the colors, green was liked the most, as it is the color of the clothing in Jannah [paradise]." Along these lines, "Allah paints his *ayats* (signs of nature) in a tapestry of green all over the world" (Abdul-Matin 2010, 47). Lastly, the color green is deeply connected to growing, fertile things, an element considered somewhat miraculous given the origin of Islam in the arid areas of the Middle East (Erzen 2011, 128).

Many of these natural, plant-based themes are also expressed more directly in the structural elements of the kramat itself. The superstructure, for example, maintains one large central "onion" dome which is painted green with a scalloped yellow cap that resembles the bud at the

3.2 Nature's Aesthetic

base of a flower; four smaller onion domes also adorn each corner of the structure. In addition, the placement of the building allows the major areas of the superstructure to receive sunlight, dispersed by the surrounding trees to generate a dappled effect on the marbled surfaces of the exterior courtyard. Thus, this "interplay of light and shadow connects architectural spaces with the dynamics of the physical and natural world, the season, and hours of the day" (Pallasmaa 2015, 23). Importantly, this aesthetic also subscribes to Ibn al-Haytham's historical definition of beauty (*al-husn*) in which color and light are the primary components for creating aesthetic harmony through a balance of visual elements as a reflection of "the omnipotence of God" (Necipoğlu 1995, 188–189; 192). Light is also emphasized through the material of the superstructure courtyard itself, its white marble shaded by white umbrellas that resemble sails floating across a dappled surface.

This aesthetic also extends to the interior of the space, which is softly lit by natural light coming in from small windows in each wall and a small chandelier highlighting the grey marble surface tiles and red carpet of the flooring. The walls are sparsely decorated but do contain a handful of images, including one of Mecca and a poster produced by students from a local school, and a bookshelf containing various copies of the Qur'an sits in the corner. The tomb itself is located in the middle of the space at an odd angle to accommodate an orientation toward Mecca and is composed of a rectilinear space created from black granite, a seemingly immovable presence positioned slightly askew but nonetheless fundamentally harmonious with the structure through the application of geometric principles: a rectilinear tomb lying within a rectilinear space over which a circular dome rests on a pendentive system. The tomb itself might be interpreted as a type of rocky outcropping within this lush vegetal environment, its formidable presence gesturing to the longevity of both rock and earth as natural forms and the saint himself as an eternal presence. The geometric symmetry also relieves any structural tension, particularly because all elements seem to complement the hidden body that lies in state in this environment as the primary focus and performer in the space (Erzen 2011, 128). Importantly, visitors to this shrine are given multiple spaces in which to enact a masjid, each of which is intimately connected to the natural aesthetic of both the site and the surrounding landscape, generating a spiritual experience that is intimately embedded in the embrace of the natural world.

Similar natural elements deployed in different ways are found in another nearby kramat containing the body of Sayed Mahmud, one of Sheikh Abdurahman Matabe Shah's primary religious advisers (Figure 3.2a and 3.2b). Located at a place previously called Islam Hill, a visit to

148 3 The Masjid as Environmental Advocate

Figure 3.2 a and b Kramat of Sayed Mahmud, Constantia, South Africa, 2018.
Images by the author.

the site used to require a fair amount of physical effort to get there on the part of the faithful, given its location on an incline leading up to the base of Table Mountain. This in many ways made a journey to Sayed Mahmud's not only an all-day affair but almost a mini-pilgrimage in and of itself, forcing visitors to move over and through the natural world to arrive at their destination (Jaffer, Essack, and Davids 2010, 27).

The kramat itself is located in a large open area surrounded by a wall; one enters the grounds through a gate that mimics the exterior superstructure of the kramat form itself, which is located within the complex. Through the gate, one has a direct line of sight to the kramat, which stands against the backdrop of Table Mountain, a view that is framed by the gate. Once through the gate, one follows a wide graveled path stretching up to the kramat superstructure, which is lined with widely spaced trees that border a well-cultivated garden area containing fruit trees and other edible and otherwise functional plants. The edges of the path are also lined with the graves of Mahmud's followers, creating various spiritual stopping points along the primary path to the mausoleum of Mahmud. A courtyard has also been created in front of the structure that one must cross in order to climb the steps up to it to enter the kramat; this courtyard also contains one of the oldest sundials in the Cape region, evoking a primordial sense of time and the passing of the sun.

Within the context of the kramat, landscaping provides important aesthetic and spiritual buttressing for the superstructure itself, drawing on some of the earliest approaches to generating Islamic masjid space, particularly with regard to the form of the "garden." Gardens were often located on masjid grounds and, because mosques constituted one of the primary axes around which work and life revolved in early Islamic communities, it is perhaps not surprising that most mosque structures maintained gardens on their grounds in reference to numerous descriptions in the Qur'an which describe God's garden as paradise (Alarslan Uludas and Adiloglu 2011, 44–96). Nature as a driving theme in form and décor was also deployed to create highly aesthetic immersive landscapes within these areas whose purpose was to enable communion with God through the medium of his earthly (and heavenly) creations. Qur'anic Surah 56: 27–33 remarks: "Those on the right hand – happy shall be those on the right hand! They shall recline on couches raised on high in the shade of thornless sides and clusters of lote-tree; amidst gushing waters and abundant fruits, unforbidden, never ending."

Along these lines, the construction and organization of the garden also reflected various elemental components highlighted in the Qur'an. Water is an element that has already been discussed, with many gardens deploying water as a major physical and conceptual theme, maintaining water canals and central pools arranged in aesthetic and occasionally symbolic channels. In addition, water often acted as climate control in these areas, absorbing heat from the often intense sunlight of equatorial regions while also keeping the air within the garden humid and thus conducive to plant growth. In addition to water, trees and other plants were not only seen as symbolic but were also deployed as a form of climate control, both trapping moisture and providing shaded areas for garden goers. Historically, they also may have acted as a windbreak, as well as providing privacy for garden users.

Importantly, however, the garden was seen as an ideal environment, akin to heaven on earth, and such implications are also noted in the Qur'an. "Whereas those who believe and do right actions, such people are the Companions of the Garden, remaining in it timelessly, forever" (Surat al-Baqara, 82). In addition, these gardens also gesture toward an environmentalist impulse that has long underscored Islamic practice and belief. Early Muslim hospitals utilized gardens with the intention of creating an "environment of healing" for their patients that was not only based on physical requirements, but emotional and psychological ones as well, as these were thought to benefit from a natural environment (Finlayson 2001, 78). Therefore, nature over time and space has maintained a strong grasp on the Islamic imagination as not only an aesthetic element but also a significant theological component whose importance is highlighted numerous times in Qur'anic verse and the hadith. Thus, nature and the natural environment have long been woven into the sacred environments of the Islamic faith.

Along these lines, unlike the previous kramat, which resembled a smaller mosque structure in its formal and decorative design, the kramat of Mahmud is a three-tiered structure whose walls are composed almost entirely of windows, enabling a visual connection between the interior space and exterior natural areas. Not only does this allow light into the space, but it also creates the feeling of being in the open air, the glass dissolving an interior/exterior separation and enabling the landscape itself to act as the kramat's space-making apparatus. Light is particularly significant here, as it is intimately associated with creation in Islamic belief. Direct comparisons are drawn between light and God, such as in Qur'anic Surah 24:35, which states:

Allah is the Light of the heavens and the earth. The parable of His Light is as a niche and within it a lamp, the lamp is in glass, the glass as it were a brilliant star, lit from a blessed tree, an olive, located neither to the east nor of the west, whose oil would almost glow forth (of itself), though no fire touched it. Light upon Light! Allah guides to His Light whom He wills. And Allah sets forth parables for mankind, and Allah is All-Knower of everything.

Within mosque spaces themselves, some architects even used light as a structural element, the earth's rotation and shifting light patterns throughout the day illuminating different areas of the interior at certain times, often in accordance to the schedule of the *salat* (Renard 1996, 79). Likewise, Allah is thought to create from "pure light." But light is also key to life itself, a necessary element to aid in the growth of the natural world and thus continue the legacy of God's creation.

In addition to light as a natural aesthetic and symbolic element, the structure of the kramat itself plays with natural geometries, beginning with a square base followed by an octagonal band that eventually culminates in a dome spanning the width of the ceiling. The dome is supported by a modified squinch/pendentive system and its visual transition from octagonal shape to square platform is eased by the addition of a series of half domes that decorate each corner and which function in a type of fractal design, a visual and an organizational theme common in Islamic design that has a basis in natural form.[3] Fractals are series of figures, units, or components whose form is statistically related to one another and often occur in seemingly chaotic but often miraculously rational and systematic ways within natural forms such as snowflakes, crystals, and galaxy formations. Other examples of fractal constructs in nature include river flow patterns and even the construction of DNA molecules, making fractals a fundamental organizing principle in numerous natural processes. Fractals are also intimately connected to mathematical systems, geometry being foremost among them, which has long held a core position in the structural manifestations of the Islamic faith. Gülru Necipoğlu's study of a Persian manual of architectural design developed between the fifteenth and sixteenth centuries known as the Topkapi Scroll reveals the dominance of geometry in the development of not only ornamentation and surface embellishments but also the design of complex vaulting and dome systems, building elevations, and even floorplans. Importantly, Necipoğlu underscores the symbolic multivalence of these forms as gestures to both advances in scientific and mathematical knowledge generated during the medieval Islamic period and informing Islamic spatial production over time and space into the contemporary period, as well as

---

[3] One of the most notable fractal forms in early Islamic architectural traditions is the muqarnas. Developed in the tenth century and occurring almost simultaneously in areas ranging from North Africa and southern Spain to Armenia and present-day Iran, muqarnas is a fractal-based vaulting system that is constituted of repetitive miniaturized units called alveoles that are often based on the basic miniaturized form of the structural units they decorate, whether it is a squinch, a corbel, or a pendentive. Adorning the undersides of structural elements such as domes and arches, the repetition of muqarnas units in tightly organized patterns creates a superstructure that has been described as "cellular" and "stalactite-like" in form; others have called it a "honeycomb" vault (Finlayson 2001, 71), and some have even compared its "insubstantial" kaleidoscopic appearance, the patterning of light and shadows "dissolv[ing] its mass" as reminiscent of flowing water (Tabbaa 1985, 63; 67).

to ideological views regarding visual abstraction and contemplative spiritual acts.

Along these lines, the period from the ninth century to the sixteenth century that most scholars call the "Islamic Golden Age" was notable for its advances in astronomy, mathematics, medicine, and geography, in addition to the subfields of optics, mechanics, and, importantly, geometry. All of these elements contributed to the understanding of the properties of space and its measurement. These developments also had important implications for the study of optics; increased understanding of the components of magnification, reflection, and refraction enabled the development of apparatuses/lenses toward focusing light and enabling a mathematical standardization of these systems. Likewise, Muslim scientists and theologians began questioning the nature of matter, eventually theorizing that "matter was neither eternal and immutable nor infinite in composition, but rather composed of particles which cannot be divided any further" (Tabbaa 1985, 38). This view of the natural environment at the atomic/molecular level, enabled by advancements in fields such as geometry, played an important role in advancing natural sciences like geology and astronomy, given that "geometric order underlies the structure of all things from molecules to galaxies, and in the circumambulating of the sacred mosque at Makkah" (Kahera 2002, 332). Geometry and fractal forms also helped create a bridge between the natural world and architectural practice, leading geometry to not only act as a governing principle to the structural components of these buildings but also a symbolic system that enabled the expression of the *tawhid* at an infinitely reproducible level. Geometry also produces forms that are, to quote Necipoğlu, "devoid of cultural specificity" (Necipoğlu 1995, 83), a universalism that not only speaks to the collective oneness of God over all, but also to its intimate connection with the natural as an equally essential element to humanity and thus a natural partner in the construction of spiritual spaces of the faith.

With regard to the kramat, each geometric component in this structural design can be interpreted to represent a repetition and intersection of form and space on multiple scales, which also adds an important symbolic component in one's experience of this building. Circles in Islamic traditions are typically considered "the perfect form" and are thus associated with the divine – God and the heavens – while the square represents a more earthly dimension, namely the four cardinal directions in the world. From these two forms derive most additional forms, including the polygon (Erzen 2011, 130). Not only can the relationships between these forms be seen in Islamic decoration, but they also make up the structural designs of many mosques and have even been applied to the planning and urban layout of sacred cities like Touba in Senegal.[4] In addition, this combination of geometric forms in a system of standardized symmetrical dimensions represents a beauty achieved through "proportionality and harmony ... obtain[ed] between the particular properties," or the "proportional combination of congruent shapes" (Necipoğlu 1995, 190). Geometry in the Islamic spatio-visual tradition has long been viewed as a somewhat transcendental system that maintains a "purifying role ... in uplifting the mind to contemplate higher forms of understanding" (Necipoğlu 1995, 190). Forms whose basis lay along geometric lines have a particular sensual quality as the "intermediate position between immaterial higher realities and the confused material objects of the world of the senses" (Necipoğlu 1995, 191). As such, these forms evoke an abstracted sacred experience not based on conscious familiarity but on experiential form and subsequently meditative reflection.

These geometric elements appear on both the exterior and the interior of this structure, which, like the previous kramat, has a bookshelf containing Qur'ans, as well as benches embedded in the walls and plaques detailing the history of this particular saint. The carpet in this structure is not red but grey, and reaches halfway up the wall to cover the benches which are also decorated with red pillows. The interior walls are white with yellow trim, with a bright green dome overhead. Instead of black granite, the tomb of the saint is clad in white marble, making the interior space very bright and light-filled. In fact, within the interior of this space light becomes an almost tangible presence, the white stone of the tomb seeming to capture light and make it into an actual object, in many ways affecting one's spatial experience of the interior space by "turn[ing] light into a substance that has a sense of other-worldly mystery" (Pallasmaa 2015, 28).

In addition, unlike the previous kramat, which was rectilinear on the interior, this kramat has a rounded interior that encourages circulation within the space and around the central tomb. This references not only the devotional repetition of circumambulation around structures such as the Ka'ba in Mecca during the Hajj and potentially even various *dikhre* practices among the Sufi, but also the natural organic form of the spiral and the aforementioned repetitions of circular forms in nature, the most obvious being the rotation of the earth and the movement of the planets. In this way, "the movement of the body and its experience

---

[4] For more information on this topic, see Eric Ross, *Sufi City: Urban Design and Archetypes in Touba* (Rochester Studies in African History and the Diaspora), University of Rochester Press, 2006.

[proprioception] could refer to both cosmic and spiritual movements" (Erzen 2011, 130). Adding to this experience is the previously mentioned fact that the structure does not have solid walls but instead has a series of large full-pane glass panels that allow the walls to fall away and adds lightness to the structure. The exterior landscape thus becomes the "walls" of this structure, allowing nature to create space, which again links to the numerous references to paradise in the Qur'an as being fundamentally embedded in the natural world, specifically the ideal of the garden.

Interestingly, this approach to the "natural aesthetic" is mirrored in a different way by the ablution structure that is located immediately to the right of the kramat and connected to it by a rose-covered trellis. The tilework decoration on this structure, which features flowers, vines, and other organic forms, provides an interesting complementary decorative counterpoint to the kramat not only through the representation of a different type of decorative program, but also through the use of an artistic technique that in many ways speaks to a history of decorative tradition within the Islamic tradition in which architectural "skins" were crafted for structures via the utilization of tilework and mosaic that recreated organic forms and scenes from nature onto a two-dimensional plane. Appearing variously as singular images or sometimes complex abstracted tableaux, these vegetal patterns – in conjunction with calligraphy and geometry-based patterning – covered numerous surfaces throughout the early Islamicate and were drawn largely from other established regional traditions coming out of Byzantium and Iran (Metropolitan Museum of Art 2001). Floral designs and garden scenes, punctuated with feats of Islamic architectural engineering such as houses and palaces, were common not only in masjid structures but also on portable objects like textiles and containers (Finlayson 2001, 77). Particular plants also came to have their own symbolism, the roses in the aforementioned kramat trellis becoming a popular symbol in Persia for "the union of the soul and God ... [whose] ... thorns of earthly life must be endured to obtain the beauty of paradisiacal union with the flower, the Beloved" (Finlayson 2001, 77–78). Likewise, recurring organic forms could be seen across buildings, such as the "vine scroll" whose decorative patterning allowed it to be deployed in multiple contexts due to its flexible application and its continuous, repetitive visual form. Often created using gilding, frescoes, and mosaic composed of glass tiles and precious stones, these compositions created jewel-like atmospheres that in many ways acted as an extension of the exterior natural world, creating a sensual, wondrous interpretation of the Garden to which all faithful believers were destined to go.

3.2 Nature's Aesthetic

Importantly as well, both these exterior garden environments and interior intimate spaces create a numinous sensescape oriented around elements of the natural world, "numinous" used here to reflect a combination of not only the physical and the metaphysical but also man and nature as "distinctly different, yet intrinsically interwoven," an element that "exudes in particular forms derived in our shared subconscious." As a concept that holds that the sacred "is embedded in all things" (Price 2015, 248), the numinous is deeply embedded in the sensescapes produced by early Islamic architecture, particularly that of the mosque, as a microcosm of the natural world recreated through an architectural medium in which man is seen to share a harmonious and mutually beneficial relationship with nature. This process creates intrinsic connections to the *tawhid*, as a three-dimensional sensorial representation of the oneness of God as the creator of all things and universal in His power. In doing so, it creates a harmonious vision of not only the natural world but man's place in it and in relationship to it, standardizing this "good environmental image" (Kahera 2008, 92) not only as a representation of spiritual belonging but also an ideal to which humanity should strive toward by living a life of faith.

Thus, the carefully cultivated landscape around the kramat, whose infusion of organic formalism is positioned against the dramatic backdrop of Table Mountain, is itself a spiritually charged geological feature, an idyllic, almost utopic spiritual environment. In fact, the natural beauty of the place has prompted other individuals to visit and even attempt to conduct other spiritual activities here, which have been firmly prohibited. Within the environment, the kramat functions as both a central focus of spiritual practice and as part of a broader natural landscape designed to both accommodate and encourage human perception and appreciation of the natural world as God's creation through its mimesis of an idyllic garden saturated with spiritual significance.

Yet this natural aesthetic has been taken even further in the context of kramat sites that eliminate the presence of an architectural superstructure all together. Such sites hold to the idea of nature as paradise and, in doing so, utilize natural elements and landscaping as the singular spatial components of constructing a spiritual kramat space. Kramats like those of Sayed Abdul Aziz, Tuan Dea Koasa, and Tuan Ismail Dea Malela are three such examples whose "architecture" is composed of trees, rocks, air, greenery, and water. Importantly, these three sites, in which the tomb itself is the only pseudo-structural element, often appear out of nowhere in the natural environment, not only abiding by the dictum that saints should be buried where they pass, but also giving these kramats a type of experiential spontaneity that often classifies one's interaction with the natural world, particularly in the context of the sublime in nature, as that which is both awe-inspiring and fear-inducing in its power. The sublime in nature is also at play in the fact that these sites exist at the mercy of nature, exposed as they are to both time and the elements. Some of this plays into their spiritual charge: there are numerous miraculous tales of these sites being able to withstand even the fiercest weather conditions. And located as many of them are on the sides of mountains, on the shores of beaches, and in the middle of forests, their removal from the world of man in essence "makes the viewer an insider and participant in the ... event instead of merely viewing the work" (Pallasmaa 2015, 22). Their brutal simplicity and their highly ascetic treatment in the face of the power and beauty of the natural landscape gives them a meditative capacity that comes from their withdrawal into nature and the subsequent quiet, which in itself is a sublime spiritual and aesthetic element that "make[s] us conscious of our fundamental solitude" (Pallasmaa 2015, 28). The situation itself generates a "primal stillness.... And as man is always frightened by remains, so he is frightened by the remains of silence" (Picard 1988, 145; 212; in Pallasmaa 2015, 28). This of course fits with the idea of nature being the kramat's fundamental architectural construct in that "The language of architecture is the drama of tranquility ... [and] ... Great architecture is petrified stillness, silence turned into matter" (Pallasmaa 2015, 29). Such architecture is meant to make one internally focused, a necessary state with which to engage in acts of devotion.

Despite the role that kramats have played in the Western Cape region as sites of history and religious identity, however, they have experienced some pushback in the contemporary period, mainly from a growing conservative population which feels that the appearance of shrines comes perilously close to adopting a form of idolatry, and even polytheism in that the body of the saint becomes less of intermediary between an individual and Allah and more of a divine power in and of themselves. Such concerns are not specific to the kramats of Cape Town, but are in fact being leveled at shrines around the continent and indeed the world; similar arguments have been made against those in Harar Jugol, as mentioned in Chapter 2. Yet pushing back against this is the fact that the spiritual aspect of the kramats in Cape Town is evoked not necessarily just through the individual, event, or inspiration that informed its creation, but through its evocation of "a feeling of transcendence beyond the conditions of commonplace and the normality of meanings" (Pallasmaa 2015, 19). As Pallasmaa notes: "A sacred space projects experiences in which physical characteristics turn into metaphysically charged feelings of transcendental reality and spiritual meanings" (Pallasmaa 2015, 19). Thus, the kramats evoke sacredness not only through concept, but through particular sensory languages that collectively evoke the "numinous" (Pallasmaa 2015, 19).

3.3 Holy Ground: Earth, Biomimesis, and Environmental Design in the Djenne Mosque

Spaces like the Cape's kramats take nature as the primary canvas on which they base the masjid experience; in addition, nature also provides the necessary raw materials and landscape to craft these spaces of spiritual devotion. Yet natural inspiration can come in a variety of forms, not only through the utilization of nature as an aesthetic and symbolic form, but also nature as a source of design and engineering solutions to the problem of enclosed space. The growing popularity of biomimetic design, from the Greek words *bios* (life) and *mimesis* (to imitate), lies in the fact that its structural systems look to nature and its various structural systems to generate solutions to problems of building structurally solvent spaces. Known also variously as biological design and biomorphism, biomimetic design as it applies to architecture focuses on generating sustainable approaches to built design along the lines of principles that govern ecological and environmental systems. There is also the idea that man-made structural systems should work collaboratively with rather than against natural forces and elements in a type of symbiotic relationship and, in doing so, bring about a particular type of synergy between the two as well as an awareness of humanity's intrinsic place within this natural system.

The Djenne mosque in Djenne, Mali, has the potential to be considered in such a way, not only representing a potential application of a "biologically-derived" process "using traditional materials to copy the shape and forms of nature" through material, form and symbolic resonance (Armstrong 2010, 79), but also pointing to the fact that such approaches to the built environment are not new. The Djenne mosque has existed in one iteration or another for at least seven hundred years and the fact remains that the idea of biologically derived structural systems is common in all cultures of the world (Figure 3.3a and 3.3b). Scholars in ancient Greece held the view that nature offers:

perfect models of ... harmonious balance and proportion between parts of a design ... [embodying] ... qualities of wholeness, of integrity, of a unity in structure such that the parts all contribute to the effect or purpose of the whole, and no part may be removed without some damage to the whole. (Steadman 2008, 9)

And fundamental to the reality of these biological architectures is that these forms embody both a visual and a functional coherence, maintaining an

158   3 The Masjid as Environmental Advocate

(a)

(b)
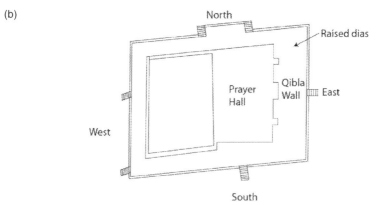

Figure 3.3 a and b The Great Mosque of Djenne. Image by BluesyPete. Own work, CC BY-SA 3.0. Floorplan by the author.

aesthetic harmony whose beauty derives from both its natural origins and its superior design based on a "survival of the fittest" system of selection (Steadman 2008, 9–10).

The site of the first iteration of the Djenne mosque, the historical city of Jenne-Jeno, was initially established around 250 BCE as a rudimentary market site for Djenne's nascent agricultural production, later developing into a thriving urban and cultural metropolis on a par with its legendary sister city Timbuktu (Newman 1995, 109). This original site was eventually abandoned in favor of Djenne's current location, potentially as a result of the overwhelming presence of "non-Muslim practices" which were unsettling to the newly converted Islamic population of the early fifteenth century (Insoll 2003, 328).[5] Today, Djenne stands as both a spiritually significant space and a UNESCO World Heritage Site, home to slightly over 30,000 residents and located on a floodplain in the inland Niger River Delta that for part of the year becomes an island, giving Djenne the dubious honor of being dubbed the "Venice" of Africa (Bourgeois and Pelos 1996, 128).

The mosque itself, which has experienced various demolitions, reconstructions, and relocations over its 700-year history, is located in Djenne's main market square and acts as an architectural, cultural, and spiritual centerpiece to the community. Located on a wide platform that sits nearly three feet above ground level and thus protected from erosion by the annual rains, Djenne's eastern face or dominant façade borders the town center. Previously a marsh area that was filled in by the French colonial administration in the early days of their occupation, it now acts as the community marketplace, a soccer field, and oftentimes an informal social area for the community.

The mosque itself sits on a dais constructed of earthen bricks that are held together by an earthen mortar and covered with clay plaster. The general thickness of the walls ranges from one-and-a-half to two feet, with denser areas located near the bottom to absorb the full weight of the structure. Its four facades are adorned with rounded pinnacles, engaged pillars or pilasters, and bundles of palm sticks called *toron* that are built into the sides of the walls as aerators that wick moisture from the interior walls and act as scaffolding for the replastering and reparation events that occur on a yearly basis. It has been suggested by Maas and Mommersteeg that the formal differences that exist between the northern and southern faces of the mosque reflect "a general disparity in wealth between these two halves of the town" (1992, 115; in Marchand 2015, 125). Three massive rectilinear towers buoy the *Qiblah* wall, and the central tower incorporates a staircase leading to a perch on the roof where the *muezzin* calls to faithful to prayer.

The space itself is accessed by six staircases lined by thick mud walls that ascend the platform on which the mosque is built. The complex also contains the rectangular tombs of two saints that are each located in front of the *Qiblah* wall (Marchand 2015, 124). Once inside the space, the exterior world falls away as one is enveloped by the large, quiet, dimly lit interior of the mosque prayer hall, which measures fifty meters by twenty-six meters and maintains ceilings that are at least twelve meters high (Marchand 2015, 125). Ninety large, earthen pillars subsequently divide the space into a hypostyle hall "like a platoon of giant dominoes," creating

---

[5] This view is still speculative, but supported by strong multidisciplinary evidence.

160   3 The Masjid as Environmental Advocate

a series of "long, narrow corridors that traverse the building north–south and east–west" (Marchand 2015, 126). Because this organization regulates the number of faithful that the mosque can contain during Friday prayers, additional individuals are accommodated within a courtyard located on the western side of the complex which is surrounded by additional galleries that function as women's space (Marchand 2015, 126; 127).

Importantly, the structure, with its distinctive aesthetic style and unique conceptual program, is commonly interpreted as an architectonic synthesis of spirituality: an Islamic construct defined by the visual and conceptual standards of local architectural practices and styles, which has resulted in a structure reflective of the complex political, social, and spiritual conversations that have defined the identity of this area. It is generally thought that Koi Konboro (dates unknown), Djenne's twenty-sixth king and the first to convert to Islam in the early thirteenth century, was responsible for creating the initial Djenne mosque. Various accounts have Konboro either transforming his palace into the first Great Mosque of Djenne, or tearing down his palace to have a mosque erected in its place (Prussin 1986, 182).[6] Currently there are two main areas in Djenne that are thought to be the primary locations of the various "Great Mosques" that have occurred over time, the first being the original location of Konboro's palace, and the second being the area where the current mosque now stands. It has been speculated that, after its initial construction, the first mosque may have stood for six centuries until it was demolished during the iconoclastic reign of Sheku Amadou at the beginning of the 1800s, but this assumption is still debated and many alternative theories abound.[7] Yet it is important to mention one key figure in this long narrative: the legendary Mansa Musa (1312–1337), king of the Malian Empire who, after his pilgrimage to Mecca in the fourteenth century, constructed numerous mosques throughout the region, yet with an observant eye to the religious pluralism of his subjects.[8]

---

[6] Little is known about the appearance or structure of this first mosque as no drawings remain and other sources of information such as oral histories or historical narratives are "for various reasons unsatisfactory" (Bourgeois and Pelos 1996, 129).

[7] Prussin believes that Malaha Tanapo, the first chief of Djenne and a non-Muslim, tore down Konboro's mosque and later built another on the secondary site (Prussin 1986, 182).

[8] Some credit Musa with the creation of the *Sudonaise* style, seen in a majority of the traditional mud domestic and religious structures in Djenne, both then and now. As these structures share similar stylistic characteristics, it is important to note that many of them manifest similar spiritocultural connotations to that of the mosque although on a less monumental scale. The use of mud as a construction material in both sacred and domestic structures highlights spiritual resonances between the two as specific examples of communicative cultural space with the attendant binary issue of public (secular) vs. private (sacred) designated areas. Further highlighting mud's particular resonance are

Pre-Islamic spiritual systems in the region are thought to have been based primarily on agricultural cycles that were dependent on environmental conditions and seasonal changes throughout the year. In addition, ancestral entities remained active within this system as residents of the earth and active mediators with regard to agricultural prosperity, fecundity, and renewal within the realms of communal life (Prussin 1982, 204). Thus, earth as both a source of sustenance and as an abode of the ancestors provided a nascent platform on which subsequent spiritual systems in the region were constructed. Many of these spiritual systems also inspired structural forms like shrines and various "ancestral" mounds, which were designed to privilege the presence of ancestors and solicit their blessings, and they were often placed near the entrance to familial compounds. Another spiritually charged form found adjacent to and sometimes incorporated within these forms was the familial granary, a structure responsible for ensuring the livelihood of a family and community from one agricultural cycle to the next, and whose construction from earth was symbolically protective as well. Auspicious designs often decorated the outsides of these structures, many referencing anthropomorphic female attributes with a full granary being called a "pregnant" granary in reference to their life-giving presence. Thus, in each case, earth is equated with ancestral abodes, communal life, and spiritual protection (Prussin 1982, 204–205).

With this in mind, during the broader period of the Malian Empire, many of these pre-Islamic traditions make formal appearances on numerous mosque forms throughout the region, Djenne included, whose pillars and pinnacles lining the walls of the structure serve as an evocative formal reference to ancestral presence and the centrality of earth as a source of life. And by incorporating large earthen mounds into the mosque architecture as a nod toward the West African tradition of the ancestral pillar, Mansa Musa and the rulers that followed contributed to the creation of a mediated structural form that spoke to both Islamic and indigenous spiritual paradigms (Morris and Blier 2004, 190). Through this iconographic program, the mosque style not only acknowledged its syncretic origins, but also promoted the structural development of a more ideologically honest form of architecture that reflected the true nature of the communal religiocultural condition at the time.[9]

---

commercial or business structures in the area which, while representing this style via the formal aspects of pinnacles and embellished entrances, are typically composed of cement.

[9] These earthen mounds also provide an interesting contribution to the discussion of material signification. As earth embodies the abode of the ancestors and thus signifies the power of the ancestral presence, it would seem that form fulfills a largely secondary or subordinate role in this signification hierarchy as it necessarily bows to the material. This is not to say that the function of formal composition is entirely suppressed; rather, the myth "impoverishes it, it puts it at a distance, it holds it at one's disposal ... the meaning loses its

Yet because of the malleable characteristics of its primary medium, earth, the mosque can also be interpreted further as not just a form but an environmental event, indeed an ongoing physical process defined by its continuous interaction and collaboration with nature, a reality that challenges conventional architectural notions of stasis and continuity. Mud structures tend to "melt" after the rainy seasons of the Sahel and thus must be maintained regularly in order to retain their shape and structural integrity. Because the physical alteration of an earthen form provides a visual indication of the progression of time via changing textures, formal anomalies, and shifting surface characteristics, the "life cycle" of a structure is thus not only measured in terms of these material-oriented shifts, but also the resulting periodic maintenance. This maintenance typically occurs on an annual basis, and has assumed ceremonial aspects informed both by culturally specific social cycles within the community and by the spiritual components involved in the maintenance components themselves. Yet this collective phenomenon in many ways contradicts a canonical architectural premise that Donald Preziosi calls the "property of object-permanence" (Preziosi 1979, 6) which holds that the lasting aspects of architectural forms are often assumed to be "sustained note[s] in an ongoing and dynamic orchestration of signs," with the typical physical longevity of a structure preserving the signifier in a way that verbal rapport and other forms of abstract communication cannot (Preziosi 1979, 6). While the material form of the Djenne mosque obviously maintains its structural integrity for longer than a word or gesture, its earthen medium still signifies primarily from the base of its ephemeral, living nature and, as such, its resulting dynamic aspects are recognized, accommodated, and even celebrated in the seasonal activities that surround its maintenance, particularly the annual replastering of the structure by the community.

This renovation activity is in many ways a "material celebration" of the structure, occurring on an annual basis in a festive tradition that has been described as "as cyclical as the harvest" in which the individuals of the community apply "new mud like balm on weathered skin … [to] … heal the erosion of annual rains" (Bourgeois and Pelos 1996, 60). This regenerative process not only safeguards the mosque's physical form, but also signals agricultural revitalization after the Sahelian rainy season. Additionally, the mosque's renewal allows the community to refresh their spiritual ties with the earth and their Islamic faith, a pilgrimage

---

value but keeps its life, from which the form of the myth will draw its nourishment" (Barthes 2013, 118). One could also reasonably conclude that form in this secondary role may have acquired resonance from its association with its medium; thus, the mound itself would be unable to resonate at a sustainable level were it not for its specific earthen composition.

made possible by the laborious, mud-spattered replenishment of Djenne's earthen surface. Prussin calls such activity a "salvation event in which human experience is re-created and renewed" (Prussin 1999, 424), and indeed, via this act, the enduring ideologies of the Djenne mosque and community are reaffirmed through the recognition of the mosque as a living spiritual and architectural organism.

The replastering of the mosque is an extremely important communal occasion that occurs on a day deemed auspicious by the elders of the community in consultation with the community masons who study almanacs, lunar calendars and, importantly, the various environmental and climatic conditions of the area before making a final decision (Marchand 2015, 117; 129). As such, the event acts as "the focal point around which Djenne society, identity, and knowledge has been continually renewed and reinforced" (Marchand 2015, 117). The occasion of the replastering itself involves various neighborhood communities competing to resurface their section of the mosque the fastest, with the very act of resurfacing itself seen as an act of devotion that encourages the renewal and rejuvenation of communal ties through the laborious, mud-spattered replenishment of Djenne's earthen surface. Thus, as a collective exercise, this act reaffirms spiritual ties with Islam, the earth, and the ancestors in a communion made possible through the resuscitating of the mosque's physical structure; one might even consider this a pilgrimage event made manifest through prayer and ritualized action.

This discussion positions Djenne as a living structure, a structure that responds to its environment in an organic fashion and in this way it maintains a number of diverse environmentally embedded components. For one, the form and material of the mosque exists in an active call-and-response relationship with the environment. The surface of the mosque is composed of positive (form) and negative (void) spaces that recede and advance like a geometric tide and create a formal composition that not only resembles the numerous zoologically inspired mask countenances of the region and thus suggests a deep intimacy with nature (Prussin 1986, 186) but is also an effective tactic for minimizing erosion. Aiding this process is the inclusion of ostrich eggs atop the delicate pinnacles of the earthen towers, which not only protects them from erosion but provides an added symbolism via a localized reference to prosperity (Bourgeois and Pelos 1982, 9–10). Lastly, the utilization of earth as a building material in this area of the Sahel, which is characterized by hot days, cold nights, and little rain, is highly efficient given earth's natural thermodynamic efficiency. Specifically, the insulating properties of earth allow structures built from it to maintain a moderate to cool interior temperature during the day while releasing the stored heat into the interior at night

3 The Masjid as Environmental Advocate

when temperatures drop significantly. In addition, because structural stability requires thick earthen walls to maintain the structure's weight, the *toron* are necessary to maintain structural solvency (Apotsos 2012, 7). All of these elements create a balance (*mizan*), which remains one of the fundamental qualities of spiritual space as a sign of God (*ayat*) (Abdul-Matin 2010, 60). It is also noteworthy that the first mosque, built by the Prophet Muhammed, was a simple earthen structure whose pillars and *minbar* were made from palm trunks, a space that not only heeded the Qur'anic call to exercise moderation but also utilized natural resources in the most efficient way possible (Aburawa n.d.).

Yet efficiency not only lies within form and material, but also within the design process itself. Some have speculated that Djenne and other stylistically similar architectural forms in the region have taken aesthetic and functional inspiration from other structures that appear naturally in the landscape in this region, one of which may have been *termitaria*, or the tall earthen mounds that function as dwelling spaces for the insect species *Termitidae*, also known as the termite (Figure 3.4a and 3.4b). There are

Figure 3.4 a and b Visual comparison between Djenne's Great Mosque and a West African termitarium from Ghana.
Image of Great Mosque of Djenne by Francesco Bandarin. UNESCO World Heritage Site, listed as Old Towns of Djenné, CC BY-SA 3.0-igo.
Image of termitarium by Shawn Zamechek from Philly, USA. CC BY 2.0.

more than 2,500 termite species in the world, with more than 1,000 existing in Africa. Of those 1,000, many are large mound builders (*macrotermes*) and construct *termitaria* up to five meters high (Huis 2017). *Termitaria* across the West African savannah bear an undeniable spatiovisual resemblance to architectural forms like Djenne and suggest the possibility of processes of structural mimicry and formal assimilation, points of formal connection that are also supplemented by various systems of belief with regard to termites and their importance to various cultures and communities over the region. Some cultures view termite colonies as symbols of fertility and prosperity, with their nests acting as the abodes of ancestral figures and other spiritual beings (Henderson and Umunna 1988, 33–34). The Igbo cultural group of Nigeria, for example, have viewed *termitaria* as not only an ancestral abode, but also the dwelling spaces of *djinn*, Islamic spiritual entities thought to be neither good nor evil and able to take forms both human and animalistic, which remain fundamentally connected to elemental aspects of nature. Because of this, termite mounds, particularly the earth used to craft them, have long been the primary building material of *Mbari* structures, which are large earthen "houses" crafted in response to a community problem or disaster such as sickness, crop failure, etc. Although there is little evidence that such structures are still constructed in the contemporary period, historically they were intended to act as offerings to the deity Ala to request her intervention. In addition, because of the time, energy, and expense that they entailed, *Mbari* were rarely built more than once a generation. When they were constructed, however, these structures used termite earth as their primary construction material, both because of its physical properties – it is, in the words of Hendersen, "superior modeling clay" – as well as its associations with the spirit world as the space from which masquerade spirits emerge and in which the ancestors reside (Henderson and Umunna 1988, 32–33). Workers dug deep into termite mounds to harvest the clay used in *Mbari* structures, and this deep clay was known as "yam food of mother earth," a title that crafted an intimate connection between "mother earth" and *termitaria* and, importantly, pointed to a broad-based value system oriented around the importance of the natural environment (Cole 1982, 57–58; 72–100; in Henderson and Umunna 1988, 33). This clay was then used to craft the numerous sculptures within a *Mbari*, representing all aspects of Igbo life. After the *Mbari* was completed and unveiled to the populace, it was left to naturally disintegrate back into the environment, its purpose and its impact on the surrounding landscape fulfilled.

Such resonances are also not specific to West Africa or Africa in general. The Rayalaseema region of India, for example, contains a town – Puttaparthi – that literally translates to "multiplier of termite mounds" and its origin story is centered around termite mounds and the protective snakes often associated with them (Rigopoulos 2014, 117–119). In many areas in rural India, in fact, termite mounds are regarded as intensely spiritual sites where "oaths are taken by touching it, and boundaries are marked by naming it." In some cases, these mounds come to stand for the idea of a sacred mountain and sometimes as a phallic symbol for Shiva (Rigopoulos 2014, 120).

But another reason termites and their architectural constructs are held in such esteem in areas of West Africa in particular has to do with their structural success within the often harsh environments of the Sahel. *Termitaria* are complex to say the least in that they are constantly adapting and evolving in response to changing conditions. In some ways, the structure of a termite mound resembles the neural highways of the brain, synapses forming, terminating, and shifting in response to various circumstances in the context of a dynamic living system (Henderson and Umunna 1988, 31). Not only are termites incredibly prolific – one queen can produce up to 36,000 eggs a day, a total of 13 million eggs per year – but their nests extend far beyond the often significant visual indication of the mound which rests above ground. Termites often tunnel downwards forty meters into the earth to bring up both water and minerals (Henderson and Umunna 1988, 31–32) and build their structures predominantly out of area earth and fecal matter, as well as a glue-like substance they secrete from their own bodies to create a hard, packed, largely waterproof surface (Denny and McFadzean 2011, 118).

But perhaps one of the most interesting components about these structures is their dynamism, in the sense that the mound is constantly reforming and evolving in response to the external environment like some type of "giant lung." The channels, tunnels, and chimneys built into the mound reveal an intricacy and ingenuity in engineering that uses natural forces and processes to actively circulate and exchange air, which in turn actively controls the interior climate of the structure as well as the level of carbon dioxide (Denny and McFadzean 2011, 127–128). Avenues and tunnels are opened and closed frequently to regulate heat and humidity, with chimneys designed to vent carbon dioxide produced by the nest. Thus the mound is inherently responsive to both interior and exterior environments and acts as a mediator toward maintaining balance between these two worlds, enabling colonies and *termitaria* to potentially exist indefinitely. In fact, the recent discovery of a 4,000-year-old termite colony in northeastern Brazil supports the sustainability and longevity of these systems, not only because of the age of the colony but also the fact that the colony is composed of a network of over 200 million distinct mounds, many of them roughly ten feet high, twenty feet wide at the base and regularly spaced at thirty- or forty-foot intervals. Incredibly, these mounds cover an area roughly the size of Great Britain and can be seen from space (Martin et al. 2018).

The Djenne mosque maintains interesting resonances with such natural architectures on a number of levels, the first obviously being structural. The Djenne mosque, like many termite mound forms in West Africa, maintains a thick base that gradually narrows into a series of tapered pillars which not only makes it appear to grow organically from the ground but also promotes structural stability. In addition, this tapering aspect, in conjunction with the undulating surfaces that both the mosque and the *termitaria* maintain in the form of protruding and receding surface depths, also reduces erosion by minimizing friction caused by wind and rain. The next similarity between these two forms is material. Djenne is made entirely of earth and the surface of the mosque has been traditionally smoothed with a hard plaster made from specific types of mineral-rich earth, including lime deposits and calcium from fish bones left in nearby riverbeds after the floodwaters recede. Various types of dung are also included, whose components actively slow annual erosion, mimicking a similar composition to those of termite beds, where earth is processed using a substance secreted by the termite's body to generate a hard, almost cementlike, waterproof exterior surface. In addition, the timbers incorporated into the sides of the mosque not only act as scaffolding but also as a type of channel for moisture to escape from the interior, similar in both form and function to the vents and chimneys that termites build at strategic spaces in the mound structure to not only support the structural integrity of the mound but also to maintain interior climate control. The interior of Djenne is also climate controlled not only through the building material but also through a series of vents piercing the ceiling and typically covered with porcelain tops, again referencing the utility of the spires that often decorate the upper portions of termite nests. These spires and vents within *termitaria* are also regularly plugged and unplugged by workers to account for shifting environmental conditions on the exterior as well as air quality within the mound itself.

Such elements contribute to the idea that both the Djenne mosque structure and *termitaria* constitute living architectural systems, "living" in the sense that, like an animate organism, they both engage in respiration, growth, and evolution over time and often in response to their dynamic interaction with the physical environment. Indeed, with regard to Djenne and the biological influences that it may have incorporated as a mode of generating productive interactions and responses to the natural environment, Djenne as an architectural system could be said to be engaging in forms of biomimicry or biomimetics. Referencing the condition of acting or imitation, biomimetics/biomimicry is broadly defined as an engineering system or solution based on an imitation of nature in which natural models and structures are used to solve human problems. Biomimetics are seen to provide particularly durable models of being in the world given they have been subject to the tests of time, evolution, and natural selection and thus represent highly adapted structures that have been subject to rigorous tests.

With regard to biomimetics as a system of human production, numerous contemporary products and materials are the result of natural inspirations. Swiss engineer George de Mestral, inventor of Velcro, got the idea in 1941 after observing the ways in which burrs became lodged in dog fur via tiny hooks along the barb's edge. Likewise, contemporary engineers are taking inspiration from the aerodynamic qualities of whale fins and flippers when designing more efficient wind turbines. Architecture, in particular, has been impacted by biomimetic systems in terms of finding sustainable structural solutions that both support contemporary living and minimize environmental impacts. Indeed, *termitaria* have not only functioned as a potential source of inspiration for Djenne, but also for other structures both around the world and in other parts of Africa as well. The Eastgate Mall in the capital city of Harare, Zimbabwe, for example, is an office and shopping complex that was designed in 1996 by architect Michael Pierce, who is largely considered to be one of the foremost tropical architects working today. Pierce's primary concern with this design was how to both minimize the economic burden of the structure by offsetting the costs of climate control and other ecologically relevant issues, while also embedding it in its cultural and historical context. Climate control was a particular problem given the fact that Zimbabwe is largely a savannah region that experiences a wide range of climatic shifts; these shifts constitute one of the primary financial drains in large building projects such as this due to the energy-intensive heating and air-conditioning requirements they entail. In taking *termitaria* as his inspiration, Pierce subsequently designed the structure so that, like Djenne, it incorporated heat-absorbing material as well as chimneys from which hot air could be vented in the evening, and floor vents that enabled cool air to enter with the use of fans. These fans also actively circulate air throughout the building during the day and it has been estimated that the building itself uses 35 percent less energy than six typical Harare buildings combined, saving the owner upwards of $4 million in energy costs (Architects for Peace n.d.).

Yet in constructing this space, Pierce also looked to the regional architectural history of the area, specifically the use of native stone and masonry in architecture with the intention of making the structure a collaborative cultural construct (Architects for Peace n.d.). The term "Zimbabwe" in the Karanga dialect of Shona actually means "large houses of stone," and one of the most revered heritage sites in Zimbabwe is that of Great Zimbabwe, a large architectural complex built between the eleventh and fifteenth centuries composed of meticulously fitted stonework. In reference to this site, the mall itself has a stacked, heavily carved masonry look, its porous surfaces in many ways resembling the strategic stacking of multiple-sized stone bricks that characterize the stonework at Great Zimbabwe.

As such, the Eastgate Mall represents a similar structural approach to biomimetic design potentially also encapsulated within the Djenne mosque and is one of a growing number of emergent environmentally oriented spaces whose guiding principles are deeply embedded in current discourses of responsible resource utilization and construction practices and materials that are low impact and "sustainable." But questions remain about the long-term success of such projects from a global standpoint given the variety of histories and discourses that inform them. Indeed, the various ways in which environmentalism has been defined and deployed in the context of architecture and other "sustainable" projects leads to the ultimate conclusion that, to quote Chidester and Linenthal, "nature, in its human meaning and significance, is a cultural product" (Chidester and Linenthal 1995, 13).

Along these lines, ideas of sustainability and conservation have in some cases come to rub up uncomfortably against contemporary conceptualizations of heritage (addressed in Chapter 2), particularly with regard to conflicts between environmentally sensitive design and the "regimes of representation and regulation" enacted by heritage governing bodies whose focus on preservation is often ironically at odds with the necessary dynamism of ecologically sensitive constructs (de Jorio 2016, 97). The Djenne mosque and many of the surrounding community residences were inscribed on UNESCO's world heritage list in 1988, which has led to the subsequent regulation of not only Djenne's mosque structure but also various domestic spaces throughout the city of Djenne. This has generated a number of problems with regard to the city and the mosque, not only as a residential and commercial environment but also as a built landscape that maintains a light footprint on the surrounding environment.

Charlotte Joy notes that "UNESCO ... decreed that the whole town should stay materially the same and rejects new technologies that would help home owners cope with the yearly cost of maintaining their homes" (Joy 2007, 3; in de Jorio 2016, 103). Likewise, de Jorio notes that

"UNESCO literature reiterates the importance of keeping intact a certain town atmosphere." With regard to Djenne, this meant that "the restoration of Djenné must conform to the aesthetic criteria of Sudanese architecture (e.g., imposing facade, a certain decorative pattern), maintain the spatial organization of the lived-in space (e.g., an interior partitioned into small spaces arranged around an interior courtyard), use local materials (mud, karite, rice hulls, etc.), and use specific construction techniques – mastered by a specialized group of masons" (de Jorio 2016, 103).

These regulations had the effect of preventing the expansion of homes to accommodate contemporary furnishings and discouraging "the creation of living spaces to accommodate changing ideas of cleanliness, hospitality, and prestige" (de Jorio 2016, 105). Likewise, the use of contemporary materials and technological advancements has also been frowned upon as they "either contradict UNESCO guidelines or serve as expressions of bad taste ... contributing to the city's cultural decline" (de Jorio 2016, 106). The addition of "neon pipes" on one of the four facades of the Great Mosque, as well as the installation of electric fans and plastic (rather than ceramic) pipes in the interior, have been largely disparaged (de Jorio 2016, 106).[10]

But perhaps the most troubling aspect of this situation with regard to its environmental impact is the fact that this "museological approach in the handling of the city's patrimony" (de Jorio 2016, 107) may have robbed both the mosque and its localized context of a crucial element that contributed to its capacity to function as an environmentally responsive structural system: its ability to change or evolve over time and space and in terms of form and material (Apotsos 2012, 2). Shifts in agriculture and the Djennenke economy have resulted in changes to the materials utilized in architectural construction. Contemporary mud bricks are not only created in different shapes than they had been in the past, but are also composed of substandard materials and even stray bits of garbage, and this led to a decrease in durability (Joy 2007). Likewise, the mosque has been unable to respond to changing ecological conditions that include a drop-off in lime and calcium deposits in the river bed; this has meant that securing the necessary construction materials (as designated by UNESCO's preservation guidelines) has become more costly, as has securing the services of masons to do the job and, in addition, according to Charlotte Joy, the required skilled labor has all but disappeared due to the dissolution of

---

[10] UNESCO does not provide financial support for such maintenance projects, which is largely funded through local and state-based programs as well as a handful of international organizations and entities.

"traditional kinship structures" (Joy 2007, 153). All of this has also had an effect on the structure as a faith-based form, in that the structure, to quote Marchand, is not just an "aesthetic object for historical preservation" but also a "place of prayer" and as such "a building constructed, maintained, and, one might add, perpetually transformed by its community" just as spaces are perpetually transformed into masjid when ritualized actions take place (Marchand 2015, 139). By removing the agency of the people who engage in this transformative process, the mosque itself runs the risk of not only failing to resonate with its community but also failing to function as an ecologically responsive form that in turn follows the environmentalist tenets of the Islamic faith.

By selecting a "trace of a memory," structurally speaking, to be preserved as "definably authentic" heritage (Rowlands 2007, 134), authentic heritage has become less about process and relationships and more about appearances in which structural forms are frozen in commemoration to a subjective interpretation of history, also known as memory. Ironically, an important aspect of memory is also forgetting; in this sense, the primary purpose of memory is to adjust or tweak the past in order to supplement the present, creating a specific, highly personalized narrative that says more about the current sociopolitical context than a past cultural milieu (Lowenthal 1985, 210). This not only reflects a highly "romantic notion of culture" that implies "a view of culture as neatly defined, distinct, unique, and fundamentally unchanging" but also transforms space into "a permanent museum" (de Jorio 2016, 103), a space singled out for control and presentation in a manner that is distinctly political in nature and reflective of "new regime[s] of value" (Fontein 2000, 86).

From an environmental standpoint, the structure's relationship with the landscape and its community as an ecologically complementary space is suffering through this stasis. By arresting its ability to evolve, Djenne's current heritage program may in fact have undermined the mosque's most fundamental signifying tool with regard to religious identity and environmental impacts, leading to the question of whether the mosque has been able to remain "in tune" with the cultural voice of the Djennenke community and the ecological environment in which it exists (Apotsos 2012, 2).

3.4 Technology and Emergent Environmentalism in Tanzania's First Eco-Mosque

These tensions represent an important element of masjid design as not only an environmental project, but also a holistic enterprise that addresses multiple interlocking elements of social, environmental, and spiritual identity. This has also led to new considerations of what constitutes a truly sustainable masjid space, and such considerations have subsequently informed the development and current success of what is thought to be the continent's only green-technology-based eco-mosque, which is located in Tanzania and forms part of the broader complex of the Children's Eco-Village, a nonprofit community for predominantly orphaned girls that was established in 2010 in the small town of Kisemvule on the outskirts of Dar es Salaam. The Children's Eco-Village was founded by a UK-based charitable organization called Islamic Help, which was established in 2003 as an organization dedicated to alleviating poverty and suffering through a variety of programs that have ranged from providing emergency assistance in the context of natural and man-made disasters to the development of sustainability and environmental programs, among others, to disenfranchised communities on a global scale. Islamic Help has operated at a strictly local level in collaboration with local stakeholders and volunteers who provide a majority of the motivational impetus behind the success of these programs (Islamic Help n.d.) Thus far, Islamic Help has assisted communities in more than twenty countries, with the Children's Eco-Village being one such project, focusing on environmental sustainability at a holistic level.

Founded in 2010, the Childrens' Eco-Village is located on a thirty-acre parcel of isolated fertile land given to the group by a local donor. The purpose of the village itself is to care for vulnerable children, typically orphans, from around the region, which is one of the reasons that the village itself is located somewhat off the beaten path in a protected natural area. Statistics in this area are telling in that sub-Saharan Africa is home to an estimated fifty-three million children who are without either of their parents; Tanzania is home to 3.1 million of these children, almost half of whom have been orphaned due to HIV/AIDS (Islamic Help n.d.). Within this group, girls are particularly at risk in that they are most likely to experience abuse and neglect due to long-standing cultural gender biases. Thus, at this point in time, the village is a single-sex facility aimed at ameliorating the historical plight of girls and young women.

Within the village, the girls receive education and care in the context of a familial setting that "replicates everyday villages, communities and family life." In terms of the village, this aspect is oriented around five key principles: 1. Each child has a "mother"; 2. Each child grows up alongside "siblings" as a natural family unit; 3. Each child has a dedicated "home" space; 4. Each child grows up in and is supported within the context of a "village" environment; and 5. This support continues into

3.4 Technology and Emergent Environmentalism

adulthood. Through this model, the children in the village become active community members who also play a key role in the successful operation of the village itself. Programs and events are undertaken to integrate these children into the surrounding communities, not only as a mode of socialization but also as a way of establishing wider communal networks and connections based on shared communal and faith-based values (Ngolola 2017).

Many of the environmental and spiritual lessons the children absorb are made manifest in the village's eco-mosque, which was the first building to be built on the village campus and is an unprecedented structure on the continent, said to be the "only mosque in Africa designed completely on green technology" (Islamic Help n.d.). The eco-mosque would also set the campus standard for building in an Islamically motivated, green, holistic manner (Figure 3.5a and 3.5b). The mosque itself lies at the entrance to the village, allowing it to be used by both village residents and members of the surrounding community alike and, true to the holistic aims of the village, it is a spiritual space open to those across faiths as "a serene space of prayer or quiet reflection" (Islamic Help n.d.). In addition to being the structural anchor of the community, the mosque acts as the social and spiritual foundation of the village where one not only experiences religious services, but also is able to access counseling and engage in "social and cultural interaction, discussions and debates" (Islamic Help n.d.). Importantly, the mosque is a space not only of interfaith collaboration but also intercultural support, a complement to its additional role in creating awareness of the importance of a healthy environment. Thus, the mosque "represents a built reflection of the ethos of the Children's Eco Village providing an environmentally friendly backbone to the community with environmental features and a unique union of the local community and their faith based responsibility as caretakers of their natural environment" (Islamic Help n.d.). This is an unprecedented architectural model in Tanzania that will hopefully be reproduced in other areas as a model intersection of faith and environmental consciousness.

The structure itself makes uses of a number of green technologies from the outside in. Completed in 2012 and able to hold up to 160 individuals, the conceptualization of the mosque from start to finish was one solely focused on its environmental and social footprint. In terms of the exterior space surrounding the mosque, the land has been carefully cultivated for both spiritual and functional purposes. It contains a number of fruit-bearing trees and plants that benefit from a series of water sources within the grounds and which create a pleasant micro-climate. In addition, the placement of vegetation in this area is also meant to create a pleasing, meditative aesthetic in a way that speaks to Qur'anic verses of the garden

174   3 The Masjid as Environmental Advocate

(a)

(b)

Figure 3.5 a and b Eco-mosque, children's village, Kisemvule, Tanzania, 2018.
Images by the author.

as a space of paradise and one of mankind's responsibilities to care for. Importantly, this landscape benefits directly from the water system in place at the mosque, which uses recycled water from ablutions to feed the surrounding landscape. The eco-mosque maintains three water-collection tanks, each holding around 2,000 liters of water, that enable

3.4 Technology and Emergent Environmentalism

the performance of *wuḍū* or the cleaning of the body in preparation for prayer. The wastewater resulting from the process is then collected and fed to the surrounding landscape in an irrigation scheme, which saves around 225 liters of water daily (Ngolola 2017). But the importance of water in this context is also spiritual. Cleanliness in the Islamic faith is of great importance and is undertaken five times daily in preparation for prayer and in specific sequences, which is the ablution process (Mokhtar and Ahmadi 2005, 1). This process is described in the Qur'an: "O you who believe! When you prepare for prayer, wash your faces, and your hands (and arms) to the elbows; rub your heads (with water); and (wash) your feet to the ankles (Qur'an Surah 5:6)" (Abdul-Matin 2010, 134). The state of purity must be maintained before prayers are said, and certain actions can "contaminate" the body and thus make it unsuitable to engage in the act of *salat*. Thus, the importance of water is that it renders one ready to leave the mundane world behind and enter the realm of the spirit through prayer (Abdul-Matin 2010, 135). This points to the power and importance of water not only as a symbol of faith but also as a key component in one's physical and spiritual preparation for communion with the divine. The power of water is expressed in the Qur'an, such as in Surah 13:17: "He sends down water from the skies, and the channels flow, each according to its measure" (Abdul-Matin 2010, 133). In fact, to many, water is considered *ayat*, or a sign of God, and it is perhaps not coincidental that water plays a key spiritual role in many faith-based traditions, such as baptism in the Christian tradition, which signifies a rebirth into a life of Christ, and *mikyah* and *netilat yadayim* in the Judaic tradition, the first of which is a ritual bath utilized to achieve a "state of spiritual purity" and the second a form of hand washing done before eating challah (Abdul-Matin 2010, 117).

The importance of water in the faith also points to the importance of conserving water as a necessary spiritual element. Currently, the mosques in both Mecca and Medina recycle wastewater or "grey water" as a mode of offsetting the extreme drain on water resources during the annual Hajj season. As the "largest gathering of people on the planet for one purpose," the Hajj is a major religious event in which millions of Muslims flock to the desert environment of Saudi Arabia to fulfill one of the most important pillars of the faith. The limited potable water resources in the area prompted the Saudi Arabian government to issue a *fatwa* or religious ruling that treated water waste must be recycled for use in *wuḍū* (Abdul-Matin 2010, 59–60). The delivering of a *fatwa* on this issue held a great deal of symbolic power as well, underscoring the idea that this type of environmental stewardship was not only acceptable, but also important and preferred. As Abdul-Matin notes: "If the most important mosques in the world can issue an edict that sets a precedent for rethinking how we manage critical systems, then mosques all over the world can be transformed, and we can all better honor the trust (*amana*) we have with God" (Abdul-Matin 2010, 59–60). Likewise, "If the Earth is a mosque, then seventy percent of our mosque is water" and thus water management becomes a preeminent issue in spaces such as the mosque (Abdul-Matin 2010, 119).

The concerns governing the exterior area surrounding the eco-mosque are also extended to the interior architecture, which has been designed with a number of elements in mind. The first is noise pollution. In the contemporary period, there are few active *muezzin*s save those in rural areas or small communities who still regularly call the *adhan* (call to prayer) without the benefit of a microphone or a prerecording. In many communities, particularly large-scale urban areas like Dar es Salaam, the call to prayer is done via microphone or prerecording and is blasted across the landscape, generating a type of "noise pollution" that some have compared to that of urban traffic congestion. Likewise, mosques both large and small often use microphones and speakers on the interior so that sermons can reach all those present. The eco-mosque in contrast has been designed to produce a natural interior echo that allows voices to easily carry and thus erases the need for additional sound technology (Islamic Help n.d.) (Ngolola 2017). In addition, the mosque has been built on a raised platform and has a number of large windows, which benefits the interior space in two ways. Both the positioning and the windows allow for the introduction of natural air flows and ventilation to not only circulate the interior air but also cool it by enabling the release of hot air through exterior vents and the introduction of cool air through vents closer to the floor, reducing the need for fans or other forms of energy-dependent circulation or cooling, although they are present should the need arise (Islamic Help n.d.; Ngolola 2017). For those elements in the mosque that are energy dependent, the structure is fully powered by solar energy produced by panels mounted on the roof, and these fuel the interior lights, plumbing, and fans (which, again, are only activated when needed).

The architectural components of this space also act as a teaching tool for those who utilize it. As Ramadhan Makuka, current imam of the eco-mosque, notes:

Although I have extensive religious knowledge, being at the eco-village has enabled me to make a connection between the religious teachings and the environment. I never knew about permaculture. But being in the Village has enabled me to understand this method through training programs and courses and now, I am teaching others regarding the importance of being protectors of the environment. (Islamic Help n.d.)

Imam Makuka not only serves on the village's advisory board but is also a key figure in the spiritual health of the village. As such, the mosque acts as a structural manifestation of the broader mission of the village as an exercise in holistic sustainability and a microcosm of the village's larger architectural and environmental scheme.

The village is based on ideals of sharing and enabling access of mutual resources and there are many examples of this. The primary water source for the communities surrounding the village is located in the area of the village itself, so the village has constructed water wells in surrounding areas to enable communities to have access to potable drinking water. In addition, village children have been engaged in a "Trees for Change" campaign with the intention of both preserving the area's ecology and providing an additional source of sustenance; to date they have planted over 30,000 trees in local communities. Also, the village itself supports local orphans not living in the village space through the provision of food and other care requirements throughout the year, with food provisions also extended seasonally to local families in need (Ngolola 2017). The village also engages in environmental advocacy work in surrounding communities in the form of training and development projects not only to offset further environmental destruction but also in order to catalyze and strengthen the broader regional economy whose livelihood in the form of food, medicine, employment, etc. depends on the health of the environment. Through these connections, communities are being educated on the effects of climate change and modes of resilience to enhance food security and thus help reduce "the cycle of poverty," as well as in sustainability projects like bee-keeping and responsible farming methods (Islamic Help n.d.).

The lifestyle implemented within the village is one focused on sustainable living practices "based on the principles of faith (Qur'an and Sunnah)" (Islamic Help n.d.). The environmental mission statement of the village declares that its residents "believe in creating a sustainable society by coexisting in harmony and balance with the environment through observing the rights of nature" (Islamic Help n.d.). Based on this, the village has in place a number of preservation practices and procedures designed to create a symbiotic relationship with the surrounding natural environment. Regarding the village composition, each structure on the grounds from the children's homes to the administrative units are constructed to be energy efficient, low maintenance, and "light" in terms of their environmental footprint, making use of functional shading as well as natural ventilation systems and also solar and wind energy. There are also plans for a biogas plant, which will harness the methane produced by livestock in the village (which provide important nutrients for the children living in the village), and convert it into a clean carbon-neutral source of fuel for cooking, with the remnants used as an organic fertilizer (Ngolola 2017).

The landscape of the village has been cultivated using sustainable methods through the use of waste and water management. The total daily water requirement of the village hovers around 5,000 liters, including drinking water and washing, as well as watering livestock and cultivating the gardens. The village has numerous systems in place to meet these requirements. Not only does it maintain two boreholes, water being pumped from the ground using solar and wind power, but rainwater is also harvested from roofing systems to ameliorate the strain on the borehole supply. In addition, water from washing and cooking is reused through a simple system of placing water outlets on tilted concrete surfaces from which the water funnels into a channel system that subsequently delivers it to various garden plots and growing spaces near the domestic spaces. In addition, trees known for their water-retention properties have been planted in specific areas, with the spaces around them being uncultivated to preserve this retention. The campus also maintains a series of ponds that capture water from precipitation and human use and support a population of both fish and water fowl (Ngolola 2017).

Regarding cultivation, the nutrient-poor soil of the village requires additional enrichment in order to make it suitable for planting. One pseudo-experimental method currently being deployed in the village is "permaculture," a term that is derived from "permanent agriculture" and involves recuperating soil using natural ecological systems and processes. It is a broad philosophy of which green architecture is a part, and also includes modes of rehabilitating land through the use of organic fertilizers, water harvesting, rotational farming, and creating a cultivated landscape that in many ways attempts to mimic a natural ecological development. Tanzanian law requires that all orphan-related projects and spaces be fenced as a security measure, but the fence surrounding the village is multi-use in that it also acts as a scaffolding for a vertical gardening system (Ngolola 2017). In addition, the village maintains an active wormery, which not only supports the bird and fish population in the village but also enables the development of organic compost ("vermicompost") via the digestion process of earthworms, and the resulting compost contains an average of five times the amount of nitrogen, seven times the amount of phosphorous, and eleven times the amount of potassium found in regular soil (Islamic Help n.d.). Likewise, a maggot farm is in the works which will complement the wormery by breaking down meat waste into additional organic compost and continuing support for the bird and fish population, with adult flies being trapped before they escape into the environment. The village has also developed an additional eco-project called Farm Plastic, under the direction of local innovator Laurian Mchau, in which plants are grown in repurposed plastic containers using recycled cardboard that is first allowed to decompose and, through this process, becomes a fertile growing medium/compost material for these plants. Lastly, the village also subscribes to the practices of *himā* and *haram* as defined in the Qur'an, a *himā* being a private field or reserved pasture protected against intrusive farming or deforestation activities. With regard to its relationship with *haram*, or that which is forbidden, Surah Al-Baqarah 1.49, narrated by An-Nu'man bin Bashir, notes:

I heard Allah's Apostle saying, "Both legal and illegal things are evident but in between them there are doubtful things and most of the people have no knowledge about them. So whoever saves himself from these suspicious things saves his religion and his honor. And whoever indulges in these suspicious things is like a shepherd who grazes near the *himā* [private pasture or property] of someone else and at any moment he is liable to get in it. (O people!) Beware! Every king has a *himā* and the *himā* of Allah on the earth is His illegal things. Beware! There is a piece of flesh in the body if it becomes good, the whole body becomes good but if it gets spoilt the whole body gets spoilt and that is the heart."

This is in contrast to an area denoted *haram* or protected for other purposes related to human activity. In either case these natural areas are protected or set aside, predominantly for the purpose of conservation but also as an expression of man's acknowledgement of his role as steward over God's creation. In this way, the Qur'an from the beginning has dictated a form of natural conservation, which the village has followed in setting aside certain areas of the complex to develop naturally. There have been positive results from this. Over the past few years, a natural spring has formed and now runs through the village, fed by water that has been maintained by unmediated tree growth (Ngolola 2017).

Yet the mosque and the village are not only intended to model good environmental practices that privilege nature as a resource; they are also intended to collectively act as a social resource. Just as the mosque provides a space of peace and support, the village is designed to be a welcoming supportive environment where one receives education as well as emotional support as part of a distinct community, all returning back to the holistic approach to sustainability. With support figures like "house mothers," in addition to the construction of a family unit among staff and children, a community has been built based on trust, mutual respect, and responsibility to one's self, to those around one, and to the natural environment.

Increasingly, this has become a popular model and has caught on in other East African areas, such as in another children's eco-village in Soy, Kenya, operated by the One Heart Foundation. The village is similar to Islamic Help's eco-village in that it strives to be completely self-sustaining, but it is constructed along the lines of traditional Maasai architecture, which also has a very light environmental footprint, constructed as it is of local materials like mud brick and bamboo, which each have ameliorative thermodynamic qualities. On addition, its organization along the lines of a historical Maasai community emphasizes the character of "community" through the intensive use of shared space, with some small renovations to the original organizational plan to accommodate the necessary housing and institutional facilities. Designed by O2 Design Atelier of Malaysia, which approaches projects largely from the perspective of social context and environmental awareness, the One Heart campus is designed to "positively" contribute "to society" and help "improve lives" (O2 DA 2018).

Both projects are also representative of a broader national movement currently underway in Tanzania that focuses on environmental sustainability as a key component in the country's National Strategy for Growth and Reduction of Poverty (NSGRP) or MKUKUTA (Mkakati wa Kukuza Uchumi na Kupunguza Umaskini Tanzania; Assey et al. 2007, ii). In fact, this plan focuses on the environment as "a foundation for sustainable growth and poverty reduction" and has played a role in a number of current national policies such as the National Environmental Policy[11] and the Environmental Management Act[12] (Assey et al. 2007, ii–iii). This represents a shift from

---

[11] This policy, adopted in 1997, identifies six primary environmental concerns – land degradation, deforestation, loss of wildlife habitats and biodiversity, lack of accessible, good quality water for both urban and rural inhabitants, deterioration of aquatic systems, and environmental pollution, particularly in urban areas – in addition to outlining their contribution to the current poor quality of life for Tanzanian citizens, particularly in urban areas (Assey et al. 2007, 5).

[12] The Environmental Management Act, introduced in 2004, takes the National Environmental Policy further in that it clarifies the roles of local and national government offices and administrations in the areas of "environmental planning and management; pollution prevention and control; environmental information, research and public participation; international obligations; compliance and enforcement; environmental management tools including environmental impact assessment, strategic environmental assessment, and economic instruments; and environmental quality standards." In addition to this, it has catalyzed the codification and standardization of various "environmental management tools" toward enabling and streamlining cooperative action

previous political strategies which considered environmental awareness to be unimportant, even detrimental, to broader goals of economic development and the reduction of poverty (Assey et al. 2007, 5).

This increase in governmental awareness and support has led to the development of other organizations which have thus far attempted to approach environmental awareness from multiple perspectives, some of them even architectural. The Tanzania Green Building Council, founded in 2014, was created with the intent of "driving the sustainable development of Tanzania's built landscape" through partnerships and collaborations between both the government and the private sector (TGBC n.d.).[13] Defining green buildings as "healthy buildings that highlight the reduction of impact on the environment as well as improve the well-being of the individual through efficient design and infrastructure, adapted to the climate as well as resources of the country," the Council highlights not only the different ways that buildings can be made more efficient (water harvesting, use of drought-tolerant plants, ventilation, solar panels, etc.) but also the unique problems facing green building projects in developing countries. Specifically, they highlight the fact that green buildings in such contexts must necessarily utilize a holistic approach so that sustainability is not only being addressed from an environmental and technological standpoint, but also one that privileges the social, economic, and cultural identity of a context. In other words, green building techniques must be applied in a manner that generates ownership over the process by the target community, while also empowering them through their participation in the process (TGBC n.d.).

3.5   Conclusion

Islam has long been firmly embedded in environmental conversations, approaching intersections of nature and sacred space from aesthetic, biomimetic, technological, and contextually focused perspectives. Indeed, the variety of environmentally focused Islamic forms in Africa in many ways seems to reflect the sheer diversity of structural approaches possible in crafting a new environmental architectural iconography based on faith and the earth. Not only do such approaches provide "the operating manual for spaceship earth" (Jencks 2004, 106), but also give form to an "experience of sacredness ... irrespective of canonical symbolization" (Pallasmaa 2015, 21). As Pallasmaa notes: "the artistic and architectural

---

between government branches and agencies toward enacting various programs and initiatives regarding environmental planning (Assey et al. 2007).

[13] It should be noted that the website of the Tanzania Green Building Council is no longer active.

experience of spirituality, detached from deliberate devotional purposes, seems to arise from a nameless and unintentional mental origin, the individual existential experience, which is initiated by a sensitized encounter of the self and the world through the artistic work" (Pallasmaa 2015, 21). Thus, architectural elements combined with environmental complements in many ways can become the mediators of the spiritual.

The Children's Eco-Village, along with Cape Town's kramats and the Djenne mosque, each address in their own way what has been one of the primary criticisms of ecological projects in the contemporary period: many are ill-fitted to the local environmental, cultural, and historical identity of the community. In fact, many sustainable/environmental projects are launched with minimal community input and collaboration and, thus, many modern templates for ecological architecture, most of which are positively bristling with sustainability-based materials and technology, fail to resonate with their context and thus ultimately fail. Considering nature within the construction of space and the ways in which one interacts in a spiritually performative manner with that space will inevitably be diverse. Thus, challenging existing so-called "global" environmental paradigms toward articulating one's own environmental/spiritual identity in the face of a predominantly "Western" ecological rhetoric is key. To quote Sarah Jaquette Ray, "To theorize an inclusive environmentalism, it is necessary to ask whether environmentalism's others can articulate – and even more importantly achieve – their own claims without 'performing' or mimicking mainstream models and discourse" (Ray 2013, 180). This can be accomplished though the realization that individuals are "both continuous and distinct from nature, both individual selves (who are different from nature) and ecological selves (who are part of nature)" (Warren 2015). Thus, many emergent discourses in Islam are focusing on how to "green" masjid space in accordance with Qur'anic environmental doctrine, promoting the philosophy that "green" masjid spaces should not be only ecologically sustainable, but must also focus on the social and spiritual sustainability of the space in accordance with the multiple roles that mosque space can serve.

The case studies presented in this chapter represent an "inclusive environmentalism" that demonstrates the diverse ways in which communities individually "encounter and define environmental concerns" and incorporate natural design elements toward generating structural responses and solutions from a multitude of perspectives (Ray 2013, 180). Along these lines, as Sarah Jaquette Ray notes, "An inclusive environmentalism can emerge only when it is fed by many, varying, and even competing estuaries of concern" (Ray 2013, 181), a process that not

3.5 Conclusion

only generates equity between humanity and the natural world, but also connects the two using interpretive models that are fundamentally synergistic in nature. Along these lines, the diverse articulations of environmentalism that occur within the space of masjids on the continent, only a few of which we have seen, not only align with contemporary tenets of environmental discourse through the lens of spatial form, but also reaffirm faith-based knowledge and principles that underscore Islam as an ecologically sensitive system of belief.

Such a focus also privileges "the plurality of global [Islamic] cultures," enabling the opportunity for "multiple-coding" in which stylistic choices can be made while still privileging an underlying environmental focus (Jencks 2004, 101). Indeed, masjid architecture could potentially address the issues that humankind is facing as a collective species, providing an architectural "iconography of the present," in the words of Charles Jencks (2004, 101), that catalyzes the development of diverse nature/architecture combinations where controlled cultivation of the natural environment is accomplished in line with architecture that is carefully curated to minimize its ecological footprint. By intimately intertwining the structure with its environment, future masjids will function as spaces that not only emphasize the potential for collaborative relationships between architecture and nature[14] but also utilize an aesthetic paradigm that represents a "modern face of Islam" which promotes a universal message of ecological sensitivity.

---

[14] By positioning nature as "one great mosque," in the words of Mahmutćehajić (Mahmutćehajić 2006, 39), one not only has to rethink the implications of what "masjid" implies in this context but also the fact that "nature" is fundamentally a cultural invention and thus "could not stand as a stable, independent term" (Chidester and Linenthal 1995, 7).

4 Masjids on the Move: Mobility and the Growth of "Portable" Islamic Space

The masjid is a mobile space catalyzed by performance and thus perpetually "in transit" with the bodies that activate its existence.

4.1 Introduction

Although it may seem obvious at this point, the masjid is a fundamentally mobile space. In other words, it exists as a plastic spatialization of action between bodies and ritualized movement, or the "animation of... places by the motion of a moving body" (Augé 1995, 80). Yet in thinking of masjids as mobile space, one must also extend this consideration to assess how masjids can function within larger dynamic flows that currently define the contemporary reality of people, objects, concepts, spiritual ideologies, and space on the continent. In other words, in thinking about the masjid, one must question both what it means to be "in motion as a relational affordance between the senses, objects and kinesthetic accomplishments" while also simultaneously considering the politics of *im*mobility that occur through physical and imposed restraints, limitations, and containments (Sheller 2011, 2). As Sheller and Urry note, "there are new places and technologies that enhance the mobility of some peoples and places and heighten the immobility of others, especially as they try to cross borders" (Sheller and Urry 2006, 207), which fundamentally relates to "issues of movement, of too little movement or too much, or of the wrong sort or at the wrong time" (Sheller and Urry 2006, 208). At the heart of it, mobility exists as a different condition of being (or in some cases, *non*being) for different individuals, and thus a rigorous examination of the masjid as mobile space requires a consideration of the concept of mobility and what it means to be transitory, itinerant, and "on the move."

Many consider mobility to be a defining characteristic in the contemporary period of people, objects, concepts, ideologies, and even space. Indeed, it has become such a defining element that scholars have posited

4.1 Introduction

the presence of a "mobility turn" that emerged in the 1990s as a result of the realization that individuals, spaces, and ideas were increasingly coming to be defined by porous geographic boundaries, dynamic social movements, and advancing technology which allowed for multiple types of intersections, encounters, and transformations. Indeed, movement not only across local boundaries but national and even continental borders has now become a general practice, creating new forms of territoriality shaped by different types of interpenetrative flows including "migration, commerce, communication technologies, finance [and] tourism" (Taleb 2005, 51), but also a general situation of "dwelling-in-traveling" wherein one's sense of identity as being rooted to stationary space evolves to the point that identity becomes embedded in the social, political, cultural, and spiritual flows of movement and transience that characterize today's "heterogeneous modernity" (Clifford 1997, 2–3).

Mobility theories are also increasingly breaking down the idea of a "national" domain by "challeng[ing] conventional notions of borders, boundaries, nations, and community" and "redefining the relationship of the global, transnational, and the local" (Taleb 2005, 18). Thus, they constitute a form of pushback against ideas that individuals are fundamentally embedded in predemarcated terrains and that "place" is a physical concept to which people, ideas, cultures, identities, and realities are irrevocably tethered. Such ideas take their basis from established schools of thought that have positioned "sedentarism" or residence as "the manner in which humans should inhabit the earth" à la the dwelling theories of Martin Heidegger, and thus constitute a normative state of being. In addition, the idea of "place-ful-ness" became associated with a type of authenticity based on a humanistic sense of territorialism fundamentally rooted in proto-imperial Enlightenment thought. "Abnormal" conditions of being, on the other hand, were defined by "distance, change, and placelessness" (Sheller and Urry 2006, 209).

A key scholarly figure in this discussion has been Arjun Appadurai,[1] who has noted that the binaries of center/periphery and middle/marginality are increasingly dissolving in the face of "fluid, transnational space produced by 'ordinary' people" (Taleb 2005, 18). This has led to the creation of various "scapes," according to Appadurai (1996), which are characteristic of "the advent of a potent postcolonial cultural perspective that reflects more on the disruptive, conflict-filled heterogeneity of this

---

[1] Another early social scientist to push back against such ideas from a spatial perspective was French anthropologist Marc Augé, who addressed the concept of mobility through space, specifically the conceptualization of the "nonplace," a nonplace being "a space which cannot be defined as relational, or historical, or concerned with identity" (Augé 1995, 77–78).

disordered post-modern world than on the homogenizing effects of global interdependence and consciousness" (Taleb 2005, 50). Further, Appadurai notes that the development of multiple types of "hybrid" identifications has catalyzed a process called "glocalization" through which local identity is increasingly nuanced by global forces, flows, exchanges, and interplays (Taleb 2005, 50). Importantly, this means that cultures and identities based on specific localities are becoming increasingly "deterritorialized," not bound to a specific location and more informed by the "constantly increasing volume and velocity of global dissemination of information, images, and simulacra that is a diffusion of cultural traits gone wild" (Taleb 2005, 51). Thus, the question should be asked: in this day and age, where locality and bounded space only play partial roles in the formation of identity, a process that itself is fundamentally dynamic and evolving, how does an individual, a community, or a nation form and define itself? How are relationships between individuals established through means other than territorial belonging? And how are spaces established to accommodate, produce, and reinforce these new shapes of identity and community as modes of not only creating an inclusive congregation but also differentiating it from others who are nonmembers?

Important to note at this point, however, is that mobility paradigms are not new, nor do they hold that geopolitical states have become obsolete in favor of a "single system of mobile power ... a 'smooth world,' deterritorialized and decentered, without a center of power, with no fixed boundaries or barriers" (Sheller and Urry 2006, 209). Instead, mobility privileges an idea of "liquid modernity," with global flows and scapes acting as modes of examining "how social entities comprise people, machines, and information/images in systems of movement" and renovate ideas of modernity from the "heavy and solid" to the "light and liquid ... in which speed of movement of people, money, images, and information is paramount" (Sheller and Urry 2006, 210). Such approaches have especially shed light on the increasingly unpredictable collisions that are occurring between individuals and spaces that have resulted in the emergence of different types of identities, realities, and practice, particularly with regard to spirituality and performing one's spiritual identity in an increasingly mobile world. Such approaches demonstrate that being mobile and engaging in performative spirituality are not mutually exclusive, that such practice can in fact be a form of "dwelling-in-motion" with mobile spaces acting as "place of and for various activities" on the move and able to be "assembled and reassembled in changing configurations" as a response to changing conditions (Sheller and Urry 2006, 214; 216).

4.1 Introduction

This chapter addresses three such examples of mobilized spiritual space that privilege the reality of today's "on the go" performing body as it creates masjid space that is fundamentally fluid and malleable in nature. Dakar's *car rapides* constitute one such example of mobile masjids that not only represent the spiritual identities of their passengers but also engage in dialogue with the urban, spiritual environment around them. As mobile masjid space, these vehicles are saturated with spiritual power in the form of the numerous spiritual images imprinted on their surfaces, images that not only charge the vehicle with *baraka*, but that activate spiritual memory in their passengers and, in doing so, enable them to participate in a type of mental performance of spirituality (even if it's just a prayer to Allah for a safe trip).

Beyond mobile masjid spaces, however, are also fixed masjid spaces that "presuppose" mobility; in other words, there are "interdependent systems of 'immobile' material worlds" where mobility is supported and localized (Sheller and Urry 2006, 210). The increasing number of airport masjid spaces on the continent serve to support the spiritual practices of Muslims on the move by functioning as "places of in-between-ness," representing "neither arrival nor departure" but instead constituting a "pause" in the movement and circulation of people, pulling them out of the "relay" for a moment to constitute them, however briefly, as "coherent [spiritually performative] human subjects" of faith (Urry and Larsen 2011, 35). As such, these spaces are key to enabling Muslim practitioners to be mobile, even as they constitute an important emergent element of immobilized infrastructure.

That being said, the very concept of space itself has also experienced shifts in reality that move it from an area that is solidly "in the world" to an area beyond it. The emergence of the virtual world and the digital spaces within has catalyzed a shift in considerations not only of what space is, but how human beings interact with it. Along these lines, the appearance of virtual masjids such as that of Touba provide an interesting glimpse into the nature of what spirituality will entail moving forward, particularly with regard to how people perform a spirituality that is not physically but virtually embodied.

Each case study in this chapter thus positions the masjid as a place/nonplace that creates a shared spiritual identity through different types of mobility, generating a fluid *ummah* that is by nature physically and socially transient yet spiritually continuous. Importantly as well, it highlights the relationship between space, people, and performance in a way that is not physically, socially, or geographically rooted, but that can move, shift, and transplant itself in multiple forms and places. "In the new mobilities paradigm," Sheller and Urry note, "places themselves are seen as travelling, slow or fast, greater or shorter distances, within networks of human and nonhuman agents. Places are about relationships, about the placing of peoples, materials, images, and the systems of difference that they perform" (Sheller and Urry 2006, 214).

4.2   Dakar's *Car Rapides* and the Idea of a Vehicular Masjid

Car Rapides, sometimes known as "dead bodies rolling" and even "flying coffins" because of their high accident rate,[2] are public transportation vehicles active in Senegal's capital city of Dakar and have a distinctive history within this city not only as a symbol of urban identity but also as a visuospatial phenomenon that has defined and reconfigured patterns of movement, flow, and stasis within the city itself. They are fundamental contributors to the spiritual charge of Dakar as a predominantly Muslim religious space through the Islamic iconography that is encrusted on every surface of these vehicles, transforming them into moving shrine forms that careen through the streets of Dakar. As a space of "dwelling" or "corporeal inhabitation," the *car rapides* are "experienced through a combination of senses and sensed through multiple registers of motion and emotion" (Sheller and Urry 2006, 216), elements enhanced by their flashy ornamentation, which leaves a ghostly image (or one might say a spiritual residue) on the eye as they whip past, so that one is not quite sure what was real or imagined. In this way, each becomes a uniquely spiritual vehicle of experience.

Car rapides have been iconic fixture of public transport for more than half a century, arriving shortly after World War II as delivery vehicles before eventually evolving to accommodate passengers (Diouf 2002, 45). Because Dakar is a highly visual city and Islamic spirituality plays such a pervasive role in the everyday life of Dakarois, *car rapides* compose one of the many visual and spatial systems relating to the faith that have become largely hegemonic in this urban area. Billboards, street art, pictorial images sold by vendors, mosque forms, prayer mats in marketplaces: all weave the distinctive religiosensual fabric of the city, allowing those who are regularly exposed to them to read them fluently and potentially dismiss them just as quickly as part of the mundane backdrop of this hyperspiritualized urban space. *Car rapides* are potentially read just as casually as one of any number of mobile spaces that clog Dakar's roadways on a daily basis and simultaneously act as mechanisms for

---

[2] This colorful piece of knowledge came to me as my colleague Mame Laye Mbengue and I were driving through the city and were almost crushed in between two of these vehicles racing through the streets.

4.2 The Idea of a Vehicular Masjid

delivering images of spiritual resonance and thus spiritual power to the surrounding urban landscape.

Regarding the vehicles themselves, most if not all of them are Renaults, whose successive models – Gallion, Guilette, and Saviem – have continuously arrived in Senegal secondhand from France over the past thirty or forty years. These vehicles typically arrive in Senegal already in rather bad shape, having outlived their usefulness in France, and are kept alive and on the streets of Dakar through a series of ingenious mechanics and creative engineering solutions that involve the gradual replacement of parts, the replacement of the engine multiple times, and of course numerous repaintings and other bodywork. In addition, because some of the parts for the particular models of trucks are no longer available, contemporary mechanics have had to retrofit alternative parts from other vehicles as a solution, leaving very little of the original bus left over time. Currently there are somewhere between 2,000 and 2,500 *car rapides* active in Dakar, although this number might be conservative. They are typically owned by companies within the city, although sometimes private individuals own them as well, and the names of owners are often featured in the decoration on the truck. Some drivers have even been able to buy their trucks and occasionally become very successful fleet owners (Tacq 2003).

Car rapides were named as such because when they were first introduced, they offered a much faster mode of transport than the horse-drawn cart (which is still somewhat ubiquitous in the suburbs of Dakar) (Tacq 2003). Yet *car rapides* are only allowed to operate in certain areas of the city, namely the side streets and sections of the older areas that have not been subject to expansions in roadway infrastructure. This is largely due to their propensity to break down and clog the roads when picking up passengers. But because of their constrained range of movement, these vehicles have created pockets of space in the city where one is constantly exposed to the images of these trucks that collectively form a selective imagescape within the capital city, where the parameters of encounter with these moving visual symbols of culture and religious identity are strictly demarcated. Indeed, they remain iconic in the contemporary period for both their brightly painted exteriors, their reckless road behavior, and the "passengers and conductors [who] sometimes perilously hang off the backs and sides of the overcrowded vehicles" (Quist-Arcton 2016).

But to understand the relevance of these vehicles and the spiritual environment they create, it is important to understand the history of the city itself as a fluid urbanscape that has in many ways crafted and been crafted by these vehicles. The region itself had long been part of the trans-Saharan trade networks, exchanging goods, services, individuals, and cultural systems across vast regions and geographies, with Islam arriving sometime around the eleventh century as a result of this trade (Farivar 2011, 77). Its presence would be felt especially within the regional kingdoms of the dominant power brokers of the area at the time, primarily the Wolof, the Sereer, and the Fulbe kingdoms, with the Wolof Empire becoming the dominant political power in the region around the mid-fifteenth century. This is also around the time that the Portuguese arrived off the West African coast and there has been speculation that the name "Senegal" in fact derives from a possible Portuguese misinterpretation of the Wolof phrase *sunu gaal*, which means "our canoe" (Farivar 2011, 77). Although Muslims were by no means a dominant group in this context, they were the only largely literate class, which gave them access to very specific social and political positions within society, from the seventeenth to the nineteenth centuries, when some of the first Muslim towns (including those that would eventually become Dakar) began to emerge in the region (Ross 2006, 121).

When the Wolof Empire collapsed in the early seventeenth century, regional Muslim leaders began to fill the power vacuum left behind, and became increasingly powerful in the seventeenth and eighteenth centuries during which the areas and islands off the coast of Senegal came to be colonized by successive European nations, including the French, the Portuguese, the Dutch, and the English. Many of the spaces and forts they would establish along the coast would also become the staging sites for the collection and transfer of enslaved individuals across the Atlantic, the infamous Gorée Island off the peninsula of Dakar being one of them. The threat of enslavement was a major impetus for many local populations to flock to the Islamic faith, which came to be viewed as "a refuge for the powerless, who were the primary victims of the violence and insecurity spurred by the slave trade, dynastic wars, and French encroachment" (Babou 2007, 31; in Foley 2010, 22). Along those lines, the Muslim towns that had begun to emerge during this period were seen as a type of spatial sanctuary, largely because the clerics who administered them had important resources at their disposal, i.e. "manpower in the form of student labor" to create well-protected communities (Ross 2006, 122).

The continuation of this situation into the nineteenth and early twentieth centuries would also eventually catalyze the growth of a series of Sufi orders (*tariqah*) – specifically the Qâdiriyyah, the Tijaniyya, the Muridiyya, and the Layenne orders – some of whom, like the Qâdiriyyah, were imported in the eleventh and twelfth centuries from North Africa and the Middle East (Ross 2006, 131). Others arose after the 1880s and were organized around the personality cults of local holy men such as Cheikh Amadou Bamba (1853–1927) (Muridiyya), al-Hajj Umar Tall (c. 1796–1864) (Tijaniyya),

4.2 The Idea of a Vehicular Masjid   191

and Seydina Limamou Laye (1845–1909) (Ross 2006, 250). By this period, the French had firmly established a colonial foothold in the territory, appointing the first French governor of Senegal in 1895. Through jihad-based military action and other more peaceable forms of resistance, these brotherhoods began pushing back against French domination and eventually came to be viewed as a threat to the French colonial administration, which took various steps to remove power from these movements. In one case, leader of the Muridiyya order, Amadou Bamba, was exiled by the French, once to Gabon from 1895 to 1902 and again to Mauritania from 1903 to 1907. Interestingly enough, during each period, Bamba was said to have performed miracles that not only increased his popularity among his followers but also drew additional people to the faith.

By the late 1950s, numerous continent-wide movements toward independence under the leadership of highly charismatic leaders like Kwame Nkrumah, Julius Nyerere, and in Senegal's case, Leopold Senghor, led to a series of watershed moments. In 1960, Senegal and Mali merged to form the independent federation of Mali, which unfortunately collapsed within two months, after which Senegal successfully became recognized as an independent country on June 20 of that same year, with Leopold Senghor becoming the newly independent nation's first democratically elected president (Foley 2010, 29–30). Senegal was one of seventeen nations that gained independence in 1960 and was followed by over twenty more in the following decade or two, with much of the initial success of these transitions to independence being facilitating by rulers like Senghor.

Regarding the aforementioned Sufi brotherhoods, each has grown proportionally to the population since independence and acquired various interests in a number of economic, cultural, and educational enterprises. As Eric Ross notes, Sufi brotherhoods not only in Senegal but throughout the Islamicate hold to a similar hierarchical structure that governs religious leadership and brotherhood administration. At the pinnacle is the *khalīfah* (caliph or leader) who constitutes the "spiritual head of the order and representative of its founding shaykh" and, in the context of Senegal, is a direct male descendent of the founder of the order. Below the caliph are familial subgroups whose leaders are also known as "caliphs," which means that oftentimes the head of the order is known as the caliph general. From these sub-caliphs, as it were, come the Cheikhs (*muqaddams*), who are typically responsible for the administrative work required to keep the brotherhood functioning while the caliphs engage in more spiritual exercises. The role of Cheikh is also passed through the male familial line, with those below them either being students of the faith (*taalibes*) or general adherents (Ross 2006, 134). This hierarchal structure is necessary for the brotherhoods to accomplish their various functions, which include meeting the educational and devotional needs of their members while also networking with other brotherhoods and secular governmental agencies to advocate for the group. They also mobilize resources for the numerous spiritual events that they each must host and for charitable activities as well (Ross 2006, 135). Many have developed healthy international communities as well, creating "satellite" brotherhood communities around the world which support the growth and maintenance of brotherhood "capital cities" like Touba for the Muridiyya, Tivaouane for the Tijaniyya, and a variety of others (Ross 2006, 251). Likewise, each has created a complex identity system formulated through the establishment of pilgrimages and other sacred collective events, educational institutions, mosques and other religious buildings, and even charitable organizations. The brotherhoods have collectively emerged as "among the most important forces of urbanization and urban development" in the country, perhaps due to their historical role in the creation of new community settlements from an established foundation of clerical lineages (Ross 2006, 251–252).

As such, the various layers of Sufism that each brotherhood applies to the fabric of urban areas like Dakar create a series of sites "where differences in living Islam are enacted" and made manifest (Janson 2011, 102). As such, the city becomes a space of diversity, defined on the one hand by established "moral orders and ontologies" as well as "movements of commodities, ideas, and forms ... [as well as] ... the traffic of objects, sounds, and colors within the city" (Wilhelm-Solomon et al. 2017, 2; 18) toward creating an intricate Islamic cartography.

Part of this Sufi-based cartography are the *car rapides*, whose visual program is composed both of decorative textual script and image-based compositions that collectively generate sensual experience (Figure 4.1a and 4.1b). The truck's base decoration begins with three basic colors – blue, white, and yellow – which are mandated by the city government as identification and differentiation from other urban transportation operators (Tacq 2003). These colors provide the base background for the subsequent mix of text, pattern, image, color, and abstracted form that is applied to the surface, much of it geared toward the expression of religious identity.[3] In fact, the decorative program is so intensive that in many ways it seems to express the type of *horror vacui* mentality that is sometimes found on mosque-based architectural envelopes in Dakar

---

[3] Although a vast majority of the trucks are decorated along the lines of a Muslim religious identity, there are in fact a handful of "Christian" trucks that are equally exuberant and feature popular religious figures like Saint Christopher as well as Christian religious symbols including crosses, doves, and the Bible.

Figure 4.1 a and b Views of *car rapides*, Dakar, Senegal, 2018. Images by the author.

such as the Massalikoul Djinane, whose adornment seems to dissolve the very surface underneath it via the decorative weight of its surface embellishment.

In terms of the themes behind the decoration, the Islamic faith is central, expressed through word, image, and sometimes sculptural construct. Perhaps one of the first visual elements one sees when facing a *car rapide* is the text *Alhamdoulillahi*, translated variously as "Praise be to God" or "Thank you God."[4] These words of praise are painted using a specific font supposedly invented by truck painter Moussa Tine, who began decorating buses in the 1970s (Tacq 2003). The font, composed of black block lettering with a red "shadow" underneath, is a ubiquitous, defining textual design facet on the front of *car rapides* everywhere in Dakar not only because of its visual clarity but also because one must always put one's "best face forward." In addition to this "introductory" text as it were, *car rapides* also often feature the names of religious leaders such as Cheikh Amadou Bamba or Khalifa Ababacar Sy, as well as the names of holy towns like Touba and Tivaouane, often located on the front of a *car rapide* and scrawled across the metal frame above the windshield in large block letters. These elements often speak to the specific religious orientation of the owner.

In addition, in the context of the decorative programs of *car rapides*, text and image occupy similar visual conditions in that the type of literacy required to read and interpret both is not necessarily based on an understanding of linguistic mechanics but a visual association between the image of text and its message. Thus, while many Dakarois might not be able to understand the linguistic mechanics of the Arabic phrase *Alhamdoulillahi*, the word image acts as a visual object whose connection with the idea of praising God has become firmly cemented. To borrow from Elias's classification of a similar scenario associated with textual images in Pakistani trucks, "Theirs is a form of contextual literacy that does not allow them to read the newspaper and write basic letters as the census data claims they can, but does enable them to recognize certain important words and phrases, the majority of which are of religious significance" (Elias 2011, 41). In other words, text in this case "functions visually" as an image-based icon (Elias 2012, 281).

---

[4] The term/phrase "Alhamdulillah" or "praise be to the God" is used universally across the global Islamicate to convey greetings, begin prayers, and bestow blessings. Because of its broad usage, the term has been transliterated to accommodate diverse linguistic interpretations, subsequently resulting in a seemingly infinite variety of linguistic iterations of the term, many of which are phonetic in nature and include *hamdullah*, *hamdala*, *al ham du allah*, *al hamdu lillah*, *hamdoullah*, and the aforementioned *Alhamdoulillah*.

4.2 The Idea of a Vehicular Masjid

Next to religious text, religious imagery typically takes the appearance of architectural forms and notable religious figures. Regarding architectural forms, importantly most of the architectural forms included do not represent universal Muslim spaces like the Ka'ba or the mosque in Medina, but instead speak to regional architectural structures, most notably the Great Mosque in Touba and, in particular, Touba's main minaret entitled Lamp Fall, named after Amadou Bamba's most powerful and devoted disciples, Cheikh Ibra Fall. Most often, these architectural images appear as sculpted metal forms that have been attached to the roof rack either at the front or the back of the truck, sometimes both. The metal composition itself may be only "loosely" architectural in the sense that it is a largely two-dimensional construct that has been cut from metal sheets and decorated with paint and additional metal ornamentation. Rarely is the cutout itself an exact contour of the minaret or mosque form. Yet their repetition in the context of not only truck imagery but also that of drawings, paintings, murals, and other forms of visual representation around the city give it a legibility that is aided by the presence of text that identifies the particular religious identity associated with the structure. Thus, this form acts as a simplistic quotation that plays on established visual schemata for recognition rather than an exact visual duplication of the form to evoke the genre of "spiritual construct."

With regard to religious figures, rarely in the contemporary period does one see actual paintings of religious figures on the bodies of *car rapides*. Dakar's enormously prosperous market in posters and decals of important religious figures has provided a convenient source of adhesive imagery, which has allowed a proliferation of religious figures to come to adorn multiple services. With regard to *car rapides*, these decals often appear directly in the center of the windshield and are of various sizes, some the size of a postcard, others seeming almost life-size. But, importantly, these figural decals are almost always black and white, allowing them to show up with clarity against the windshield and enabling one to distinguish various features that, like the aforementioned architectural constructs, maintain a certain visual legibility based on their near constant usage across visual media in the city.

The one other space on the vehicles where one will typically find representations of religious figures is on the interior, according to the taste and religious views of the driver. Ranging from a photocopied image of a particular saint taped to the back of the driver's seat to a virtual wall of posters of religious figures from the various brotherhoods in Senegal, the interior space of the truck is the exact opposite of the exterior. Typically painted a single color (often a dark blue or green), the only visual embellishment beyond the people who ride in the cab itself are these images, which in many ways creates a somewhat charismatic space with regard to religious belief, allowing these images to become a visual locus during one's commute. And through their singular presence and watchful gaze, perhaps they bestow *baraka* on the passengers, as well as a sense of surveillance which, according to local practice, is another reason such images are included. Because passengers have been known to argue, fight, or engage in other questionable behavior in the backs of some of these buses, it is thought that the all-seeing eyes of these various Cheikhs, saints, and religious leaders create something of a panoptic gaze within the enclosed space of the truck. Others feel it is pseudo-blasphemous to introduce the images of these saintly figures into the dirty, smelly, largely profane interior space of the *car rapide*. Yet this creates an interesting juxtaposition of the sacred and secular. Within the context of the *car rapide*, the sacred has in many ways become commodified as a decorative element meant to attract customers, and the secular has come to coopt religious devices as a mode of capitalizing on their "contagious *baraka*," i.e. their ability to manifest blessing and protection on the forms they are applied to (Elias 2011, 26).

Yet perhaps the most religiously ambiguous representations on *car rapides*, however, are not necessarily the figures represented, but parts of figures, specifically eyes, which not only appear in significant numbers on the front of a truck but also along the sides. There is significant speculation as to who, or perhaps what, these eyes actually are, although most seem to agree that they occupy a symbolic space between the religious and the talismanic. One of the most well-known "functions" of these images seems to be protection against what most term "the evil eye." The phenomenon of the evil eye exists in multiple cultures and religious traditions around the world and is predominantly concerned with the belief that a malign power can be transferred through a jealous, covetous, or even admiring gaze. The belief in the malignant power of a covetous gaze is so pervasive in fact that numerous culturally embedded formulas have been created over time to protect against it, ranging from specific utterances warning the evil eye away to the creation of specific amulets designed to repel its power. Some protective objects seen in trucks to this end, for example, are toddler shoes hanging from the roof (it is believed that childish innocence can offer the truck protection from harm) (Graziano 2014, 27), and cow tails hanging from the bumper, cow tails having been traditionally used as fly whisks and thus able to "shoo" evil away (Nice 2018). In addition, almost every *car rapide* includes as part of its design program a pseudo-diamond-shaped rectilinear form on each side of the bus. Although it has obvious aesthetic value, it also has visual resonance with numerous regional traditions involved in the visualization of *hatumeres*, or "magical squares," whose specific configuration was intended to add protection and blessing to the surfaces on which they appeared. As such, this form can be found on embroidered clothing, Qur'anic boards, architectural forms, and even jewelry. Yet this square is one of any number of other potential protective objects that might include various flags, items from regional Sufi shrines, and blessed objects that act in a similar capacity.

Visual symbols have also been deployed in this manner and the symbol of the eye is perhaps one of the most pervasive across the Islamic world. Similar belief systems exist in Senegal and thus the deployment of eyes as not only a constant but also a copious visual feature on *car rapides* is perhaps not a surprise. Supposedly introduced by Moussa Tine, who was also responsible for the development of the *car rapides*' "font" and undoubtedly a number of other decorative devices on these trucks, these eyes were specifically intended to combat the evil eye along the lines of area traditions that had people wear protective amulets around their necks and waists while also engaging in protective behaviors like avoiding eye contact to prevent the establishment of a malignant connection (Graziano 2014, 24–25). Yet over time, the symbol of the eye has evolved in that it has gained additional identities, including becoming the eyes of Cheikh Amadou Bamba, whose own eyes in the only photograph available of him are mysteriously hidden and are thus seen to provide proof of his ownership of a mystical sight that precluded the necessity of actual physical eyes.[5] Because of his mystical sight, Bamba is not only capable of defending against the evil eye but also capable of seeing road obstacles that the truck driver cannot, thus potentially protecting the truck and its inhabitants from unfortunate disasters. Along these lines, the presence of eyes, particularly in the front of the truck, may also act as a complement to the ubiquitous presence of the saintly decal gracing the windshield, giving an actual identity to the "eyes" that seem to be staring out from the bus so intently and thus giving the "face" of the bus an actual identity.

Yet the anthropomorphization of these trucks may have other less spiritual components as well. As one artist notes, "It's just like my face with a nose and a mouth – with an extra pair of eyes at the back" (Quist-Arcton 2016). In addition, for every spiritual icon or talisman present on these vehicles, there seem to be an equal amount of contemporary, secular, and even merely decorative talismans, with some symbols occupying dual roles across each category. In addition to religious text

---

[5] For more information on this, see Allen F. Roberts, Mary N. Roberts, and Gassia Armenian, *A Saint in the City: Sufi Arts of Urban Senegal* (Los Angeles: UCLA Fowler Museum of Cultural History), 2006.

adorning the truck such as *Alhamdoulillahi*, there is also text indicating the name or the company of the owner, often with mention of the RTYE or the Regroupement des Transporteurs de Yoff l'Environnment, the association of *car rapide* owners whose inclusion of the acronym is a sign of their membership in the organization (Graziano 2014, 26). Likewise, every bus is required to scrawl "transport commune" along the side for licensing and identification purposes. In terms of images, three of the most dominant are horses, eagles, and lions.

The horse's inclusion speaks to both historical and symbolic elements. Historically, horses have been considered one of the fastest modes of transport, as well as a symbol of the brave exploits of Lat Dior Ngoné Latyr Diop, known as Lat Dior, who was a resistance leader and a king in his own right and who fought against French colonialism from the back of his famous horse Maalaw. There is a contemporary statue of Maalaw at the center of a roundabout a short distance from the Grand Mosque in Dakar. Thus, the inclusion of horses speaks not only to their speed (thus framing *car rapides* potentially as "contemporary horses") but also their role as one of the first modes of rapid transportation in the region (Graziano 2014, 24).

The eagle, in contrast, speaks less to Senegal's history than it does to an appreciation of strength and power, which the bird embodies. In addition, through its inclusion in the truck's decorative program, the image might also potentially transfer some of those qualities (or at least their ideals) to the vehicle itself in a way similar to the mode through which religious symbols transfer blessing and protection (Graziano 2014, 24). The lion, on the other hand, is considered a national symbol of Senegal, present on the Senegalese coat of arms and is even part of the nickname for the Senegalese national soccer team; thus it comes as no surprise that one occasionally sees a lion holding a soccer ball in one paw on *car rapides* and a cut-out metal world cup trophy screwed in to the luggage rack of the truck.

Perhaps one of the most interesting and increasingly pervasive visual symbols one sees on *car rapides* in the contemporary period, though, is that of the Nike swoosh, representing not only a general appreciation for athleticism but also a deep embeddedness in contemporary global branding, fashion, and popular culture. Occasionally paired with the words "Air Jordan," Nike paraphernalia is pervasive in Dakar and thus has incorporated itself easily and seamlessly into Dakar's modern visual culture. Yet its inclusion on the *car rapides* not only speaks to a certain contemporary sensibility, but also potentially to the ornamental properties of the design itself as a somewhat abstract form that can nonetheless be deployed in an aesthetically pleasing manner.

4.2 The Idea of a Vehicular Masjid

There are a number of visual elements present on *car rapides* that are included merely to enhance the artistic merit of the truck, one reason for this being that more attractive *car rapides* tend to be favored by customers. Thus, in some cases, *car rapides* become covered in streamers, flags, and even LED lights trailing after them down the road. Other designs that grace these trucks for beautification purposes are of the vegetal variety, with any number of floral and fruit-based designs applied to various surfaces. The meanings behind these images beyond their aesthetic appeal have been variously explained as referring to the beauty of rural vegetation (Graziano 2014, 25), exhorting the health value of fruit and green vegetables, and even being reflective of embroidery traditions often done by "good girls from good families" (Rainfoy 2015). There is also a possible religious element here, particularly in the case of pineapples, which are a highly common image on these trucks and have in some more popular Islamic traditions been linked to ideas of hospitality.[6] Apples have also been loosely connected to ideas of luck and success, but as one driver noted, "Everyone likes apples. Why not paint them?" (Nice 2018).

Both sacred and secular decorations tend to be applied in a symmetrical manner in a way that increases their visual appeal, leading to a consideration of the organization of design and the strategies of image placement behind it. Specifically, the design of the truck seems to subscribe to "a system which strengthens their function" (Lefebvre 1989, 217). The preponderance of imagery and attachments on a *car rapide* are typically found on the front, as are the most religiously and talismanically direct symbols, because "This is the part of the truck which is seen first by God and the supernatural spirits when it drives" (Lefebvre 1989, 217). This is a system that seems to govern the decoration of every *car rapide* with few, if any, deviations. Similarly standardized is the aforementioned *Alhamdoullilah*, which appears across the front directly below the windshield with invocations of specific religious figures and spaces appearing directly above the windshield. These elements are often accompanied by vegetal flourishes, religious symbols like the star and crescent, or design extensions that include previously mentioned metal cutouts of forms that range from Lamp Fall to a World Cup trophy. As such, the front space of the *car rapide* becomes the "most semiotically charged part of the truck, where (largely unstated) strictures govern the placement and content of decoration more so than anywhere else on the vehicle" (Elias 2011, 96).

---

[6] Graziano also notes that two pineapples often appear on either side of the frontal *Alhamdoullilah* text, signaling two regional areas in and around Senegal – Guinea and the Casamance – which are notable for their pineapple production (Graziano 2014, 26).

The sides subsequently become extensions of the general design strategy presented on the face of the truck, providing a "continuity of information" (Elias 2011, 151), whose inclusion and arrangement of visual elements not only place the truck firmly within the iconographic system of *car rapides* more generally but also reveal variations in style, decorative embellishment, and text that position the vehicle firmly within the context of the individual owner in addition to "within the wider world in a geographic or societal sense" (Elias 2011, 93).

Moving from the front to the sides, the previously mentioned figure of the horse can usually be found next to the driver's-side door, whereas the eagle typically occurs in the lower right-hand side of the vehicle close to the rear. Centrally placed is the diamond-shaped design, topped with text which identifies the truck as a communal transport vehicle. Decorative elements found in the surrounding space of this design include eyes, Nike swooshes, and vegetal decorations, all of which, as noted, are designed to maximize the visual plane and create an exciting eye-catching composition.

The rear of the bus is perhaps the most visually unexciting, possibly because this is where people typically enter and exit the bus and also where an *apprenti* (driver's helper or assistant), who collects the money and orients the passengers, typically stands; this is also where decoration would be most likely to get damaged, requiring more repairs than the rest of the truck, which typically gets repainted every three years or so. Because of this, visibility is often obscured either by the presence of bodies, wear to the area, or physical damage. Yet just as the front of the bus constitutes an introductory textual surface on which to inscribe religious affiliations and proclamations, the back constitutes a space of closure for the bus's textual narrative. One often sees the phrase *Yala Yana*, which loosely translated means "God is wise," or *Sope Naby*, which also praises God. One might also see the last name of the owner of the truck, or even a repeat of *Alhamdoulillahi*, which in this case, according to the truck artist Nice, refers to the fact that "God must always be the beginning and end in everything you do" (Nice 2018). In addition, such phrasing reinforces the protective aspect that these spiritual evocations are intended to accomplish, particularly in light of the *car rapides'* rather dismal safety record.

Additional decorated elements on the *car rapides* include the wheels, the rear-view mirrors, the fenders and bumpers, and the roof rack, but it is important to note that the design elements of the truck itself cannot be viewed independently. They must be viewed as a collaborative, collective semiotic system that is "greater than the sum of their individual parts or decorative motifs" (Elias 2011, 111). The trucks not only stand as icons to the religious identity of the region, but also statements of individual modern identity not only of the owner, but of those who patronize the *car rapides* and share equally in a contemporary global society influenced by Nike swooshes and World Cup glory. Thus it pays to turn attention to the individuals who are responsible for dictating the visual realm in which these vehicles exist as moving statements of religious, cultural, and personal identity.

While the visual program is usually created according to the specifications of the owner, it is the truck artist whose individual creative style is responsible for the end result. *Car rapide* artists typically make their living engaging in the visual embellishment of various surfaces, ranging from *car rapides* and other vehicles to the sides of walls and houses, as well as everyday objects like trunks. Thus, the visual compositions they create are intimately related to the shape, contour, texture, and function of the object or vehicle that they are embellishing. Their designs are also often governed by established iconographic standards and compositions which are enhanced and made unique by their own individual interpretation of the systems in place. With regard to *car rapides*, the same artists typically work on the same trucks year after year, meticulously recreating the same decorations over and over again so that the truck's visual identity and its iconic connection to its owner remains intact over time. Yet despite this meticulous attention to detail, small changes and shifts do occur, which allow the visual identity of the truck to evolve slowly over time.

Truck art as an occupation is usually rooted in a family tradition, like many traditional artisanal skillsets. One truck artist named Kalidou Diallo, who is known by his nickname "Neyoo," was first taught the trade by his uncle and then by his cousin (Quist-Arcton 2016). Every painted decoration on the truck is done by hand with car paint that has been individually mixed to achieve specific hues. In the area of the Gare Routiere Lat Dior, where most of the bodywork on the city's *car rapides* occurs, there are also numerous workshops where various removable truck parts like bumpers, fenders, grills, and luggage racks are decorated before being attached to the vehicle.

Each artist has their own particular style and though at first glance each truck appears to be some minor variation of the same design, there are subtle differences in color, composition, and execution that act as a type of artist's signature. Almost every truck artist knows the "style" of his competitors and can identify at a glance the decorative composition of the work of an artist established in Dakar. Along these lines, there is a great deal of competition between truck artists in Dakar, which creates a certain guardedness with regard to sharing trade secrets like painting technique and the mixing of color. But the true effect of the style of the truck artist is far more subtle. Indeed, even as many if not most of the visual compositions are created in the context of a highly repetitive standardized system of representation, the ways in which they are perceived and the subtle differences in style and technique "give rise to symbols and symbols give rise to thought" (Elias 2011, 125). Despite this, the systematization of iconography remains important. Alain LeFebvre notes that:

[the artist's] message must be understood by everyone, and the motifs have to be clear in their symbolism. A new abstract language would have the opposite effect, because cryptic signs cannot immediately inform about the trucker's identity and personality. The decorations would lose their strength if reading them required too many intellectual speculations. One should be able to read a truck like a poster, rapidly and easily, with a symbolism known by everyone. (Lefebvre 1989, 218)

As such, legible symbols remain, albeit adjusted in ever so subtle ways to suit the needs and creative designs of the artists. "It is through his layout of known motifs, his capacity to compose with or without taking the given frames into account, and his self-confidence in the drawing itself that a painter becomes popular" (Lefebvre 1989, 218).

But to zoom out for a moment from the specifics of the *car rapides'* decorative program, it is the visual system itself that constitutes a mode of "emplacement" for *car rapides* as part of the city's religious and cultural identity (Elias 2011, 93). The repetition of forms, which subsequently creates an easily recognizable, readable semiotic system, is not arbitrary but a strategic aspect of Dakar's larger visual and spatial program, while also acting as a collaboration between three different personalities: the owner, the driver, and the artist. These decorative programs do not preclude or condemn the production of representational art. Jamal Elias notes that Islam is often incorrectly viewed as "somehow less 'visual' than others and more attuned to words and text;" however, Elias rightly points out that this not only inappropriately places "text" and "image" in a binary relationship but it also privileges a certain fundamentalist imagery with regard to Islam that rarely occurs within "the actual lived forms of Islam" (Elias 2011, 12; 15). Rather, these decorations allow for "the hybridization and heterogeneity that is essential to modern existence" (Elias 2011, 15).

In this way, the *car rapide* acts as a mode of creating "alternative expressive spaces" within the city's visual topography (Elias 2011, 9), which in itself has allowed these forms to bleed over into other aspects of Senegalese visual and consumer culture as well. Tourists can now buy metal trunks decorated in the manner of *car rapides* (some even have wheels) along with smaller, locally made, wooden toy versions of

4.2 The Idea of a Vehicular Masjid

the *car rapides*, which are available in nearly every market in the city. Thus, the *car rapides* have come to experience alternate modes of commodification via their transformation into craft and a "folkloric" appendage "of the national and multinational capitalist system" (García 2000, 76). Likewise, the experience of a *car rapide* ride itself has come to be seen in some ways as an "authentic" cultural experience; tourists coming into Dakar, particularly the French, often ride on *car rapides* as part of a broader Senegalese "cultural education" (Menbue 2018).

Yet another way the *car rapide* has been commodified as a cultural production has been through the lens of the Western museum. Notably, in 2015, a *car rapide* entitled "Bonne Mere" (Good Mother) left Dakar for the Musee de l'Homme in Paris to be displayed as part of the museum's permanent installation. The truck itself underwent massive amounts of renovation in a collaboration between a number of artists ranging from sheet metal workers to upholsterers to painters. The result of this work is a *car rapide* that, while maintaining many of the systematic adornments that define *car rapides* in Dakar as visual objects, contains additional images and text that do not constitute part of the design oeuvre of *car rapides*. Tragic scenes from Senegal's history, including the killing of Senegalese troops by the French during World War II, and the tragic sinking of the "Joola," a ferry boat which was carrying nearly 2,000 people when it sank off the coast of the Gambia in 2003, are featured on the Bonne Mere in a strange and somewhat bizarre innovation on the *car rapides'* established visual program. Additional drawings of wrestlers (referring to Senegal's national sport) along with a yin and yang symbol, topped by the image of a religious leader surrounded by his students (*talibes*) are only a handful of examples of the various ways in which this bus was specifically crafted to function as a "frieze of Senegal" (Rainfoy 2015). This is according to Dr. Alain Epelboin, an anthropologist affiliated with Le Centre National de la Recherche Scientifique in France, and Ndiabou Sega Toure, the Director of Studies at the French Institute for Foreign Students (IFE) at the Cheikh Anta Diop University in Dakar (UCAD), the two specialists who catalyzed this project (Rainfoy 2015). Yet in generating this broad visual program, the Bonne Mere was actively displaced from the tradition that made *car rapides* a reflection of Dakar's urban personality and became instead a carefully choreographed visual object curated for a non-Senegalese audience as a type of cultural fetish object, which explains its inclusion in one of the more controversial neocolonial museological spaces in the world and its display alongside various Africa-based and Afro-Islamic objects of spiritual import.

Yet perhaps such an event is fortuitous, given the fact that the Senegalese government is currently trying to phase out *car rapides* and replace them with safer, more reliable transport. Although many Dakarois see *car rapides* as smelly, noisy, unsafe, and fundamentally trite, they maintain an important position in Dakar's transportation system as one of the cheapest modes of public transportation; thus, their potential phasing out poses a problem to the same public that sees them as a nuisance. It is because of this that some believe that *car rapides* still have a fairly decent lifespan in front of them; until a commensurate transportation option arises, *car rapides* will continue to have a role in the urban landscape, not only in a functional sense but also as an important part of Dakar's urban visual/spiritual landscape.

There is one aspect of the *car rapide*'s visual program that has yet to be addressed, however, and that is the fact that these images, when experienced in the urban setting, are not stationary. They are in a state of motion and thus it must be asked what effect this has on not only their visual presence but also their semiotic one in terms of their contribution in shaping the urban space into that of an Islamic city. It is in this way that the discussion of the *car rapides* comes to intersect with that of the space of the masjid, not only because of the highly charged nature of the vehicle itself, but because of the performative bodies that inhabit it and interact with its visual and spiritual program. Regarding the realities of these bodies as they interact with *car rapides* within the city space, Lapidus notes, "The distribution of persons within a metropolitan community is never capricious" (Lapidus 1969, 172). People self-organize across multiple spaces according to numerous types of self-orienting strategies, many of which overlap and cross-pollinate to create a vast intersectional space where people constantly traverse the borders and boundaries of the multiple communities to which they belong and constantly form, reform, and reconstruct space along those lines. Or, to quote Vertivec (2015, 14): "Urban dwellers ... have developed a kind of agility and ability to live simultaneously in many different spheres" (quoted in Wilhelm-Solomon 2017, 14) and they use spatial tools such as *car rapides* to make this reality possible. Thus, just as every individual stands as an intersectional being, every space must also be intersectional (a lesson learned in Chapter 1) and, within the context of the city, the various roles and realities that people and by association space occupy create a vast matrix of interlocking, connecting, and sometimes competing components that collectively contribute to the larger social and functional reality of an urban space.

As Malcomess and Wilhelm-Solomon note "Religious space is ... not simply large-scale spatial production or control, but encompasses the errant movement of urban residents as they cross the city" (Malcomess and Wilhelm-Solomon 2017, 58). Thus, it would make sense that the modes through which urban bodies accomplish this movement also have a direct effect on crafting religious aura, with repetitive design elements in spaces like *car rapides* calling to mind performances of ritual prayer, the counting of beads, and the undertaking of various forms of *dikhre*. The routes taken by these buses on a daily basis as they go round and round within a circumscribed urban subspace evokes the circumambulation of religious spaces that takes place in religious contexts ranging from regional shrine pilgrimages to the great Hajj in Mecca. The widespread and consistent presence in the city of *car rapides* also endows them with a pseudo-psychological aspect as well in terms of the response they elicit from their surrounding viewers. Although many Dakarois view *car rapides* as (unpleasant), overly familiar, and largely unremarkable inhabitants of the city's urban environment, their hegemonic visual presence has come to function as part of Dakar's general *habitus* and thus a type of urban truth for the city's inhabitants, who themselves compose their identities along similar organizational guidelines as those applied to *car rapides'* external surfaces. Indeed, one might see the *car rapide* as a type of mechanistic metonym for many contemporary citizens of Dakar: a complex combination of religious propaganda, cultural/historical engagement, and global popular encounter on the exterior, with an interior focused on one's moral life and those religious figures who govern it. In this way, *car rapides* could be classified as moving shrines requiring a level of engagement for them to function as such.

Yet *car rapides* also enable the performance of prayer (albeit not an ideal one) as it is so often undertaken within the mobile lifestyles that an urban space requires. For those who dwell in motion, accomplishing daily prayers as part of living one's religion while on the move requires a specific approach to the idea of masjid space that nonetheless allows one to exist comfortably as both a Muslim and a modern individual. As such, *car rapides* also reflect a specific type of separation from the surrounding urban landscape that places those who inhabit them simultaneously within two different temporal frameworks. In other words, Muslim travelers exist simultaneously as both a part of contemporary urban society on the one hand and as part of a temporally embedded global religious community on the other. In addition, not only do *car rapides* maintain a visible, modern Muslim-ness, but they are repeated in bulk across numerous locations in the cityscape, a key element in the spiritual support of individuals on the move who often do not know where they will be at any one point during their daily shifts. With regard to performing prayer, urban dwellers have come up with any number of modes of accomplishing this, from making use of garages and restaurants, to utilizing the sides of the road to fulfill their spiritual duties, providing the area is clean and there is no evidence of illicit or *haram* behaviors. Such situations occur in every major urban landscape, and solicit a variety of diverse opinions with regard to those who must make use of these liminal prayer spaces. Some find them perfectly acceptable ("The ground is clean because Allah made it" and "God knows what is in my mind"; Smith and Bender 2004, 82; 85). Some, particularly those whose occupation depends on their mobility such as taxi drivers, note that the street is a preferred area because they "can't lose the time" in finding an alternate location (Smith and Bender 2004, 85). Thus, in this case, "time, rather than space, was of the essence," creating an important conceptualization of mobile masjid space as one that is not only performance based, but time based as well (Smith and Bender 2004, 85).

Individuals engage in spiritual practice in *car rapides* and they do so in ways that "demonstrate the practical, innovative impulses of devout Muslims to continue their religious practices in spite of working conditions that might make this difficult" (Smith and Bender 2004, 90). Surrounded by spiritually charged images in a communal atmosphere that is established through mobile space, the space of a *car rapide* provides an "ethically responsive sensorium" that enables passengers to "live as devout Muslims in a world increasingly ordered by secular rationalities" through their evocation of "affective-volitional responsiveness" from, in this case, the traveler. As Charles Hirschkind notes in his study of Egyptian taxi drivers and the effect of devotional cassette tapes, perceptual media create a type of spiritual sensescape in which individuals sense with the spiritual self rather than the secular self and, in doing so, incorporate the body as a whole in "a complex synthesis of disciplined moral reflexes." With regard to Hirschkind's collaborators, they "understood the degree of benefit achieved through sermon[s] ... to be proportionate to the depth of moral sensibility they were able to bring to the act" (Hirschkind 2001, 624). As a visual sermon, the *car rapide* becomes separate from the surrounding environment as a space-making strategy and part of lived religion within the urban landscape, the ever-evolving nature of which requires new spiritual forms of spatial manifestation that are in tune with an urban sensibility composed of equally spiritual and secular considerations.

Car rapides as masjid spaces are also in dialogue with other similarly mobile masjid spaces around the world whose "space in transit" reality comes in a variety of different forms. Boeing's new "Inflight Prayer Space" concept, for example, establishes a "private zone" for passengers looking to practice their religion without removing seats. This space not only provides a screened area but also a "foldable foot-washing tray into

4.2 The Idea of a Vehicular Masjid

the wall of the lavatory" and a light indicating, much in the same way a lavatory does, whether or not a prayer space is "occupied" (Reals 2018).[7] Likewise, other airlines instruct passengers to remain seated while praying, incorporating prayer movements as much as one is able within the confines of one's seat, indicating that such practice is possible and, in some situations, the only possible mode of engaging in *salat*.

Masjids as moving vessels have also taken form on the ground. In Jakarta, the capital of Indonesia, traffic gridlock has become such a problem that it has sometimes prevented individuals from engaging in *salat* during prayer times. This has led to the creation of a "mosque-mobile" that travels through the city and parks at some of the busiest places to provide all the necessary spatial accoutrements for prayer. Painted a resonant green and white, the sides of the van open up to create a small platform from the imam can lead the sermon, and prayer rugs with space for up to 100 people are rolled out in front of the van. A water tank for ablutions and appropriate attire for women are provided. The van is owned and operated by the Archipelago Mosque Foundation and the Adira Sharia, which "provides Islamic-compliant financing for motor vehicles." This type of moving space has also increasingly been deployed at sporting events and other occasions where accessing an appropriate space may become a challenge, with the idea of movable mosques in the form of large trucks being considered for the 2020 Olympics Games in Tokyo (Siregar 2016).

Thus, each of these spaces are defined by the fact that they exist between public and private, sacred and mundane, aspects that are dictated by the people that move both around and through them. *Car rapides* act as mobile objects whose adornment represents an important contribution to the urban landscape as a delivery mechanism not only for moving bodies but for moving images. In fact, one might say that they can only fulfill their masjid function if they "appear or are used in an appropriate way, a phenomenon that constitutes informal consecration through use" (Elias 2011, 122) in that a particular performance, movement, or active intent catalyzes the object, i.e. truck, into action. Gregory Starret uses the example of a keychain with a religious inscription, which, when rattling around in one's pocket with the rest of the loose change and lint, remains somewhat spiritually neutralized. Yet once out of the pocket and the key inserted into the ignition, "the

---

[7] The idea of an onboard prayer space is not a new idea. Many airlines from Muslim-majority regions have long included "in-flight prayer rooms" on their planes, especially on long-haul flights during which individuals will inevitably either cross over time zones or will be unable to disembark between prayer times.

keychain serves to protect the vehicle, its passengers and contents from misfortune" (Elias 2011, 122).

Likewise, the physical reality of moving images as being somewhat unstable and narrative in function, in a way akin to a comic strip or the image frames of a film, also creates a more multisensory spiritual experience for those participating in Dakar's urban environment. *Car rapides* provide streaks of sacredness that disrupt the monotonous urban landscape and draw the eye to their adornment, which is repeatedly imprinted on the mind every time a *car rapide* goes by. One might see the words *Alhamdoullilah* a hundred times a day, followed by a cloud of black smoke and an *apprenti* hollering out the next stop. Eyes constantly pass and surveil bystanders as these trucks careen down the street, streamers and cow tails flapping in the breeze. One may even get a glimpse of a religious figure peeking out from one of the side windows. Thus, these vehicles "move between points of view, zooming in from wide to close, in some instances remaining distant" (Wilhelm-Solomon et al. 2017, 23) and, in doing so, establish constantly shifting levels of intimacy and spiritual resonance not only in sight but also in experience, as bodies move with and are moved by these vehicles. To again quote Jamal Elias, vehicles such as *car rapides* "transform the landscape into a checkerboard of moving religious and cultural tableaus, mobile talismans through which the truckers protect themselves and their livelihood" (Elias 2011, 124). And as they imprint on those who watch them pass, they deposit ideas and images of spirituality on the landscape and in the minds of the individuals who inhabit it.

4.3 "Pray"-Over: Airport Mosques, Liminality, and the Traveling Body

These masjid spaces are not only in dialogue with other masjid spaces around the world but also other forms of liminal masjid spaces whose in-betweenness comes in a variety of different forms. Such spaces not only enable individuals "on the move" to be both physically and spiritually engaged but they also enable "various kinds of meeting-ness" while in transition (Sheller and Urry 2006, 219). In other words, they represent spaces "where people coexist or cohabit without living together" (Augé 1995, 110; in Sheller and Urry 2006, 219) and thus enable the development of space removed from place and the development of a community connected by their very transience.

One such space is the airport masjid space, which, like the airport itself, is, to quote Gottdiener, "a place of transmission of people (and objects) into global relationships ... that facilitates the shrinkage of the globe and

4.3 Airport Mosques and the Traveling Body

the transcendence of time and space" (Gottdiener 2001, 10–11; in Sheller and Urry 2006, 219). In contrast to the *car rapides*, these are spaces of immobility; yet such spaces are paradoxically key to increased systems of fluidity. In fact, just as the mobile spaces of the *car rapides* masjid requires the immobile platform of the depot as a supporting infrastructure for both the space and the individuals who utilize and activate the vehicle, masjid spaces can also act as immobile platforms or spaces of stability for moving, unstable bodies in a state of transience. Such masjid spaces are key to contemporary ideas of mobility in that they are not only produced through the practices of users themselves but also through the movements of users across time and space, becoming a place that occurs neither at the beginning nor the end of a journey, but over the course of the journey, a condition from which it derives its fundamental reality. Indeed, such spaces derive their identity from the moment-to-moment fabric of lives in motion – "the trails produced through lived practices of users" (Bassett 2007, 158–159) – and as such constitute a type of liminal space that may be physical in nature but are nonetheless dislocated from the currents of everyday life through their existence as a result of travel and movement. The airport masjid is one such liminal space that raises new questions relating to location, mobility, space, and transversal.

The emergence of the airport mosque space and indeed airports themselves has occurred less as a result of social, cultural, and political timing and more as a result of advancing transportation technology in the form of flight, which has subsequently led to the development of particular forms of architectural structuration related to the airport and associated spaces, and a deemphasis on terrestrial geographies as relevant boundaries. Indeed, as borders and boundaries between national spaces become increasingly porous, "slippages" have begun to occur within previously contained spaces as the number of multicultural encounters and intersections taking place in these liminal spaces increases. This has led the spaces themselves to both represent and reaffirm the body in motion as having a liminal identity in and of itself, a body in transit whose own mobile "geography" of identity travels through spaces like the airport masjid, activates them through a deposit of spiritual identity in the form of performance, and then leaves. Then again, the spaces themselves exist in a liminal state, waiting for the next body to activate them through purposeful performance. It is this element, in fact, that makes these spaces such a dynamic manifestation of modern life. Not only do these spaces become "trans" or even "supra" national spaces because of their removal from ideas of geography as a mode of identity-making, they also represent "spatial transformations produced by the economy of late capitalism," which in this case focuses on "the movement of peoples rather than the flow of capital and commodities" (Taleb 2005, 17). As such, spaces like the airport masjid call into question rooted ideas of territory, habitus, and place identity as an intimate connection between a specific space and the way in which an individual defines themselves.

To understand the liminal identity that lies at the heart of the airport masjid, however, it is important to first understand the airport itself as a liminal construct, which not only problematizes the idea of place as a concept but also how "place" itself is made manifest in these spaces. Airports have long existed as an "'in-between' space between one's point of origin and destination" (Huang, Xiao, and Wang 2018, 2); thus, while airports are not necessarily a "nonplace" so to speak, they are characterized by, to quote Francesco Pellizzi, a certain "nondirectional fluidity" as a "place of transient inhabitation" (Pellizzi 2008, 334). Thus, while they themselves constitute a "place" in the direct sense of the term, their interiors remain largely placeless, "their standardized facilities and similar shops and restaurants ... easily let[ting] passengers forget where they are" (Huang, Xiao, and Wang 2018, 1). Indeed, the standardized ritual of the security process marks this transition into liminality, particularly in the context of international terminals, where passengers pass through the symbolic and legal boundaries of immigration to enter into a space "legally outside the country while still physically in the airport" (Huang, Xiao, and Wang 2018, 4). In fact, Pascoe notes that the concept of boundary or perimeter dissolves in the context of airports as they function "as a national frontier ... in the middle of a country" (Pascoe 2001, 34; in Huang, Xiao, and Wang 2018, 4).

Much of this abstract reality is also made apparent in the architecture of the airport. Just as passengers who are swallowed behind the barrier of security reemerge in a "land of nowhere" (Kasarda and Linday 2011, 97; in Huang, Xiao, and Wang 2018, 4), airport organization and aestheticization reinforces what one might call an abject placelessness. Huang, Xiao, and Wang note Rowley and Slack's 1999 examination of airport departure lounges, during which they found a "high degree of 'sameness' across different airports, such as similar facilities, low load environments, a consistent range of retail outlets, and the dominant presence of international brands" (Huang, Xiao, and Wang 2018, 4). Huang et al. note that this lack of distinctiveness may cause passengers to "easily forget where they are and experience a sense of timelessness and placelessness" (Huang, Xiao, and Wang 2018, 4). Because of this, many feel that contemporary airports have become sanitized spaces devoid of the "broad emotional sweeps" associated with travel and associated experiences of joy, sadness, anxiety, and "the mythic flavor of the traditional journey" (Pellizzi 2008, 331). In fact, the airport has been described as

4.3 Airport Mosques and the Traveling Body

a place of "extreme sensory deprivation ... which is in every way similar to the one transited through previously (without truly departing) so that nothing qualitative separates the arrival from the departure and the time itself of the journey becomes reversible" (Pellizzi 2008, 342).

The idea of the airport as a "place-non-place of air" (Pellizzi 2008, 342) may also explain the association of the airport with derivative descriptors such as "airport" art, or what have been traditionally seen as:

> (relatively) cheap objects that sometimes affected a false patina of traditional use but had been recently made, with Western techniques and tools, and only or mainly for sale to "foreigners" a term that in Early English, together with that of "strangers," referred to those outsiders who had no right to speak, argue, make their voice heard, that is, to the socially mute. (Pellizzi 2008, 334)

Treated with disdain by those of "culture," these aesthetic forms were, and in some cases still are, fundamentally liminal constructs as befitting their tag "airport" in that they not only exist as largely repetitive, derivative forms but also because they exist betwixt and between established and emergent intellectual narratives, lacking and in many ways rejecting what most would consider "standardized classification" as kitsch often does.

Even the localizing, embedding display elements that can now be increasingly found in airport spaces around the world fail to soften the "impeccable, impersonal, and anesthetized mask" (Pellizzi 2008, 338) of spaces like airports as a type of mono-topia. The early transcendent elements associated with flight and the feelings of almost-spirituality they evoked have now been made structurally manifest in the sleek verticality of many airport structures and their vast interior spaces that not only stand in marked contrast to the largely horizontal orientation of railway and bus depots (whose structures seem to mimic their various directional trajectories), but also reflect the "unearthly suspension" of air travel generally (Pellizzi 2008, 332). This type of sleek, modernized structure also seems to reflect the essential indifference associated with contemporary mass air travel, a highly individualized process in which people move through space, the commonality of the act enabling a resistance to the formation of any type of *communitas*. This type of individual apathy is also enforced through the panoptic nature of airport space both in the form of security and the various spatial layers they establish to filter spatial participants and also spectatorship that occurs between passengers themselves. The latter in particular creates the liminal experience of deconstructing socioeconomic boundaries between individuals sharing the same spatial experience of the airport. In this case, passengers become "the spectators ... as well as the spectacle"

212   4 Mobility and "Portable" Islamic Space

each enacting and responding to a variety of different gazes and surveillance (Huang, Xiao, and Wang 2018, 8; 10).

Such characteristics find stark representation in the space of Ethiopia's primary national airport, Bole International Airport, and the masjid space located within its international terminal (Figure 4.2a and 4.2b). Located three miles outside the city center of Addis Ababa, Bole International Airport (previously called Haile Selassie I International Airport) is both the hub of the country's national air carrier, Ethiopian Airlines, which was founded in 1946, and the home of Ethiopia's Aviation Academy. The airport's history officially began in the early 1960s when it was determined that a new airport with extended runways was needed to accommodate the increasing size of large-scale international carrier aircraft. Since then, the airport has undergone a series of expansions and renovations designed to heighten security, increase carrier capacity by accommodating more air traffic through the addition of more runways, and make the experience of Bole more amenable to consumers (Ethiopian Airlines n.d.).[8] With regard to Bole's international terminal, it is currently the largest passenger terminal on the continent (with South Africa's O. R. Tambo coming in a close second), and is purportedly able to handle up to 3,000 passengers an hour (allAfrica 2003). Opened just ahead of a key summit which brought together Africa's main political leaders in 2003, the terminal cost around $75 million dollars and was intended to establish Addis as "the aviation capital of Africa" (Ethiopians 2001).

Consisting of a parking garage, a shopping thoroughfare, a series of restaurants, and airline-based lounges, Bole's international terminal was designed by Al-Kharafi and Sons, a Kuwaiti company, and managed by British firm Fitchner. Composed primarily of glass and steel, the terminal itself has two stories, the lower story being primarily functional in nature as a corridor for passenger movement, support, and customs, while the upper story is oriented toward commercial and consumer enterprises. Yet despite the gleaming aspirational modernist aesthetic that the international terminal was to embody, as a vision of the future it has largely fallen to the wayside. Dingy, dirty, and smoke-filled, the terminal itself is composed of two long corridors that parallel each other and are separated by an architectural partition containing a handful of basic restaurants, duty-free and souvenir/curio shops, and airline lounges. Because many international connections out of Addis have extensive layover periods,

---

[8] In January of 2019, Ethiopian prime minister Abiy Ahmed inaugurated the opening of Bole's new expanded international terminal, which cost upwards of $363 million dollars and will effectively triple Bole's passenger capacity, enabling it to accommodate up to twenty-two million passengers on an annual basis as compared to the seven million passengers it can currently handle.

Figure 4.2 a and b Bole International Airport, Addis Ababa, Ethiopia, masjid and ablution station, 2018. Images by the author.

there are also a small number of dedicated open-air rooms containing chairs and reclining surfaces which allow travelers to rest without having the leave the airport in search of a hotel. There is also a notable Chinese influence within the terminal in terms of restaurants and shops, undoubtedly due to the number of active Chinese contracts and construction projects currently underway in Ethiopia's capital city.

Importantly, the terminal is also a site of high visibility and surveillance. Airport security roam the corridors regularly, and most of the retail and resting spaces in this area are open to public view, with the only private areas being offered by individual airline lounges and bathrooms located at each end of the terminal. Also at one of the terminal ends is the sole Muslim prayer area (masjid), located just off the busy, noisy concourse next to a Chinese-owned, duty-free liquor store, and consisting of two small rooms, one for women and one for men, set side by side. Each measuring around six feet by fifteen feet respectively, these masjid spaces are open-air in the sense that both are framed by dry-wall-based, flimsy partitions with no ceiling; instead, the spaces open up to the systems of steel struts and roofing that soar far overhead. Likewise, the partition separating this prayer area from the concourse outside is made of glass that is only partially obscured by both a shelf for shoes and an opaque covering that conceals the lower half of the wall. The interior of the prayer space is composed of dirty, deep red carpet with a handful of prayer mats strewn about the small space and a hastily printed sign that says simply "Qibla" tacked to the far wall as an indication of the direction of Mecca. The most "official" element of this space is a plaque placed near the entrance wall of each room which says *rabbana atina fid-funya hasanatan wa fil akhirati hasanatan waquina adhaban-nar,* which constitutes one of the most important *dua* prayers of supplication that is repeated several times a day and translates as "Oh our Nourisher, provide us with good things in this world / Oh our Nourisher, provide us with good things in the Next Life / Oh our Nourisher, save us from the torments of fire."

With a door that does not close, this space provides little to no separation from the exterior world and is open – visually, physically, and psychologically – to the noise, smoke, and commercial activity surrounding it. As a space that fails to provide removal from the secular chaos of the terminal, it is perhaps not surprising that most people who visit this space (as observed by the author) choose to sleep in these rooms rather than to pray. This sense of surveillance, visibility, and a general lack of spatial purity is heightened by the fact that the ablution facilities for these spaces are located on the other side of the corridor next to the bathrooms and in full view of (and almost creating a hazard for) passengers strolling up and down the concourse. Not only does this generate a potentially unwanted audience when engaging in

4.3 Airport Mosques and the Traveling Body

wudhu, but those whose intent is to pray run the risk of potentially contaminating themselves as they cross back over to the masjid.

The state of these masjid spaces within the context of the Bole international terminal is perhaps unsurprising, given the fact that Islam is a minority religion in Ethiopia and in the past has occasionally rubbed up uncomfortably up against the more dominant Ethiopian Orthodox Christianity. Yet the airport itself does not appear to contain any additional multifaith or Christian prayer spaces, the implication being that the masjid constitutes a necessary space for accommodating passenger needs.

Thus, the treatment of this space in terms of its visual, spatial, and geographic identity within the context of the terminal not only speaks to its liminal identity as a space devoted to bodies engaged in both spiritually ritualized as well as transportation-oriented movement but also its reality as a space subject to subtle and not-so-subtle controls that involve surveillance and visibility. As such, it is a space that is at once inclusive and exclusive, devoted to Muslim bodies dedicated to engaging in prayer but subsequently letting all terminal inhabitants participate in this act through the application of a consumptive gaze on both the space and the people who inhabit it. Importantly, the act disempowers the masjid as a spatial occurrence removed from the exterior world, crafting it into a functioning active nonplace where those who view, inhabit, and utilize the space are anonymous within a larger intersection of coincidental movement and identity. Thus, the Bole international terminal's "prayer space" functions as an anticipatory masjid surrounded by nonplace infrastructure that fails to support or affirm its endeavor.

Such feelings can also create a sense of alienation not only in terms of spatial design but also in terms of location, with the Bole prayer space located inconspicuously at the end of a corridor with little indication of its presence or care put into its appearance or the comfort of its users. In contrast, some airport masjid spaces such as that in Dar es Salaam's Julius Nyerere International Airport, originally the Dar es Salaam International Airport, are a dominant element. Located directly past security up the escalator, the masjid is a central component to the terminal space, a highly modernistic glass and metal cube located centrally among the rows of seats where passengers wait to disembark. The masjid itself is also denoted by a number of large green signs that depict a standardized image of a mosque and, for those who are still confused, the word "MOSQUE" is written underneath in English in capital letters. The exterior of the mosque itself also repeats this on each window.

Unlike other airport prayer spaces, this prayer space displays a set of guidelines for those entering the prayer space. Specifically, no eating, no sleeping, no smoking, and no noise is permitted within the space, creating an environment that is vastly different from that of spaces like the one in Bole International Airport and others, where individuals will sometimes chat quietly (provided no one is praying), nap, and play with their children. In addition, unlike this prayer space, other masjid spaces are often located away from main thoroughfares in out-of-the-way spaces and hallways. This typically makes them underused and ambiguous in their location and structure, particularly in the newer airports on the continent. As Andrew Crompton notes, one often has to hunt for these spaces, located as they are in inconspicuous places, around corners, and down obscure hallways. While they may be located either landside or airside, they are rarely located alongside shops, restaurants, and other spaces of commercial activity. More often than not they are located near parking garages, next to out-of-the-way restrooms, and sometimes close to the airport's administrative offices (Crompton 2013, 477).

The Muslim prayer space in Johannesburg's O. R. Tambo International Airport (South Africa) is located outside the terminal building in a space between the escalators leading to the terminal building and the parking garage (Figure 4.3a and 4.3b). Originally founded in 1952 as the Jan Smuts International Airport (named after Apartheid-era prime minister Jan Smuts), it was renamed the Johannesburg International Airport in 1994, and then the O. R. Tambo International Airport in 2006 after Oliver Reginald Tambo, a South African revolutionary who served as the president of the African National Congress (ANC) from 1967 to 1991 and was a close friend and colleague of Nelson Mandela. As one of the continent's busiest airports, the Tambo underwent massive renovations in preparation for South Africa's hosting of the FIFA World Cup in 2010. Not only was passenger capacity increased and the international terminal expanded, but a new central terminal, designed by Osmond Lange Architects and Planners, was constructed along with an extensive multilevel parking area.

It is in this parking area where Tambo's Muslim prayer spaces are located, one for males and one for females. Not only are these prayer spaces located outside the actual terminal building itself but signage within the terminal building directing one to these prayer spaces is unclear and indeed there are individuals working at the information booths who are unfamiliar with the location. Despite their obscure placement, however, the prayer rooms themselves are beautifully and efficiently constructed, as befitting an airport that saw some 130,000 Muslim soccer fans pass through its space in 2010 (Hudson 2010).[9] Set

---

[9] The following description is of the female prayer area only. Inquiries about the male prayer area yielded information that would indicate the two are similarly aligned in terms of spatial organization and décor.

4.3 Airport Mosques and the Traveling Body

Figure 4.3 a and b O. R. Tambo International Airport, Johannesburg, South Africa, women's masjid, 2018.
Images by the author.

behind a clearly labeled opaque glass door, one first enters into a cubical containing shelving for shoes on the left and a three-person ablution station toward the back wall. The stark white walls are softened by the off-white marbled floor tiles and drainage area. Moving around the corner,

218　4 Mobility and "Portable" Islamic Space

one enters the actual prayer space, composed of white painted walls and wood paneling that extends halfway up the wall. The floor mats are a beige complement to these wooden highlights, containing repetitive simplistic blue arches each further accentuated with a central florette. Wooden shelving is also present toward the *Qiblah* wall and contains a number of Qur'ans. Perhaps the most interesting thing about this space, however, is the *Qiblah* wall itself. It is marked by both a wooden panel that is modestly ornamented with a rectilinear form and an abstracted floral design at the top. But the central focus on this wall is a digital clock that sits at the apex of the wooden *Qiblah* panel, almost flush with the ceiling. This organization emphasizes the importance of time, both secular time in the sense that people at airports tend to have places to go, and sacred time with regard to the time and length of one's prayer. Thus, in the context of two notably timeless spaces – the airport and the masjid – within this space, time seems to regain some of its lost importance, displayed in a way that marries its spiritual and secular importance within the context of this borderland space.

A similar type of grounding occurs within the masjid space of Dakar's new Blaise Diagne Airport, located about forty kilometers outside the capital city and named after an early mayor of Dakar who was also the first Senegalese French political leader to hold a position in the French government. Inaugurated in 2017 after numerous setbacks to replace Dakar's former international airport, the Léopold Sédar Senghor International Airport, which had become too small to serve the country's traveling needs, the airport is designed to handle three million passengers a year (at least, in this first phase) and was predominantly funded by the Saudi Binladin Group, a multinational construction conglomerate, which has also undertaken airport projects in Malaysia, the United Arab Emirates, and the Maldives.

The prayer rooms of Diagne Airport are located inside the terminal building, which means one has to pass through security to access them (Figure 4.4a and 4.4b). They are located along the broad pedestrian walkway, and feature prominently next to one of two possible restroom stops within the terminal itself while also being isolated from the handful of commercial venues present within the terminal. This location is significant and necessary as there are no ablution facilities within the prayer room; the bathrooms are required to function in this capacity. The entrances of the prayer rooms are directly visible from at least half of the gates in the terminal, meaning they are some of the first things people see when they disembark and some of the last things people see when they leave. This visual emphasis not only points to the primacy of Islamic identity within Senegal, but also the necessity of accommodating this

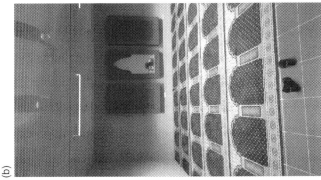

Figure 4.4 a and b Blaise Diagne International Airport, Dakar, Senegal, masjid interior and exterior, 2018. Images by the author.

identity within one of the most spiritually diverse, multicultural types of space in the world.

The two prayer rooms, one for males and the other for females, exist side by side, each accessed by an innocuous-looking door above which is a small sign indicating their purpose. Although the door itself is solid wood, there is a small pane of glass present in each one which allows passersby brief glances into the interior of the spaces. The interiors of the rooms are beautifully and simply rendered, with a tiled space located in the front of the room where one leaves shoes before moving into any one of the numerous arched-carpet "units" to partake in prayer. The front of the room features a pseudo-tryptic of two wooden latticework screens flanking a wooden-framed faux arch in the middle of which sit various copies of the Qur'an. This arch also acts as the *Qiblah*. Perhaps the most notable element of this space, however, is the quiet simplicity of the color scheme. Muted blue walls are offset by the warm tones of the wooden screens and supported by green and gold carpeted floors. The carpet designs take the construct of the arch and lay it horizontally across the floor toward creating both vertical and horizontal architectural space highly conducive to the prayer act. In addition, such a color scheme has interesting resonances with the natural world, the presence of wooden vertical elements, soft blue wall coloring, and a vibrant green and gold carpet all pointing toward attempts to eliminate the idea of a contained interior in favor of a natural world outside, which has often been identified as the ideal environment for prayer.

The *Qiblah* of the prayer rooms is in complete harmony with the geometric organization of the airport terminal space. The rooms themselves are not oddly trapezoidal to accommodate the *Qiblah*, nor is the *Qiblah* indicated by a corner or other asymmetrical element in the space. Although there is no evidence to indicate that this played a role in the considerations for the design of this new airport space, it is an interesting coincidence that, in a country whose population is 99 percent Muslim, Senegal's new international airport is oriented toward the *Qiblah*.

Whether or not the direction of the *Qiblah* was a consideration in the orientation of this new airport space, the potentially aspirational nature of its masjid design is significant for its progressive approach to the idea of Muslim masjid prayer spaces, which so often fall by the wayside during the design stage of airport planning. Leah Gordon, a photographer of many of these peripheral spaces, notes that many architects she spoke with indicated that, more often than not, these spaces were not designed by leading architects but were often passed on to firm interns (Morris 2017). These spaces – composed of churches, chapels, mosques, and even, in the case of San Francisco, a yoga space – in Gordon's view often serve as "a powerful counterpoint to the rigid design of airport duty-free shops and food courts," yet often "feel incongruous in these temples of Modernism ... [as] ... small, pre-Enlightenment pockets of faith, frenzy, fear and doubt" (Morris 2017).

Yet, whereas the industrial repetitiveness of airport environments results in a feeling of alienation and apathy, the "familiarity" of a prayer space by its very nature may in some ways have the opposite effect. As Courtney Bender notes:

> while these simple airport prayer spaces may be an "afterthought," they are quite *similar* kinds of afterthoughts and importantly maintain a dedicated separation from the airport as a meaningful space. These spaces rarely cater to the individual concerned with flight anxieties and other secular i.e. mundane concerns related to the here and now. Instead, they are focused on the individual "whose prayer is ... brought on ... by the obligations of a faith that does not change, no matter the ground on which the traveler treads." (Bender 2014)

Such is the nature of airport masjids and their particular reality within the space of the contemporary airport.

In many ways, the masjid model transcends airport space through the meaningful exploitation of space and performance. Muslims pray five times daily during periods dictated by the position of the sun and the length of the prayer. Because of this, prayer might happen when one is at work, visiting friends or family, or traveling. As such, in many Muslim majority countries, prayer spaces are ubiquitous in a variety of different public spaces (Mokhtar and Ahmadi 2005, 2). When a Muslim attends to prayer within an airport mosque space, thus, they essentially reground the timelessness of the airport space within the rhythms of the sun's movement and reestablish a connection to one's position in a daily routine that is oriented around the passing of time. Through this process of "locating oneself in space and time," the site itself becomes regrounded in the chronostream, a natural flow of time that pushes back against the place-based and temporal vacuum of the airport space.

But how does a religious space like the masjid, in all its specificity, sanctity, and performative intent, relate to the growing existence of multi-faith prayer spaces within airports? What are the different types of relationships that are formed? In some cases, such as that of the Cape Town International Airport in South Africa, the two exist side by side, both literally and metaphorically (Figure 4.5a and 4.5b). Both are located within a parking garage, neither being privileged over the other. In addition, although relatively hidden from the spectator gaze of travelers, cameras line the concrete hallway in which they are located and the airport police station is located in this area as well, creating a sense of

222   4 Mobility and "Portable" Islamic Space

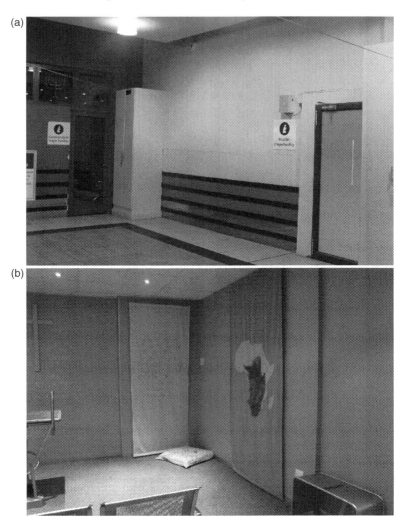

Figure 4.5 a and b Cape Town International Airport, interior and exterior of the multifaith prayer space, Cape Town, South Africa, 2018. Images by the author.

overwhelming surveillance which seems at odds with the general purpose of these spaces to begin with. Yet the lack of specificity with regard to the supposed universal nature of the multifaith space creates a stark contrast with the singular focus of the Muslim space, as it would perhaps against any other mono-devotional space. Even more strange is the fact that, as

4.3 Airport Mosques and the Traveling Body

mentioned above, in Cape Town's international airport, the Muslim and the multifaith prayer space exist side by side; yet as a multifaith prayer space, the masjid has essentially been doubled in this case, making the multifaith space an interesting experiment in hybrid spirituality.

Cape Town airport's multifaith prayer space seems to represent a somewhat strange combination of multiple religions, including Islam, although as previously mentioned there is a dedicated Muslim prayer space next door. It is essentially a Christian space that contained nods to other religions such as Judaism and Islam, as evidenced by the variety of religious texts including the Bible, the Torah, and the Qur'an present on the shelves within. This is despite the fact that the bookshelf itself is created in the shape of a cross. In addition, a metal cross also hangs on the wall at the very front of the room, flanked by white banners, each containing a story concerning Jesus. Another cross, a wooden one, hangs on an adjacent wall, making the space decidedly partisan despite a surface treatment of diverse religious icons. Enforcing this element, beside this cross, the following words are stenciled onto the wall in gold against a red background: "In the beginning there was a word and the word was with God and the word was God" (John 1:1), followed by "All things were made through him and without him nothing was made that was made. Within him was life and the life was one light of men" (John 1:3–4) and "And the light shines in the darkness and the darkness did not overpower it" (John 1:5). While these are obviously biblical quotes, they seem purposeful in their universal application not only to all religions but also to universal ideas concerning the nature of hope and resilience. A map of Africa appears opposite this cross as another unifying device, at least for those from the continent.

This inclusion/exclusion dichotomy of faith also extends to the exterior of the room, where the multifaith space and the specifically Muslim designated prayer space stand side by side. Although the doorway leading into the dedicated Muslim space is opaque, disallowing any visual penetration (and holding inquisitive researchers at bay for fear of causing offense), the multifaith prayer space is open, its glass etched with various symbols related to faith, some direct, like the outline of a menorah, others less so with the presence of a loaf of bread (possibly referring to a biblical parable) and what appears to be a sheaf of wheat. The furniture in the room appears to be repurposed metal airport lounge chairs and the front podium/altar space seems to have been crafted from similarly repurposed materials, not only giving the space a pseudo-modernist flair but also subtly emphasizing its connection to the surrounding airport space, a space of gleaming metal steel and sleek forms. The primary color palette of the room is soft grey and blood red, which again can be taken as a reference to the blood of Christ, which he shed for humanity's sins. This connection to humanity is strengthened by the presence of a red-framed chalkboard next to the bookshelf, full of scrawls of various visitors to the space sharing comments such as "Meditation will give you peace" (in all capital letters) or "I need power from God to overcome the inequalities of this earth." This is interesting because it provides a sharp contrast to the bland homogeneity of the rest of the space as "significant as presence" or "evidence of the presence of the Other in the form of traces of other people" (Crompton 2013, 492), this presence becoming meaningful and endowing the space with a visual fossil record of past life.

Beyond the books, the only other gesture to additional faiths within this space is a small pillow set in a corner near the front of the room where Muslims can perform prayers in the direction of the *Qiblah*. It is interesting as well that airport signs directing one to this space depict a figure praying to a distant unidentified object, which variously resembles a lamp or a minaret, a symbol that could be construed in a number of different ways (a Muslim praying toward a minaret in Mecca, a Christian praying toward an altar form, or a Jewish individual praying toward the *mizrach* or an abstracted wall ornamentation representing the eastern direction of Jerusalem). The vague arbitrary nature of this form not only creates a sense of ambiguity with regard to what exactly is being represented by it, but also tends to create a feeling of nonchalance and even superfluousness with regard to the individuals it is intended to accommodate.

Along these lines, however, an important distinction must be made with regard to *multifaith* prayer rooms like that of Cape Town's International Airport, which provide space for the practice of multiple religions, and *interfaith* spaces, which promote the practices of spiritual worship as being equal across religions, and this has to do with the idea of *communitas*. To quote Andrew Crompton, "In an interfaith encounter people of different faiths meet as equals around a table, with multi-faith they do not necessarily meet at all" (Crompton 2013, 494). This creates two very distinct incidents of (or lack of) *communitas*. In multifaith spaces, every individual is a singular individual and as such, engages in individualistic practices within a space, so much so that the multifaith space itself becomes further divided into separate enclaves through the performative barriers of spiritual practice and performance. This might be based on the historical fact that there are few precedents for individuals of multiple faiths praying together (although such occasions have occurred sporadically across time).

Importantly, no one truly knows where the idea of a multifaith space originated. Crompton notes that very few were built before the year 2000, with the oldest potentially being the multifaith space in the airport in Vienna, which was established in 1988 (Crompton 2013, 477). Thus, not only is the precedent for multifaith spaces obscure, but so too are the architectural and interior designs that have been created to represent it. There are examples of what might be called bi-faith spaces throughout history, such as the space currently occupied by the Great Mosque of Damascus, whose multiple realities over time, first as a temple to Jupiter and then as a cathedral of St. John, made it religiously significant to a number of faiths and at one time it accommodated both Christians and Muslims as a space of worship. In addition, during World War II in various US Army bases, collaborative prayer spaces were created for both Christian and Jewish individuals to use, not necessarily due to any religious motivations but more as a cost-saving device, a morale boast, and possibly to my mind a way to curb any potential anti-Judaic sentiment among the non-Jewish military personnel (Crompton 2013, 478). As these spaces developed into more universal spaces in the latter half of the twentieth century, they began to become increasingly vague both conceptually and architecturally, almost becoming modern "art spaces" in a way that seemed to deemphasize people in favor of the space as the main focus of attention (Crompton 2013, 478).

Yet even within the seemingly equitable spaces of airports such as that of Cape Town, different types of prayer space come to the fore, defined by their ability to either include through the use of a plethora of icons from multiple faiths or exclude through either the abnegation or careful division of said icons (Crompton 2013, 479). Although individuals in interfaith spaces may perform spirituality together, the nature of a space designed to represent universal "timeless truths," if done with equal attention to all faiths, necessarily becomes devoid of any (Crompton 2013, 494). This is one reason that so many faith spaces in airports around the world have become "empty white rooms ... [as] ... the default solution." Courtney Bender further notes:

> In contrast to many mid-century modern buildings where empty spaces connoted a universal sense of the holy, and even in contrast to earlier examples of airport chapels, the iconoclasm of airport prayer rooms is not a "positive" vision of what multi-faith entails. It is, rather, a default, whereby architects try to prevent these spaces from being "meaningful in an inappropriate way." (Bender 2014)

These newly mundane spaces are characterized by banality, repetitiveness, and a fundamental lack of aura that Crompton calls "the architectural equivalent of ambient noise" (Crompton 2013, 474). With regard to Cape Town's multifaith space, individuals pass through the space like ships in the night, with the religious identity of the room itself depending solely upon its current occupant. The fact that "they can go from Islamic to Christian by changing a mat for a chair" (Crompton 2013, 480) raises the fundamental question: is it the essence of a multifaith space (and the sheer impossibility of it even) that naturally produces this type of pseudo-iconoclastic space? Or is it the conceptual flexibility of the masjid that enables it, as a spatial paradigm/apparatus, to overcome the challenges an airport environment represents? Crompton notes that these characterless white rooms have emerged as the lesser evil because "there is an assumption that we should not be exposed to symbols of other people's faith if that can be avoided" (Crompton 2013, 474). This is made abundantly clear in Cape Town International Airport by the presence of a movable sign at the entrance of the multifaith prayer space that read: "Prayer in Progress: Cape Town International Airport would like the apologize for any inconvenience caused." That a private act taking place in a removed space could be the cause of "inconvenience" for those in the area seems odd and somewhat off-putting, again reemphasizing the idea that an airport space is truly a space of secular modern life and travel with religious spaces somewhat apologetically located in out-of-the-way spaces so as the preserve the sensibilities of passengers and the image of the airport as a space of technological advancement and modernity, two things fundamentally removed from religious practice.

Perhaps the presence of a multifaith space itself is in some ways an attempt to downplay the role of religion by universalizing it to the point of obscurity. Crompton notes that "Multi-faith can be seen as a response to a globalized world in which social life is torn from its locality and we interact with absent others rather than face to face" (Crompton 2013, 476–477). In many ways, this seems to reflect the identity of the airport as a space itself: a universally neutral, i.e. equitable (in theory), port of global intersection, exchange, transversal, and interpersonal isolation as per its modernist roots, which largely reject cultural and geographic embeddedness and try to follow self-styled "universalist" principles. Indeed, multifaith spaces tend to resemble a lobby or even a departure terminal, a fundamentally liminal space where people spend time "in between," whether that is between spaces, activities, or destinations; it, like the airport in which it is contained, essentially becomes a nonspace. It would seem that in such a world, a space like the masjid would be an ill fit. But it is precisely because of the masjid's fundamental characteristics that it can exist in this capacity as a space meant to be iconographically "neutral," a space that can disappear and reappear as needed, a space that maintains a fundamental mobility and flexibility in formation, a space that only requires a direction and a performance to be enacted, and a space that is fundamentally unembedded in any specific geographical area save the one it faces during prayer times. In the contemporary period, it is possible that time is one of the only constants and the masjid brings this to the fore even as the environment of the airport tries to efface it.

A masjid is not a masjid without the performance of prayer to activate it or provoke it into being. Without this act, a room remains just a room. As the photographer Leah Gordon notes, "I soon realized that the physical actions of Muslim prayer are transformative. This utilitarian space was swiftly transformed into a charged and magical space" (Morris 2017). While the use of term "magical" is inappropriate in this context, Gordon has nonetheless picked up on the distinctive shift in reality that a room undergoes when it becomes a masjid. And this shift is made all the more emphatic within an airport space as a space designed to elide such spiritual connotations. What is more is that the performance of prayer in an airport masjid creates an interesting occurrence of "movement within movement," in which a space like the airport, which itself is defined by mobile anonymous bodies, becomes both nuanced and recontextualized through the specificity and intent of the prayer movement (Coleman and Eade 2004, 18). Likewise, it is also through this movement that another element antithetical to the ideological connotations of the modern airport emerges: the establishment of a sense of *communitas*. The isolation often promoted by airport architecture dissolves in the space of the masjid and the company of like-minded spiritual people who, despite inherent differences of class, race, or nationality, nonetheless leave these multiple identities and the negotiations they require with regard to one's additional political social, and cultural identities outside the door with their shoes. Part of this, of course, is made possible by the actual separation of mosque space from the rest of the airport space. This space not only acts as an island of spirituality and a refuge for Muslims seeking to reaffirm their spiritual identity through both prayer and interaction with like-minded Muslims, but also an area that, while being a public space, is nonetheless intended to provide a boundary between Muslim and non-Muslim. Boundaries in the context of Muslim space have long been organized both formally and informally to create partitions based on gender, social hierarchy, occupation, and other elements. Regarding the presence of non-Muslims in Muslim space, there is disagreement among Islamic scholars and jurists with regard to a universal ruling on this matter, with passages from the Qur'an indicating that the presence of "idolaters" in the mosque is forbidden but with no clear definition given of an "idolater." There are also accounts in the hadiths in which non-Muslims were allowed to pray in Muslim prayer spaces and vice versa (Hassner 2007, 139). Thus, most communities have developed local guidelines with regard to these matters based on the history and ideologies of the area.

However, even though there are rarely clear directives forbidding non-Muslims from entering into this Muslim space, its often peripheral placement alongside parking garages and down obscure hallways and its lack of visual accessibility via the presence of doors or oblique glass all present an image of guarded space that filters individuals who traverse into the interior. In some ways, this makes airport masjids something of a "borderland," in the words of James Clifford, in that these spaces are at once "blocked" to outsiders but "permitted" to Muslims, "policed" by airport surveillance and the spectator gaze but also "transgressive" in their lack of interior surveilled space (Clifford 1997, 8). The masjid is not only a physical borderland, but a spiritual and psychological one as well, where "people of different races occupy the same territory, where under, lower, middle and upper classes touch, where the space between two individuals shrinks with intimacy" (Anzaldúa 1999, 19; in Ewing 1998, 262). And while not all airport masjid spaces, particularly those on the continent, maintain this type of binary inclusionary/exclusionary aesthetic, as Gordon notes, there is a shift in atmosphere when one enters this space and surveys the Arabic signage, the basins for ablution, and the highly embellished carpets. In this way, masjids become independent territories within airport space, also due to the fact that, during the act of prayer, one is connected to Mecca via a spiritual umbilicus and through the sense of *communitas* established not only with fellow devotees in the prayer space itself but with the millions of Muslims who all face Mecca as a collective focus of their spiritual performance.

Along these lines, the nature of the prayer space become insignificant. The idea that airports should also act as displays for the local history and culture of their location has no relevance with regard to these prayer spaces. In fact it is in this area where masjids perhaps have the most in common with the streamlined aesthetic of contemporary airport spaces in that their neutrality shifts focus to the importance of prayer, as all masjid spaces should be oriented. This makes airport masjid spaces liminal but in a very strange way. Ideally a masjid space should be a space devoid of contextual elements that could distract from the prayer act. In essence, masjid spaces should be "placeless," just as airports in many ways have become. Yet, simultaneously, masjid spaces are fundamentally embedded *in* place, largely through the performance of prayer which makes the space both alive and dialed in to the holy city that constitutes their focus five times daily and remains a destination that Muslims are required to journey to at least once in their lives. So masjids in essence are unlocated spaces within unlocated spaces (airports), while nonetheless being

4.3 Airport Mosques and the Traveling Body

inextricably tethered to a space located outside. Individuals exist in the mundane liminal space of the airport before entering into the spiritually liminal space of the masjid and subsequently become tethered in time and space through the performance of the prayer act that extends space outside the airport toward Mecca. It is this simultaneous interior/exterior geography that grounds them within the purposeful place-ness of their spiritual identity. In this case, both the meaning and purpose of travel become insignificant as one engages in their spiritual journey.

Most major international airports around the world now contain Muslim prayer spaces, largely to accommodate the fact that Islam is the fastest growing religion in the world. Because of the global nature of these prayer spaces and the increasingly global character of the airport spaces in which they appear, it is becoming far more difficult to find prayer spaces that speak to the specific context of their geographical location. Prayer spaces in major African capitals are no different and are often distinguished predominantly by their newness, which typically creates differences in size, technology, and appearance.[10]

Despite their differences in location and design, however, all of these spaces are nonetheless connected by their removal from the secular mundane space of the airport. Whether composed of a new prominent chamber within the terminal, a hidden away room by a parking garage, or a dingy partition along a noisy concourse, each actively creates an idea of boundary and separation and attempts to apply a different identity to an island of space within the place-based and temporal vacuum of the airport. Another element that each space has in common is their visual representation on the various signs, both obvious and obscure, directing individuals to their location. The signs in many ways carry as much symbolic weight as the spaces themselves given that through them Islamic space is rendered/reified within a two-dimensional visual image that takes any number of forms across various contexts. In Dakar, the signage identifying prayer spaces is composed of text accompanied by a small square inside of which is an abstracted genderless form kneeling down with head bent. In Dar es Salaam, the word "mosque" is placed centrally and complemented by a rendered generic mosque outline composed of a large green square topped with a dome and a crescent shape.

---

[10] I should note that I held myself to specific standards when entering and photographing these spaces. I never entered a space that was occupied by someone in the act of prayer. If an individual was present but not praying (sleeping or napping was the most common activity I encountered), I first asked if they would mind my presence as a non-Muslim. Depending on their response, I then either took a picture of the space without them in the frame or I asked if I could take a picture of the space with the understanding that they would not be photographed.

Johannesburg features a somewhat similar design although more abstracted: a singular dome with an abstract minaret sits inside a bright yellow circle, mimicking the color scheme of most of the other signage in the airport. Interestingly, the signage for mosque space at Addis Ababa airport is perhaps the most theologically appropriate of them all, the prayer space itself being rendered textually rather than through an image, and written in both English and Amharic. While this use of symbols may seem somewhat unimportant on the face of things, the symbols nonetheless chart an important geographic journey through the space of the airport and in many ways actively overlay the airport space with a spiritual cartography for the faithful to follow. This "journey within a journey" in many ways layers the airport space with alternate and more complex paths of movement and being within the mosque space that act as affirmations of identity, with these symbol in many ways "perform[ing] both the structural task of presenting a worldview, closely associated with the belief system of the religion in question, as well as establishing justification for certain behavior" (Tayob 1999, 5). The presence of these symbols and the masjid space they refer to act as mutual confirmations of a specific worldview visible only to those who seek it through the active demarcation and summoning of space. Although symbolic representations in each space are different, they nonetheless actively produce the same sacred cartography within the space of the airport, using figures of bodies praying and iconic structures to conjure a spiritual cartography while also providing a pilgrimage route to a sacred space.

Thus, the airport masjid constitutes a mode through which contemporary Muslims in Africa (as one of the fastest growing Muslim areas in the world) are navigating a contemporary global condition defined by mobility, finding points of intersection between spirituality, modernity, and space. Airport masjid spaces on the continent are necessarily in conversation with spaces around the globe precisely because of the liminal nature of the airport space as a space out of place with the world, repeated on multiple geographies and thus fundamentally in dialogue with each other across the cultural, national, and spiritual spectrum. Airports are spaces in which "worlds collide" (Crompton 2013, 477); yet masjid spaces maintain a more universal nature. Within a masjid space, one is no longer in Senegal or South Africa or Ethiopia or Tanzania; one is embedded in prayer. And importantly, one is embedded in prayer while being simultaneously in transit, occupying the in-between space of the airport. The individual, like the masjid, is thus in process, removed from the stream of being in the world precisely because one has journeyed to the spiritual world through the temporary confluence of body, space, and performance.

4.4 Spiritual Space as Digital Terrain: Virtual Touba and the Creation of Online Masjid Space

Such a categorization can also be applied to the virtual experience, a conceptualization of space that has been growing in the contemporary period with advances in digital technology and has in some cases eliminated the need for physical space as a place of interaction and performance. Thus far over the course of this chapter, the masjid has been addressed as a space that is occasional, condition, mobile, and ephemeral. It is within such spaces, according to Pablo Neruda, that "authentic communication and understanding occur" (Barrie and Bermudez 2008, 4) and thus such spaces are as "real" as the "material" spaces of built forms like mosques. But it is also important to think through immateriality in space in a more literal sense, particularly in a day and age where technology has actively propagated a "time–space compression" that has not only connected people and generated networks in unprecedented ways across the globe but has also supported, as mentioned previously, a "speeded-up 'liquid modernity'" (Urry and Larsen 2011, 30) that has dematerialized the spatial realm in somewhat unpredictable ways. Characterized by incorporeal (virtual) travel, simultaneous presence in multiple digital locations, and instantaneous access to vast quantities of data, space has come to take on new meanings and existences within today's digital terrain in response to different types of "flow," be it people, information, commodities, or ideologies. And it is with regard to ideology that virtual space has experienced one of its more interesting contemporary manifestations, particularly with regard to spirituality and the emergence of a virtual masjid.

Spiritual space has historically been characterized as a tangible physical geography that has specific features and even occasionally demarcations, which help it branch into the reality of place. Such definitions require reimaginings, however, in the contemporary period (much like the masjid does) to not only accommodate the advent of the spatial turn (as discussed in the introduction) but also the contemporary implications of modernization, globalization, and the rise of digital space as an authentic realm of existence. With the development of contemporary spatial programs like Geographic Information Systems (GIS), scholars are increasingly able to spatially visualize vast quantities of information, leading to the idea that spatialization is more than just a tool but is also an interpretive apparatus that could be applied across disciplines toward conceptualizing conditions of existence.

With regard to the convergence of these contemporary ideas of space and spirituality, liminality has come to represent a particularly effective method of conceptualization. Although it has been addressed throughout this chapter as a condition of existing in a state of betweenness or transition, the term was first introduced as an anthropological concept by Arnold van Gennep in 1909 in his work *Rites de Passage,* which sought to examine religious and initiatory rites not in terms of the stages one occupies in this event as they move from start to finish, but in terms of how one transitions between these stages. Van Gennep was particularly interested in the space individuals occupy during these transitory "no name" transversals. These, van Gennep suggests, are rites in and of themselves, which he termed "transition rites" as a type of middle tier in a three-stage process that importantly has none of the sharply defined contours or definitions of the beginning and end stage (Thomassen 2009, 14). Essentially, the individual is "in process," as is the space they occupy, which can perhaps be characterized as a type of threshold, fundamentally defined by its anticipatory nature and its "in-between" status.

Since van Gennep's work, scholars such as Victor Turner have refined concepts of the liminal to the point of negating the necessity of "transition" as a key defining element of liminality. In fact, most contemporary scholars hold that the liminal need not necessarily "involve a resolution of a personal crisis or a change in status" (Thomassen 2009, 15); in fact, it may potentially stand as an end goal or condition in and of itself. With regard to discussions of the masjid, the liminal has particular significance in that the concept of the masjid holds that the whole of the earth is waiting in anticipation of human intent to pray. Thus a fundamental component of a masjid's essential being is liminality, an omnipresent in-between space evoked at specific times and through various acts. Importantly, the essential reality of the masjid as a liminal space has in many ways made it an ideal spatial construct for contemporary intersections of globalization, movement, and technology as a space able to take on less tangible dimensions as a mental, conceptual, or imaginative construct. The most recent addition to the masjid's reality in the contemporary period is that of the digital masjid, a cutting-edge utilization of virtual terrain. And, importantly, one of the fastest growing "polities" with regard to utilization of media and digital technology is the African continent.

In terms of communications platforms, Africa currently maintains over 400 million active users, making it a larger market than North America (Essoungou 2010). Indeed, one of the major developments that has fueled this uptick in categories such as cellular phone use are social media platforms which have enabled people to simultaneously interact at unprecedented speeds across unprecedented distances. Facebook, Twitter, and YouTube are particularly popular platforms; Facebook is in fact the most

4.4 Spiritual Space as Digital Terrain

visited website on the continent and has even overtaken what some might consider "traditional" digital platforms such as email. With more than 15 percent of Africans online visiting Facebook, the continent has even surpassed Asia in terms of active Facebook users. Mobile internet use on the continent is the highest in the world and some predict that Africa will be setting future trends in usage (Essoungou 2010).

In addition to acting as social platforms for interaction, these sites also function as political and economic platforms as well, with individuals such as Zambian author and economist Dambisa Moyo having more than 26,000 Twitter followers and political candidates in Cote D'Ivoire posting campaign updates and propaganda on Facebook and Twitter (Essoungou 2010). This has led people like Jon von Tetzchner, co-founder of Opera, the world's most popular internet browser for mobile phones, to speculate that the "mobile Web is beginning to reshape the economic, political and social development of the continent" (Essoungou 2010).

Adding to this is the development of "homegrown platforms" designed by African programmers to "keep the African online conversation going" and the increased availability of internet platforms in a variety of major African languages like Swahili, Zulu, and Hausa (Essoungou 2010). Google recently developed a service specific to East African Swahili speakers called Baraza ("meeting place" in Swahili) to enable interaction and knowledge-sharing between Swahili speakers (Essoungou 2010). But regardless of the regional specificity of these programs, one cannot just talk about continental users as a contained group; they are part of a global movement toward broad-based online internet usage. Indeed, the development of the aforementioned services is important because it highlights the nature of the impetus driving internet usage not only in Africa but perhaps around the world, which is, to quote Caroline Bassett, "the sense of creating a shared, inhabited space" (Bassett 2007, 140).

The idea of space within the virtual world has been increasingly framed as one that combines "virtual modernity and physical modernity" into an unprecedented new spatial apparatus. With regard to the digital masjid as it is emerging within "virtual" Africa, it has begun to shift conceptualizations of the "real" in terms of "real spaces" and "real relationships" and how the two are constituted.

One well-developed example of this is Touba, located about 200 miles east of Dakar. Touba is the holy city of the Muridiyya order established by Cheikh Amadou Baba, the founder of the group. The city itself was founded in 1887, although its construction didn't begin until after Bamba's death in 1927 (Ross 2006, 222). Touba has been compared to Vatican City and Jerusalem in terms of its spiritual importance to its founders, its founding (like so many other important spiritual sites in the Islamic tradition) the result of a miraculous occurrence. The city was revealed to Bamba under a giant *mbeb* tree by the archangel Gabriel during one of Bamba's spiritual retreats during which he went into the wilderness and meditated for long periods of time while practicing extreme asceticism. Gabriel told Bamba that the very spot on which he stood was "chosen" to be the site for "a spiritual metropolis of universal significance" and this spot would later be where the great mosque of Touba would be built (Ross 2006, 224).

The name "Touba" also has spiritual significance. In Wolof, *tuub* means "to convert" or "to do penance," a similar meaning to the Arabic term *tawba* which means "repentance" (Coulon 1999, 199). But Touba (also spelled Tuba) in the Islamic tradition is also the name of the Tree of Paradise, mentioned in the Qur'an Surah 53:14 as the *sidrat al-muntaha* or the "Late-tree of the Extremity" which marks the gate between the earthly and heavenly realms and is "the closest one can possibly approach God" (Coulon 1999, 223). The tree is also said to embody "eternal bliss and also ... life and death" with an individual's name written on each leaf along with their good and bad deeds, which are preserved until the day of judgment. Thus, to quote Eric Ross, Touba "represents the idea not only of Paradise but also of access to Paradise," its roots extending down into the netherworld and its branches supporting the kingdom of heaven (Ross 2006, 223). It also represents the "actualization" of Bamba's mission as a leader and teacher of any *murid* (aspirant) who chose to follow the path of Islam (Ross 2006, 224). It is perhaps not surprising then that Touba as both a tree that spans human and divine realms with branches stretching across eternity and incorporating each person within it, and as a space for the education and edification of the faithful, gives itself so readily to virtual interpretation within the seemingly eternal flows of cyberspace.

As an actual space, Touba today is the second-largest urban area in Senegal, containing over half a million people. It has been vigorously maintained both spiritually and spatially, with the Mouride brotherhood enforcing a strict code of behavior (no alcohol, no tobacco, no secular music, no games, no parties, etc.) through the presence of *gendarmes* (military officers) stationed at various points in the city including its entrances and exits, and who often search travelers coming into the space (Ross 2006, 245). Such control is but part and parcel of the broader power that the Muridiyya order wields both in Touba and across the numerous territories both in Senegal and abroad who follow the Mouride way. This in many ways makes Touba not only a spiritual space but a political space too, manifesting the complete control of the brotherhood over its followers and their spaces (Ross 2006, 222).

4.4 Spiritual Space as Digital Terrain 235

Figure 4.6 The Great Mosque of Touba and the Lamp Fall minaret, Touba, Senegal, 2018.
Image by the author.

Regarding these spaces, perhaps the most iconic space in Touba is the Great Mosque (Figure 4.6). Oriented in the direction of Mecca, the mosque sits in the center of the city on a raised platform and has seven minarets and four domes,[11] the green dome marking the mausoleum of Cheikh Amadou Bamba. It is also surrounded by the mausolea of other Mouride caliphs, each tomb shaped to resemble the Ka'ba and spaced around the Great Mosque so that one circumambulates the complex as one visits each tomb. Each past caliph has attempted to add a new element to the mosque as a way to "make their mark" in a real physical sense on the structure as part of their legacy, whether it is the cladding of the walls in pink marble from Italy, or the refurbishment of the prayer hall ceiling in pseudo-fresco via artists imported from Spain. Thus, the mosque is always in a transitional state, constantly evolving

[11] The Grand Mosque previously had five minarets, but two more were added by previous caliphs and constitute the last minarets that Touba will be able to sustain, largely because the Grand Mosque in Mecca has seven minarets and Touba cannot be "greater" than the mosque in Mecca. Thus, unless one falls down, another minaret cannot be built. In addition, one cannot tear down a minaret to build another one because such wanton destruction of a mosque is forbidden, and it would also represent destroying another caliph's contribution to the structure.

236   4 Mobility and "Portable" Islamic Space

under the direction of the current caliph. As I was told by one attendant, "Come back in five years and it will be completely different!" (Traoré 2018).

Perhaps the most notable visual element of the mosque, however, is its central minaret, known as Lamp Fall, after one of Bamba's most loyal and devoted followers, Cheikh Ibra Fall. Oftentimes, when one sees images of Bamba, one sees an image of Ibra Fall next to him as well. Lamp Fall is eighty-seven meters high, far taller than needed to call the faithful to prayer, Eric Ross points out, and thus maintains an important symbolic element as "a visible concrete manifestation of the Tree of Paradise" (Ross 2006, 226). Its iconic status means that Lamp Fall has almost achieved a similar type of visual legibility as the various saints in Senegal have, appearing on the sides of *car rapides*, posters, and other visual material around the country (Ross 2006, 226). It can also be seen from great distances given the flatness of the Senegalese landscape and thus acts as a strikingly visible geographic marker of the city (Ross 2006, 226–227). Importantly too, Lamp Fall acts as an architectural representation of both the *mbeb* tree where Bamba first received his vision and the Tree of Paradise, and thus functions as a *qutb* or a type of spiritual center around which the earthly world rotates (Ross 2006, 227).

Such spiritual and metaphoric considerations have also played a large role in the how the city has been spatially organized over time as a direct spatial manifestation of "the application of Sufi principles and concepts" (Ross 2006, 2). Specifically, the design of Touba presents an overlay of rectilinear and circular elements in the form of streets, compounds, and *khalwahs* or spaces where Bamba "purposefully and indelibly imprinted his spiritual desire onto the landscape" (Ross 2006, 51) that all center on the mosque, the combination of which references the form of the *khâtim*, which means "seal" in Arabic and refers to a site that "places an inhabitant in a position of receptivity for empowering forces or *baraka*" (Apotsos 2016b, 13). Indeed, the avenues and routes of activity throughout the city all actively channel human movement toward the mosque as the spiritual center of the city and the point around which the Muridiyya order itself revolves. This "squaring of the proverbial circle," in Eric Ross's words, not only enables the city to represent a larger divine plan but also represents "an ideal social order" through the "judicial application of the principles of urbanism" (Ross 2006, 256). All the compounds, neighborhoods, and suburbs of Touba submit to the larger rectilinear/circular organization of the city and thus the will of God. This has the additional important effect of demonstrating the "fractal" nature of Touba's spiritual power in that it exists and flows through everything in Touba, from the smallest house to the Grand Mosque itself, thus "transcend[ing] the different compartments into which life is so often subdivided" and proving the point that life can be lived holistically through the spiritual lens that Touba offers (Ross 2006, 256).

Interestingly, this organizational scheme is expanding not only with the ever-increasing creep of Touba into the outlying suburbs as its population grows, but also via the development of a major highway "artery" – Ila Touba – currently under construction that will link Dakar directly to Touba almost like a type of umbilical cord. One of the reasons for this, of course, is the crowds that clog Senegal's highways every year as pilgrims journey to Touba for the Grand Maggal; lack of safety and traffic control leads to dozens of people dying each year on the trip. There are also a number of helipads popping up in and around the city for religious leaders and individuals of means to come and go as they like. Indeed, it is rapidly coming to pass that "all roads lead to Touba" with the Mourides themselves "recognize[ing] no limits to Touba – *de jure* or *de facto*" (Ross 2006, 227; 247).

Thus, the reality of Touba not only as a major urban area but also the spiritual heart of the Muridiyya order is expressed in a crystalline manner through its organization and deployment of space, all of which was designed to position Touba as "the gate to Paradise." Not only does the formulation of Touba reference spiritual principles set down by Bamba, but also pulls from older ordering systems for precolonial capital cities in West Africa where palaces and administrative structures were located in the central part of the city, often at the site of a great palaver tree (*penc* in Wolof), which not only stood as a landmark for the community itself but was also a site for community discussions and decisions ("palaver" meaning "lengthy discussion") (Ross 2006, 231). Here the symbol of the tree continues to function in Touba as not only a "celestial" object but also "a religious reincarnation of the political *penc*" (Ross 2006, 231).

For all of this, however, Touba exists in the contemporary period as a wholly modern city, dynamic and evolving despite the static connotations so often associated with spaces defined by religious visions. Thus, it makes sense that Touba's expansion in recent times has not only been physical but also digital. If Touba is indeed the tree whose branches touch every aspect of life and whose presence knows no borders or boundaries, then Touba finds a natural complementary environment within the virtual world. This becomes particularly apparent in the context of Touba's main annual pilgrimage event, the Grand Maggal, during which Touba is flooded both physically and virtually with pilgrims seeking to partake in the blessing of the city.

The Grand Maggal, "Maggal" coming from a Wolof term meaning "to make something grow" (*magg*) and, loosely translated, meaning "to commemorate" (Babou 2007, 200), has been described as a "ceremonial rite which affirms the identity and power of the brotherhood in the context of Senegalese society and also in regard to the state" (Coulon 1999, 206). Along these lines, if Touba constitutes the ideal city, then the Grand Maggal is "a festival of Utopia, the celebration of a model of social and urban organization which is sharply distinguished from the harsh realities of daily life in Senegal" (Coulon 1999, 206–207). Regarding the pilgrimage itself, the event brings millions of people into the spiritual capital for a five-day period. The origin of the Maggal began with the death of Bamba and the assembling of Bamba's followers at the command of his son and successor Serigne Moustapha M'Backe to honor his memory. The next caliph, Falilou M'Backe, would subsequently change the date of this event to instead mark the date of his exile to Gabon, the reason being that it was through such trials and persecutions that Bamba was able to receive his spiritual calling while at the same time actively resisting French colonial imperialism (Coulon 1999, 200). Today, pilgrims journey to the Maggal, pay a "pilgrimage" fee of around 1000CFA which is used for mosque maintenance and food for pilgrims,[12] and then proceed to engage in a number of rites, ceremonies, and recreational activities over a five-day period. The main task of most pilgrims coming to Touba is to visit the mausoleum of the founder Bamba and receive his blessing or *baraka,* something that one can gain by merely entering into a holy space; the entirety of Touba is considered holy ground, with *baraka* becoming steadily more concentrated as one approaches the Grand Mosque and Bamba's Mausoleum (Coulon 1999, 201). Because of the holiness of the tomb of Bamba, followers often queue up for hours, held in check by the Baye Fall, or followers of Bamba's most ardent spiritual lieutenant, Ibra Fall, who in this case act as "veritable warrior-monks" (Coulon 1999, 201). In addition to visiting Bamba's tomb, pilgrims typically visit the mausolea of the past caliphs who all share in Bamba's *baraka* as his direct descendants and are also buried on the grounds of the mosque in a circular arrangement. There are other potential sites for visitation, such as the Well of Mercy, a miraculous spring created by God whose water is said to heal and bless; many pilgrims bottle water from the well to carry home with them, often for those who need it and were unable to make the trip. Also popular is a visit to the Mouride library, where many of the writings of Bamba and other Mouride scholars are kept (Bamba's writings are also said to have their own sort of power),

---

[12] If individuals can't afford to pay the "pilgrimage" fee, oftentimes they will instead do volunteer work in the mosque, such as sweeping the floors, moving carpets during prayer times, and other tasks.

as well as the new university. Within this period, followers also make time to visit their own personal spiritual advisers – Cheikhs within the Muridiyya order – who each maintain a home in Touba and are in residence during the pilgrimage to host their advisees. The pilgrimage is also a time when religious music in the form of hymns, praise poetry recitations, and historical renderings is celebrated, often performed throughout every night of the pilgrimage (Coulon 1999, 202). There are also other, lesser spiritual events and activities that occur during the pilgrimage. For example, there are political components to this event that involve the Mouride leadership welcoming officials from the national government to Touba as a type of "mutual recognition" of societal power (Coulon 1999, 202). The pilgrimage also constitutes a good time to shop. In fact, Christian Coulon notes that a visit to Touba's market, one of the largest in the country, is almost as "obligatory" as some of the spiritual visits themselves (Coulon 1999, 203). Due to the fact that Touba does not tax, many of the prices in the Touba market are lower than those around the country; thus pilgrims return home after the pilgrimage "weighed down with goods which they have bought at low prices and which, moreover, have a special prestige because they were purchased in the holy city itself" (Coulon 1999, 204). This gives the pilgrimage to Touba a more festive feeling, a type of excess, that only fully manifests during this time of the year. And it is through this collaboration of the spiritual, the political, and even the consumerist, that the identity of Touba is confirmed as a city of not only spiritual but also popular devotion.

Touba's online identity takes on similar attributes during the Maggal process as an extension of Touba's reality as an ever-expanding "territory," "territory" in this case being defined as "a theoretical framework derived from the geographic projection of a society's structures and values" (Guèye 2003, 610–611). Yet, cyberspace is merely the newest mediascape in a continuous timeline of New Information and Communication Technologies, or "NICT" to coin Guèye's terminology, that have been used in Touba which not only "eliminate constraints on the realities of distance and space" (after all, because "Touba is carried in their hearts," the Mourides do not recognize borders or boundaries when it comes to the Holy City) but also create a continuous territory throughout the mediascape in Senegal and beyond. Radio and television have long served as platforms for extending Touba's spiritual, sensorial, and political reach, often drawing large Mouride audiences, particularly during grand events like the Maggal. Indeed, broadcasting events and speeches at the Maggal are highly strategic undertakings in that the content is shaped to reflect not only the power of the brotherhood itself but also the "proselytizing mission that the sect continues to direct at the world at large." Such soundscapes are even reproduced in the form of mobile media like video cassettes which are sold in areas of high Mouride concentration (Guèye 2003, 612), although there are now also online music platforms like Touba Radio that stream music. Yet, media like radio, television, and their mobile derivatives have long served as an important component of the "marabout–disciple relationship," not only acting as a unifier of collective Mouride identity due to the reach of NICTs, but also a mode of reaffirming the power and reach of the brotherhood at large (Guèye 2003, 613). Similar modes have long defined experiences of the pilgrimage. Audio and video cassettes have long acted as "carriers of the images and sounds from pilgrimages, religious events, the messages of the Khalif, and religious speech" (Guèye 2003, 615). But the digital realm constitutes an increasingly emergent frontier among Mourides as a mode of communication, interaction, and importantly, spiritual identity and performance.

One of the first online undertakings by a Mouride group was that of the Hizbut Tarqiyya, which began as a social organization of Mouride students in the 1970s at the University of Dakar. Eventually, the group based itself in Touba, where it became defined by its particular approach to life and spirituality, namely one that privileged "modernism and activism" as part of its missionary work (Guèye 2003, 621). In the 1980s, as a way of more closely monitoring the Tariqa's adherents, the group acquired a set of computers and set up a member database, the first Mouride group to do so; they were subsequently praised "for [their] adoptions and exploitation of this 'miracle'" (Guèye 2003, 622). Along these lines, the group adopted a new approach to the idea of brotherhood in general, with members receiving training in computer literacy and the utilization of internal communications networks that highlighted and stressed achievements while also offering audio and visual sources for members (Guèye 2003, 622). Thus, Hizbut Tarqiyya became the first to craft an online space for its members that would become a defining component of their spiritual identity.

Importantly, in 1999 this group launched a web platform designed to coincide with the Grand Maggal in order to "promote cultural values espoused by Mouridism and around which Hizbut Tarqiyya's entire educational system is organized, via the Internet" (Guèye 2003, 622). Htcom.sn provides an almost overpowering visual space of stationary and moving images, notifications, videos, and contextual information on Amadou Bamba, Islam more broadly, Mouridism, the city of Touba, its Grand Maggal, and the Maouloud (the night of the birth of the Prophet Muhammed). There are also audio archives of each major Mouride

4.4 Spiritual Space as Digital Terrain

pilgrimage event over the past ten years including the Grand Maggal to Touba, the Porokhane Maggal (where Bamba's mother is buried), various Ramadan events, and the Maouloud. Video files available include the most recent Friday sermons at the Grand Mosque of Touba as well as speeches delivered at various pilgrimage events, documentaries, Islamic news coverage of global issues like climate change and traditional medicine, and even tutorials on cooking meals during Ramadan. The archive is massive and one can scroll seemingly forever through this complex array of video and audio material. One can also take a "guided tour" of the Hizbut Tarqiyya (provided one has an Adobe Flash Player) in which one is treated to a small moving slide show of Tarqiyya people and places along with an outline of their mission, activities, history, and importantly, contacts not only in Senegal but throughout the world. The image gallery also features a visual history of the group, with classifications like "cultural identity," "information and communication technology," and "administration." It is a remarkably organized yet highly complex and deeply contextualized cyberspace that surrounds the visitor both visually and metaphorically with what one might consider both the essential elements of the Mouride faith as well as the day-to-day activities of Mouride life. Importantly, the Hizbut Tarqiyya have also used traditional means and symbols to sanctify this online space through many of the same modes that physical spaces have been similarly blessed in dense urban spaces like Dakar, specifically by including images of Amadou Bamba.

Images of Bamba abound in Touba cyberspace, and do so in a similar fashion to which they appear within the physical environment, being both repetitive and ubiquitous (Figure 4.7a and 4.7b). With regard to the physical environment, the faces of Bamba and other religious leaders peek out from behind corners and through shop doors around the city; in other places they tower over city dwellers in central areas like a type of anthropomorphic skyscraper. These images are thought to contain spiritual power, as described in the previous discussion of *car rapides*, that has been variously interpreted as "charisma" or even "aura," both qualities seen as evidence of the image containing *baraka* or "blessing." According to the Oxford English Dictionary "aura" is a Greek derivative meaning "breeze" or "breath," thus closely associating it with the idea of life, animation, and presence (OED 1982, 565 in Roberts and Roberts 2002, 56). As an image endowed with "breeze," thus, these saintly representations subsequently possess "the capacity to produce a response, bestow well-being, and protect its viewers" (Roberts and Roberts 2002, 56). Roberts and Roberts also point out that Walter Benjamin's contributions to the discussion of "aura" have led works such as saintly images

242   4 Mobility and "Portable" Islamic Space

Figure 4.7 a and b Images of Chlekh Amadou Bamba on a shop building in Dakar and the home page of the Hizbut Tarqiyya, Senegal, 2018. Images by the author.

to not only become connected with idea of authenticity but also become endowed with "the ability to look at us in return" (Benjamin 1988, 188; in Roberts and Roberts 2002, 56). In doing so, they are able to transmit *baraka* through the "weight, opacity, and

4.4 Spiritual Space as Digital Terrain

substance" of their visual representation (Baudrillard 1983, 22–23; in Roberts and Roberts 2002, 56).

At the time of writing (September 2019), the home page of the Hizbut Tarqiyya site features a photograph of the iconic figure of Bamba, who stands on the high left of the page next to a miniaturized version of Touba's Grand Mosque. Moving across the page, one sees crowds of believers gathered on the platform outside the mosque at dusk along with an image of the current caliph general, who is given equal visual weight as Bamba and acts as a visual counterpoint/complement book-ending the visual program of the page. As one navigates to other areas of the site, this upper banner remains the same, greeting the visitor each time they move from link to link. The bottom of each webpage features a similar green banner structure to the top, only this time the banner features only the figure of Amadou Bamba, robed and anonymous, placed in the center of the banner in front of a small, standardized version of Touba's main minaret, Lamp Fall, which appears in a medallion. Contact information for Hizbut Tarqiyya appears in small, unobtrusive text on the right-hand side. The repetition of this organizational structure not only actively defines the identity of the space for visitors to the site, but also emphasizes the borders and parameters of the site "space," each new "land" within being framed and defined by this configuration as a mode of marking territory. In addition, each territory containing the image of Bamba, the Grand Mosque, and the current caliph subsequently becomes a "blessed" space, separating this site as spiritually charged from others that are not so "authenticated." In some ways, this cyberscape constructs Touba and Mouridism as a virtual pseudo-utopia for Mourides just as it acts as a spiritual utopia in the physical landscape, framing Mouridism as an emergent form of "migratory religion in which new territorialization is constantly renewing and reshaping the religion's symbols" (Guèye 2003, 611).

Touba's Grand Maggal further activates this cyberscape as a space of spiritual practice and congregation through the inclusion of live-streaming video feeds from multiple locations around the city. These feeds not only capture important ritual events and ceremonial occasions, but also the movement and interactions of thousands of visiting pilgrims, who walk to and fro across the feed, sometimes noticing the camera and waving happily, other times paying no heed to it. One in essence becomes a participant in this flow as one takes the place of the camera, sometimes being noticed, sometimes not, but always watching, observing, and occasionally being interacted with through a smile, a joyful wave, or a passing glance. It is through such elements that these sites create a "virtual community," or as Ameli says, a community of "conscious and selective origin" without the limiting imposition of "real space" (Ameli 2009, 218). Indeed, cyberspace might be said to enable more streamed modes of communication by "provid[ing] the opportunity to anyone to attend in the space individually and without any interruption in communication" while still enabling the possibility, if so desired, of "being in a crowd" (Ameli 2009, 223).

It is also through these feeds that one is transported across space while also being able to inhabit multiple spaces at once. One can watch individuals arrive in Touba by train, car, etc. and be out in the street with the milling masses or present during a sermon delivered by one of the many religious leaders in attendance. One can listen to reports on the various events going on at different sites or can witness/participate in ongoing prayers from a remote location. What is important about the idea that a pilgrimage can be experienced online is that it supports Jill Dubisch's statement that "pilgrimage ... as a ritual form [is] particularly suited to the postmodern era" (Dubisch 2014, xvi). As individuals increasingly engage in the pilgrimage act for largely individualized motivations and needs, cyber-pilgrimage platforms like that of the Hizbut Tarqiyya construct a necessary experiential apparatus to enable an "encounter" with the spiritual space of Touba in a way that not only fits comfortably with the realm of modern virtual existence but also enables the continuous affirmation of Mouride identity through the elimination of time and distance. One's "presence" in Touba is simultaneous and immediate when one engages in a virtual pilgrimage to a cyberspace of power. To quote Olalquiaga, within the virtual realm, the self "becomes a ship that can sail fluidly through different times and places, always moving and changing" (Olalquiaga 1992, 32; in Adams 1997, 166). Importantly, even though these virtual selves tend to move and interact according to their own impulses and motivations, in the context of cyber-pilgrimage sites like Touba, "they find themselves synchronized automatically with a host of other [pilgrims]" through their channeled online experience (Adams 1997, 164). The shift and alteration of moving images in real time not only creates an attentive tone for the visitor but is also an enticement to those who long for participation rather than the continuous transmission of information.

Thus, perhaps unsurprisingly, Touba as a virtual territory and the diversity of sites that now cover the Touba pilgrimage is also expanding and in many ways is reflective of the pilgrimage event itself, bringing different people together from all over the world to participate in a shared experience of spiritual performance and identity. In addition to the web platform first provided by Hizbut Tarqiyya, there is now a general Mouride site – Mourides.com – which focuses on all aspects of Mouride identity, with a constant newsfeed streaming across the top of the website announcing important dates, events, awards, and occasions. There are also links on this page to the Mouride YouTube channel, Mourides TV, as well as a link to the YouTube channel – Darou Minane TV – of the current caliph general. Facebook has also become a particularly important social platform, particularly during the pilgrimage season when one can see minute-to-minute posts by people there and people can post onto the site from elsewhere as well in a directly interactive, immediate relationship enhanced by images, videos, and status updates. This ability to post and therefore interact is particularly relevant given that cyberspace in contrast to real space seems to enable people to come together in a more comprehensive, fluid manner. As Paul Adams notes, "Community created through shared experience recalls a form of magical union, like the taking of communion in church: Many persons join in a single body through an act of symbolic consumption" (Adams 1997, 164). Thus, there is almost a transcendent element to this communal interaction, a leaving of the physical body where one interacts not through physical apparatuses but through the mind and heart made manifest as data in a space that is both contained within the perimeters of Mouride spirituality but also infinite within that space as well.

There is also a dedicated Maggal site managed by the Culture and Communication Commission of Touba and run by the organizing committee of the Touba Maggal. Along with a pilgrimage "program" of important events, it is here that one can also access live streams from Maggal TV Direct. In each case, the visitor is not only treated to information about the event itself, but also the "synaesthetic experiences of movement, color, touch, and emotion" which are all actively processed by the viewer not in the abstract but through a grounding in "the actual sensual experience of the body as a complex of culturally honed perceptual capacities," produced through the sensual familiarity established by being a member of this specific religious community (Hirschkind 2001, 629).

But in considering the idea of cyber pilgrimage in Touba, it becomes important to examine the nature of pilgrimage as it exists or possibly is developing in the virtual plane. A pilgrimage can be defined as both a process and ritualistic event that is involved with the pursuit of a sacred ideal. Because of the simultaneously collective and individual nature of this event and definition of this ideal, pilgrimages in essence become "busy intersections ... where a number of distinct social processes intersect" (Rosaldo 1989, 17; in Dubisch 2014, X). Importantly, pilgrimage is distinctive precisely because of its visibility. As Turner and Turner note, "If mysticism is an interior pilgrimage, pilgrimage is exteriorized mysticism" (Turner and Turner 1978, 6–7; in Dubisch 2014, xii). Indeed, in many cases the process of the pilgrimage itself, which often involves masses of people converging onto a single space, is rich in symbolic meaning. Turner and Turner also discuss the evolutionary process that a pilgrimage catalyzes within a participant, who separates from their previous sociospiritual space to enter into the rarified environment of the pilgrimage sites to subsequently engage in an act or series of acts that promote personal transformation. Once the transformation has been accomplished, the participant returns to their previous space but at a different sociospiritual level, the result of not only the respiritualization process a person has undergone, but also the symbolic social capital one derives from said experience (Dubisch 2014, xii). Important to catalyzing the aforementioned actions toward promoting personal transformation, however, are numerous important symbolic elements, features, and props that create the necessary spatial apparatus for transcendence to take place. Such features can include "symbolic structures, religious buildings, pictorial images, statuary, and sacralized features of the topography" (Turner and Turner 1978, 10; in Dubisch 2014, xii) and also importantly the sacred narrative of the area, all of which are present for the benefit of one's individual and collective encounter, interaction, and response to these features and to each other. Through these elements, the site of the pilgrimage itself assumes additional realities not only as a spiritual space but also a liminal space, a space out of time and place that in some ways might even compare to a spiritually charged Brigadoon.

When occurring in a spiritual capital city or a dedicated space isolated from other spaces of potential conflict, pilgrimage events make the typical hegemonic landscapes of an already spiritually charged sites hyperspiritualized; in other words, the spiritual meanings and messages that exist in plain sight in this everyday environment suddenly become recharged with spiritual resonance. In many ways, this speaks to the pilgrimage theories of Turner and Turner (1978) in which a pilgrimage is accomplished through both a separation from and a transformation of "daily life patterns" (Dubisch 2014, XX). Yet this separation is not only physical and psychological, but also temporal as an individual "reorients" themselves to engage in "a multiplicity of relationships to the past ... [and] to historical, prehistorical, and imagined traditions of the sacred" (Dubisch 2014, XX).

Pilgrimages thus constitute a potentially interesting event for "online" consideration, as it were, in that, as Ralph Schroeder notes, "while on-line text-based ritual lacks physical presence, the interaction of text, graphics, video and sound open up a range of ritual possibilities that may have profound consequences for the symbolic expression of religiosity"

4.4 Spiritual Space as Digital Terrain

(Schroeder, Heather, and Lee 1998). In addition, the fact that time-based religious practices such as prayer and pilgrimage become ubiquitously available and simultaneous through online platforms makes mass, mobility-driven events not only possible, but also possibly more accessible as well, allowing an individual "to be connected with a crowd 'out of place'" and engage in "a virtual ceremony through a 'virtual religious act'" (Ameli 2009, 221).

Another pilgrimage event that has gained an increased online presence has been the Hajj to Mecca, an annual occurrence that attracts millions of faithful, with more coming every year. Although the Hajj represents one of Islam's primary pillars of faith, i.e. followers must attempt to complete the Hajj at least once in their lifetime, there are many for whom the Hajj is not possible, often because the cost of getting to Mecca can be extreme, especially for followers from poorer areas. In addition, the elderly and infirm may not have the physical capacity to make the trip and, increasingly, women are opting not to go because of the growing number of sexual assaults and harassment they experience during the event. In addition, the Hajj has become an enormous, crowded affair, with some saying that they were unable to reap the spiritual benefits because of the sheer masses of people who flood the holy area each year. While an online pilgrimage experience could probably never replace the Hajj, for those unable to attend it might, however, offer both a commensurate spiritual experience as well as a sense of participating in the congregational aspects of the event.

To this end, Saudi Arabia's Ministry of Culture and Information has created two digital platforms that are intended to provide information for both pilgrims journeying to Mecca and those not able to attend the Hajj during a given year. In addition to providing livestreams at various holy sites around the city, the annual website Hajj.org (typically the web address changes from year to year, i.e. Hajj2017.org, etc.) includes extensive real-time coverage of the full five-day event, including the ceremonies, sermons, and speeches given, as well as information about various sites, updates on times, and general news about the goings on in the city. Another platform, SaudiWelcomesTheworld.org, allows pilgrims to share personal photos from the event and has a gallery devoted to pilgrims undertaking the Tawaf or the circling of the Ka'ba in the Grand mosque. In addition, the Islam Channel broadcasts live from all of the major events during the Hajj and can be accessed online. Through this comprehensive approach to documenting (often minute by minute) the Hajj experience, these platforms in some ways create a "multi-layered physical geography," that approaches the Hajj from multiple trajectories, spaces, and angles of experience simultaneously. Through this, the Hajj as a spiritual experience becomes dimensional and "affords particular forms of sensory engagement to users, who experience themselves as both weightless and prostheticized within virtual space in distinctive ways" (Bassett 2007, 134).

Thus, in many ways, both Mecca and Touba exist online as they do in the real world: as spiritual spaces that become heightened presences on a seasonal basis and act as specific points of reference for followers of the faith both in Senegal and around the world. In this sense, pilgrimage becomes both an event and a "structural concept" that classifies as "a particular type of journey that makes sense only within a particular ordering of [digital] space" (Couldry 2007, 66–67). Within this virtual space are specific constructs, patterns, sources, and images that all maintain deep religious resonance and help structure spiritual identity as it is felt, lived and, importantly, practiced. Thus, online platforms like those mentioned above can be said to create the necessary conditions for the construction of an online pilgrimage experience that exists as a different but potentially complementary alternative to the real experience.

However, this is not to say that such digital spiritual spaces are without their problems, particularly in Senegal. One potential problem with an online pilgrimage experience is a lack of familiarity with the computer interface; computer illiteracy can be highly alienating to any type of online experience that requires one to forget about one's physicality. Interestingly, of all the countries in West Africa, Senegal has shown the most promise in terms of its citizens becoming cyber-fluent, having one of the highest usage rates in all of sub-Saharan Africa and "the second highest level of international bandwidth among countries below the Sahara (trailing only South Africa)." In addition, the relatively high education rate in the country and its working political and economic infrastructure have placed the country in a good position to emerge as a leader in virtual experience (Farivar 2011, 74). Although there is no established Wi-Fi network in Senegal, internet access is provided in a number of individual spaces including from workplaces, homes, and places of business (Farivar 2011, 73). The Internet is obviously more common in urban areas and cybercafes began to appear in increasing numbers in urban areas across the country in the early 2000s (Farivar 2011, 82). Increased familiarity with virtual platforms has also been aided by groups such as the Hizbut Tarqiyya, with platforms such as Facebook and YouTube having the potential to familiarize digital interfaces to the point where they are not only normalized but also hegemonic as they have become in other parts of the world (Ameli 2009, 225).

Yet another potential downside of the virtualization of pilgrimage events like that of Touba, however, is that it could effectively "industrialize" the event, not only neutralizing its spiritual uniqueness through the mundane ability to gain simultaneous immediate access but also making such occasions commonplace and mass produced. Along these lines, Wertheim offers an important point that speaks to this element in that "how we conceive of space reflects how we think about ourselves, since they mirror each other" (McRobert 2007, 95). As both products and producers of our own space, we in turn govern our experiences of that space and how it subsequently shapes our identities. Yet through the contextualization of the faith, these sites enable visitors to subsequently deploy this contextualization within the world of images, audiovisual materials, news, and information they offer toward creating not only a legitimation of the visitor as an active participant in the faith but also authenticating themselves as a purveyor of these elements. Through their organization around the key site of Touba as well, these sites virtualize a physical space into a digital masjid arena, transforming its reality so that Touba as a place exists on two planes of existence, the physical and the virtual, and gives people the tools to exist and participate simultaneously on two planes as well.

Many of the online spaces that have developed around the experience of the Grand Maggal in Touba also importantly fit with the defining characteristic of the pilgrimage as defined by Turner, i.e. "special individual journeys to distant places associated with common values." Further, Nick Couldry notes that:

online space ... is so vast, indeed effectively infinite, that any number of "special journeys" to its obscure corners would seem possible, suggesting a vast pluralization of pilgrimage opportunities in the "online world." An advantage, prima facie, would seem to be that online space is not a vast chaos, but a domain where all journeys are potentially traceable: there are determinable routes by which we can reach even very obscure sites. We can imagine in principle "online journeys" taking on at least some features of offline pilgrimage. the uncertainty of arrival, anticipation, relief at arrival, a sense of discovery and affirmation on arrival. (Couldry 2007, 70)

And with regard to the Mourides, each and every site contains the visage of Bamba who, as a whole figure, a shadowy face, and even just a pair of shaded eyes, becomes a liminal figure in the digital realm, his presence transformed into a type of virtual bodily imprint that in turn constitutes proof of presence and blessing in the virtual realm as he does in the physical one. As A. A. Aziz notes, "Murid sacred space is defined with the spiritual guide or sheikh of the Muridiyya order, Amadu Bamba, and his ability to convey *baraka* (the gift of grace) to any place with which he came into contact" (Babou 2007, 200–201). Thus, his inclusion on the "walls" of online spaces creates a series of digital footprints as Bamba increasingly colonizes online space into masjid space through the forward momentum of Mouridism, spreading his blessing through visual form and virtual action within the growing territory of Mouride online space. The visage of Bamba indeed could act as a mechanism toward the mapping of online Mouride space: an iconic form who constitutes the singular most territorializing visual apparatus of the Mouride brotherhood and represents the ever-watchful omnipresent power of God in the lives of Mourides, or at least those who are online. Thus, to adapt Cheikh Anta Babou's commentary on Mouride sacred space, by creating "sites of Murid memory" within the digital landscape through celebratory events like the Grand Maggal, Mourides are "seeking to stretch the tariqa's space"; thus, the establishment and growth of these online masjid spaces "is central to the articulation and revision of memory, and through it the writing and rewriting of history" (Babou 2007, 215).

Sites like Touba, among others, do provide multiple possibilities for different conceptualizations of masjid space to emerge in the digital realm. Touba has been described as "the supreme expression of this sense of 'communitas'" (Coulon 1999, 206). It is an enormous emotional gathering of pilgrims who have come together at the spiritual and geographic center of their faith to share in the celebration and veneration of their sainted founder and thus reaffirm their commitment to the faith and their spiritual identity among diverse but like-minded followers in a "syntony," to use Michel Maffessoli's term, in which "individuals in contact with one another ... fuse their individuality into a strong sentiment of their belonging to a collective Us" (Maffesoli 1988, 113; in Coulon 1999, 206). Thus, Touba online is a type of heart space or soul space where the body is left behind in favor of the mind and spirit wandering and practicing faith as "electronically extended bodies" through established spaces like virtual Touba and its digital spatial territories (Mitchell 1995, 167; in Adams 1997, 167). Touba online might even be termed a type of "liquid architecture" in which its ever-expanding virtual spaces connected through links and tabs can be thought of as "interconnected rooms opening up to realms of other rooms in open-ended, never-ending kaleidoscope fashion" (McRobert 2007, 103).

The "virtuo-real" space of Touba represents a potential solution to what Travis Price and Randall Ott predict is the future of architectural reality – "homogenized buildings augmented by nostalgically watered-down exterior decorating" which culminates into "one monochromatic, bland whisper" (Price 2015, 249). Because our environments shape us just as we shape our environments, the virtual could become the next spatial platform of human existence, although Price and Ott warn against the potential for a "vacuous virtual, electronic reality that not only

4.4 Spiritual Space as Digital Terrain

alienates us but, more dreadfully, numbs us to our environment and our fellow humans" (Price 2015, 249). Many feel in fact that architects should be designing "for subjects imparted with two bodies, the real and the virtual one ... [because] ... they are part of what constitutes today's physical presence." Thus it becomes possible that contemporary and future expectations with regard to one's spatial environment might only be met via the digital realm (Picon 2004, 119).

If prayer is a meditative act that involves performative action, new masjid spaces oriented to support alternative types of action and experience are one of the primary motivating factors behind the now expansive reach of the current digital world into contemporary reality. As Bassett notes, "the Internet architecture was settled, colonized, inhabited, navigated, surfed, and linked by the practices of its users" (Bassett 2007, 141), a formative event that subsequently created a digital "geography" that was somewhat patchwork in nature but importantly organic and spontaneous in its production. Its subsequent expansion has now created a space that is fundamentally anticipatory in nature. Thus, the digital realm has become the ultimate example of a liminal space, not only because of its general intangibility but also because of its fundamental reality as being always "in process" and "in transit." In fact, these aspects of digital life have come to be synonymous with modern life in general, as individuals increasingly exist in between spaces or in transit from one area to another.

The true potential of virtual masjid spaces like Touba's lies in the fact that many scholars are coming to believe that the "intensification" of one's virtual experience is in many ways akin to a type of spiritual sensuality, made possible through one's sensorial removal from the "real" world (Ameli 2009, 224). Another aspect of cyberspace that approaches the spiritual is offered by Margaret Wertheim, who compares the philosophical binary of physical space vs. cyberspace to that of physical space vs. nonphysical/metaphysical space adopted by Christian philosophy during the Middle Ages (McRobert 2007, 93–94). Both, Wertheim contends, maintain a particular mystical quality, with cyberspace having the capability to become a "new spiritual space" or a "realm for the soul." In a particularly poetic turn of phrase, cyberspace has the potential to become "a new immaterial space where techno-spiritual dreaming can occur" (McRobert 2007, 94). Such considerations have also led to a number of additional eschatological metaphors including the possibility of "cyber-immortality," "digital eternity," and a cybernetic body that is able to return in a coded "hypercorporal synthesis" just as Jesus Christ did in similarly exalted form (McRobert 2007, 94).

At its base, however, the masjid remains a space devoid of structural parameters and oriented around purpose. In the contemporary period, advances in communications and technology have fundamentally shifted our conceptualization of time, space, and distance, all elements that are not only fundamental for perceptions of architectural form but also definitive of one's experience within a masjid construct (Imdat 2006). Thus, the question of whether or not one actually needs a physical space in which to engage in religious practice remains.

4.5 Conclusion

Within the context of this chapter, mobility theory has acted as the theoretical and interpretive basis for the analysis of multiple types of emergent Afro-Islamic spiritual spaces in the contemporary period. Yet, it is not without its problems with regard to conceptualizations of the masjid. As has been addressed, the masjid as a space is fundamentally based on the intent and performance of the individual, which is why any space can be a masjid. Yet the nonplaces of the aforementioned examples have the effect of reducing the individual to their current action, i.e. passenger, commuter, virtual user, etc. How do these identities, in which an individual is "relieved of his usual determinants" (As 2006, 103), interact or potentially interfere with the identity of the individual as a purposeful unique prayerful body, i.e. masjid maker? Does the "solitude and similitude" (As 2006, 103) that comes from existing within a nonspace as a nonindividual fundamentally depower an individual's ability to actively catalyze spiritual space? In addition, because nonspaces are "there to be passed through … [and are thus] … measured in units of time," how does one navigate living in "the urgency of the present moment" with the time/space removal required of engaging in masjid activity (Augé 1995, 104)?

In dealing with this, it pays to recenter "the corporeal body as an affective vehicle through which we sense place and movement, and construct emotional geographies" (Sheller and Urry 2006, 216). Each body creates a different experience of masjid space based on the filtering of multiple perspectives and lens of experience and movement, which highlight the complexity of individual experience in relation to space and spiritual performance and how each interacts and entwines through mobility. Thus, with regard to spiritual spaces on the move, "we are not dealing with a single network, but with complex intersections of 'endless regimes of flow', which move at different speeds, scales, and viscosities" (Sheller and Urry 2006, 213).

Mobility theories in many ways reverse established binaries of center/periphery created by these assumed relationships and established

4.5 Conclusion

movement and the forces driving them as a type of moving center that encounters, interacts, and sometimes pushes back against other moving centers in a type of dynamic, shifting Venn diagram. As Africa and the rest of the world moves "in more dynamic, complex and trackable ways than ever before, while facing new challenges of forced mobility and uneven mobility, environmental limits and climate change and the movement of unpredictable risks" (Sheller 2011, 1), mobility paradigms and the masjids that result from them create new conceptualizations of space where even a "'passing stranger' can feel at home" (Augé 1995, 106).

Each of these case studies represent toolkits that African Muslims are deploying as part of their lived faith to not only help facilitate spiritual practice as they dwell in motion but also "demonstrate the practical, innovative impulses of devout Muslims to continue their religious practices in spite of working conditions that might make this difficult" (Smith and Bender 2004, 90). In other words, these space-making strategies represent a mode through which ephemeral, even occasional masjid space is established as part of lived religion within the landscape, the ever-evolving nature of which requires new spiritual forms of spatial manifestation that are in tune with a contemporary sensibility composed of equally spiritual and secular considerations.

This generates an even larger spiritual cartography defined by a trans-spatial identity that moves away from the binary models of center/periphery and homeland/frontier toward framing the world as masjid as "a zone of intercultural contact and interchange [and I would add movement]" (Chidester and Linenthal 1995, 25). Importantly, the performative action that makes such spaces possible is one replicable anywhere and everywhere. To quote Metcalf, "It is themselves and their fellow Muslims as embodiments of Muslim ritual and practice, that define any place as Muslim space." The fact that Mourides, for example, "carry Touba in their hearts" means that "Marseilles or Manhattan are ultimately indistinguishable" (Metcalf 1996, 11). Yet even as these spaces replicate, they continue to travel and transform in a continuous process of reinvention and reimagining. Thus, even as human identities are "written onto the environment" through space and in some ways enable us to "look back to read our lives between the brick and mortar," a space "inextricably bound up with our sense of self" does not mean such space cannot be moved, replicated, or transformed (Reaven and Zeitlin 2006, 334). With regard to the masjid, the fact that "sacred space" does not exist in Islam means that all spaces exist in a type of spiritually fluid state ready to emerge as the need arises. Although certain spaces like Mecca orient one in space, one continues to move around in relation to it in a way that "undermines the logic of the nation and at the same time ... seeks to transcend the logic of the nation" (Taleb 2005, 39). It is here where the notion of *ummah* rises to the forefront. As a collective unit of faithful followers on the path of Islam, the *ummah* exists "without the physical boundedness that nation implies" toward "transcending national state boundaries and instead linking all Muslims to this symbolic community" (Taleb 2005, 39). Such relationships provide natural complements to the idea of mobile space, whether it be vehicular, infrastructural, or virtual in nature. The *ummah*'s lack of geographic boundedness enables a perfect example of Benedict Anderson's imagined community in which temporality and a shared destiny create a collective sense of belonging. Masjid spaces in the various mobile forms addressed in this chapter actively support this global collective in that they do not generate strong divisions between interior/exterior, center/periphery, or homeland/frontier. Such binaries are subverted and deconstructed by masjids as spaces that move within, between, and around worlds and do not claim a homeland; thus, those that exist within the spatial experience of the masjid also do not experience displacement. Regarding space, thus, masjids function as "lens through which [scholars] could interrogate the politics of landscape, identity, and memory" in a way that privileges the mobility of the contemporary world while also anchoring space in the performance of prayer (Della Dora 2015). As spaces that accommodate bodies moving between destinations, masjids are both spiritual spaces and also spaces of temporary habitus, areas of encounter that exist in the frontier-like nonspaces between centers and peripheries. They are zones of contact that exist as staging areas for the traversal of borders and boundaries.

Conclusion
Looking to the Future: The Masjid as a Space on the Edge

Throughout this volume, masjids have been positioned not only as space but also as an interpretive lens through which to view Islam not only as a condition of being but also a mode of place-making and in fact interpreting the world. This has not only allowed diverse communities to come together in ways that were not previously thought to be possible, but it has also allowed communities to expand outwards, creating satellite societies that are physically separated yet nonetheless intimately connected and thus contained within a spiritual community, creating a "highly variegated ecology of Muslim experience" (Mandel 1996, 147). The volume has covered numerous masjid spaces in Africa that have either existed over a significant period of time or are just beginning to make their presence known. As representative mechanisms, these masjids not only actively reproduce diverse iterations of Islamic identity in Africa over time and space, but also adapt within these contexts in response to an evolving spectrum of influences, ideologies, and interventions that have each played important roles in shaping the contours of Islamic identity and practice within specific regional contexts. Importantly, these spaces challenge established ideas of space and architecture by generating progressive discussions of the masjid in terms of what it is and how it manifests in contemporary Africa as well as around the world. Such conversations are just beginning and will progress into the future as social, political, cultural, and spiritual identities continue to evolve. Thus, masjids must be seen, read, interpreted, and privileged as contextually embedded structural manifestations of the ways in which time and transformation have been allowed to act upon the environment, as well as spatial strategies and/or solutions to the problem of performing Muslim identity within the diverse contexts of Africa both now and moving in the future.

Such spaces must also be seen as modes of creating dialogue within increasingly diverse Muslim environments, able to accommodate and respond to the ebbs and flows of society as fluid blueprints of political, cultural, and socio-spiritual identity. As a spatial formula characterized by mobility, flexibility, and a fundamentally metabolic nature, the masjid as a space on the edge is deeply embedded in contemporary conversations about modernity, space, and what it means to be a Muslim in the contemporary period. As such, it continues, as it always has, to rub up uncomfortably against established ideas of built form and the interpretive methodologies that have been applied to it. As space, process, symbol, and assertion, masjids not only stand as a symbol of Muslim identity in Africa, but as an active affirmation and progression of identity toward an unknown but undoubtedly edgy future.

In addition, such considerations also stress the importance of the conceptual evolution of concepts like architecture, religion, and specific constructs like the masjid, which no longer exist as just usable spaces, but also as symbols in multiple forms. Beyond two-dimensional images and three-dimensional constructs, each of these entities exist as four-dimensional territories of simultaneous movement and communication. They exist as form, text, image, and now pixel, reflective of the true reality of space as it exists in the contemporary period. While individuals like Price may see these spaces as liminal in the sense that they teeter on the edge of oblivion, these are in actuality spaces on the cutting edge, liminal in that they transgress borders and boundaries and exist in between given spaces that are still "frontier" in many ways. Indeed, as Caroline Bassett notes: "The cultural history of the Internet is all about the promise of a space" (Bassett 2007, 132) and, importantly, these spaces are increasingly constructed through the narratives of themes and ideas like Islam. Bassett notes de Certeau, who said that "to write a story is to make a space" (Bassett 2007, 132). "Stories … traverse and organize places; they select and link them together; they make sentences and itineraries out of them. They are spatial trajectories" (de Certeau 1984, 115; in Bassett 2007, 132). Importantly, these spatial stories must reflect the reality of religions like Islam which evolve not only through changing ideological viewpoints, but also through the media by which they are transmitted. Religions such as Islam have always depended on media such as text, speech, and structure to "make the spiritual and the transcendental more accessible for believers" (Melice and Pype 2009, 16). Because of this, Annie Melice and Katrien Pype note, "The moving image, the printed word and the materiality of the television set, the camera, or any other medium may acquire a sacred power similar to that of diviners, spiritual mediums and power objects" (Melice and Pype 2009, 16). The rise of virtual space thus is the next step in a continuum of media that have long made sacred space a usable apparatus for the faithful.

Yet these spaces are further articulated through the stories and narratives of social relationships, and such narratives are not only produced through the practices of the users themselves but also through the movements of users across time and space and the places they create, not only at the beginning and the end but also over the course of the journey and the moment-to-moment fabric of their lives – "the trails produced through lived practices of users" (Bassett 2007, 158–159). These spaces constitute another type of liminality, spaces that may be physical in nature but are nonetheless somehow dislocated from the currents of everyday life through their existence as a result of travel and movement. These types of liminal spaces breed new questions relating to location, mobility, space, and transversal, and highlight the fact that to understand the conceptual, physical, and idealized depth of spatial genres like the masjid, one cannot restrict interpretations to a single form, area, or construct, but must in fact consider the entirety of the spatial landscape that they compose.

Collectively these spaces, particularly within the diverse contexts of the African continent, not only "mak[e] visible the contestation of territories … [and] … the proximities of different practices" (Wilhelm-Solomon et al. 2017, 23) but also create a multitude of spiritual essays that narrate history, memory, and identity, their sheer number and pervasiveness collapsing the separation between the spiritual and the everyday through the proliferation of mediums, genres, symbolisms, and spatializations. This gives voice to the fact that any space can be "masjid" depending on intent, and it is through this intent that "a simple site of activity becomes a *place* endowed with the 'distinct potencies' of connotative significance" (Casey 1987; Roberts and Roberts 2002, 73). Masjid spaces are not fixed spaces; they actively fluctuate in response to contemporary conditions, circumstances, and ideologies, with certain histories, politics, social identities, and causes emerging more strongly in some times and places than others in the context of specific situations and conditions of being. Space does not exist as a void or vacuum to be filled, but instead is created by a series of relationships and performances and is thus invested with symbolic meanings and messages in a way that demonstrates that "the place is inseparable from the consciousness of those who inhabit it" (Daniels 1985, 151; in Taleb 2005, 14). Space and the architectures, landscapes, and image fields that compose it thus actively function as "symbolic fields," "maps of meaning," "ways of seeing," and, importantly, documents and even types of text (Thrift 1989, 151; in Taleb 2005, 14). Thus space is defined both by its inner dimensions and the relationships that occur between area and inhabitant, as well as its exterior dimensions in terms of its relationships with the spaces around it and how people move between these spaces.

While this is not a new development, it has important ramifications in the contemporary period within vast, diverse, mobile terrains like Africa, whose Muslim populace not only maintains diverse histories, traditions, and spiritual practices that have evolved in unique ways over time, but have also absorbed various influences, hierarchies, and ideologies into their own narrative topographies not as disruptions but as modes through which spiritual identities come into their own as contemporary modes of being in the world. Along these lines, such modes are constantly being reworked, resulting in diverse arrays of spatial production, performance, and movement, all of which are firmly embedded in and responsible to the modern realities of life on the continent.

Thus, the creation of masjid space is a multi-tiered process that reflects a tableau of "the linkages of macro processes with the texture and fabric of human experience" (Taleb 2005, 20). Regardless of the lack of what some might call a "formalized" structure, these spaces nonetheless maintain a unity that takes its very rationality from the diverse spectrum of identities in modern society. In turn, such identities create saturated spaces that are constructed according to specific ideas about the relationships and interaction between sacred and secular. As such, the masjid as a concept focuses less on the rarefied examples of self-consciously performative Islamic practice and more on "Islam as a lived reality" or the way in which "Islam is (re)negotiated in everyday living" (Janson 2011, 102). In unpacking the various quotidian ways that Muslims are "in the world" on a daily basis in Africa, *Islam mondain* becomes a mode of understanding the unique ways that Islam has been contextualized within the context of an urban area. "Living Islam," thus, becomes a mode of considering religion not as a component of a social system but, to quote Janson, "part of the actual world in which Muslims live" (Janson 2011, 101). The masjid stands as the spatial mobilization of this identity, a mediator between spiritual and mundane worlds, a symbol of faith, and a representation of the social, political, and cultural flows that force contemplation of the role of spirituality in contemporary society and what the future of Islam in Africa might entail.

As a site "both abstract and concrete, lived and conceived, an arena of practice and an arena of thought" (Guest 2012, 220), the masjid in contemporary Islamic Africa constitutes a type of code, which, in the words of Abdulkader Tayob, "can be compared with technical and functional codes used in everyday life, through which things get done, ideas thought, and social groups formed" (Tayob 1999, 9). Along these lines, diverse "Islams" not only create diverse masjid sites but also reflect different ideas of space (Nuttall 2004, 741). To quote Nasseema Taleb, "The recurrent, serial production of new spaces, practices, and patterns is accompanied by ... new experiences of space and time" (Taleb 2005, 15), allowing it to encompass both physical and virtual constructs or "the conceptual and the lived" (Guest 2012, 222). The masjid as a trans-Muslim structural order thus creates a spatial realm removed from the world which maintains its integrity through a consistent adherence to ritual law and subsequent "transformative potential of its user" (Della Dora 2015).

Bibliography

Abbink, Jon. 1998. "An Historical-Anthropological Approach to Islam in Ethiopia: Issues of Identity and Politics." *Journal of African Cultural Studies* 11 (2): 109–124.

———. 2008. "Muslim Monasteries? Some Aspects of Religious Culture in Northern Ethiopia." *Aethiopica: International Journal of Ethiopian Studies* 11: 117–133.

Abdul-Matin, Ibrahim. 2010. *Green Deen: What Islam Teaches About Protecting the Planet*. San Francisco: Berrett-Koehler.

Aburawa, Arwa. n.d. "Eco-Mosques: Building Green Houses of Worship." *Sisters Magazine*. Accessed December 3, 2017. www.sisters-magazine.com/building-a-green-house-of-worship/.

Accra. 2014. "ACCRA, Ghana National Mosque, U/C." Skyscraper City (website). May 14. Accessed September 9, 2019. www.skyscrapercity.com/showthread.php?p=119517657.

Adams, Bert D., and R. A. Sydie. 2001. *Sociological Theory*. Thousand Oaks, CA: Pine Forge Press.

Adams, Paul C. 1997. "Cyberspace and Virtual Places." *Geographical Review* 87 (2): 155–171.

AFP. 2012. "Agenda Items 2 and 4." Report of the United Nations High Commissioner for Human Rights on the Situation of Human Rights in Mali. Human Rights Council, January 7.

———. 2016. "Cape Town's Gay Mosque Provides Rare Haven." *News 24*. October 31. Accessed December 30, 2017. www.news24.com/SouthAfrica/News/cape-towns-gay-mosque-provides-rare-haven-20161031-62.

Ahmad, T., M. J. Thaheem, A. Anwar, and Z. U. Din. 2016. "Implications of Stereotype Mosque Architecture on Sustainability." *Procedia Engineering* 145: 96–103.

Ahmed, Abdul. 2018. Interview by Michelle Apotsos (February 10).

Ahmed, Hussein. 2007. "Reflections on Historical and Contemporary Islam in Ethiopia and Somalia: A Comparative and Contrastive Overview." *Journal of Ethiopian Studies* 40 (1/2): 261–276.

Ahmed, K. G., and L. Elgizawi. 2009. "Two Versions of 'New Gourna' and the Dilemma of Sustainability in New Urban Communities in Egypt." *Sustainable Development of Planning* 120: 691–701.

Ahrends, P. 1996. "Public Architecture and Settlement: Architectural Practice in South Africa." *AA Files* 31: 72–78.

Alarslan Uludas, Burcu, and Fatos Adiloglu. 2011. "Islamic Gardens with a Special Emphasis on the Ottoman Paradise Gardens: The Sense of Place Between Imagery and Reality." *Online Journal of Communication and Media Technologies* 1 (4): 44–96.

allAfrica. 2003. "Ethiopia: State of the Art Airport Terminal Opens." allAfrica (website). January 22. Accessed July 15, 2019. https://allafrica.com/stories/200301220109.html.

Ameli, Saied Reza. 2009. "Virtual Religion and Duality of Religious Spaces." *Asian Journal of Social Science* 37 (2): 208–231.

ANCBS. 2014. "Mission Report: Civil-Military Assessment Mission for Malian Heritage, January 13 to 19, 2014." Association of National Committees of the Blue Shield, January.

Appadurai, Arjun. 1996. *Modernity at Large: Cultural Dimensions of Globalization.* Minnesota: University of Minnesota Press.

Apotsos, Michelle. 2012. "Holy Ground: Mud, Materiality, and Meaning in the Djenne Mosque." *Rutgers Art Review* 27: 2–12.

— 2016a. *Architecture, Islam, and Identity in West Africa: Lessons from Larabanga.* New York: Routledge.

— 2016b. "New Meanings and Historical Messages in the Larabanga Mosque." *African Arts* 49 (4): 8–23.

— 2017. "Timbuktu in Terror: Architecture and Iconoclasm in Contemporary Africa." *International Journal of Islamic Architecture* 6 (1): 97–120.

Architects for Peace. n.d. "Curriculum Vitae: Mike Pierce." Architects for Peace (website). Accessed September 17, 2016. www.architectsforpeace.org/mickprofile.php.

Archnet. n.d. "The Great Mosque at Kilwa – Kilwa Kisiwani, Tanzania." Archnet (website). Accessed August 7, 2019. https://archnet.org/sites/3779.

Armstrong, R. 2010. "Biological Architecture." *Forward: The Architecture and Design Journal of the National Associates Committee* 110: 77–82.

As, Imdat. 2006. "The Digital Mosque: A New Paradigm in Mosque Design." *Journal of Architectural Education* 60 (1): 54–55.

Asad, Talal. 2009. "The Idea of an Anthropology of Islam." *Qui Parle* 17 (2): 1–30.

Asscy, Paschal, Stephen Bass, Blandina Cheche, David Howlett, George Jambiya, Idris Kikula, Servacius Likwelile, et al. 2007. *Environment at the Heart of Tanzania's Development: Lessons from Tanzania's National Strategy for Growth and Reduction of Poverty – MKUKUTA.* Vol. 6. London: International Institute for Environment and Development.

Augé, Marc. 1995. *Non-Places: Introduction to an Anthropology of Supermodernity.* Translated by John Howe. London and New York: Verso.

Avni, Gideon. 2007. "From Standing Stones to Open Mosques in the Negev Desert: The Archaeology of Religious Transformation on the Fringes." *Near Eastern Archaeology* 70 (3): 124–138.

Aziz, A. A. 2016. "Execution of Contemporary Islamic Architecture Through Design: The Cyberjaya Green Platinum Mosque Project in Malaysia." In *WIT Transactions on the Built Environment, Volume 159*, edited by C. A. Brebbia and A. Martinez Boquera, 11–21. Southampton: WIT Press.

Paper presented at the 1st International Conference on Islamic Heritage Architecture and Art (IHA).

Babou, Cheikh Anta. 2007. "Urbanizing Mystical Islam: Making Murid Space in the Cities of Senegal." *The International Journal of African Historical Studies* 40 (2): 197–223.

Badaru, Comfort. n.d. "Cultural Heritage – Urban Dynamics: Zanzibar, Bagamoyo, Dar es Salaam." Report on conference held at the Goethe Institute, November 4. https://aat.archi/publication/view/cultural-heritage-urban-dynamics/.

Baderoon, Gabeba. 2019. "Reading the Hidden History of the Cape: Islam and Slavery in the Making of Race and Sex in South Africa." In *Slavery in the Islamic World: Its Characteristics and Commonality*, edited by Mary Ann Fay, 37–50. New York: Palgrave Macmillan.

Barrie, Thomas, and Julio Bermudez. 2008. "Introduction – Immateriality in Architecture." *Journal of Architectural Education* 62 (2): 4–5.

Barthes, Roland. 2013. *Mythologies*. New York: Hill and Wang.

Bassett, Caroline. 2007. *The Arc and the Machine: Narrative and New Media*. Manchester: Manchester University Press.

Bauman, Zygmunt. 2004. *Europe: An Unfinished Adventure*. Cambridge: Polity Press.

Baydar, Gülsüm. 2004. "The Cultural Burden of Architecture." *Journal of Architectural Education* 57 (4): 19–27.

BBC. 2009. "Religions: Hijab." BBC (website). September 3. Accessed January 3, 2018. www.bbc.co.uk/religion/religions/islam/beliefs/hijab_1.shtml.

Becker, Felicitas. 2006. "Rural Islamism During the 'War on Terror': A Tanzanian Case Study." *African Affairs* 105 (421): 583–603.

Belkhir, Jean Ait, and Johnella E. Butler. 1998. "Introduction: Environmentalism and Race, Gender, Class Issues." *Race, Gender, & Class* 6 (1): 5–11.

Bender, Courtney. 2014. "The Architecture of Multi-Faith Prayer: Airport Multi-Faith Prayer Rooms." Reverberations: New Directions in the Study of Prayer. SSRC Forums (website). August 4. Accessed September 26, 2017. http://forums.ssrc.org/ndsp/category/the-architecture-of-multi-faith-prayer/.

Bennett, Tony. 1996. "The Exhibitionary Complex." In *Thinking About Exhibitions*, edited by Reesa Greenberg and Bruce W. Ferguson, 81–112. Sussex: Psychology Press.

Bergdoll, Barry. 2007. "Of Crystals, Cells, and Strata: Natural History and Debates on the Form of a New Architecture in the Nineteenth Century." *Architectural History* 50: 1–29.

Bhabha, Homi K. 1994. "Of Mimicry and Man: The Ambivalence of Colonial Discourse." In his *The Location of Culture*, 85–92. New York: Routledge.

Bhatt, Ritu, and Alka Patel. 1998. "How Buildings Divide and Unite Us: The Case of Mandal (Gujarat, India)." *Thresholds* 17: 47–51.

Binte-Farid, Irteza. 2013. "Kramats in Cape Town: Telling Stories of Slavery, Defiance, and Identity." *Avicenna – The Stanford Journal on Muslim Affairs* 3 (1): 12–14.

Bird, Michael, and Zeynep Sentek. 2015. "Revealed: Turkey's Massive Global Mega-Mosque Plan." The Black Sea (website). September 29. Accessed

Bibliography

September 9, 2019. https://theblacksea.eu/_old/mirror/theblacksea.eu/index340e.html?idT=88&idC=88&idRec=1211&recType=story.
Bissell, William Cunningham. 2005. "Engaging Colonial Nostalgia." *Cultural Anthropology* 20 (2): 215–248.
Bokhari, Abdulla Yahia. 1980. "Some Notes on the Development of Contemporary Islamic Architecture (Extract)." *Ekistics* 47 (280): 76–77.
Boswell, Rosabelle. 2008. "Scents of Identity: Fragrance as Heritage in Zanzibar." *Journal of Contemporary African Studies* 26 (3): 295–311.
Boudier, Jean Paul, and Trinh T. Minh-ha. 1998. *Drawn from African Dwellings*. Indianapolis: Indiana University Press.
Bourgeois, Jean-Louis, and Carollee Pelos. 1982. "Magnificent Mud: Mosques in Mali." Edited by Hasan-Uddin Khan. MIMAR 3: Architecture in Development 3, 9–15.
———. 1996. *Spectacular Vernacular: The Adobe Tradition*. New York: Aperture Foundation Inc.
Böwering, Gerhard, Patricia Crone, and Mahan Mirza. 2013. *The Princeton Encyclopedia of Islamic Political Thought*. Princeton: Princeton University Press.
Bowker, Sam. 2016. "From Tin Sheds to Temples: The Past, Present, and Potential of the Australian Mosque." *The Guardian*. September 22. Accessed August 5, 2019. www.theguardian.com/world/2016/sep/23/tin-sheds-temples-past-present-potential-australian-mosques.
Braukämper, Ulrich. 1984. "On Food Avoidances in Southern Ethiopia: Religious Manifestation and Socio-Economic Relevance." *Proceedings of the Seventh International Conference of Ethiopian Studies*, edited by Sven Rubenson, 429–446. Addis Abeba: Institute of Ethiopian Studies; Uppsala: Scandinavian Institute of African Studies.
Buchli, Victor. 2015. *The Anthropology of Architecture*. London: Bloomsbury Academic.
Casey, Edward. 1987. "Place Memory." In his *Remembering: A Phenomenological Study*, 181–215. Bloomington: Indiana University Press.
Chidester, David, and Edward Linenthal. 1995. "Introduction." In *American Sacred Space*, edited by David Chidester and Edward Linenthal, 1–42. Bloomington: Indiana University Press.
Clifford, James. 1997. *Routes: Travel and Translation in the Late Twentieth Century*. Cambridge: Harvard University Press.
CMRM. n.d. "Vision and Mission." Claremont Main Road Mosque (website). Accessed July 24, 2019. https://cmrm.co.za/vision-and-mission/.
Coleman, Simon, and John Eade. 2004. *Reframing Pilgrimage: Cultures in Motion*. London: Routledge.
Collison, Carl. 2017. "Queer Muslim Women Are Making Salaam with Who They Are." *Mail & Guardian*. February 10. Accessed September 28, 2017. https://mg.co.za/article/2017-02-10-queer-muslim-women-are-making-salaam-with-who-they-are.
Connery, W. 2000. "Within the Walls of Ethiopia's Islamic City of Harar." *World and I* 15: 184–191.
Couldry, Nick. 2007. "Pilgrimage in Mediaspace: Continuities and Transformations." *Etnofoor* 20 (1): 63–73.

Coulon, Christian. 1999. "The Grand Magal in Touba: A Religious Festival of the Mouride Brotherhood of Senegal." *African Affairs* 98 (391): 195–210.

Creighton, Oliver. 2007. "Contested Townscapes: The Walled City as World Heritage." *World Archaeology* 39 (3): 339–354.

Crenshaw, Kimberlé. 1989. "Demarginalizing the Intersection of Race and Sex: A Black Feminist Critique of Antidiscrimination Doctrine, Feminist Theory and Antiracist Politics." *University of Chicago Legal Forum* 1989 (1): 139–167.

Crompton, Andrew. 2013. "The Architecture of Multifaith Spaces: God Leaves the Building." *The Journal of Architecture* 18 (4): 474–496.

Currier, Ashley. 2012. *Out in Africa: LGBT Organizing in Namibia and South Africa*. Minneapolis: University of Minnesota Press.

Daragahi, Borzou. 2015. "The Secret of Turkey's Ever Expanding Mega-Mosques." Buzzfeed News (website). December 15. Accessed September 9, 2019. www.buzzfeednews.com/article/borzoudaragahi/the-real-reason-turkey-is-building-so-many-mosques.

Davary, Bahar. 2016. "'King-Slaves' in South Africa: Shrines, Rituals, and Resistance." In *Hagiography and Religious Truth: Case Studies in the Abrahamic and Dharmic Tradition*, edited by Rico G. Monge, Kerry P. C. San Chirico, and Rachel J. Smith, 137–151. London: Bloomsbury Academic.

Davidson, Naomi. 2012. *Only Muslim: Embodying Islam in Twentieth-Century France*. Ithaca: Cornell University Press.

Davis, Richard H. 2005. "Iconoclasm in the Era of Strong Religion." *Material Religion: The Journal of Objects, Art, and Belief* 1 (2): 261–268.

――― 2009. "The Rise and Fall of a Sacred Place: Ayodhya over Three Decades." In *Culture and Belonging in Divided Societies: Contestation and Symbolic Landscapes*, edited by Marc Howard Ross, 25–44. Philadelphia: University of Pennsylvania Press.

de Jong, Ferdinand. 2007. "A Masterpiece of Masquerading: Contradictions of Conservation in Intangible Heritage." In *Reclaiming Heritage: Alternative Imaginaries of Memory in West Africa*, edited by Ferdinand de Jong and Michael Rowlands, 161–184. Walnut Creek: Left Coast Press.

de Jorio, Rosa. 2016. *Cultural Heritage in Mali in the Neoliberal Era*. Chicago: University of Illinois Press.

de Vere Allen, James. 1974. "Swahili Architecture in the Later Middle Ages." *African Arts* 7 (2): 42–47; 66–68; 83–84.

――― 1989. "The Kiti Cha Enzi and Other Swahili Chairs." *African Arts* 22 (3): 54–63; 88.

Deccan Herald. 2016. "Badriya Jam'a Masjid to Be Zero Energy Mosque." *Deccan Herald*. January 16. Accessed August 9, 2019. www.deccanherald.com/content/523278/badriya-juma-masjid-zero-energy.html.

Della Dora, Veronica. 2015. "Introduction: Sacred Space Unbound." *Society and Space*. June. Accessed August 5, 2019. https://societyandspace.org/2015/06/12/virtual-issue-13-sacred-space-unbound/.

――― 2016. *Landscape, Nature, and the Sacred in Byzantium*. Cambridge: Cambridge University Press.

Demoz, Abraham. 1969. "The Many Worlds of Ethiopia." *African Affairs* 68 (270): 49–54.

Denny, Mark, and Alan McFadzean. 2011. *Engineering Animals: How Life Works*. Cambridge: Harvard University Press.

Desplat, Patrick. 2005. "The Articulation of Religious Identities and Their Boundaries in Ethiopia: Labelling Difference and Processes of Contextualization in Islam." *Journal of Religion in Africa* 35 (4): 482–505.

Dickinson, Daniel. 2005. "Eco-Islam Hits Zanzibar Fishermen." BBC News (website). February 17. Accessed February 23, 2017. http://news.bbc.co.uk/2/hi/africa/4271519.stm.

Dilley, Roy. 2011. "'Daaira,' Devotional Acts, and the Transformation of Space in Senegal, West Africa." *Anthropos* 106 (1): 185–192.

Dillon, Brian. 2011. *Ruins*. Cambridge: MIT Press.

Diouf, Ibou. 2002. "Comme car rapide ou les tentatives d'intégration du transport artisanal." In *Les transports et la ville en Afrique au sud du Sahara: Le temps de la débrouille et du désordre inventif*, edited by Xavier Goddard, 43–56. Paris: Karthala Editions.

Donley-Read, L. W. 1990. "A Structuring Structure: The Swahili House." In *Domestic Architecture and the Use of Space*, edited by S. Kent, 114–126. Cambridge: Cambridge University Press.

Dubisch, Jill. 2014. *Pilgrimage and Healing*. Tucson: The University of Arizona Press.

Dyke, Kristina van. 2005. "Beyond Monument Lies Empire: Mapping Songhay Space in Tenth to Sixteenth Century West Africa." *RES: Anthropology and Aesthetics* 48: 33–44.

Ebron, Paulla A. 2009. *Performing Africa*. Princeton: Princeton University Press.

Economist. 2012. "Prayers and Playthings: Making Money from Believers." *The Economist*. July 14. Accessed September 25, 2019. www.economist.com/international/2012/07/14/prayers-and-playthings.

Edensor, Timothy. 2005. "The Ghosts of Industrial Ruins: Ordering and Disordering Memory in Excessive Space." *Society & Space (Environment and Planning)* 23 (6): 829–850.

Elias, Jamal J. 2011. *On Wings of Diesel: Trucks, Identity and Culture in Pakistan*. Oxford: Oneworld.

———. 2012. *Aisha's Cushion: Religious Art, Perception, and Practice in Islam*. Cambridge: Harvard University Press.

El-Khatib, Abdallah. 2001. "Jerusalem in the Qur'an." *British Journal of Middle Eastern Studies* 28 (1): 25–53.

El-Zein, Abdul Hamid. 1977. "Beyond Ideology and Theology: The Search for the Anthropology of Islam." *Annual Review of Anthropology* 6: 227–254.

Emerick, Keith. 2014. *Conserving and Managing Ancient Monuments: Heritage, Democracy, and Inclusion*. Suffolk: Boydell and Brewer.

Erzen, Jale Nejdet. 2011. "Reading Mosques: Meaning and Architecture in Islam." *The Journal of Aesthetics and Art Criticism* 69 (1): 125–131.

Essoungou, André-Michel. 2010. "A Social Media Boom Begins in Africa." *United Nations Africa Renewal Magazine*. December. Accessed November 10, 2017. www.un.org/africarenewal/magazine/december-2010/social-media-boom-begins-africa.

Ethiopian Airlines. n.d. "About Us: History." Ethiopian Airlines (website). Accessed July 15, 2019. www.ethiopianairlines.com/corporate/company/about-us/history.

Ethiopians. 2001. "The New Bole International Airport Terminal Due to Open in May 2001." The Ethiopians (website). March. Accessed April 3, 2018. www.ethioopians.com/bole_airport.htm.

Ewing, Katherine Pratt. 1998. "Crossing Borders and Transgressing Boundaries: Metaphors for Negotiating Multiple Identities." *Ethos* 26 (2): 262–267.

——— 2010. "Exim Tower/SPASM Design Architects." Archdaily (website). August 7. Accessed October 17, 2017. www.archdaily.com/72087/exim-tower-spasm-design-architects.

——— 2012. "Extremists Destroy Historic Shrines in Timbuktu, Mali." RT (website). July 1. Accessed August 6, 2019. http://rt.com/news/islamists-destroy-timbuktu-mali-131/.

Farivar, Cyrus. 2011. *The Internet of Elsewhere: The Emergent Effects of a Wired World*. New Brunswick: Rutgers University Press.

Ferguson, James G. 2002. "Of Mimicry and Membership: Africans and the 'New World Society.'" *Cultural Anthropology* 17 (4): 551–569.

Finlayson, C. 2001. "Behind the Arabesque: Understanding Islamic Art and Architecture." *Brigham Young University Studies* 40 (4): 69–88.

Flood, Finbarr Barry. 2002. "Between Cult and Culture: Bamiyan, Islamic Iconoclasm, and the Museum." *The Art Bulletin* 84 (4): 641–659.

Foley, Ellen E. 2010. *Your Pocket Is What Cures You: The Politics of Health in Senegal*. New Brunswick: Rutgers University Press.

Fontein, Joost. 2000. *UNESCO, Heritage, and Africa: An Anthropological Critique of World Heritage*. Occasional Papers 80. Edinburgh: University of Edinburgh, Centre of African Studies.

Furman, Adam Nathaniel. 2017. "Adam Nathaniel Furman's Democratic Monument." *An Interior Magazine*. Fall. Accessed September 24, 2019. https://aninteriormag.com/adam-nathaniel-furmans-democratic-monument/.

Gaffney, Patrick. 1992. "Popular Islam." *The Annals of the American Academy of Political and Social Science* 524: 38–51.

Gamboni, Dario. 1997. *The Destruction of Art: Iconoclasm and Vandalism since the French Revolution*. London: Reaktion Books.

——— 2011. "Targeting Architecture: Iconoclasm and the Asymmetry of Conflicts." In *Der Sturm der Bilder: Zerstörte und Zerstörende Kunst von der Antike bis in die Gegenwart*, edited by Uwe Fleckner, Maike Steinkamp, and Hendrik Ziegler, 119–137. Berlin: Akademie Verlag.

García, Canclini N. 2000. *Transforming Modernity: Popular Culture in Mexico*. Austin: University of Texas Press.

Ghana Friendship and Solidarity Association. 2017. "AkraFurqan Complex." AkraFurqan Camii Ve Külliyesi (website). Accessed September 21, 2019. www.accrafurqan.com/tr/akrafurkan-kulliyesi.html.

GhanaWeb. 2014. "Accra Gets a New Mosque." GhanaWeb (website). August 13. Accessed September 9, 2019. www.ghanaweb.com/GhanaHomePage/NewsArchive/Accra-gets-new-Central-Mosque-321031#.

Golombek, Lisa. 1983. "The Resilience of the Friday Mosque: The Case of Herat." *Muqarnas* 1: 95–102.

Goolam, Vahed. 2000. "Indians, Islam and the Meaning of South African Citizenship: A Question of Identities." *Transformation: Critical Perspectives on Southern Africa Transformation* 43: 25–51.

Graziano, Alicia. 2014. "Alhamdoulillah: The Use of the Car Rapide as a Living Symbol of Senegal." Independent Study Project (ISP) Collection (Paper 1911). SIT Digital Collections (website). Accessed February 17, 2021. http://digitalcollections.sit.edu/isp_collection/1911.

Grosz-Ngate, Maria Luise, John H. Hanson, and Patrick O'Meara. 2014. *Africa*. 4th ed. Bloomington: Indiana University Press.

Guest, Gerald B. 2012. "Space." *Studies in Iconography* 33: 219–230.

Guèye, Cheikh. 2003. "New Information & Communication Technology Use by Muslim Mourides in Senegal." *Review of African Political Economy* 30 (98): 609–625.

Hagen, Victor W. Von. 1942. "Natural History of Termites." *The Scientific Monthly* 54 (6): 489–498.

Haider, Gulzar. 1996. "Muslim Space and the Practice of Architecture: A Personal Odyssey." In *Making Muslim Space in North America and Europe*, edited by Barbara Metcalf, 31–45. Berkeley: University of California Press.

Hammond, Andrew. 2012. *The Islamic Utopia: The Illusion of Reform in Saudi Arabia*. London: Pluto Press.

Haney, Gina, Jeff Allen, Erica Avrami, and William Raynolds. 2011. "New Gourna: Conservation and Community." World Monuments Fund (website). May. www.wmf.org/publication/new-gourna-village-conservation-and-community.

Harari Regional State Cultural Heritage and Tourism Bureau. 2015. "Harar." Addis Ababa: Harari Regional State Cultural Heritage and Tourism Bureau.

Harrison, Rodney. 2013. *Heritage: Critical Approaches*. New York: Routledge.

Hassner, Ron E. 2007. "Islamic Just War Theory and the Challenge of Sacred Space in Iraq." *Journal of International Affairs* 61 (1): 131–152.

Hecht, E. D. 1987. "Harar and Lamu: A Comparison of Two East African Muslim Societies." *TransAfrican Journal of History* 16: 1–23.

Henderson, Richard N., and Ifekandu Umunna. 1988. "Leadership Symbolism in Onitsha Ogbo Crowns and Ijele." *African Arts* 21 (2): 28–37; 94; 96.

Hendricks, Muhsin. 2010. "Islamic Texts: A Source of Acceptance of Queer Individuals into Mainstream Muslim Society." *The Equal Rights Review* 5: 31–51.

Hirschkind, Charles. 2001. "The Ethics of Listening: Cassette-Sermon Audition in Contemporary Egypt." *American Ethnologist* 28 (3): 623–649.

Hoel, Nina. 2013a. "Feminism and Religion and the Politics of Location: Situating Islamic Feminism in South Africa." *Journal of Gender and Religion in Africa* 19 (2): 73–89.

——— 2013b. "Sexualising the Sacred, Sacralising Sexuality: An Analysis of Public Responses to Muslim Women's Religious Leadership in the Context of a Cape Town Mosque." *Journal for the Study of Religion* 26 (2): 25–41. Accessed August 17, 2017. www.scielo.org.za/scielo.php?script=sci_arttext&pid=S1011-76012013000100003.

hooks, bell. 1984. *Feminist Theory: From Margin to Centre.* Boston: South End Press.

Huang, Wei-Jue, Honggen Xiao, and Sha Wang. 2018. "Airports as Liminal Space." *Annals of Tourism Research* 70: 1–13.

Hudson, Alexandra. 2010. "South Africa Muslims Look to Welcome Muslim Fans." Reuters (website). June 16. Accessed July 15, 2019. www.reuters.com/article/us-soccer-world-muslims/south-africa-muslims-look-to-welcome-muslim-fans-idUSTRE65F2VU20100616.

Huis, Arnold van. 2017. "Cultural Significance of Termites in Sub-Saharan Africa." *Journal of Ethnobiology and Ethnomedicine* 13 (8): 1–12.

Hyung-Jun, Kim. 2007. *Reformist Muslims in a Yogyakarta Village: The Islamic Transformation of Contemporary Socio-Religious Life.* Canberra: Australian National University Press.

Insoll, Timothy. 2003. *The Archaeology of Islam in Sub-Saharan Africa.* Cambridge: Cambridge University Press.

Islamic Help. n.d. "Children's Eco-Village: Visioning Document." Accessed February 15, 2017. www.ihelpglobal.org/wp-content/uploads/2018/04/Childrens-Eco-Village.pdf.

Ismail, Farhana. 2015. "Struggling to Find God in a Shared Space." *Mail & Guardian.* September 19. Accessed August 6, 2019. https://mg.co.za/article/2014-09-19-the-prophets-mosque-was-a-space-shared-by-men-and-women.

Iziko Museums. 2017. "Moffies." New Year Carnival in Cape Town (exhibition). Iziko Museum (Slave Lodge), Cape Town, January.

Jackson, Michael. 2005. *Existential Anthropology: Events, Exigencies, and Effects.* New York: Berghahn Books.

Jaffer, Mansoor, Razia Essack, and Achmat Davids. 2010. *Guide to the Kramats of the Western Cape.* Cape Town: The Cape Mazaar (Kramat) Society.

Janson, Marloes. 2011. "Living Islam Through Death: Demarcating Muslim Identity in a Rural Serahuli Community in the Gambia." *The Journal of the Royal Anthropological Institute* 17 (1): 100–115.

Jarzombek, Mark. 2006. "Sustainability: Fuzzy Systems and Wicked Problems." *Log* 8: 7–12.

Jawondo, Ibrahim Abdul Ganiyu. 2012. "Architectural History of Ilorin Mosques in the Nineteenth and Twentieth Centuries." *Social Dynamics* 38 (2): 303–313.

Jeenah, Naeem. 2001. "'A Degree Above ....' The Emergence of Islamic Feminisms in South Africa in the 1990s." Master's thesis. University of Witwatersrand.

Jencks, Charles. 2004. "Towards an Iconography of the Present." *Log* 3: 101–108.

Jensen, Steffen. 2005. "Above the Law: Practices of Sovereignty in Surrey Estate, Cape Town." In *Sovereign Bodies: Citizens, Migrants, and States in the Postcolonial World,* edited by Thomas Blom Hansen, 218–238. Princeton: Princeton University Press.

Jones, Dorian. 2015. "Does Turkey Aspire to the Leadership of the Islamic World?" Qantara (website). Accessed November 10, 2017. https://en.qantara.de/content/turkeys-mosque-building-programme-does-turkey-aspire-to-the-leadership-of-the-islamic-world.

Jones, Paul. 2006. "The Sociology of Architecture and the Politics of Building: The Discursive Construction of Ground Zero." *Sociology* 40 (3): 549–565.
    2011. *The Sociology of Architecture: Constructing Identities*. Liverpool: Liverpool University Press.
Joseph, Roger. 1981. "The Semiotics of the Islamic Mosque." *Arab Studies Quarterly* 3 (3): 285–295.
Joy, Charlotte. 2007. "'Enchanting Town of Mud': Djenne, A World Heritage Site in Mali." In *Reclaiming Heritage: Alternative Imaginaries of Memory in West Africa*, edited by Ferdinand de Jong and Michael Rowlands, 145–160. Walnut Creek: Left Coast Press.
Kahera, Akel Ismail. 2002. "Gardens of the Righteous: Sacred Space in Judaism, Christianity, and Islam." *CrossCurrents* 52 (3): 328–341.
    2008. *Deconstructing the American Mosque*. Austin: University of Texas Press.
Karim, Sulmaan. 2015. Interview by Michelle Apotsos (April 2).
Karnouk, Liliane, and P. J. Vatikiotis. 1988. *Modern Egyptian Art: The Emergence of a National Style*. Cairo: The American University in Cairo Press.
Khairul, Arnaz. 2016. "Vote for Cyberjaya Mosque for the Plan International Award 2016." *New Straits Times*. May 1. Accessed April 10, 2018. www.nst.com.my/news/2016/05/142777/vote-cyberjaya-mosque-plan-intl-award-2016.
Khan, Hasan-Uddin. 1990. "The Architecture of the Mosque: An Overview and Design Directions." In *Expressions of Islam in Buildings*, edited by Hayat Salam-Liebich, 109–127. Singapore: Concept Media/The Aga Khan Award for Architecture.
Khan, Shahrukh. 2014. "Ancient Causes of a Modern Conflict in Mali." *Harvard Political Review*. March 23. Accessed August 6, 2019. http://harvardpolitics.com/world/ancient-causes-modern-conflict-mali/.
Khan, Shubnum. 2017. "South Africa's Untold Success Story: A Christian Nation's Peaceful History with a Muslim Minority." *Huffington Post*. April 17. Accessed August 6, 2019. www.huffingtonpost.co.uk/2017/04/09/south-africas-untold-success-story-a-christians-nations-peac_a_22032852/?guccounter=1&guce_referrer=aHR0cHM6Ly93d3cuZ29vZ2xlLmNvbS8&guce_referrer_sig=AQAAAA_W7qjlV9cUTuTPPOXuDXKEhojod c12ymPJzb_yRtiq0MCuak9zo63Ou.
Khumalo, Juniour. 2017. "Soweto's Oldest Mosque: A Place of Solace and Suspicion." Soweto Central: A Project of the 2017 Wits Honours in Journalism Class. Accessed March 10, 2018. http://sowetocentral.africa/sowetos-oldest-mosque/.
Kugle, Scott Siraj al-Haqq. 2014. *Living Out Islam: Voices of Gay, Lesbian, and Transgender Muslims*. New York: New York University Press.
Lambert, Léopold. 2017. "Introduction: Colonialism as a Continuous Process, Architecture as a Spatial Apparatus." *The Funambulist* 10. Accessed August 6, 2019. https://thefunambulist.net/articles/introduction-colonialism-continuous-process-architecture-spatial-apparatus-leopold-lambert.
Lambourn, Elizabeth. 2006. "Brick, Timber, and Stone: Building Materials and the Construction of Islamic Architectural History in Gujarat." *Muqarnas* 23: 191–217.

LaNier, R., and D. A. McQuillan. 1983. "The Stone Town of Zanzibar: A Strategy for Integrated Development." Unpublished working document. Commissioned by the United Nations Centre for Human Settlements.

Lapidus, Ira M. 1969. "Varieties of Urban Experience: Contrast, Coexistence, and Coalescence in Cairo." In *Middle Eastern Cities: A Symposium on Ancient, Islamic, and Contemporary Middle Eastern Urbanism*, edited by Ira M. Lapidus, 159–187. Berkeley: University of California Press.

Larsen, Kjersti. 2008. *Where Humans and Spirits Meet: The Politics of Ritual and Identified Spirits in Zanzibar.* New York: Berghahn Books.

Lassner, Jacob. 2017. *Medieval Jerusalem: Forging an Islamic City in Spaces Sacred to Christians and Jews.* Ann Arbor: University of Michigan Press.

Lefebvre, Alain. 1989. "The Decorative Truck as Communicative Device." *Semiotica* 75 (3–4): 215–227.

Leichtman, Mara A. 2015. *Shi'i Cosmopolitanisms in Africa Lebanese Migration and Religious Conversion in Senegal.* Bloomington: Indiana University Press.

Loimeier, Roman. 2013. *Muslim Societies in Africa: A Historical Anthropology.* Bloomington: Indiana University Press.

2016. *Islamic Reform in Twentieth-Century Africa.* Edinburgh: Edinburgh University Press.

Lowenthal, David. 1985. *The Past Is a Foreign Country.* Cambridge: Cambridge University Press.

Łykowska, Laura. 2011. "Complementary Oriental Cities, the Case of Harar and Dire Dawa (Eastern Ethiopia)." *Rocznik Orientalistyczny* 64: 31–37.

Mahida, Ebrahim Mahomed. 1993. *History of Muslims in South Africa: A Chronology.* Durban: Arabic Study Circle.

Mahmutćehajić, Rusmir. 2006. *The Mosque: The Heart of Submission.* New York: Fordham University Press.

Malcomess, Bettina, and Matthew Wilhelm-Solomon. 2017. "Valleys of Salt in the House of God: Religious Re-Territorialisation and Urban Space." In *Routes and Rites to the City: Mobility, Diversity and Religious Space in Johannesburg*, edited by Matthew Wilhelm-Solomon, Peter Kankonde Bukasa, Bettina Malcomess, and Lorena Núñez, 31–60. London: Palgrave Macmillan.

Mancini, JoAnne M., Keith Bresnahan, and Christina Schwenkel. 2014. *Architecture and Armed Conflict: The Politics of Destruction.* London and New York: Routledge.

Mandel, Ruth. 1996. "A Place of Their Own: Contesting Spaces and Defining Places in Berlin's Migrant Community." In *Making Muslim Space in North America and Europe*, edited by Barbara Metcalf, 147–166. Berkeley: University of California Press.

Marchand, Trevor H. J. 2015. "The Djenne Mosque: World Heritage and Social Renewal in a West African Town." *APT Bulletin* 46 (2/3): 4–15.

Martin, Stephen J., Roy R. Funch, Paul R. Hanson, and Eun-Hye Yoo. 2018. "A Vast 4,000-Year-Old Spatial Pattern of Termite Mounds." *Current Biology* 28 (2): R1292–R1293. Accessed August 8, 2019. www.sciencedirect.com/science/article/pii/S0960982218312879.

Marty, Martin E, and R. Scott Appleby. 2004. *Accounting for Fundamentalisms: The Dynamic Character of Movements.* Chicago: University of Chicago Press.

Matthee, Heinrich. 2008. *Muslim Identities and Political Strategies: A Case Study of Muslims in the Greater Cape Town Area of South Africa, 1994–2000*. Kassel: Kassel University Press.
Mazrui, Ali A. 2005. "The Re-Invention of Africa: Edward Said, V. Y. Mudimbe, and Beyond." *Research in African Literatures* 36 (3): 68–82.
McClanan, Anne, and Jeff Johnson. 2005. "Introduction: 'O for a Muse of Fire ….'" In *Negating the Image: Case Studies in Iconoclasm*, edited by Anne McClanan and Jeff Johnson, 1–12. Aldershot: Ashgate.
McGregor, Andrew. 2012. "Intervening in Mali: West African Nations Plan Offensive Against Islamists and Tuareg Rebels." The Jamestown Foundation (website). July 5. Accessed May 5, 2015. www.jamestown.org/single/?no_cache=1&tx_ttnews[tt_news]=39553#.VUV_42ZrXsA.
McRobert, Laurie. 2007. *The Essence of Cyberspace and Immersive Virtual Spatiality*. Toronto: University of Toronto Press.
Meier, Prita. 2009. "Objects on the Edge: Swahili Coast Objects of Display." *African Arts* 42 (4): 8–23.
— 2016. *Swahili Port Cities: The Architecture of Elsewhere*. Bloomington: Indiana University Press.
Melice, Anne, and Katrien Pype. 2009. "Religion and Mobility in Africa and in the African Diaspora." *Forum* 30: 10–16.
Menbue, Mame Laye. 2018. Interview by Michelle Apotsos (April 12).
Metcalf, Barbara. 1996. "Introduction: Sacred Words, Sanctioned Practice, New Communities." In *Making Muslim Space in North America and Europe*, edited by Barbara Metcalf, 1–27. Berkeley: University of California Press.
Metropolitan Museum of Art. 2001. "Vegetal Patterns in Islamic Art." Heilbrunn Timeline of Art History. Metropolitan Museum of Art (website). October. Accessed October 2, 2018. www.metmuseum.org/toah/hd/vege/hd_vege.htm.
Michelet, Jules. 1875. *L'Insect*. Edited by Chris Curnow, Tom Cosmas and Distributed Proofreaders. London, November 26. Reproduced in e-book form in 2013.
Mir-Hosseini, Ziba. 1999. *Islam and Gender: The Religious Debate in Contemporary Iran*. Princeton: Princeton University Press.
Mohamed, Abdı Ahmed. 2018. Interview by Michelle Apotsos (February 9).
Mohanty, Chandra Talpade. 1991. "Under Western Eyes: Feminist Scholarship and Colonial Discourses." In *Third World Women and the Politics of Feminism*, edited by Chandra Talpade Mohanty, Ann Russo, and Lourdes Torres, 51–80. Bloomington: Indiana University Press.
Mokhtar, Ahmed, and Aminah Ali Ahmadi. 2005. *Design Guidelines for Ablution Spaces in Mosques and Islamic Praying Facilities*. Sharjah: American University of Sharjah.
Morris, Frances. 1921. "Prayer Rugs." *The Metropolitan Museum of Art Bulletin* 16 (12): 252–255.
Morris, James, and Suzanne P. Blier. 2004. *Butabu: Adobe Architecture of West Africa*. New York: Princeton Architectural Press.
Morris, Kadish. 2017. "Photographing Prayer Spaces in Airports Around the World." *AnOther Magazine*. August 21. Accessed September 26, 2017. www

.anothermag.com/art-photography/10094/photographing-prayer-spaces-in-airports-around-the-world.

Mortada, H. 2011. *Traditional Islamic Principles of Built Environments*. London: Routledge.

Myers, Garth Andrew. 1994. "Making the Socialist City of Zanzibar." *American Geographical Society* 84 (4): 451–464.

———. 1997. "Sticks and Stones: Colonialism and Zanzibari Housing." *Africa: Journal of the International African Institute* 67 (2): 252–272.

Nabudere, Dan Wadada. 2001. "The African Renaissance in the Age of Globalization." *African Journal of Political Science* 6 (2): 11–28.

Nageeb, Salma. 2007. "Appropriating the Mosque: Women's Religious Groups in Khartoum." *Africa Spectrum* 42 (1): 5–27.

Necipoğlu, Gülru. 1993. "Challenging the Past: Sinan and the Competitive Discourse of Early Modern Islamic Architecture." *Muqarnas* 10: 169–180.

———. 1995. *The Topkapi Scroll: Geometry and Ornament in Islamic Architecture*. Santa Monica: Getty Center for the History of Art and the Humanities.

Newman, James L. 1995. *The Peopling of Africa: A Geographical Perspective*. New Haven: Yale University Press.

Ngolola, Saidi. 2017. Interview by Michelle Apotsos (October 20).

Nice. 2018. Interview by Michelle Apotsos (April 2).

Nimtz, August H. 1980. *Islam and Politics in East Africa: The Sufi Order in Tanzania*. Minneapolis: University of Minnesota Press.

Nooter, Nancy Ingram. 1984. "Zanzibar Doors." *African Arts* 17 (4): 34–39; 96.

Noyes, James. 2013. *The Politics of Iconoclasm: Religion, Violence, and the Culture of Image-Breaking in Christianity and Islam*. London: I. B. Tauris.

Nuha, N. N. Khoury. 1998. "The Mihrab: From Text to Form." *International Journal of Middle East Studies* 30 (1): 1–27.

Nuryanti, Wiendu. 1996. "Heritage and Postmodern Tourism." *Annals of Tourism Research* 23 (2): 249–260.

Nuttall, Sarah. 2004. "City Forms and Writing the 'Now' in South Africa." *Journal of Southern African Studies* 30 (4): 731–748.

O2 DA. 2018. "One Heart Foundation Orphanage and Children Eco-Village Published in Belgian Magazine Bouwkroniek." O2 DA (website). January 19. Accessed September 23, 2019. www.o2designatelier.com/single-post/2018/01/19/Our-project-One-Heart-Foundation-Orphanage-and-Children%E2%80%99s-Orphanage-Center-published-in-Bouwkroniek-Magazine.

Oberauer, Norbert. 2008. "'Fantastic Charities': The Transformations of Waqf Practice in Colonial Zanzibar." *Islamic Law and Society* 15 (3): 315–370.

Ohmoto-Frederick, Ayumi Clara. 2009. "Lyotard, Beckett, Duras, and the Postmodern Sublime (review)." *Comparative Literature Studies* 46 (3): 549–552.

Omer, Spahic. 2008. "Towards Understanding Islamic Architecture." *Islamic Studies* 47 (4): 483–510.

Open Mosque. n.d. "Mission and Vision." The Open Mosque (website). Accessed September 12, 2017. http://theopenmosque.co.za/mission-vision/.

Othman, Zulkeplee, Rosemary Aird, and Laurie Buys. 2015. "Privacy, Modesty, Hospitality, and the Design of Muslim Homes: A Literature Review." *Frontiers of Architectural Research* 4 (1): 12–23.

Pallasmaa, Juhani. 2015. "Light, Silence, and Spirituality in Architecture and Art." In *Transcending Architecture*, edited by Julio Bermudez, 19–32. Washington, DC: Catholic University of America Press.

Patel, Samir S. 2014. "Stone Towns of the Swahili Coast." *Archaeology* 67 (1): 42–49.

Pellizzi, Francesco. 2008. "Airports and Museums: New Frontiers of the Urban and Suburban." *RES: Anthropology and Aesthetics* 53/54: 331–344.

Pellot, Brian. 2016. "Queer Muslims Find Solace and Solidarity at South Africa Retreat." Heinrich-Böll-Stiftung (website). November 4. Accessed August 14, 2017. https://za.boell.org/2016/11/04/queer-muslims-find-solace-and-solidarity-south-africa-retreat.

Petersen, Andrew. 1999. *Dictionary of Islamic Architecture*. London: Routledge.

Picon, Antoine. 2004. "Architecture and the Virtual Towards a New Materiality." *PRAXIS: Journal of Writing + Building* 6: 114–121.

Pietz, William. 1985. "The Problem of the Fetish, I." *RES: Anthropology and Aesthetics* 9: 5–17.

Preziosi, David. 1979. *The Semiotics of the Built Environment: An Introduction to Architectonic Analysis*. Bloomington: Indiana University Press.

Price, Travis. 2015. "Architectural Quests into the Numinous." In *Transcending Architecture*, edited by Julio Bermudez, 247–255. Washington, DC: Catholic University of America Press.

Price, Zeena. 2016. "(Re)Configuring Ruin: The Sacred Poetics of Rubble in the Photography of Scott Hocking." Master's thesis. Radboud University.

Primiano, Leonard Norman. 1995. "Vernacular Religion and the Search for Method in Religious Folklife." *Western Folklore* 54 (1): 37–56.

Prussin, Labelle. 1968. "The Architecture of Islam in West Africa." *African Arts* 1 (2) (Winter): 32–35, 70–74.

———. 1982. "West African Earthworks." *Art Journal* 42 (3): 204–209.

———. 1986. *Hatumere: Islamic Design in West Africa*. Berkeley: University of California Press.

———. 1999. "Non-Western Sacred Sites: African Models." *The Journal of the Society of Architectural Historians* 58 (3): 424–433.

Purkayastha, Bandana. 2012. "Intersectionality in a Transnational World." *Gender & Society* 26 (1): 55–66.

Quadir, Tarik Masud. 2013. *Traditional Islamic Environmentalism: The Vision of Seyyed Hossein Nasr*. Lanham: University Press of America.

Quist-Arcton, Ofeibea. 2016. "If You Think This Bus Has an Eye on You, You're Right." All Things Considered (NPR) (website). March 20. Accessed September 23, 2019. www.npr.org/sections/goatsandsoda/2016/03/20/470951358/if-you-think-this-bus-has-an-eye-on-you-youre-right.

Rabbat, Nasser. 2002. "In the Beginning Was the House: On the Image of the Two Noble Sanctuaries of Islam." *Thresholds* 25: 56–59.

Rainfoy, Claire. 2015. "A Fast Bus to the Museum: What the Bodywork of These Machines Says About the History of Senegal." Jeune Afrique (website). August 18. Accessed August 2, 2017. www.jeuneafrique.com/256991/economie/rapide-disparait-de-circulation-entre-musee/.

Ray, Sarah Jaquette. 2013. *The Ecological Other: Environmental Exclusion in American Culture*. Tucson: University of Arizona Press.

Reals, Kerry. 2018. "Boeing's Inflight Prayer Space Concept Catering to Religious Needs." Aviation Week Network (website). February 28. Accessed September 25, 2019. https://aviationweek.com/aircraft-interiors/boeings-inflight-prayer-space-concept-catering-religious-needs.

Reaven, Marci, and Steve Zeitlin. 2006. "Introduction: Urban Remembrance." In *Hidden New York: A Guide to Places That Matter*, edited by Marci Reaven and Steve Zeitlin, 335–340. New Brunswick: Rutgers University Press.

Renard, John. 1996. "Comparative Religious Architecture: Islamic and Hindu Ritual Space." *Religion and the Arts* 1 (3): 62–88.

Revault, Philippe, Serge Santelli, Raphael Alessandri, Nadia Ammi, Nadege Bonnet-Chelhi, Pauline Bosredon, and Emma Greiner. 2006. "Harar Jugol." Nomination of Properties for Inclusion on the World Heritage List. Harari People's National Regional State.

Rigopoulos, Antonio. 2014. "The Construction of a Cultic Center Through Narrative: The Founding Myth of the Village of Puttaparthi and Sathya Sāī Bābā." *History of Religions* 54 (2): 117–150.

Rihouay, Francis. 2014. "Timbuktu Seeks Rebirth After Islamist Militants' Destruction." Bloomberg (website). March 31. Accessed September 20, 2014. www.bloomberg.com/news/articles/2014-03-30/timbuktu-seeks-rebirth-after-destruction-by-islamist-militants.

Rizvi, Kishwar. 2015. *The Transnational Mosque: Architecture and Historical Memory in the Contemporary Middle East*. Chapel Hill: University of North Carolina Press.

Roberts, Allen F., and Mary Nooter Roberts. 2002. "A Saint in the City Sufi Arts of Urban Senegal." *African Arts* 35 (4): 52–96.

Ross, Eric. 2006. *Sufi City: Urban Design and Archetypes in Touba*. Suffolk: Boydell and Brewer.

Rowlands, Michael. 2007. "Entangled Memories and Parallel Heritages in Mali." In *Reclaiming Heritage: Alternative Imaginaries of Memory in West Africa*, edited by Ferdinand de Jong and Michael Rowlands, 127–144. Walnut Creek: Left Coast Press.

Saine, Abdoulaye. 2011. "Islam and the 'Global War on Terror' in West Africa." In *Globalization and Sustainable Development in Africa*, edited by Bessie House-Soremekun and Toyin Falola, 404–420. Rochester: University of Rochester Press.

Salvatore, Armando. 2015. "Modernity." In *Islamic Political Thought: An Introduction*, edited by Gerhard Bowering, 135–151. Princeton: Princeton University Press.

Santelli, Serge, and Philippe Revault. 2004. *Harar: A Muslim City of Ethiopia/Harar: Une cité musulmane d'Éthiopie*. Paris: Maison & Larose.

Schacht, Joseph. 1965. "Notes on Islam in East Africa." *Studia Islamica* 23: 91–136.

Schroeder, Ralph, Noel Heather, and Raymond M. Lee. 1998. "The Sacred and the Virtual: Religion in Multi-User Virtual Reality." *Journal of Computer-Mediated Communication* 4 (2). http://onlinelibrary.wiley.com/doi/10.1111/j.1083-6101.1998.tb00092.x/full.

Seemungal, Martin. 2015. "Is Cape Town's Women and Gay-Friendly Mosque a Sign of New Muslim Attitudes?" PBS News Hour (website). May 9.

Accessed August 14, 2017. www.pbs.org/newshour/show/cape-towns-gay-women-friendly-mosque-sign-re-interpretation-muslim-faith.

Seibert, Thomas. 2015. "Turkey's Mosque-Building Diplomacy." Al-Monitor: The Pulse of the Middle East (website). February 13. Accessed September 21, 2019. www.al-monitor.com/pulse/originals/2015/02/turkey-mosque-building-soft-power.html.

Selamta. 2018. "Cradle of Culture." *Selamta Magazine* Jan.–Feb.: 38–53. https://www.selamtamagazine.com/stories/cradle-of-culture?_k=bWFtb0BldGhpb3Nwb3J0cy5jb206OjVhNGE0MmFmYjQ4NjI.

Shaikh, Sa'diyya. 2003. "Transforming Feminism: Islam, Women, and Gender Justice." In *Progressive Muslims: On Gender, Justice, and Pluralism*, edited by Omid Safi, 147–162. Oxford: Oneworld.

Sheller, Mimi. 2011. "Mobility." *Sociopedia*. doi:10.1177/205684601163.

Sheller, Mimi, and John Urry. 2006. "The New Mobilities Paradigm." *Environment and Planning A: Economy and Space* 38 (2): 207–226.

Siregar, Kiki. 2016. "'Mosque-Mobile' Makes Praying Easier in Gridlocked Jakarta." Business Insider (website). July 5. Accessed September 25, 2019. www.businessinsider.com/afp-mosque-mobile-makes-praying-easier-in-gridlocked-jakarta-2016-7.

Smith, Elta, and Courtney Bender. 2004. "The Creation of Urban Niche Religion: South Asian Taxi Drivers in New York City." In *Asian American Religions: The Making and Remaking of Borders and Boundaries*, edited by Tony Carnes and Fenggang Yang, 76–97. New York: New York University Press.

Smith, Laurajane. 2010. *Uses of Heritage*. London: Routledge.

Solomon, Robert C. 1985. "On Kitsch and Sentimentality." *The Journal of Aesthetics and Art Criticism* 49 (1): 1–14.

Sonn, Tamara. 1994. "Middle East and Islamic Studies in South Africa." *Middle East Studies Association Bulletin* 28 (1): 14–17.

Sourdel, Dominique, Janine Sourdel-Thomine, and Caroline Higgitt. 2007. *A Glossary of Islam*. Edinburgh: Edinburgh University Press.

Steadman, Philip. 2008. *The Evolution of Designs: Biological Analogy in Architecture and the Applied Arts*. London: Routledge.

Steele, James. 1997. *Sustainable Architecture: Principles, Paradigms, and Case Studies*. New York: McGraw-Hill.

Stieber, Nancy. 2003. "Editorial: Architecture Between Disciplines." *Journal of the Society of Architectural Historians* 62 (2): 176–177.

Stifin, P. 2012. "The Resonating Voice: Materialities of Testimony at Ground Zero." Presentation to The Cultural Studies Association General Meeting, San Diego, March.

Strom, Karen M. n.d. "Puye Cliff Dwellings: A Project of the Santa Clara Indian Pueblo." Puye Cliff Dwellings Walking Tour Brochure. Accessed April 23, 2018. www.hanksville.org/voyage/misc/puye.html.

Tabbaa, Yasser. 1985. "The Muqarnas Dome: Its Origin and Meaning." *Muqarnas* 3: 61–74.

Tacq, Filiep. 2003. *Proceeding #1: The Dakar Car Rapide – An Endangered Species*. Maastricht: Jan van Eyck Academie.

Taleb, Nasseema. 2005. "Muslim Identity and Gated Community Development in Durban." Master's thesis. University of KwaZulu Natal.
Tarsitani, Belle Asante. 2009. "Revered Vessels: Custom and Innovation in Harari Basketry." *African Arts* 42 (1): 64–75.
Taussig, Michael. 2012. "Iconoclasm Dictionary." *TDR: The Drama Review* 56 (1): 10–17.
Tayob, Abdulkader. 1999. *Islam in South Africa: Mosques, Imams, and Sermons*. Gainesville: University of Florida Press.
——— 2011. "Islam and Democracy in South Africa." *Focus: The Journal of the Helen Suzman Foundation* 62: 20–24.
TGBC. n.d. "About the Tanzania Green Building Council." Tanzania Green Building Council (website). Accessed November 16, 2016. http://tzgbc.com/.
Tharoor, Ishaan. 2012. "Timbuktu's Destruction: Why Islamists Are Wrecking Mali's Cultural Heritage." *Time*. July 2. Accessed August 7, 2019. http://world.time.com/2012/07/02/timbuktus-destruction-why-islamists-are-wrecking-malis-cultural-heritage/.
Thomassen, Bjørn. 2009. "The Uses and Meanings of Liminality." *International Political Anthropology* 2 (1): 5–27.
——— 2012. "Timbuktu Shrine Destruction a 'War Crime.'" *The Telegraph*. July 2. Accessed September 2, 2016. www.telegraph.co.uk/news/worldnews/africaandindianocean/mali/9369271/Timbuktu-shrine-destruction-a-war-crime.html.
Tonna, J. O. 1990. "The Poetics of Arabo-Islamic Architecture." *Muqarnas* 7: 182–197.
Traoré, Madou. 2018. Interview by Michelle Apotsos (April 9).
Turner, Simon. 2009. "'These Young Men Show No Respect for Local Customs': Globalization and Islamic Revival in Zanzibar." *Journal of Religion in Africa* 39 (3): 237–261.
Turner, Victor, and Edith Turner. 1978. *Image and Pilgrimage in Christian Culture*. New York: Columbia University Press.
UNESCO. n.d.a. "Harar Jugol, the Fortified Historic Town." UNESCO (website). Accessed August 24, 2017. https://whc.unesco.org/en/list/1189/.
——— n.d.b. "Safeguarding Project of Hassan Fathy's New Gourna Village." UNESCO (website). Accessed January 14, 2019. https://whc.unesco.org/en/activities/637/.
Urry, John, and Jonas Larsen. 2011. *The Tourist Gaze 3.0*. London: SAGE Publications.
van der Hoorn, Melanie. 2009. *Indispensable Eyesores: An Anthropology of Undesired Buildings*. New York: Berghahn Books.
Vellinga, Marcel. 2006. "The Inventiveness of Tradition: Vernacular Architecture and the Future." *Perspectives in Vernacular Architecture* 13 (2): 115–128.
Vered, Amit, and Christina Garsten. 2015. "The East as a Complex Religious Field." In *Checkpoint, Temple, Church and Mosque: A Collaborative Ethnography of War and Peace*, edited by Jonathan Spencer, Jonathan Goodhand, Shahul Hasbullah, Bart Klem, and Benedikt Korf, 20–44. London: Pluto Press.
Verkaaik, Oskar. 2013. *Religious Architecture: Anthropological Perspectives*. Amsterdam: Amsterdam University Press.

Visit 2 Ethiopia Tourism Marketing and Promotions. 2015. "Harar." Visit 2 Ethiopia Tourism Marketing and Promotions. Addis Ababa.

Walker, Bethany J. 2004. "Commemorating the Sacred Spaces of the Past: The Mamluks and the Umayyad Mosque at Damascus." *Near Eastern Archaeology* 67 (1): 26–39.

Warren, Karen J. 2015. "Feminist Environmental Philosophy." In *Stanford Encyclopedia of Philosophy*, edited by Edward N. Zalta. Summer. Accessed April 15, 2019. https://plato.stanford.edu/entries/feminism-environmental/.

Watson, Donald. 2001. "Environment and Architecture." In *Discipline of Architecture*, edited by Andrzej Piotrowski and Julia Williams Robinson, 158–172. Minneapolis: University of Minnesota Press.

Weisenfeld, Gennifer. 2012. *Imaging Disaster: Tokyo and the Visual Culture of Japan's Great Earthquake of 1923*. Berkeley: University of California Press.

Wellington, Nii-Adziri. 2017. "Crises in Contesting Identities in Islamic Sacral Architecture: A Reflection on the Hagia Sophia in Accra, Ghana." Paper presented at the 17th Triennial Symposium of African Art, held at the Institute of African Studies, University of Ghana, Legon, August 8–13.

Wilhelm-Solomon, Matthew, Lorena Núñez, Peter Kankonde, and Bettina Malcomess. 2017. "Routes and Rites to the City: Introduction." In *Routes and Rites to the City: Mobility, Diversity and Religious Space in Johannesburg*, edited by Matthew Wilhelm-Solomon, Lorena Núñez, Peter Kankonde Bukasa, and Bettina Malcomess, 1–30. London: Palgrave Macmillan.

William, F. A. Miles. 2004. "Conclusions." *African Studies Review* 47 (2): 109–117.

Women's Environment and Development Organization. 2013. "Prioritizing the Intersection of Women's Rights and Empowerment, Gender Equality, and Sustainable Development." Women's Environment and Development Organization. January 6. Accessed February 13, 2019. https://wedo.org/prioritizing-the-intersection-of-womens-rights-and-empowerment-gender-equality-and-sustainable-development/.

Wright, Richard, and Mark Ellis. 2016. "Perspectives on Migration Theory: Geography." In *International Handbook of Migration and Population Distribution*, edited by Michael J. White, 11–30. Dordrecht: Springer.

Wynne-Jones, Stephanie. 2010. "Remembering and Reworking the Swahili Diwanate: The Role of Objects and Places at Vumba Kuu." *The International Journal of African Historical Studies* 43 (3): 407–427.

Zbidi, Monika. 2013. "A Call to Eco-Jihad." Environment and Ecology (website). Accessed February 23, 2017. http://environment-ecology.com/religion-and-ecology/738-the-call-to-eco-jihad.html.

Zeleke, Meron. 2014. "'We Are the Same but Different': Accounts of Ethiopian Orthodox Christian Adherents of Islamic Sufi Saints." *Journal for the Study of Religion* 27 (2): 195–213.

Index

'Abd al-Salām, 'Abdallāh Qād ī ', 34
Abida, Ay (sheikh), 98–99
Abu Hanifa, 40
Accra, Ghana, 116–130. *See also* Blue Mosque
Achmat, Midi, 50
Adams, Paul, 245
Africa. *See also* LGBT+ rights; masjid; *specific countries*; *specific topics*
  Islam in
    construction of, 12–18
    context for, 12–18
    culture of, 12–18
    early origins of, 12
    spatial environment of, xi
  online access and participation in, 232–233
  on homegrown platforms, 233
African National Congress (ANC), 55, 216
Afrikaner Resistance Movement, 45
Afrocentricity, masjid and, 20–27
  in critical heritage studies, 23–24
  eco-criticism and, 24–25
  environmentalism and, 24–25
  intersectionality and, 22–23
Afro-Ottoman style mosques, 24, 117, 130
afterlife, 75–76
Aga, Sedefhar Mehmet, 24, 119
Ahmad, Ali, 138
Ahmed, Abiy, 212
AIDS. *See* HIV/AIDS
airplanes, as masjid spaces, 206–207
airports, as masjid spaces, 187, 208–230
  architecture of, 210–211
  Blaise Diagne International Airport, 218–220
    prayer areas in, 220
  Bole International Airport, 212–215
  Cape Town International Airport, 221–224
    multifaith prayer space, 223–228
    as community space, 227–228
    connection to secular elements of airport, 229–230
  liminality of, 209–210, 230
  mosques in, 209–210
  O.R. Tambo International Airport, 216–218
    prayer areas, 216
  Qiblah wall in, 220–221
Akra Furqan, 119, 121
  foreign architectural styles and, 123–124
  Neo-Ottoman style, 116–118, 120–122
  Selimiye Mosque as inspiration for, 120–122
  Sultan Ahmed Mosque as inspiration for, 23–24, 120–122
  as symbol of political power, 124–126
  as soft power, 126
Al-Fitre Foundation, 22
  as affirmational space, 48–50
  Forum for the Empowerment of Women, 50–51
  Hendricks and, 45–47, 58–62
  LGBT+ rights and, 45–62
  Muslim identity and, 47
  Open Mosque and, 46–47
  origins and purpose of, 45, 58–62
  People's Mosque and, 46–47, 48
  as safe religious space, 60–61
  visibility routines and, 51–52
Ali, Kecia, 59
Amadou, Sekou, 70
Amazigh, Aissa, 49
Amissah-Arthur, Kwesi Bekoe, 122
ANC. *See* African National Congress
Angawi, Sami, 6–7
Ansar Dine, 17
  counter-masjids and, 22–23, 63–65
  Sufis and, 22–23
  in Timbuktu, 22–23, 62–65, 67–73, 74–75
  destruction of religious structures by, 68–73

Index

members of, 72
Tuareg participation in, 67–68
antigay hate speech, in South Africa, 56–57
anti-lesbian violence, 56–57
Apartheid regime, in South Africa, 35–36
  African National Congress and, 55
  anti-Apartheid organizations, 35
  Call of Islam and, 35
  heteronormative ideologies under, 54
  LGBT+ rights under, 55
  mosque construction during, 41–42
  Muslim identity during, 35–36
Appadurai, Arjun, 185–186
appropriate technology (AT), 23–24, 142–143
Arab Spring, 74
ARCCH. *See* Centre for Research and Conservation of Cultural Heritage
'Āṣ, 'Amr ibn al-, 12
Asad, Talal, 18
Ashāma, al-Najāshī, 84
AT. *See* appropriate technology
Augé, Marc, 185
authentic heritage, 171
Auwal Masjid mosque, 34
Aw Machad Mosque, 90
Aw Mansur Mosque, 90
awaach (shrines), in Harar Jugol, 95–98
'awrah (nakedness), 38–39
Axsum Empire, in Ethiopia, 84
Aziz, A. A., 249–250

Babou, Cheikh Anta, 249–250
Bamba, Cheikh Amadou, 190–191, 194, 197, 249–250
  Touba and, 233
Bassett, Caroline, 256
Beck, Ulrich, 123
Bender, Courtney, 225
Benjamin, Walter, 241–243
Bevan, Robert, 76
Bham, Maulana Ebrahim, 42
bin Bashir, An-Nu'man, 179
biomimesis. *See also* Great Mosque of Djenne
  as design approach, 157
  in contemporary architecture, 168–169
  Great Mosque of Djenne and, 168–169
  in Mali, 25
Bird, Michael, 126
Blaise Diagne International Airport, as masjid space, 218–220
  prayer areas in, 220

Bole International Airport, as masjid space, 212–215
Bourdieu, Pierre, 6
Burckhardt, Titus, 5–6
Butler, Judith, 52

Cachalia, Ismail, 35
Cape Mazaar Society, 138
Cape Town, South Africa. *See also* Open Mosque
  Moffies in, 52–53
Cape Town International Airport, as masjid space, 221–224
  multifaith prayer space, 223–228
car rapides, as masjids, 26, 187, 188–208
  anthropomorphization of, 197–198
  architectural forms in, 195
  commodification of, 203
  decorative adornment in, 192–194, 199–202
  "evil eye" imagery, 196–197
  as family tradition, 201
  of religious figures, 195–197
  dialogue with other mobile masjid spaces, 206–207
  history of, 188–189
  intersectionality of, 204
  as sacred spaces, 208
  spiritual practices in, 205–207
  prayers, 205–206
Catholic Church, in Timbuktu, 70–71
Centre for Research and Conservation of Cultural Heritage (ARCCH), 103
Chidester, David, 6
Children's Eco-Village, Kenya, 180
Children's Eco-Village, Tanzania, 25, 171–181
  as environmental model, 179–181
  founding of, 172
  green technologies in, 173–175
  interior architecture of, 176–177
  permaculture in, 178–179
  purpose of, 172–173
  sustainability of, 177–179
  water cultivation in, 178
Christianity, Islam and, 17
civil rights. *See* LGBT+ rights
clean technologies, 133
cleanliness, as element in Islamic faith, 175–176
Clifford, James, 228
colonization, Islam influenced by, 16
Couldry, Nick, 249
Coulon, Christian, 239

280 Index

Council of Muslim Theologians, 42
counter-masjids
   Ansar Dine and, 22–23, 63–65
   in Timbuktu, 73
Crenshaw, Kimberlé Williams, 28–29
critical heritage studies. *See also specific heritage sites*
   Afrocentricity in, 23–24
   theoretical approach to, 79–82
   power hierarchies in, 79–80
   UN World Heritage Convention and, 80
   United Nations Educational Scientific and Cultural Organization and, 80–81
criticism. *See* eco-criticism
Crompton, Andrew, 216, 224–226
Currier, Ashley, 45, 50–51, 53
cyber-immortality, 251

Dadoo, Yusuf, 35
Dakar, Senegal. *See also car rapides*
   Blaise Diagne International Airport as masjid space, 218–220
   prayer areas in, 220
   in trans-Saharan trade networks, 189–190
dan Fodio, Ithman, 16–17
Dar al Islam, New Mexico, USA, 24, 113
   architectural significance of, 116
   construction of, 81–82
   design commission of, 113–114
   mosque complex, 114–116
   as sustainable space, 114
Davidson, Naomi, 77
De Jorio, Rosa, 66, 77
de Mestral, George, 168
Dedeoglu, Beril, 126–127
Desai, Ebrahim, 59
Diallo, Kalidou, 201
digital eternity, 251
Din Agobarar Mosque (Grand Jami mosque), 90, 91–92, 93
Diop, Lat Dior Ngoné Latyr (Lat Dior), 198
Dire Dawa, Harar Jugol and, as sister city, 88
Djinguere Ber Mosque, 66
domestic compound. *See ksar*
Dubisch, Jill, 244
Durkee, Nooruddean, 113–114

earthen mounds, in Great Mosque of Djenne, 161–162, 164, 165–166
eco-criticism, Afrocentricity and, 24–25

eco-Islam, 136–137
   conceptual components of, 137
   Nasr and, 136–137
   recognition of, 137–138
Egypt. *See also* New Gourna
   appropriate technology in, 23–24
   Islam in
      early practices of, 12
      Rashiduns, 12
Elias, Jamal, 202
Environmental Management Act, Tanzania (2004), 180–181
environmentalism. *See also* biomimesis; Great Mosque of Djenne; kramats; sustainability
   Afrocentricity and, 24–25
   eco-Islam, 136–137
      conceptual components of, 137
      Nasr and, 136–137
      recognition of, 137–138
   gender issues and, 134–135
   gender mainstreaming, 134–135
   inclusive, 182
   multiple-coding and, 183
   in Qur'an, 132, 182
   race and, 135
   religious systems and, 135–137
      deep ecology and, 135–136
      in Islam, 136–137
   spirituality and, 136–137
   in Tanzania, 171–181
      under Environmental Management Act, 180–181
      under National Environmental Policy, 180–181
Epelboin, Alain, 203
Erdogan, Recep Tayyip, 126, 127
Ethiopia. *See also* Harar Jugol
   Axsum Empire in, 84
   Bole International Airport, as masjid space, 212–215
   Islam in, 15–16
   political instability in, 86
   UNESCO heritage sites in, 83–84
"evil eye" imagery, 196–197

faith, Islam and, 18–20
Fall, Cheikh Ibra, 195
"Far Mosque." *See* Masjid al-Aqsa
Fathy, Hassan, 105–116. *See also* New Gourna
   Dar al Islam, 24, 81–82, 113
      architectural significance of, 116
      construction of, 81–82
      design commission of, 113–114

Index

mosque complex, 114–116
  as sustainable space, 114
  as humanitarian architect, 106
  Islamic architecture and, 106–108
  on spirituality of architecture, 105–106
feminism, Qur'an and, 39–41
Ferguson, James, 129–130
FEW. *See* Forum for the Empowerment of Women
folk Islam, 18
Forum for the Empowerment of Women (FEW), 50–51
fundamentalism, in Timbuktu, 68
Furman, Adam Nathaniel, 61–62

GANADER. *See* Ghana Friendship and Solidarity Association
Gay Muslim Outreach, 58
gender equality
  in Open Mosque, 44
  as Qur'anic ordinance, 32
  in Qur'an, 37
Geographic Information Systems (GIS), 231
Getinkaya, Erdiogan, 120
Gevisser, Mark, 56–57
Ghana. *See also* Accra, Ghana;
  nongovernmental organizations in, 122
Ghana Friendship and Solidarity Association (GANADER), 122
Ghāzī, Ibrāhīm al-, 85
Gibb, Camilla, 102
GIS. *See* Geographic Information Systems
glocalization, 185–186
Golombek, Lisa, 103
Gordon, Leah, 227
Grabar, Oleg, 5
Grand Jami mosque. *See* Din Agobara Mosque
Grand Maggal pilgrimage, 237–246
  Hizbut Tarqiyya, 240–243
  Mouride identity and, 244–245, 249–250
  as online masjid space, 239–252
  origins of, 238
Great Mosque of Damascus, 225
Great Mosque of Djenne, 25, 70, 157–171
  architectural structure of, 159–161
    earthen mounds, 161–162, 164, 165–166
    inspirations for, 164–166
    Sudonaise style, 160–161
    termitarium and, 164, 165–168
  biological architecture of, 157–158
  biomimesis and, 168–169
  history of, 158–159
  as living structure, 163–164
  property of object-permanence and, 162
  Qiblah wall of, 159
  as UNESCO heritage site, 169–171
Great Mosque of Touba, 235–237
  Lamp Fall element, 235, 236
green technologies, in Children's Eco-Village, 173–175
Greenburg, Clement, 128

hadiths, in Qur'an, 40
Hagia Sophia, 119–120
Hajj, to Mecca, 6–7
  as online pilgrimage, 247–248
Harar Jugol, Ethiopia, 23, 81, 82–105
  as Africa's Mecca, 82
  Aw Machad Mosque, 90
  Aw Mansur Mosque, 90
  Din Agobara Mosque, 90, 91–92, 93
  Dire Dawa and, as sister city, 88
  ethnic composition of, 83
  as hub of Muslim saints, 95
  Islamic identity of, 84, 86–88
  Kazir Abogn Mosque, 90
  Medhane Alem Church, 91–92
  memorial spaces in, 94–96
    shrine culture and, 102
  mosque forms in, 90–94
    construction of, 91–92
  museum spaces in, 104–105
  as national heritage site, 103
  origins and establishment of, 84–86
  shrine culture in, 95–102
    architectural elements in, 96–98, 100
    awaach and, 95–98
    forms of shrines, 96
    memorialization through, 102
    Qabri and, 101
    Qubbah tombs, 96
    shrine for Abida, 98–99
    shrine for Mujahid, 97–98
  Sufism in, 86–87
  walls and boundaries for, 87–90
    evolutionary history of, 88–89
    spiritual identity from, 89–90
Hargey, Taj (imam)
  Open Mosque and, 30–32, 42, 59, 60
  veiling practice and, 30
Haroon, Abdullah (imam), 35
Harris, Neil, 71
hate speech. *See* antigay hate speech
Heidegger, Martin, 185
Hendricks, Muhsin (imam)
  Al-Fitre Foundation and, 45–47, 58–62

Hendricks, Muhsin (imam) (cont.)
 language and terminology for, 58
 People's Mosque and, 58
heritage sites. *See also specific sites*
 authentic, 171
heteronormative ideologies, in South Africa, 53–54. *See also* LGBT+ communities; LGBT+ rights
 under Apartheid regime, 54
hijab (head covering), 36
HIV/AIDS, 55
Hizbut Tarqiyya, 240–243
Human Development International (HUDAI), 122
Hussein, Nur (sheikh), 99–100

Ibn Abdelwahhab, Mohammed (sheikh), 74
Ibn Abdul-Aziz, Umar, 59
Ibn Ghalib, 117
Ibn Hazm, 40
ibn Nafi, 'Uqba, 13
inclusive environmentalism, 182
Inkatha Freedom Party, 45
Inner Circle, 61, 62
interfaith couples, in Open Mosque, 43
intersectionality
 Afrocentricity and, 22–23
 of car rapides, 204
 disenfranchisement experiences and, 28–29
 globalization and, 28–29
 LGBT+ population and, 22–23, 50
 marginalization experiences and, 28–29
 oppression and, 28–29
 theoretical development of, 28–29
  origins of term, 28
 in Timbuktu, 64–65
  administrative structure and, as polity, 64
Islam. *See also* Muslim identity; Muslims; Qur'an; *specific countries*
 assimilation of, 16–17
 Christianity and, 17
 cleanliness as element of, 175–176
 colonization and, 16
 eco-Islam, 136–137
  conceptual components of, 137
  Nasr and, 136–137
  recognition of, 137–138
 in Egypt
  early practices in, 12
  Rashiduns, 12
 in Ethiopia, 15–16
 expansion of, 14–16
 faith and, 18–20
 folk, 18
 identity and, 18–20
 "Living," 258
 in Mahgreb region, 12, 13, 15
 multiple versions of, 18–20
 orthodox, 18
 spatial environment of, in Africa, xi
 Sufi brotherhoods, 14–15
 third world-ism and, 20
 in Timbuktu, 13–14
 Umayyads and, 12–13
Islamic, definition of, xiv–xv
Islamic identity, of Harar Jugol, 84, 86–88

Jasper, Marcel, 107
Jawondo, Ibrahim Abdul Ganiyu, 142–143
Jencks, Charles, 183
Jones, Dorian, 126
Jones, Paul, 129
Joseph, Édouard Louis, 107
Joseph, Roger, 5, 116–117
Joy, Charlotte, 169–171

Ka'ba site, 6–7
 Prophet Muhammad and, 6
Kabbani, Sahl, 113–114
Kahera, Akel, 40
Kazim Muhammad (sheikh), 99–100
Kazir Abogn Mosque, 90
Kenya, 180
Khan, Hasan-Uddin, 21–22
Khoi peoples, in South Africa, 34
Konaré, Alpha Oumar, 67
kramats (shrines), in South Africa (Cape region), 25, 138–157
 architectural structure of, 146–147, 151–154
  geometric elements in, 151–153
  muqarnas, 151
 Cape Mazaar Society, 138
 contemporary response to, 156–157
 function and spiritual purpose of, 139
 history between nature and space, in Islamic practices, 141–145
  appropriate technology, 142–143
 for Mahmud, 147–150
 as pilgrimage site, 141
 Robben Island Mazaar Society, 138
 for shah, 143–145, 146
 spiritual power of, 141
 topography of sites, 139–141
  natural aesthetics of, 141, 154–156
  trees, 145–146

Index

water themes in, 145
ksar (domestic compound), 66
Kugle, Scott Siraj al-Haqq, 45, 47–48

LAGO. *See* Lesbians and Gays Against Oppression
Lamp Fall element, in Great Mosque of Touba, 235, 236
Lat Dior. *See* Diop, Lat Dior Ngoné Latyr
Latour, Bruno, 75
Laye, Seydina Limamou, 190–191
Lesbians and Gays Against Oppression (LAGO), 55
LGBT+ communities
  intersectionality and, 22–23, 50
  Moffies, 52–53
  Open Mosque and, 44
  under Sexual Offenses Act, 54–55
  in South Africa
    antigay hate speech in, 56–57
    anti-lesbian violence, 56–57
    inclusive congregations for, 57
    Muslims in, 57–60
  in Tanzania, 49
LGBT+ rights, in Africa. *See also* Al-Fitre Foundation
  Al-Fitre Foundation and, 45–62
  HIV/AIDS and, 55
  intersectionality and, 22–23
  Lesbians and Gays Against Oppression, 55
  National Coalition for Gay and Lesbian Equality, 55–56
  Open Mosque and, 44
  Rand Gay Organization, 55
  under Sexual Offenses Act, 54–55
  in South Africa, 45, 55–57
    Afrikaner Resistance Movement, 45
    Inkatha Freedom Party, 45
    National Coalition for Gay and Lesbian Equality, 55–56
    under Promotion of Equality and Prevention of Unfair Discrimination Act, 56
  as un-African, 45
liminality
  of airports, as masjid spaces, 209–210, 230
  as concept, development of, 231–232
  Van Gennep and, 232
Linenthal, Edward, 6
"Living Islam," 258
Loimeier, Roman, 11

Maghreb region, Islam in, 12, 13, 15
Mahmud, Sayed, 147–150
majalis, mihrab and, 4
Makuka, Ramadhan (imam), 176–177
Mali. *See also* Great Mosque of Djenne; Timbuktu
  Ansar Dine and, 22–23, 62–63
  biomimesis in, 25
  National Movement for the Liberation of Azawad in, 62–63
  political instability in, 62–63
  Shari'a law in, 62–63
  Tuaregs in, 68
    in Ansar Dine, 67–68
    in National Movement for the Liberation of Azawad, 62–63
Mandela, Nelson, 56–57, 216
Marcel, Alexandre, 107
masjid (place of prostration). *See also* counter-masjids; intersectionality; kramats; mobility paradigms; *specific cities; specific countries*
  Afrocentricity and, 20–27
  in critical heritage studies, 23–24
  eco-criticism and, 24–25
  environmentalism and, 24–25
  intersectionality and, 22–23
  definition of, xi, 1, 2–11
  diverse iterations supported within, xiii
  etymology of, 2
  functions of, xiii
  identities in, ambiguity of, 2–4
  Islamic hermeneutics and, 2–3
  mosque as distinct from, 2, 4–5
  as multi-tiered construct, xii
  as performative place, 2–11
    performing body in, 5–6
    position of sun and, 5
  prayer mats, 8–11
  salat and, 9–10
  in Qur'an, 2, 3
  as space, 255–259
    in Africa, xi
    creation of, 258
  theoretical approach to, xi–xvi
    case studies in, xiii–xv
    geographic variables in, xv
    methodology in, xv
Masjid al-Aqsa ("Far Mosque"), 2–3
Masjid al-Haram (mosque / masjid at Mecca), 2–3
Masjid al-Rasul (Prophet Muhammad's house site), 2–3
M'Backe, Moustapha, 238
McClintock, Anne, 53–54

Mecca. *See* Hajj; Masjid al-Haram
Medhane Alem Church, 91–92
Meer, Fathima, 35
Melice, Anne, 256
memorial spaces, in Harar Jugol, 94–96
   shrine culture and, 102
Metcalf, Barbara, xii, xv
mihrab, 3–4
   majalis and, 4
mobility paradigms, of masjids, 25–27, 252–254. *See also* airports; *car rapides*; online masjid spaces
   dialogue with other mobile spaces, 206–207
   globalization and, 25–26
   theoretical approach to, 184–188
Mohanty, Chandra, 41
Mosque of Kairouan, 13
mosques. *See also specific mosques*
   Afro-Ottoman style, 24, 117, 130
   in airports, as masjid spaces, 209–210
   forms of, in Harar Jugol, 90–94
   masjid as distinct from, 2, 4–5
   nature and, 183
   Neo-Ottoman style, 116–118, 120–122, 129–130
   origins of, 7
   Sudonaise style, 160–161
   transnational projects, 123
   in Turkey, 126–128
Mouride identity, 244–245, 249–250
Mouridism, 27
Moyo, Dambisa, 233
Muhammad (Prophet), 2
   house of, 7–8
   Ka'ba site and, 6
   Masjid al-Rasul, 2–3
Muholi, Zanele, 56
Mujahid Nur bin (emir), 97–98
muqarnas, 151
Musa, Kanku (King), 64
Musa, Mansa, 160–161
museum spaces, in Harar Jugol, 104–105
Muslim architecture, definition of, xiv–xv
Muslim identity
   Al-Fitre Foundation and, 47
   Islam and, 18–20
   Mouride identity, 244–245, 249–250
   reproduction of, xvi
   in South Africa, 35
      during Apartheid regime, 35–36
Muslim Judicial Council of South Africa, 38, 58

Muslim Youth Movement (MYM), 35–36, 58
Muslims. *See also* Muslim identity
   definition of, xiv–xv
   in LGBT+ communities, 57–60
MYM. *See* Muslim Youth Movement

Nabataeans, 142
Naess, Arne, 135–136
nakedness. *See 'awrah*
Naseef, Abdullah, 113–114
Nasr, Seyd Hossein, 136–137
National Coalition for Gay and Lesbian Equality, 55–56
National Environmental Policy, Tanzania, 180–181
National Mosque of Ghana. *See* Blue Mosque
National Movement for the Liberation of Azawad (NMLA), 62–63
natural aesthetics, of kramats, 141, 154–156
nature, as great mosque, 183
Necipoğlu, Gülru, 117, 151–152
Neo-Ottoman style mosques, 116–118, 120–122, 129–130
Neruda, Pablo, 231
New Gourna, 23–24, 81–82, 105–116
   architectural origins of, 108
   Dayr al-Bahari temple, 108–110
   floorplan of, 108–110
   government disinterest in, 111–112
   mosque at, 110–111, 112–114
   museumification of, 112
   walls in, 110–111
   on World Monuments Fund Watch, 112
New National Mosque, 116–130
NGOs. *See* nongovernmental organizations
Nkrumah, Kwame, 191
NMLA. *See* National Movement for the Liberation of Azawad
nongovernmental organizations (NGOs), 122
Nyerere, Julius, 191

object-permanence, property of, 162
Omer, Spahic, xiv–xv
online masjid spaces, 231–252. *See also* Touba
   disadvantages of, 248–249
   Grand Maggal pilgrimage, 239–252
   Hajj to Mecca, 247–248
Open Mosque, 22, 31
   Al-Fitre Foundation and, 46–47

Index

as alternative Islamic space, 32–33, 62
arson attacks against, 42
composition of attendees at, 42–43
  interfaith couples, 43
gender equality in, 44
  as Qur'anic ordinance, 32
global influence of, 43–44
Hargey and, 30–32, 42, 59, 60
  veiling practice and, 30
LGBT+ community and, 44
physical expansion of, 43
sexual equality in, as Qur'anic ordinance, 32
shahada calligraphic style in, 33–34
women in, 30–44
O.R. Tambo International Airport, as masjid space, 216–218
  prayer areas, 216
orthodox Islam, 18
Ott, Randall, 128, 250–251
Ottoman Court, 117
Ottoman Empire
  architectural styles inspired by, 117–118, 119–120, 123
    Afro-Ottoman, 24, 117, 130
    Neo-Ottoman style, 116–118, 120–122, 129–130
  Hagia Sophia and, 119–120

Pacha, Hammouda, 117
Pellizzi, Francesco, 210
People's Mosque, 46–47, 48
  Hendricks and, 58
permaculture (permanent agriculture), 178–179
Pierce, Michael, 168–169
pilgrimage
  to Ka'ba site, 6–7
  to kramats, 141
place of prostration. *See* masjid
prayer mats, 8–11
  salat and, 9–10
Preziosi, Donald, 162
Price, Travis, 128, 250–251
Promotion of Equality and Prevention of Unfair Discrimination Act, South Africa (2000), 56
Prophet Muhammad. *See* Muhammad
Prussin, Labelle, 14
Pype, Katrien, 256

Qabri (dedicated space next to shrine), 101
Qaddafi, Muammar, 63
Qiblah wall, 3, 119
  in airports, 220–221

in Great Mosque of Djenne, 159
Qubbah tombs, 96
Qur'an
  environmentalist themes in, 132, 182
  feminist perspective on, 39–41
  gender equality in, 37
    in Open Mosque, 32
  hadiths in, 40
  masjid in, 2, 3
  preservation themes in, 81
  Qiblah wall in, 3
  sexual equality in, 32
  Touba in, 234
  women in, 37

Rabbat, Nasser, 79, 102
Radio Islam, 38
Rand Gay Organization (RGO), 55
Rashid, Hussein, 44
Rashiduns, 12
Ray, Sarah Jaquette, 182–183
religion, as social framework, 19–20
RGO. *See* Rand Gay Organization
Rida, Abadir Umar ar, 89
rights. *See* LGBT+ rights
Rio Earth summit, 133
Rites of Passage (Van Gennep), 232
Robben Island Mazaar Society, 138
Ross, Eric, 191, 234

Sa'diyyah (shaikh), 41, 42
Sa'idi, Abdul Hakam al- (Tuan Guru), 6–7, 139
Saine, Abdoulaye, 26
Salafism, in Timbuktu, 74–75
salat, prayer mats and, 9–10
San peoples, in South Africa, 34
Sankoré Masjid, 65, 66
Santelli, Serge, 88
school systems, in Timbuktu, 64–65
Schroeder, Ralph, 246–247
Selimiye Mosque, 120–122
Şenalp, Hilmi, 120
Senegal. *See also* car rapides; Dakar; Touba
  Sufi brotherhoods in, 190–192
  Wolof empire in, 190
Senghor, Leopold, 191
Sentek, Zeynep, 126
sexual equality, in Qur'anic ordinance, 32
Sexual Offenses Act, South Africa (1957), 54–55
Shah, Abdurahman Matabe (sheikh), 143–145, 146
shahada calligraphic style, 33–34
Shari'a law, in Mali, 62–63

286 Index

Sheller, Mimi, 25–26
Sheriff, Abdulahi Ali, 104
shrines. *See* Harar Jugol; kramats
Sidi Yahya Mosque, 66, 69–70
Sinan, Mimar, 117, 118, 119
Solomon, Robert, 128
South Africa. *See also* Apartheid regime; Al-Fitre Foundation; kramats; Open Mosque
   Auwal Masjid mosque, 34
   Cape Town International Airport, as masjid space, 221–224
   multifaith prayer space, 223–228
   Forum for the Empowerment of Women, 50–51
   heteronormative ideologies in, 53–54
   under Apartheid regime, 54
   Islam in, 34
      Call of Islam and, 35
      Council of Muslim Theologians, 42
      gender separation under, 37–39
      hijab and, 36
      Muslim identity and, 35–36
      Muslim Judicial Council of South Africa, 38
      Muslim Youth Movement, 35–36
      women's rights organizations and, 35–36
   Khoi peoples in, 34
   LGBT+ communities in
      antigay hate speech against, 56–57
      anti-lesbian violence, 56–57
      inclusive congregations for, 57
      Muslims in, 57–60
   LGBT+ rights in, 55–57
      National Coalition for Gay and Lesbian Equality, 55–56
      under Promotion of Equality and Prevention of Unfair Discrimination Act, 56
   O. R. Tambo International Airport, as masjid space, 216–218
      prayer areas, 216
   San peoples in, 34
   Sexual Offenses Act, 54–55
   Triangle Project in, 51
spirituality
   environmentalism and, 136–137
   Harar Jugol and, spiritual identity from, 89–90
   of kramats, in South Africa
      through function and purpose, 139
      power of, 141
   of Timbuktu, architectural environment as influence on, 65–67

Starret, Gregory, 207–208
Steele, James, 133–134
Sudonaise style, of mosques, 160–161
Sufi brotherhoods, 14–15
   Ansar Dine and, 22–23
   in Senegal, 190–192
Sufi identity
   in Harar Jugol, 86–87
   in Timbuktu, 30, 64–65
Suleymaniye mosque, 118–119
Sultan Ahmed Mosque, 23–24, 120–122
sustainability, 132–134
   of Children's Eco-Village, 177–179
   clean technologies and, 133
   conceptual development of, 132–133
   criticisms of, 133–134
   Dar al Islam and, 114
   Rio Earth summit and, 133
   in Tanzania, 180–181
   Tanzania Green Building Council, 181
Sustainable Architecture (Steele), 133–134
Sy, Khalifa Ababacar, 194

Tal, Umar, 16–17
Taleb, Naseema, 258–259
Tall, al-Hajj Umar, 190–191
Tambo, Oliver Reginald, 216
Tandina, Yeya, 73
Tanzania. *See also* Children's Eco-Village, Tanzania
   environmentalism in, 171–181
   under Environmental Management Act, 180–181
   under National Environmental Policy, 180–181
   Julius Nyerere International Airport, as masjid space, 215–216
   LGBT+ community in, 49
   sustainability awareness in, 180–181
   Tanzania Green Building Council, 181
Tayob, Abdulkader, 258
termitarium, 164, 165–168
Thinking Through Lesbian Rape (Muholi), 56
Third World women, 41
third world-ism, 20
Timbuktu, Mali, 62–77
   Ansar Dine and, 22–23, 62–65, 67–73, 74–75
   destruction of religious structures by, 68–73
   members of, 72
   Tuareg participation in, 67–68

Index

architectural environment of, 63–64
humanism as element of, 65–66
spiritual identity influenced by, 65–67
Catholic Church in, 70–71
counter-masjids in, 73
Djenne mosque, 25, 70
Djinguere Ber Mosque, 66
fundamentalism in, 68
intersectionality in, 64–65
  administrative structure and, as polity, 64
Islam in, 13–14
ksar in, 66
reconstruction of structures in, 76–77
Salafism in, 74–75
Sankoré Masjid, 65, 66
school system in, 64–65
Sidi Yahya Mosque, 66, 69–70
Sufi identity in, 30, 64–65
violence against women in, 73–74
Wahhabism in, 74
as World Heritage Site, 67
Timol, Ahmed, 35
Touba (holy city), 26–27, 233–246
Bamba and, 233, 242
Grand Maggal pilgrimage, 237–246
  Hizbut Tarqiyya, 240–243
  Mouride identity and, 244–245, 249–250
  as online masjid space, 239–252
  origins of, 238
Great Mosque, 235–237
Lamp Fall, 235, 236
liquid architecture of, 250
in Qur'an, 234
spatial planning of, 236–237
Touré, Amadou Toumani, 62–63, 67
Toure, Ndiabou Sega, 203
transport. *See car rapides*
trans-Saharan trade networks, Dakar in, 189–190
trees, kramats and, 145–146
Triangle Project, 51
Tuan Guru. *See* al-Sa'idi, Abdul Hakam
Tuaregs, in Mali, 68
in Ansar Dine, 67–68
in National Movement for the Liberation of Azawad, 62–63
Turkey, mosque-building in, 126–128
Turner, Victor, 232

Umayyads, 12–13
United Nations (UN)

Educational Scientific and Cultural Organization, 80–81
in Ethiopia, heritage sites, 83–84
Great Mosque of Djenne as heritage site, 169–171
World Monuments Fund, 112
World Heritage Convention Concerning Protection of World Cultural and Natural Heritage, 80
Unsal, Ozlem, 125–126
Urry, John, 25–26

van der Hoorn, Melanie, xiv
van der Leeuw, Gerard, 8
Van Gennep, Arnold, 232
veiling practices, 30
Verkaaik, Oskar, 19–20
violence, against women
anti-lesbian violence, 56–57
in Timbuktu, 73–74
virtual masjid, 231. *See also* online masjid spaces; Touba
cyber-immortality and, 251
digital eternity and, 251
Geographic Information Systems and, 231
von Tetzchner, Jon, 233

Wahhbism, in Timbuktu, 74
walls and boundaries
for Harar Jugol, 87–90
  evolutionary history of, 88–89
  spiritual identity from, 89–90
in New Gourna, 110–111
Qiblah wall, 3, 119
  in airports, 220–221
  in Great Mosque of Djenne, 159
Warren, Karen, 134
water
in Children's Eco-Village, 178
in kramats, 145
Wellington, Nii-Adziri, 127
Wertheim, Margaret, 251
Wolof empire, in Senegal, 190
women. *See also* gender equality
'*awrah* of, 38–39
Forum for the Empowerment of Women, 50–51
under Islam, separation of, 37–39
in Qur'an, 37
in South Africa
  in Open Mosque, 30–44
  women's rights organizations and, 35–36

women (cont.)
  in Third World, 41
  in Timbuktu, violence against, 73–74
World Heritage Convention. *See* United Nations
World Heritage Sites. *See also specific sites*
  local interactions at, 82
  in Timbuktu, 67

Yekouna-Amlak (emperor), 85
Yoder, Don, 19
Yonis, Fakhraddin, 88
Youssef Dey mosque, 117

Zahed, Ludovic Mohammed, 57
Zein, Abdul Hamid el-, 18
Zimbabwe, 168–169

Printed in the United States
by Baker & Taylor Publisher Services